Shak
befo
accessible, wide-ranging, and informed account of Shakespeare's history and Roman plays. It is attentive throughout to the plays as they have been performed over the centuries since they were written. The first part offers accounts of the genre of the history play, of Renaissance historiography, of pageants and masques, and of women's roles, as well as comparisons with history plays in Spain and the Netherlands. Chapters in the second part look at individual plays as well as other Shakespearean texts which are closely related to the histories. The *Companion* offers a full bibliography, genealogical tables, and a list of principal and recurrent characters. It is a comprehensive guide for students, researchers, and theatre-goers alike.

CAMBRIDGE COMPANIONS TO LITERATURE

The Cambridge Companion to Greek Tragedy
edited by P. E. Easterling

The Cambridge Companion to Old English Literature
edited by Malcolm Godden and Michael Lapidge

The Cambridge Companion to Medieval Romance
edited by Roberta L. Kreuger

The Cambridge Companion to Medieval English Theatre
edited by Richard Beadle

The Cambridge Companion to English Renaissance Drama
edited by A. R. Braunmuller and Michael Hattaway

The Cambridge Companion to Renaissance Humanism
edited by Jill Kraye

The Cambridge Companion to English Poetry, Donne to Marvell
edited by Thomas N. Corns

The Cambridge Companion to English Literature, 1500–1600
edited by Arthur F. Kinney

The Cambridge Companion to English Literature, 1650–1740
edited by Steven N. Zwicker

The Cambridge Companion to Writing of the English Revolution
edited by N. H. Keeble

The Cambridge Companion to English Restoration Theatre
edited by Deborah C. Payne Fisk

The Cambridge Companion to British Romanticism
edited by Stuart Curran

The Cambridge Companion to Eighteenth Century Poetry
edited by John Sitter

The Cambridge Companion to the Eighteenth-Century Novel
edited by John Richetti

The Cambridge Companion to Victorian Poetry
edited by Joseph Bristow

The Cambridge Companion to the Victorian Novel
edited by Deirdre David

List continues on page following the Index.

The Cambridge Companion to American Realism and Naturalism
edited by Donald Pizer

The Cambridge Companion to Nineteenth-Century American Women's Writing
edited by Dale M. Bauer and Philip Gould

The Cambridge Companion to the Classic Russian Novel
edited by Malcolm V. Jones and Robin Feuer Miller

The Cambridge Companion to the French Novel: from 1800 to the present
edited by Timothy Unwin

The Cambridge Companion to Modernism
edited by Michael Levenson

The Cambridge Companion to Australian Literature
edited by Elizabeth Webby

The Cambridge Companion to American Women Playwrights
edited by Brenda Murphy

The Cambridge Companion to Modern British Women Playwrights
edited by Elaine Aston and Janelle Reinelt

The Cambridge Companion to Virgil
edited by Charles Martindale

The Cambridge Companion to Ovid
edited by Philip Hardie

The Cambridge Companion to Dante
edited by Rachel Jacoff

The Cambridge Companion to Goethe
edited by Lesley Sharpe

The Cambridge Companion to Dostoevskii
edited by W. J. Leatherbarrow

The Cambridge Companion to Tolstoy
edited by Donna Tussing Orwin

The Cambridge Companion to Proust
edited by Richard Bales

The Cambridge Companion to Thomas Mann
edited by Ritchie Robertson

The Cambridge Companion to Chekhov
edited by Vera Gottlieb and Paul Allain

The Cambridge Companion to Ibsen
edited by James McFarlane

The Cambridge Companion to Brecht
edited by Peter Thomson and Glendyr Sacks

The Cambridge Chaucer Companion
edited by Piero Boitani and Jill Mann

THE CAMBRIDGE
COMPANION TO
SHAKESPEARE'S
HISTORY PLAYS

EDITED BY
MICHAEL HATTAWAY

CAMBRIDGE
UNIVERSITY PRESS

PUBLISHED BY THE PRESS SYNDICATE OF THE UNIVERSITY OF CAMBRIDGE
The Pitt Building, Trumpington Street, Cambridge, United Kingdom

CAMBRIDGE UNIVERSITY PRESS
The Edinburgh Building, Cambridge CB2 2RU, UK
40 West 20th Street, New York, NY 10011-4211, USA
477 Williamstown Road, Port Melbourne, VIC 3207, Australia
Ruiz de Alarcón 13, 28014 Madrid, Spain
Dock House, The Waterfront, Cape Town 8001, South Africa

http://www.cambridge.org

First published 2002

Printed in the United Kingdom at the University Press, Cambridge

Typeface Sabon 10/13 pt   *System* LATEX 2ε   [TB]

A catalogue record for this book is available from the British Library

ISBN 0 521 77277 X hardback
ISBN 0 521 77539 6 paperback

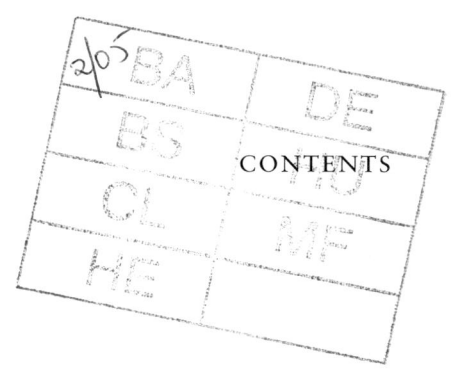

CONTENTS

FIGURES

CONTRIBUTORS

DAVID M. BERGERON, University of Kansas

MARIE-HÉLÈNE BESNAULT, University of Tours

MICHEL BITOT, University of Tours

ROBYN BOLAM, St Mary's University College, Strawberry Hill

JAMES C. BULMAN, Allegheny College, Pennsylvania

R. A. FOAKES, University of California at Los Angeles

DOMINIQUE GOY-BLANQUET, University of Amiens

STUART HAMPTON-REEVES, University of Central Lancashire

MICHAEL HATTAWAY, University of Sheffield

A. J. HOENSELAARS, University of Utrecht

JANIS LULL, University of Alaska

PAMELA MASON, The Shakespeare Institute, University of Birmingham

ROBERT S. MIOLA, Loyola College of Maryland

A. J. PIESSE, Trinity College, Dublin

PHYLLIS RACKIN, University of Pennsylvania

ABBREVIATIONS

References to Shakespeare's plays when using the abbreviation alone are to volumes in the *New Cambridge Shakespeare*, published under the general editorship of Brian Gibbons and A. R. Braunmuller. Other editions are included in the following list.

Abbreviated titles are as follows:

Ado	*Much Ado about Nothing*
Ant.	*Antony and Cleopatra*, 1990, ed. David Bevington, New Cambridge Shakespeare.
AWW	*All's Well that Ends Well*
AYLI	*As You Like It*
Cor.	*Coriolanus*, 1976, ed. Philip Brockbank, Arden Shakespeare; 1994, ed. R. B. Parker, Oxford Shakespeare; 2000, ed. Lee Bliss, New Cambridge Shakespeare.
Cym.	*Cymbeline*
E3	*King Edward III*, 1998, ed. Giorgio Melchiori, New Cambridge Shakespeare.
Err.	*The Comedy of Errors*
Ham.	*Hamlet*
1H4	*King Henry IV, Part I*, 1960, ed. A. R. Humphreys, Arden Shakespeare; *The First Part of King Henry IV*, 1997, ed. Herbert Weil and Judith Weil, New Cambridge Shakespeare.
2H4	*The Second Part of King Henry the Fourth*, 1977, ed. Peter Davison, Penguin Shakespeare; *The Second Part of King Henry IV*, 1989, ed. Giorgio Melchiori, New Cambridge Shakespeare; *Henry IV, Part 2*, 1998, ed. Rene Weis, Oxford Shakespeare.
H5	*Henry V*, 1954, ed. J. H. Walter, Arden Shakespeare; 1968, ed. A. R. Humphreys, Penguin Shakespeare; 1982, ed. Gary Taylor, Oxford Shakespeare.

1H6	*The First Part of King Henry VI*, 1990, ed. Michael Hattaway, New Cambridge Shakespeare.
2H6	*The Second Part of King Henry VI*, 1991, ed. Michael Hattaway, New Cambridge Shakespeare.
3H6	*The Third Part of King Henry VI*, 1993, ed. Michael Hattaway, New Cambridge Shakespeare.
H8	*King Henry the VIII*, 1964, ed. R. A. Foakes, New Arden Shakespeare; 1990, ed. John Margeson, New Cambridge Shakespeare; *King Henry VIII or All is True*, 2000, ed. Gordon McMullon, Arden Shakespeare.
JC	*Julius Caesar*, 1984, ed. Arthur Humphreys, Oxford Shakespeare; 1988, ed. Marvin Spevack, New Cambridge Shakespeare.
John	*King John*, 1990, ed. L. A. Beaurline, New Cambridge Shakespeare.
LLL	*Love's Labour's Lost*
Lear	*King Lear*, 1997, ed. R. A. Foakes, Arden Shakespeare.
Mac.	*Macbeth*, 1997, ed. A. R. Braunmuller, New Cambridge Shakespeare.
MM	*Measure for Measure*
MND	*A Midsummer Night's Dream*
MV	*The Merchant of Venice*
Oth.	*Othello*
Per.	*Pericles*
R2	*King Richard II*, 1984, ed. Andrew Gurr, New Cambridge Shakespeare.
R3	*King Richard III*, 1981, ed. Antony Hammond, New Arden Shakespeare; *Richard III*, 1981, ed. Julie Hankey, Plays in Performance; *King Richard III*, 1999, ed. Janis Lull, New Cambridge Shakespeare.
Rom.	*Romeo and Juliet*
Shr.	*The Taming of the Shrew*
STM	*Sir Thomas More*
Temp.	*The Tempest*
TGV	*The Two Gentlemen of Verona*
Tim.	*Timon of Athens*
Tit.	*Titus Andronicus*, 1994, ed. Alan Hughes, New Cambridge Shakespeare; 1995, ed. Jonathan Bate, Arden Shakespeare.
TN	*Twelfth Night*

TNK   *The Two Noble Kinsmen*
Tro.   *Troilus and Cressida*, 1998, ed. David Bevington, Arden
      Shakespeare.
Wiv.   *The Merry Wives of Windsor*
WT   *The Winter's Tale*

Dates given for plays (some of which are as much tragedies or romances as histories) are of first performance unless otherwise specified; many of these dates are approximate.

Other history plays, extant or lost, performed in universities, at court, or the Inns of Court, or written in Latin, can be traced in Alfred Harbage (ed.), *Annals of English Drama 975–1700*, 3rd edn (London, 1989).

1509	Accession of Henry VIII
c.1521	Skelton, *Magnificence*
1547	Accession of Edward VI
1553	Accession of Mary Tudor
1558	Accession of Elizabeth I
1562	Norton and Sackville, *Gorboduc*
1564	Shakespeare born in Stratford-upon-Avon
1566	Red Lion playhouse opens
1576	The Theatre opens
1577	Curtain playhouse opens
1582	Shakespeare marries Anne Hathaway; the license is issued on 27 November and the first child (Susanna) is born six months later
1585	Shakespeare's twin son and daughter, Hamnet and Judith, born
c.1586	Shakespeare leaves Stratford; nothing is known for certain of his life between this date and 1592, by which time he is in London; Anon., *The Famous Victories of Henry V*
1587	Rose playhouse opens
c.1587	Marlowe, *1 Tamburlaine*
c.1588	Marlowe, *2 Tamburlaine*; Lodge, *The Wounds of Civil War*
1589	Peele, *The Battle of Alcazar*

I
CONTEXTS

I

MICHAEL HATTAWAY

The Shakespearean history play

Genre

In 1623 when, seven years after Shakespeare's death, John Heminges and Henry Condell, the editors of First Folio (the first collected edition of Shakespeare's works), grouped roughly a third of Shakespeare's plays under the heading of 'histories', they confirmed a dramatic genre that Shakespeare himself seems to have endorsed: Polonius announced that 'the best actors in the world, either for tragedy, comedy, history . . .' had arrived in Elsinore (*Ham.*, 2.2.416). But Heminges and Condell also unloosed a host of critical problems – they seem to have recognised difficulties themselves. *Troilus and Cressida*, which they placed after *Henry VIII*, they entitled *The Tragedy of Troilus and Cressida*. Yet this play is not included in the Folio's 'catalogue' or index of the tragedies, which are printed after the histories. In fact many have regarded *Troilus* as a 'history', which is how it had been categorised by the publisher of its Quarto version (1609)[1] where it was entitled *The Famous History of Troilus and Cresseid* [*sic*]. In recent years critics have located *Troilus* among the 'problem plays' (plays that defy easy generic classification and which may be best approached by way of the ethical problems they explore).

Generic classification was bound to be difficult given that most of the English histories centre their action on the reign of a monarch, the narrative ending with his death. It was therefore inevitable that 'history' plays were going to be closely affiliated with tragedy. Some were initially labelled as such. The long title headings to Folio 'Histories' include *The Life and Death of King John*, *The Life and Death of King Richard the Second*, and *The Tragedy of Richard the Third: with the Landing of Earl Richmond, and the Battle at Bosworth Field*. (Forms of these titles in the volume's catalogue often vary from the above.) The Quarto title of the second of these is *The Tragedy of King Richard the Second* (1597 etc.), while the third has a running title 'The Life and Death of Richard the Third'. Only the Henry VI plays offer a 'life' from the king's childhood to his death: the others, like tragedies, take up the story of the king's reign when his career is tilting towards crisis. As the case of *Troilus and Cressida* suggests, the very titles Heminges and Condell gave these plays may not be those by which Shakespeare knew them: the play they called *The Second Part of Henry the Sixth* had been entitled in its Quarto version *The First Part of the Contention betwixt the Two Famous Houses of York and Lancaster* (1594), and the title of the Octavo version of *The Third Part of Henry the Sixth* is *The True Tragedy of Richard Duke of York and the Death of Good King Henry Sixth* (1595).

Despite this evidence, for generations it was common to regard the union of 'history' and 'tragedy' as an uneasy one: Aristotle, after all, had contrasted 'history' with 'poetry' on the grounds that the latter was more philosophic and universal, an observation endorsed by Sir Philip Sidney. A.C. Bradley's distinction between 'historical' and 'pure' tragedy led him to exclude *Antony and Cleopatra* from his influential *Shakespearean Tragedy* (1904).[2] All too often commentators concentrated on the personalities of the protagonist, marginalising 'history' and offering a moralisation of the action that occluded the politics. More recently, however, the *convergence* of history and tragedy in Shakespearean texts has been a starting point for critical analysis. Tragedy has been characterised not just by conflict between a man of high degree and his destiny or read as a tale of a 'flawed' protagonist, but has been seen to evolve from political situation. Attention has been paid not only to larger patterns of action but to values, ideologies, and institutions, and to the accidental or contingent. Rather than seeing politics emerge from history it may even be more profitable to think of history emerging from politics: historical narratives are shaped by the politics of the writers of those narratives. In theatrical productions the outcome of the action has been signalled from the beginning, perhaps so that the audience might attend to constitutional degradation or the particular chains of causation that generate the play's ending. In 2000 Steven Pimlott's *Richard II* for the Royal Shakespeare Company opened with a striking stage image: the royal throne was perched on top of a chest that became, at the end, the coffin for the king. In Adrian Noble's 1988 RSC production of '*Henry VI*' and '*The Rise of Edward IV*' (conflations of *1*, *2*, and *3 Henry VI*) the throne stood above a prison cage in which both Mortimer and King Henry were to die. In Julie Taymor's film *Titus* (2000) an induction showed a boy playing with robotic warrior toys, an index for the techno-muscular masculinity the film explores, his game presently interrupted by a massive explosion as if from a bomb outside.

Henry V is the play that is the most obvious exception to this rule. It ends, not like tragedy with a death, but like comedy with a marriage. If we read the two parts of *Henry IV* as one play, we note an ending in death, but

Figure 1   Joan of Arc (see *1 Henry VI*) leading the assault against Paris, from Martial
d'Auvergne, *Vigiles du roi Charles VII*, 1484.

Part 1, dominated as it is by the misrule of Falstaff, is also closely related to
comedy.[3]

Folio titles may be yet more deceptive: *The Famous History of the Life of
King Henry the Eighth* (1613) was, possibly, originally called '*All is True*'.
Moreover, although this play seems to be appropriately placed in order of
reign at the end of the 'histories' section of the Folio, the play was written
much later than the others and is, in its structure, more like Shakespeare's
late romances than, say, the plays about the reigns of Henry IV or Henry V.
(Romance was not a genre recognised by the Folio editors.) Sometimes
tragedies and even comedies were labelled 'histories': in 1600 a Quarto appeared entitled *The Most Excellent History of the Merchant of Venice*, and
in 1607–8, another Quarto: *Mr William Shakespeare his True Chronicle
History of the Life and Death of King Lear and his Three Daughters*. Certain
of the tragedies (*Macbeth*, *King Lear*) have among their principal sources the
chronicles by Edward Hall (1548 etc.) and Raphael Holinshed (1577 etc.)
that Shakespeare had used for his 'histories'.[4]

What have come to be called the 'Roman plays' appear in the Folio among
the tragedies – a tendentious placing given that, famously, Julius Caesar is
murdered less than half-way through the play (called in Folio *The Tragedy of*

Julius Caesar) that bears his name. Likewise *Cymbeline*, arguably a romance although categorised as a 'tragedy', has only a couple of scenes in which King Cymbeline appears. *Coriolanus* appears first among the tragedies with the title *The Tragedy of Coriolanus*. The Stationers' Register entry of 6 February 1594 for what is probably *Titus Andronicus* refers to 'a noble Roman history of Titus Andronicus' although the play is described in both Folio and Quarto as a 'tragedy'. Like these three texts, the English history plays all bear the names of individuals, but it is apparent that they too are as much about reigns as personalities – an observation that is supported by the title page of a play now ascribed at least in part to Shakespeare, *Edward III* (1595) which, interestingly, reads 'The Reign of King Edward the Third: as it hath been sundry times played about the City of London'. Moreover, it is arguable that all of the plays have at their centres political and social concerns: *Julius Caesar*, for example, exposes the fragility of republics, *Cymbeline* celebrates Empire (the word 'Britain' occurring frequently in the text, testifying to James VI and I's attempts to unify the crowns of Scotland and England),[5] and *Titus Andronicus* addresses the grotesque excesses of honour cultures and the way tyranny both generates and is generated by violence.

So, from a consideration of their titles alone, the genre of the Shakespearean history play was very undetermined. Who else had written 'history plays'? Drama in England before the first decades of the sixteenth century was almost entirely ceremonial and produced under the auspices of religious institutions. Dramatisations of biblical history and of saints' lives we know as 'mysteries' and 'miracles' respectively – few of the latter have survived. Those that were written to instil Christian doctrines of ethics, 'moralities', were allegorical, generally dramatising a battle between personified virtues and vices for the soul of mankind. (The conflict between the Chief Justice and Falstaff for the allegiance of Prince Hal is a residue of this pattern.) Both mystery and morality plays mingle the grandiose and the comic, pain and laughter – like Shakespeare's histories. But in the reign of Henry VIII new kinds of offering appeared: John Skelton's *Magnificence* (*c*.1515–1523), described on its title-page as a 'a goodly interlude', sets out the relationship between 'magnificence' and 'measure' within a court world that is defined by characters with names like 'Cloaked Collusion' and 'Courtly Abusion'. The play satirises a contemporary, the most powerful man in England after the monarch, Cardinal Wolsey. About the same time appeared political moralities with titles like *Friendship, Prudence, and Might* (offered by boy players at court in 1522) and *Lord Governance and Lady Public Weal*, a play that was obviously a political morality. Its text is lost but it was performed at Christmas in Gray's Inn 1526, by and for law students.[6] Its title suggests a perennial theme. Conflicts between, on the one hand, the material desires of the aristocracy and monarchs who required money for rule and government (or demanded it to maintain wanton magnificence), and, on the other, the necessary thrift of commoners and handicraftsmen led to charges of prodigality and waste that are represented in morals throughout the six-teenth century and given a local habitation in Shakespeare's histories. An anonymous morality, *Liberality and Prodigality*, was performed by boys of the Chapel as late as 1601. Shakespeare's 'prodigal' Richard II improvises a way of defraying the costs of putting down rebellion in Ireland and of his 'fierce blaze of riot' (2.1.33) by seizing the wealth of his uncle John of Gaunt upon the latter's death. Moral outrage could harden into a kind of class conflict: in 2 *Henry VI* we hear two of Cade's followers compare the lot of the common people with that of 'magistrates', i.e. high-ranking members of the executive:

> HOLLAND … Well, I say, it was never merry world in England since gentle-men came up.
> BEVIS O miserable age! Virtue is not regarded in handicraftsmen.
> HOLLAND The nobility think scorn to go in leather aprons.
> BEVIS Nay more, the King's council are no good workmen.
> HOLLAND True: and yet it is said, 'Labour in thy vocation': which is as much to say, as let the magistrates be labouring men; and therefore should we be magistrates.
> $\qquad$ (2H6, 4.2.7–16)

Although the mechanicals' chop-logic vitiates their conclusion, the passage reminds us of how the myth of 'merry England' was both informed by the imperative of social equality and grounded in scriptural values.

What are the characteristics of Shakespeare's histories? Shakespeare could probably count on a minimal knowledge of historical events in his audience[7] and he represented these in various ways, inevitably concentrating as much on form and genre as on story. Structurally the plays are indeed various: the earliest, the plays about the reign of Henry VI (1588–90), are chronicles of civil war, what Edmund Hall called 'intestine division'.[8] Dramatising the events of this reign involved not only making sense of, and giving a dra-matic shape to, the chroniclers' accounts of the Wars of the Roses between Yorkists and Lancastrians, but relating the surges of national politics to the persistent conflict between England and France during the Hundred Years War. Out of this wilderness of wars between barons and nations personal-ities emerge: England's doughty champion Lord Talbot, 'the terror of the French',[9] who fights a racy Joan of Arc who spouts Marlovian heroical verse; Good Duke Humphrey, brother to England's lamented hero, Henry V; the womanising Edward IV; the high-aspiring Duke of York who dies at the hands of a tigress, Queen Margaret of Anjou; and her husband, the pious

Henry VI, who achieves some tragic quality as he is slaughtered by the villainous Richard of Gloucester. In production, the parts of Joan of Arc and Margaret can be doubled, an economical way of exposing the destabilising role of powerful women. The plays invoke the populist myth of the court being infiltrated by diabolic 'politicians' – the word was newly imported from France.[10] When Richard of Gloucester in the Folio version of 3 Henry VI boasts that he will 'set the murderous Machiavel to school' (3.2.193) we recognise a popular figure who was also conjured up by Kyd and Marlowe, the totally unscrupulous bogyman. 'Machiavel' derives from Protestant writings against Italianate vice rather than from any real comprehension of the writings of Niccolò Machiavelli who lived well after the death of Henry VI. It is significant that, in the Octavo, 'aspiring Catiline' appears in place of 'murderous Machiavel', probably a player's recollection of a lost play by Stephen Gosson, Catiline's Conspiracies, performed at the Theatre about 1578. Both readings testify to the way political myths infiltrated chronicled history.

In Coriolanus one of Aufidius' serving men proclaims: ' Let me have war, say I. It exceeds peace as far as day does night: it's sprightly walking, audible and full of vent' (4.5.228–9). This matches the tone of these first histories, but they are also remarkable for their quizzical interrogation of sovereignty and the way they portray the horror and savagery as well as the glories of war, suggesting throughout, in a manner akin to the 'true' Machiavelli, that the course of human history is evidently ordained by the might of armies and the actions of particular men.

King John (1595–6) is a theatrical essay that anatomises different claims to authority and portrays a Romish intervention in English politics. One of its most prominent characters, Philip Faulconbridge, often referred to as 'the Bastard', derives from another traditional figure, the Vice of the morality plays. Richard III (c.1591) and Richard II (c.1595) concentrate more on central figures whose lives are fitted into tragic moulds. The earlier play owes as much to Seneca as to the chroniclers of English history, and its hero is constructed differently from the figure he cut in 3 Henry VI. In the play that bears his name he is a figure in whom dissimulation has distorted personality, a man whose shadow has displaced his substance. 'Shadow' was an Elizabethan designation for an actor – there is extended play with the word in 4.1 of Richard II.[11] This doubleness is associated with the fiction that a king was 'twin-born with greatness' (H5, 3.1.231), inhabiting his own body, the 'body natural', but incarnating the mystical 'body politic' which legitimated his rule and ensured succession. Play between these two 'bodies' might generate splits in personality, conflict between them, tragedy.[12] The Henry IV plays (c.1597) return to civil war, to discrepancies between public and private personalities, and lay bare conflict between monarchy and aristocracy, fathers and sons, authority figures and the unaccommodated. *Henry V* (*c*.1599) is an epic pageant that places in perspective both the glories and the moral expenditure of war. Henry's heroical venture into France may be driven by a desire for glory, but for Pistol, one of his officers, war was an occasion for plunder.

Characters recur in different plays,[13] and there can be a degree of narrative continuity, but it is probably misleading to assume that Shakespeare planned these works as a 'cycle'. The order of the plays' composition does not match the sequence of the reigns they portray, and grouping them into 'tetralogies' elides their structural differences. (The 'second tetralogy' covers the reigns of the *earlier* Plantagenets Richard II, Henry IV, and Henry V, while the so-called 'first tetralogy' yokes together, as we have seen, plays as formally different as *1–3 Henry VI* and *Richard III*.) They certainly do not possess a pattern that is directed to endings that are morally or theologically linked to their beginnings in a manner analogous to the way that the 'cycles' of medieval mystery plays progressed from creation to resurrection. But although, since 1864, there have been a number of ambitious and important linked productions of the histories as 'tetralogies' or 'cycles',[14] there is no evidence from Shakespeare's time that they were ever performed in this manner, and no evidence that he was aware of the 'cycles' of ancient Greek tragedy. Nor does it seem that he wrote them programmatically to exhibit a providential scheme that culminated in the foundation of the Tudor dynasty that is acclaimed at the end of *Richard III*. Presenting the plays as cycles emphasises elements of ritual which may dampen the political charge they delivered, and also invites audiences to consider attendance at linked performances as a celebration of a myth of Englishness, akin to a pilgrimage to Bayreuth to hear Wagner's *Ring* cycle. In fact, while Shakespeare created many touchstones for national sentiment, he also showed that, even as the state was developing, the unified nation which might validate that state was a myth. Shakespeare chronicles an age of feuding warlords and, in what may seem to be his most patriotic play, *Henry V*, reminds his audience that the motley horde of English, Irish, Welsh, and Scots that make up the king's army scarcely constitutes 'one nation'. National unity was a tactical instrument developed to sustain an expeditionary force, the creation of which was supposed to concentrate the 'giddy minds' (*2H4*, 4.3.342) of the leaders of political factions. The English monarchy was legitimated by heredity: Shakespeare shows not only alternative political systems, republics and elective monarchies, but lays out, in all their complexity and tenuousness, the devious paths by which the crown descended to Elizabeth.

For many modern theatregoers, however, Shakespeare's histories, especially when experienced as linked productions, seem to make a statement about a destiny for England. In other words, although Homer and Virgil are never primary sources, magnitude of action, grandiloquence of style, the invocation of deity, and what are taken as signs of divine intervention have suggested to critics since Coleridge relationships not only to tragedy but to epic. Coleridge considered both genres were 'founded on the relation of providence to the human will', and while

> in the epic poem fate is represented as overruling the will . . . in the drama, the will is exhibited as struggling with fate . . . The events themselves are immaterial, otherwise as the clothing and manifestation of the spirit that is working within. In this mode, the unity resulting from succession is destroyed, but is supplied by a unity of a higher order, which connects the events by reference to the workers, gives a reason for them in the motives, and *presents men in their causative character* (emphasis added).[15]

Coleridge's concentration on the way men struggle to make their own history suggests a model for interpretation that does not stress a grand design but which anatomises the English body politic and refuses the mystification of the secular and causative that occurs when claims for master narratives made by characters within the plays are taken literally. This part of Coleridge's account is not so very different from the ideal for political drama created by Bertolt Brecht with his model for epic theatre. There is so much questioning of glory in Shakespeare that we might even claim that the histories are rejoinder to Elizabethan projects for a revival of heroic poetry. In the October eclogue in *The Shepheardes Calender* Piers had sounded a clarion call for poets:

> Abandon then the base and viler clowne,
> Lyft up thyselfe out of the lowly dust:
> And sing of bloody Mars, of wars, of giusts [jousts];
> Turne thee to those that weld the awful crowne,
> To doubted [dubbed] knights, whose woundless armour rusts,
> And helmes unbruzed wexen dayly browne. (36–42)

Shakespeare implicitly asserts that if a poet is to address the ancient topics of heroism and return to the depiction of knights fighting for fame and honour, it is necessary to eschew the pieties of romance epic that emerge in *The Faerie Queene*. He delineated the duties as well as the glories of England's honour caste, and subjected monarchs, their courts, and the ideology of monarchy to a scrutiny as searching as that to which they had been exposed in the morality plays.

Truth and realism

Henry VIII may have been called 'All is true', possibly a quiet irony that disputes the content of the play in that it shows the king rewriting the history of his marriage to Katherine of Aragon.[16] We rapidly realise what a riddle that alternative title is. Although writers of history in our own age are aware that the past they map out is coloured by ideological positioning and fashioned by the kinds of narrative they are creating, all modern historians critique their sources and write discourses that are evidence-based. We assume that behind modern histories are 'facts', deduced from written or material documents, witnesses to events, or from statistical analysis. Any divagation from this kind of 'truth' would, in our own period, be unacceptable. Yet although Renaissance historians in their search for veracity went to what they took to be primary sources, particularly the historians of the ancient world, they made few distinctions between historical figures and fictive characters, and made ample use of the rhetorical device of *prosopopeia*,[17] writing speeches they deemed such figures on particular occasions might have made – or ought to have made. Such fictional histories were the stuff of popular literature as well. When Prince John denigrates Falstaff's capture of Coleville of the Dale, Falstaff retorts 'let it be booked with the rest of this day's deeds; or, by the Lord, I will have it in a particular ballad else, with mine own picture on the top on't, Coleville kissing my foot' (*2H4*, 4.1.395–8).

As Shakespeare did in the comedies, where he inserted frequent intimations of the conventions of comedy (creating 'meta-theatre'), in his political plays he addressed not only history but historiography. *Readers* of history may be encouraged to reflect upon recurrent patterns in the past, but theatre audiences watch history being made: the immediacy of the experience concentrates the mind upon the contingent, the secular, and on psychological deliberation. Moreover, given that each production is going to create particular emphases and therefore differing explanations for dramatised events, historicism may be impossible in the theatre. While St Paul may have written 'there is no power but of God: the powers that be are ordained of God' (Rom.13.1), the winning and losing of theatre battles obviously rests upon charismatic leadership and upon the right forces being in the right place at the right time. The authority of office might be subverted by the impotence of the office holder, the outcome of a staged battle may be shown to depend upon the particular sword-strokes and spear-thrusts in a fight to the death.

Although this suggests a kind of demystification or historical 'realism', Shakespeare, like his contemporaries, made no attempt to create a sense of geographical exactitude or historical authenticity by 'accurate' theatrical settings. Elizabethan playhouses were not designed for *illusion*: there was no question of constructing scenic likenesses of palace rooms or tavern 'ordinaries', formal gardens or fields for battle. When such places were evoked in dialogue, they served as what Mikhail Bakhtin called 'chronotopes',[18] 'time-places', representations of *social spaces* and not imitations of *particular places*. We are not certain how actors were dressed: it seems most likely that basic costumes were Elizabethan with some token costumes – long medieval shoes, for example – to mark historical difference. Other details obliterated that difference: clocks are referred to long before they were historically invented, Cleopatra plays billiards. Anachronism was not a failing: it may indeed have served to forge links between past and present situations. What is certain is that no play stands or falls by its historical 'accuracy'. Not all characters are historical, some were composites as with Mortimer in *1 Henry VI*,[19] others were shunted from one generation to another: Hotspur and Hal, contemporaries in *1 Henry IV*, historically were born in 1364 and 1387 respectively. 'There is figures in all things' (*H5*, 4.7.30): stage-Plantagenets could signify individuals contemporary with Shakespeare. In the Chorus to Act 5 of *Henry V* Shakespeare explicitly compares Henry's triumphant return from Agincourt to a wished-for return for Robert Devereux, Earl of Essex who, at the time of the play's composition, was in Ireland dealing with the Tyrone Rebellion. 'All is true' turns out to have other meanings that are not related to accuracy: the phrase might suggest scepticism, or it might mean that the action presented is of universal validity, a demonstration of political paradigms and not necessarily an accurate account of the deeds of one set of great women and men. (Alternatively, the title may be a rejoinder to a censor.)

Courts are represented not with painted scenery but by appropriate varieties of theatrical ritual: processions, music, formal speech. The ceremonies that sustain the state are often interrupted – that is the pattern of the arrested funeral of Henry V at the beginning of *1 Henry VI*, of Saturninus' obstruction of the investiture of Titus Andronicus, and of the moment when Richard II refuses to allow the challenge to Mowbray by Bullingbrook in 1.3 to proceed to a duel – a trial by combat that would have delivered the outcome into God's hands. Richard, for once a good strategist, intervenes to banish both men, Mowbray because he may *know* too much about the murder of Woodstock in which Richard himself had had a hand, Bullingbrook because he may *want* too much, even the crown of England.

Shakespeare, therefore, was concerned not just with chronicle and personality but with institutions: in particular with the fissures of court politics. St Augustine had famously pointed out the precariousness of what we would now call the 'state':

> Remove justice, and what are kingdoms but gangs of criminals on a large scale? What are criminal gangs but petty kingdoms? A gang is a group of men under the command of a leader, bound by a compact of association, in which the plunder is divided according to an agreed convention.[20]

From some points of view the Wars of the Roses and the earlier insurrections of Bullingbrook's erstwhile allies can be seen as chronicles of plunder, Augustinian gang-wars, and the solemn oaths that, it is claimed, seal allegiance seem more like what Augustine had in mind when he wrote of 'compacts of association'. If Shakespeare celebrates monarchical magnificence, as in the set-piece description of the Field of the Cloth of Gold in *Henry VIII*, or acclaims his audible and sprightly walking heroes, he equally offers a populist perspective on political action: he decrowns power, makes majesty his 'subject', unmasks politicians, exposes feebleness.[21] This he sometimes does by introducing scenes in different modes, in subplots and counterplots. Once Bullingbrook is firmly established on the English throne, after a long ritualistic sequence in which Richard II strips himself of the regalia that sustained his power, the newly crowned Henry IV finds himself 'monarchising' in a strange little farce written in comic couplets (5.3). Here he seeks news of his 'unruly son', Prince Hal, and has to decide between, on the one hand, the claims of the Duke of York who wants the even more unruly Aumerle, his own son, put to death for plotting against the crown and, on the other, the pleas of the boy's mother for mercy on her son's life.[22] The irony is that Henry IV as Bullingbrook himself had come to the throne by 'by-paths and indirect crooked ways' (*2H4*, 4.2.312). Fathers cannot control sons, and the Eastcheap scenes in the Henry IV plays implicitly question whether the royal writ can (or ought to) extend into the tavern. As Francis Bacon observed in his essay 'Of Empire', 'Kings have to deal with their neighbours . . . their children, their prelates . . . their nobles, their second-nobles . . . their commons, and their men of war.'[23]

The Pistol sequences in *Henry V* register not only the decease of the qualities of wit and ease incarnate in that 'second-noble' and unwilling man of war, Falstaff, but the contrast between heroic rhetoric and the actualities of politics and the battlefield, hinting the while at a causative relationship between male sexuality and military aggression. Henry V's jingoism as he departs for France is replayed in a fustian mode as Pistol takes leave of the Hostess:

> Look to my chattels and my movables.
> Let senses rule. The word is 'Pitch and pay'.

Trust none, for oaths are straws, men's faiths are wafer-cakes,
And Holdfast is the only dog, my duck.
Therefore *caveto* be thy counsellor.
Go, clear thy crystals. – Yoke-fellows in arms,
Let us to France, like horse-leeches, my boys,
To suck, to suck, the very blood to suck!   (2.3.43–50)

Pistol's rhetoric exposes the tactical considerations that may animate Henry's claim to the throne of France, made, he asserts, 'with right and conscience' (*H5*, 1.2.96). The real end of war was at best the wealth that could come from ransoms, at worst the rape of cities and wanton pillage:[24] the Battle of Bosworth in *Richard III* may be the only example of a just war in the canon. Indeed Shakespeare's protracted analysis of the nature, origins, and uses of power makes us realise that it may well be more profitable to think of these texts as political rather than 'historical' plays.

Politics

Shakespeare's 'histories' therefore are neither generically similar one to another nor bound to historical fact. They are related to history mainly by offering representations of historical figures and the creation of theatre out of historical events. Yet in another sense they are profoundly historical, addressing themselves to historical *process*, ways in which change comes about. Raphael Holinshed's *Chronicles of England, Scotland, and Ireland*, Shakespeare's principal source, offer not only stories, but colour the narrative of events with set speeches and reflections upon the course of action. Sometimes Holinshed mingles providential accounts of history with secular materialist ones of the kind associated with Livy or Machiavelli. Sometimes marginal notes offer a sardonic and populist perspective upon a grand narrative: 'an ominous marriage' beside the account of the marriage of the young Henry VI to Margaret of Anjou, or, concerning the death of the Duke of York in 3 *Henry VI* which the text likens to the Crucifixion, 'a purchase of God's curse with the pope's blessing'.[25] Hall had offered introductory essays that reflect upon the course of his chronicle and the moral nature of his protagonists, and the title of his work, *The Union of the Two Noble and Illustre Families of Lancaster and York*, proclaims the 'end' of at least one phase of history, marked by Henry Tudor's victory over Richard III at Bosworth Field.

Were the plays, like the pattern of Hall's chronicle, patriotic? A hard answer would be that there was no one 'nation' to which contemporaries might owe allegiance. Although both Shakespeare's contemporaries Thomas Nashe and Thomas Heywood bear witness to the way history plays stiffened the sinews and summoned up the blood of Englishmen,[26] there are grounds for conjecturing that Shakespeare may have provoked rather than pleased those who would control the political culture of England. At the beginning of his career, at the time of the Henry VI plays, his endeavour may even have appeared 'oppositional': on 12 November 1589 the Privy Council wrote to the Archbishop of Canterbury, the Lord Mayor of London, and Edmund Tilney, Master of the Revels, asking them each to appoint someone to scrutinise all plays performed in and about the City of London because the players had taken 'upon them, without judgement or decorum, to handle matters of divinity and state'.[27] Parts of the Henry VI plays reveal evidence of censorship by Tilney[28] – or of self-censorship by the players. History was indeed dangerous matter: it was not until 1608 that the deposition scene (4.1.154–317) was included in Quarto versions of *Richard II*.[29] Following the publication in 1599 of his *Life and Reign of King Henry IV*, the historian Sir John Hayward was almost indicted for treason, although much of his material was drawn from the writings of the Roman historian Tacitus.[30] Also in 1599 certain publications provoked a famous order by the Archbishop of Canterbury, John Whitgift, who prohibited further printing of certain named satires in verse and prose (those that had been printed were to be burnt), and commanded in particular that no history plays be printed unless they had been allowed by the Privy Council and that other plays be permitted only 'by such as have authority'.[31] All of this testifies to a widespread habit of scrutinising the past for analogues of the present, a habit of mind that derives from typological reading of the Bible. Yet the fact that the gist of that 1589 order from the Privy Council (which repeats a formula that had been used in a proclamation of 1559), was often repeated is yet another example of the way the reach of the Tudor state exceeded its grasp.[32]

What this and other encounters with the various authorities who had powers of censorship confirm – Jonson was forced to write a prefatory epistle to *Sejanus* which does not really accord with the contents of his play – is that the age did not draw a firm distinction between history and politics. This was inevitable: Cicero had celebrated history as the 'light of truth ... the mistress of life', a contradictory description that could be sharpened into a claim as threatening as the observation by a contemporary of Shakespeare that history taught 'the precepts either of politic laws or of the art of war'.[33] It was equally impossible to separate politics from religion: Richard Bancroft, canon of Westminster, seems to have promoted theatrical satires by Lyly, Nashe, and Greene against 'Martin Marprelate', the fictitious author of scurrilous pamphlets attacking the English bishops.

Historiography

Like the 'chroniclers' Shakespeare does not offer an unadorned account of act and event, nor does he separate dramatisation from commentary – Rumour as chorus in 2 *Henry IV* and the prologues in *Henry V* are the exceptions that prove the rule. His language, in verse and in prose, tells as it shows, offering not reflections *of* the past but reflections *on* the past. As the Russian director Grigori Kosintsev exclaimed, 'Who said [Shakespeare] was reflecting history? He was interfering with the present'.[34] Shakespeare, in fact, may well be the greatest political thinker of his age, addressing himself to matters such as the enigmas of empire, statehood, and nationality, to clashes between ethical and political imperatives, the possibilities for individual liberty within a society conceived of as a 'body politic' (see Menenius' parable of the belly in *Coriolanus* 1.1). He examines roles for women in political life, lays out relationships between honour, valour and policy – sometimes suggesting that women's concept of what constituted honour in men was too narrowly equated with valour, an equation that, as in *Henry VI*, *Macbeth*, and *Coriolanus*, could have disastrous consequences.[35] More generally he questioned whether nobility derived from birth or behaviour, addressed difficulties of governance in a society where information was scanty, rumour was rife, and national armies were put together out of what were essentially private militias. He drew attention to the way the level of funds in the exchequer affected the monarch's power to act, and explored what constituted the 'common weal', suggesting throughout that although monarchical power might have been acquired by 'divine right', monarchs had no absolute right to rule in a lawless manner.[36] Shakespeare may well have appreciated Alexander Pope's quipping reference to 'The RIGHT DIVINE of Kings to govern wrong' (*The Dunciad*, 1742, IV, 188).

Above all, like most 'politic historians' of the Renaissance, Shakespeare was interested in causation.[37] Earlier writers chronicled the course of human events on the assumption that they unfolded under divine control: events from the death of a king to the fall of a sparrow were demonstrations of God's providence. Accounts of prodigies and what we would take to be 'natural' catastrophes are construed by Hall and Holinshed as divinely ordained. Although Shakespeare probably believed that there was a divinity that shaped our ends, like most of his contemporaries his interest was in secondary causes, in the way men could be seen making their own history, even if the conditions were not of their choosing: 'Wisdom cries out in the streets, and no man regards it' (*1H4*, 1.2.89) proclaims Hal – he was quoting from Proverbs 1.23–4. It may well be that Shakespeare would have agreed with Francis Bacon who held that any attempt to deduce metaphysical causes from the material world served just to create 'remoraes and hindrances to stay and slug [hinder] the ship from sailing'.[38] As in the case of Hall and Holinshed, we should not look for consistency – in any one play providential explanations of historical change may coexist with secular ones. This is not surprising, given that the author is often depicting the explanations men offer themselves of historical change. The texts are polyphonic: 'the powers that be', voices of authority, attempt to legitimate their authority by avowing that they and their offices are ordained by God. These voices contend with popular voices which invoke the commonweal, demystify power, desacralise the monarchy, or expose the cost of heroic adventurism: 'there are few die well that die in a battle' (*H5*, 3.1.141). Despite the rhetoric of military leaders, many a battle in the histories does not in performance resemble a duel, a form of trial under the eye of God, but appears as a 'brawl ridiculous' (*H5*, 4 Prol. 51) or as a skirmish whose outcome has little meaning. Fights are won or lost for secular or material reasons, for 'want of men and money' as a Messenger puts it tersely at the opening of Shakespeare's first history, *1 Henry VI*. The terse words of the Messenger criticise not only the conduct of the nobility, but their self-deluding fustian style. 'Politics', a demystificatory analysis of the forces that shape events, has interrupted 'history' – at least that kind of history that derives from theology and reads human chronicles as chapters in a book of God. When, in *Henry V*, the English win a great victory over the French at Agincourt the result is presented as a miracle as disconcerting as it is glorious – the ethics of the Almighty himself seem to be questioned. In his film version, made during the Second World War, Olivier changed the number of the English dead from 'five-and-twenty' (4.8.107) to 'five-and-twenty score', presumably to make the outcome of Agincourt less embarrassing.

Although, as in *Julius Caesar* and *Richard III*, ghosts may appear and supernatural prodigies may be described, these tend to function as portents, theatrical devices to signal the course of the action. Margot Heinemann wrote, 'Prophecies, dreams, and ghosts may influence the audience's moral attitude to the action … but do not determine its course. Comments on political events are usually those of various human characters, not of the author, and the audience retains the right to judge between them.'[39] As in the tragedies, there are many moments like that when Cassius uses a familiar trope to urge Brutus to political action:

> Men at some time were masters of their fates.
> The fault, dear Brutus, is not in our stars,
> But in ourselves, that we are underlings.
>
> (*JC*, 1.2.140–2)

History is made by the decisions and actions of men and women taken at particular times and in particular circumstances.

As well as following Hall and Holinshed, Shakespeare had absorbed the influence of the Italian politic historians of the Renaissance, epitomised by the writings of Machiavelli, a contemporary of Sir Thomas More at the beginning of the sixteenth century. In the introduction to his *Discourses* Machiavelli writes of history as having to do with action and not mere knowledge. The majority of people, he says, read history passively, in order to 'take pleasure only in the variety of events' it relates, 'without ever thinking of imitating the noble actions'.[40] There is a cue for subversion there – 'if you want to learn how to become a "magistrate", read this'. Shakespearean texts, plays like *Richard III*, may demonstrate the fragility of civil society rather than a confidence in a divinely appointed order. Richard of Gloucester can destroy a state in the way a clever and malicious child can destroy a family – in fact he and Buckingham play a theatrical and childlike game of defending an imaginary Castle of England in order to dupe the Mayor of London (*R3*, 3.1). In another mode Henry V accepts the challenge of the Dauphin who sends him tennis balls as tribute and goes to France to play at war. The sport of kings becomes the scourge of peace.

All Shakespeare's history plays, with the exception of *Henry VIII*, were written during the reign of Elizabeth. Although their material derives from the English chroniclers Hall and Holinshed they may have been generated in part by a surge of interest in historiography that centred on critical rereadings of Tacitus. It is a moment of politic history that can be located about the time of the composition of Marlowe's translation of Lucan's *Pharsalia* and the publication of Sir Henry Savile's translation of Tacitus' *Histories* in 1591, printed with an epistle that, according to Jonson, was written by the Earl of Essex himself.[41] Marlowe's translation is significant because Lucan took a very sceptical view of Julius Caesar's imperial ambitions.[42] Tacitus' view of history was likewise quizzical and secular: his emperors were, unlike Shakespeare's monarchs, scarcely possessed of a mystic as well as a natural body, and his great themes were ancient liberty, and what his translator, almost certainly invoking *Tamburlaine*, called 'higher aspiring minds',[43] corruption, and modern servitude. In the epistle we read

> In these four books ... thou shalt see all the miseries of a torn and declining state: the empire usurped, the princes murdered, the people wavering, the soldiers tumultuous, nothing unlawful to him that hath power, and nothing so unsafe as to be securely innocent ... If thou dost detest their anarchy, acknowledge our own happy government, and thank God for her, under whom England enjoys as many benefits as ever Rome did suffer miseries under the greatest tyrant.[44]

'Ambition' is a key word in *Julius Caesar* and Jonson was to get into trouble by writing Tacitean history plays in the next century and during the next reign. But Tacitean matter – it is not just a question of style – can be discerned earlier. Tacitus delighted in exposing the hypocrisy of courtiers: his target was absolutism and her handmaid, theatricality. His tone was sardonic and his characters could be fantastical, like actors in a play. *Richard II*, unlike many tragedies, centres not just on one outsize character but on the conflict between two men with very different styles as actors on the political stage, King Richard and his cousin Henry Bullingbrook. As the former declines in power, figured in the moment when he cannot resist the great histrionic gesture and comes down 'like glistering Phaethon' from the walls of Flint Castle to parley with his adversary (3.3.178–83), the latter rises, designing strategic alliances with the Percy family. Bullingbrook's motives are ambiguous: is he merely ambitious, or is he concerned to prune the garden of the commonwealth (3.4) and take out the prodigal gardener? Shakespeare was always alert to a variety of historical processes and his political characters often behave theatrically – at worst being guilty of dissimulation, at best as though they are conscious of taking part in a play. Even Coriolanus says, 'I play / The man I am' (3.2.14–15). Richard III had pronounced, 'I am I' (5.3.186), in his case a blasphemous echo of God's words to Moses from the burning bush, 'I AM THAT I AM' (Exod. 3.14). With these observations in mind, we might even surmise that a classic definition of postmodernist novels as 'historiographical metafictions' well describes Shakespearean history plays.[45]

The translator of Tacitus, Sir Henry Savile, was prepared to argue that it was right to resist a tyrant, a thesis that was also propounded in political documents like the anonymous *Vindiciae Contra Tyrannos* that had emerged during the French Wars of Religion. Richard's profligacy weighed so heavily on his people as to constitute a kind of tyranny. Of Vindex, who led a rebellion against Nero, Savile wrote:

> Not upon private despair to set in combustion the state, not to revenge disgrace or dishonour, not to establish his own sovereignty, things which have moved most men to attempt; but to redeem his country from tyranny and bondage, which only respect he regarded so much that in respect he regarded nothing his own life or security.[46]

Savile then discusses Nero who stands for exotic monstrous viciousness in *3 Henry VI* (3.1.40); in *King John* the Bastard likes the English lords to 'bloody Neros, ripping up the womb / Of your dear mother England' (5.2.152–3). Another Tacitean theme is that the populace are merely 'the instruments of the ambition of others',[47] a view that might invalidate our sympathies for the followers of Cade in *2 Henry VI* or of the plebeians in the Roman plays. Theatrical representation of such sequences, however, can invalidate this scepticism.

Yet the plays have not always been read in this fashion. Earlier generations of commentators read the plays as a prolonged apologia for the Tudor dynasty. E.M.W. Tillyard, writing during the Second World War, held that Shakespeare and his contemporaries endorsed what Tillyard had earlier termed '*the* Elizabethan world picture', and in particular, that Shakespeare's history plays endorsed 'the Tudor myth [which] presented a scheme fundamentally religious, by which events evolve under a law of justice and under the ruling of God's providence, and of which Elizabeth's England was the acknowledged outcome'.[48] There are various difficulties with such a reading. First, there would have been no instructions from a variety of censors if there had not been radical disagreements in the period over the best ordering of a civil society. The execution of Roman Catholic priests during the reign of Elizabeth was an instrument of political as well as religious repression. Tillyard's reading concentrates on prophesies and on references within the text to a divinely ordained pattern for history. Yet prophesying was as much a political as a religious act, and those characters who proclaimed a divine order may have been created by Shakespeare as examples of those who used the topics of religious discourse for particular secular purposes or as figures of self-deception or even credulousness. They are not necessarily choric figures – it is notable that there are no references to a providential pattern to English history in those (comparatively few) choruses that he wrote. When the Bishop of Carlisle prophesies in 4.1 of *Richard II* he is giving an account of history that is his own – not necessarily one endorsed by Shakespeare – and he is promptly arrested for capital treason.

In Tillyard's reading the murder of Richard II becomes a kind of original sin, the consequences of which were visited upon Bullingbrook (Henry IV) and his descendants. However, as we have seen, *Richard II* and *1–2 Henry IV* were written *after* the chronicles of the Wars of the Roses in *1–3 Henry VI* and *Richard III*, and in *1 Henry VI* Shakespeare gives us an emblematic scene in which plucking of white and red roses marks the division of England's élite into factions. The iconography of the scene contains analogies with the narrative of the Fall in Genesis and may encourage a reading that stresses systemic rather than historical origins for dissent.

'Edification'

As we have seen, Machiavelli seemed to the Elizabethans to have brought into being the dystopias that Shakespeare created in the Henry VI plays and *Richard III*. It was to Sir Thomas More that men looked for the opposite vision, to More's model of a designer state in the *Utopia*. Although Shakespeare was no Utopian, never willing to share the view of those who saw things as other than they are, he did imply that men could, by thinking strategically, construct a new kind of society. Here is the canny Lord Bardolph, one of the leaders of the rebels against Bullingbrook in 2 *Henry IV*:

> When we mean to build,
> We first survey the plot, then draw the model;
> And when we see the figure of the house,
> Then must we rate the cost of the erection,
> Which if we find outweighs ability,
> What do we then but draw anew the model
> In fewer offices, or at least desist
> To build at all? Much more in this great work
> (Which is almost to pluck a kingdom down
> And set another up) should we survey
> The plot of situation and the model,
> Consent upon a sure foundation,
> Question surveyors, know our own estate,
> How able such a work to undergo,
> To weigh against his opposite.
>
> (2H4, 1.3.41–55)

The analogy is a time-honoured one, deriving ultimately from the linked Parables of the Tower Builder and the King going to War in Luke 14.28–32. Bardolph is offering a lesson in 'edification': etymologically the word means 'building' and is a recurrent metaphor in the Pauline epistles. It is around this topic, attached to the building of Solomon's Temple, that the reforming theologians who prepared the Geneva Bible in 1560 wrote their Epistle Dedicatory to the monarch.[49] Shakespeare's debt to Plutarch, Tacitus, and the Italian historians places him in the mainstream of Renaissance culture, but he owes equal allegiance to movements for reformation. Reformation, a project at the centre of the history plays,[50] whether of the individual as with Prince Hal or of the country, depends upon planning and the setting of realistic goals. As Richard Hooker wrote about 1593, 'men are edified, when either their understanding is taught somewhat whereof in such actions it behoveth all men to consider, or when their hearts are moved with any affection suitable thereunto'. Hooker goes on to praise words and 'sensible means', i.e. religious and public ceremonies, as instruments of edification.[51]

'Edification' has also to do with the craft of the playwright or maker of theatrical ceremonies. Playwrights deploy what Sir Philip Sidney, following

Aristotle, called the 'architectonic' arts, those that combined particular skills.[52] A playwright is a kind of 'architect', called upon to furnish narrative, language, and directions for the theatrical imagery that adorned his play. Out of these materials a maker of history plays builds ethical and political structures. And, as Aristotle said,

> Since politics makes use of the other practical sciences, and lays down what we must do and what we must not do, its end must include theirs. And that end, in politics as well as in ethics, can only be the good for man. For even if the good of the community coincides with that of the individual, the good of the community is clearly a greater and more perfect good both to get and to keep. This is not to deny that the good of the individual is worth while. But what is good for a nation or a city has a higher, a diviner, quality.[53]

If Shakespeare was setting out to educate his audience he offered not just moral exhortation, lessons in providential history or repetitions of Tudor propaganda, but sketched out situations and motivations in all their complexity, writing theatrical essays on political 'edification', on the possibilities of and impediments to wisdom and reformist visions.

In *King John* (1596) and the *Henry IV* plays that were written over the next couple of years Shakespeare addresses not just character conflict but the role of the monarchy in a newly emergent state. For the authors of that Geneva Epistle, the enemies of the state were papists, ambitious prelates, and 'worldlings'.[54] Shakespeare's plays ask their audience whether in fact England is governable, as they watch the monarch resisting the machinations of the papal legate Pandulph in *King John* or the destabilising prophecies of the Bishop of Carlisle in *Richard II*. In *1* and *2 Henry IV* we witness Bullingbrook's difficulties with the worldlings of his reign, notably with the Percies who had supported him. His own son is so driven by a desire to seize the crown that we may be tempted to look for a psycho-social explanation, possibly Freud's Œdipal complex, to explain it. Falstaff and his crew demonstrate that while kings might propose it is clowns who dispose. The king had two bodies: the material body of Falstaff, standing for commodity (expediency and self-interest), revelry, lasciviousness, and makes him a political figure – scarcely a focus for mere 'comic relief'. His rotundity makes him truly a 'worldling', a figure of everything that could not be accommodated within the state of England. Yet he is also, as we see from the play-scene in *1 Henry IV* (2.4), an actor, able to play the king just as well as his companion the prince. Handy-dandy, what is substantial, what is mere 'shadow'? This is the question that Shakespeare in his great historiographical metafictions wickedly but wisely refused to answer.

NOTES

I should like to thank Sarah Carter for preparing the index to this volume.

1 Some of Shakespeare's plays were individually published during Shakespeare's lifetime as smaller books, 'quartos' or, occasionally, 'octavos'. The texts these contain often differ considerably from those of the Folio. Some of them are obviously corrupt, but even the so-called 'bad quartos' contain stage directions that are useful to modern editors, because many reveal traces of early performance.

2 Aristotle 1920, ch. 9, p. 43; Sidney 1965, p. 109; Bradley 1957, p. 62; for the essay Bradley wrote about *Ant.*, see Bradley 1909, pp. 277–308.

3 See Bulman's essay in this volume, pp. 158–76.

4 See Foakes' essay in this volume. pp. 214–28.

5 For a reading of *The Tempest* as an English 'history play', see Wymer 1999.

6 See Harbage 1989, pp. 22–3.

7 See Fox 1999.

8 Hall 1809, p. 1.

9 Nashe 1958, I, 212.

10 Puttenham 1589, p. 122.

11 See Bolam in this volume, pp. 141–57.

12 See Kantorowicz 1957.

13 See in this volume, pp. 247–60.

14 See p. 230 of Hampton-Reeves in this volume; Hodgdon 1991.

15 Coleridge 1836, II, 159–60.

16 See Kreps 1999.

17 For *prosopopeia* see Puttenham 1589, p. 200.

18 See Bakhtin 1981.

19 See *1H6*, ed. Hattaway 1990, p. 64.

20 Augustine, *The City of God*, 4.4, quoted in Cox 1989, pp. 12–13.

21 See Kastan 1986.

22 See in this volume, Bolam, pp. 147–8.

23 Bacon 1865, p. 77.

24 See *1H4*, 1.3; *H5*, 3.6.100–12; *Cor.*, 1.6.

25 *3H6*, ed. Hattaway 1993, p. 213; see also Goy-Blanquet, p. 63 in this volume.

26 Nashe 1958, I, 212; Gilbert 1962, p. 558.

27 Wickham *et al.* 2000, p. 95; this order may, however, refer to anti-Martinist plays (see below) or to seditious matter in Marlowe's *Doctor Faustus*: see Clare 1990, pp. 24–59.

28 Clare *ibid.*, pp. 39–43, Clegg 1997.

29 See Bolam p. 144 in this volume; for the censorship of 'Oldcastle' (Falstaff), see Bulman pp. 160–2 in this volume.

30 See Collinson 2000a.

31 See McCabe 1981.

32 No officers were to permit interludes 'wherein either matters of religion or of the governance of the estate of the Commonwealth shall be handled or treated: being no meet matters to be written or treated upon but by men of authority, learning, and wisdom, not to be handled before any audience, but of grave and discreet persons' (Wickham *et al.* 2000, p. 51); see also minutes of 15 August 1597 (p. 102) and 10 May 1601 (p. 414).

33 Cicero, *De Oratore*, 2.9; Coignet 1586, p. 71.
34 Quoted in Hodgdon 1983.
35 See Harding 1969.
36 These matters are best explored in the working drafts made in the 1590s by Richard Hooker and published as Book VIII of his *Laws*: see Hooker 1989, pp. 139–58.
37 For a general survey of Renaissance historiography, see Woolf 1999; also Rackin 1990, pp. 6ff.
38 Bacon 1900, II.vii.7, p. 119.
39 Heinemann 1990, p. 179.
40 Machiavelli 1950, p. 104.
41 See Womersley 1991, pp. 313–42; Tuck 1993, p. 105; the epistle may have been written by Anthony Bacon.
42 See *JC*, ed. Humphreys 1984, p. 28 for evidence that Shakespeare knew Lucan.
43 Tacitus 1598, 1.4, p. 7.
44 *Ibid.*, 1591, Sig. ¶3^{r-v}.
45 Hutcheon 1988, p. 5.
46 Tacitus 1591. Sig. ¶6^{v}; see Skinner 1978, pp. 187–358.
47 See Womersley 1991.
48 Tillyard 1943; *ibid.*, 1944, p. 321.
49 Key scriptural texts are Rom.14.19; 1 Cor.10.23 and 14.3–5; 2 Cor.13.10; 1 Thess.5.11; the metaphor is found in a treatise to King James written by Francis Bacon at the time of the Hampton Court Conference (1604), *The Pacification and Edification of the Church of England* and in Jonson's *Catiline* (1.392–5) and Jonson's *Bartholomew Fair* (5.6.115–16) where it derives from Horace and Sallust.
50 See Collinson 1986.
51 Hooker 1907, I, 361.
52 Sidney 1965, p. 104.
53 Aristotle 1955, I, i–ii, p. 27.
54 Bible, (Geneva, 1560), Sig. ***ii^{r}.

2

A. J. HOENSELAARS

Shakespeare and the early modern history play

John Churchill, the first Duke of Marlborough (1650–1722), is alleged to have said that he knew no English history but what he had learned from Shakespeare. The irony of Marlborough's claim was that Shakespeare's ten history plays, covering a century and a half between them, could eclipse the infinitely broader, complex narrative of the English nation. A similar type of irony may be discerned in the modern reception of the Shakespearean history play. Here, the experience of many readers and theatre-goers with the Shakespeare histories tends to be inversely proportional to their familiarity with the genesis and history of the history play as a literary genre in an early modern European context, in England and abroad. The same individual who might now visit Blenheim Palace at Woodstock under the assumption that the Duke of Marlborough was a wealthy tobacconist, is likely also to live under the delusion that Shakespeare invented the history play. But as G. K. Hunter has rightly noted, 'Shakespeare could not, any more than God, invent *ex nihilo*.'[1] Shakespeare had predecessors but also contemporaries who practised the history play, and although it seems beyond doubt, as Richard Helgerson has argued, that 'Shakespeare did make a larger contribution to that genre than anyone else', these contemporaries provide an indispensable framework within which the unique achievement of Shakespeare may be appreciated.[2] One of the aims of this essay is to bring into focus Shakespeare's accomplishment within the immediate English contexts of the new genre. In addition, this essay seeks to position Shakespeare and the early modern project of historical drama in its no less relevant, though frequently neglected, European framework.

The English history play as practised by Shakespeare had distinct roots in the morality tradition, which produced, among other things, John Bale's *King Johan* of the 1530s, and the anonymous *Troublesome Reign of John* (1587/91), before Shakespeare wrote his own *King John* (1591/98). The life and death of King John is highly appropriate as subject matter for the earliest English history plays. Although modern readers are likely to associate his reign with the Magna Carta of 1215, the sixteenth-century stage lives of John Lackland largely concentrate on the monarch's rather fraught relationship with the puissant Church of Rome, and make little or no reference to the event that marks the beginning of the constitutional monarchy. To the Tudors, John's problematic relations with Rome recalled Henry VIII's politico-religious contention with the Pope and Roman Catholicism. Thus represented, the analogy between the two reigns enables one to recognise how the Reformation, and with it England's radical and isolated position in Europe from the 1530s onwards, induced the national self-awareness that is likely to have fostered the developing stage genre of the history play in England.[3]

King John was not the only monarch whose reign had been staged before Shakespeare turned to the material. The anonymous *Thomas of Woodstock* (1591/5) – presenting the marriage of Richard II to Anne of Bohemia, as well as the fateful assassination of his uncle Woodstock at Calais – has long been interpreted and dated as the first part of Shakespeare's *Richard II*, which has unmistakable intertextual connections with the anonymous play.[4] Also, when Shakespeare wrote his early history play on the political career of Richard III – the Yorkist who, since Sir Thomas More's prose *History* of him (1513), had been the favourite Tudor scapegoat – the playwright was really treading ground familiar to Thomas Legge, the Cambridge-based author of the Latin *Ricardus Tertius* (1579/80). In addition, there had been the anonymous *True Tragedy of Richard III* (1588–94). Shakespeare's *Henry IV* and *Henry V* play off their scope, sophistication, and epic polish against the anonymous rambling chronicle, *The Famous Victories of Henry V* (before 1588). There was also a precedent for *Henry VI* as the history of the king withdrawing from the political scene to philosophise seated on a molehill; its eponymous monarch had already appeared allegorically in the 1580s as the image of idleness, passively gazing at the nation's misery in *The Second Part of the Seven Deadly Sins*, likely to have been written by Richard Tarlton.

If in these instances we can say with near certainty that Shakespeare drew upon existing historical drama, there are also situations where it is more difficult to define the exact mode of exchange. The Jack Cade rising that Shakespeare presents in the second part of *Henry VI*, for example, has a number of striking similarities with the anonymous play about the Peasant Revolt entitled *The Life and Death of Jack Straw* (1590/3), but it is difficult to establish the exact relation between them. For its portrayal of the languid king surrounded by sycophants, *Richard II* unmistakably relies on Marlowe's *Edward II*, but as Charles Forker has rightly argued, the interrelations between Marlowe and Shakespeare via the burgeoning genre of the history play is many times more complex.[5] The most intriguing instance of

Figure 2   The murder of Thomas of Woodstock, Duke of Gloucester (see *Richard II*), from
'De la mort du duc de Gloucester et du comte d'Arundel', Jean Froissart, *Chroniques de
France et d'Angleterre*, c.1480.

overlap between Shakespeare's history plays with contemporary dramatic
material is undoubtedly that of *Henry IV* and *The True and Honourable
History, of the Life of Sir John Old-castle, the Good Lord Cobham* (1600),
which, as its title conveys, rather emphatically rehabilitates the Protestant
martyr whose name Shakespeare used for the character that became Falstaff
after complaints from Sir John Brooke, whose title, Lord Cobham, was the
same as that of the original Sir John Oldcastle.[6] In the final analysis, the
often creative and sometimes troubled connections between Shakespeare's
history plays and the other historical drama of the period suggest that the

history play – which had gradually emerged from the morality tradition, mobilised for the national, Protestant cause by Bale – was an attractively new but also potentially volatile political genre inviting different playwrights to experiment in the no-man's-land between dramatic history and state diplomacy.

In view of this widespread early modern interest in the history play, it is curious that, with few exceptions (such as *Edward II*), only Shakespeare's history plays are still read and performed, often as a category in their own right, without reference to the other contemporary plays. There may be several reasons why the other history plays seem to have faded from literary history. With their material's historically specific urgency changing in the course of time, they would also need to possess additional merits to enjoy a continuing interest. The joint political and psychological complexity of Shakespeare's history plays could account for much of his lasting appeal, although one should not underestimate the impact of the process by which Shakespeare has risen to become the national laureate whose English history plays have tended to be privileged over those of his contemporaries. In times of war, it is not the anonymous *Famous Victories* that are recycled to boost the nation's morale, but Shakespeare's *Henry V*. But there are, of course, significant differences worth contemplating.

Shakespeare's history plays are at a far remove from the folk plays of the period like Robert Greene's genre-blending *Scottish History of James the Fourth* (based on Giraldi Cinthio's *Heccatommithi*), or Anthony Munday's two instalments of *The Downfall and Death of Robert Earl of Huntingdon* (1598). Munday's two plays are set during the early reign of King John, but rather than concentrating on matters of national interest, they are constructed around the life and death of the eponymous folk hero, better known as Robin Hood, a character whom Ben Jonson relegated to the genre of comedy in *The Sad Shepherd* (1641). John Meagher has advanced the convincing argument that the folk story got out of hand as Munday wrote the two plays. This inevitably moved the scenes involving King John and his mother, Eleanor of Aquitaine, to the periphery, and even created the need for Henslowe to commission an additional play, presumably never written, on *Richard Cœur de Lion*.[7] Perhaps one of most glaring examples of romance history marginalising the monarch is Thomas Dekker's *The Shoemaker's Holiday*. Here Thomas Deloney's account of the eccentric political career of London shoemaker Simon Eyre is, in the final scene, framed by the appearance of a king who, historically speaking, should be Henry VI, but who – as his convivial behaviour and his apparent delight in tennis suggest – is really Henry V, the more popular monarch, eminently capable also of appreciating a holiday. Dekker's play is primarily a comedy, and only in the second instance, with dauntless anachronism, does the play elect the monarch most suitable to rule the festive nation.

With the exception of *Henry VIII*, the period covered in Shakespeare's history plays invariably antedates 1485. For quite a number of his contemporaries in the theatre, however, the history of England continued beyond the end of the Wars of the Roses, and they developed a wide variety of plays using materials bearing on the more recent Tudor era. Samuel Rowley, still in an implausible, ballad-like manner, stages Henry VIII in *When You See Me, You Know Me* (1604), where the king comes to London in disguise to pick a hand-to-hand fight with Black Will who is suspected of murdering two merchants at the London Steelyard.[8] More serious is the treatment of Tudor history in Thomas Dekker and John Webster's *Sir Thomas Wyatt* (1602), dealing with the troublesome succession at the death of King Edward VI, the defamation of his rightful heir Lady Jane Grey, and the ominous ascent to the throne of the Catholic Mary Tudor, against whose marriage to Philip II and whose denial of religious freedom it is that Sir Thomas Wyatt speaks, fearless that his 'liberal tongue', as the queen terms it, might offend.

When, in 1603, Queen Elizabeth died, and the ban on portraying living monarchs no longer applied to her, Thomas Heywood was quick to produce his two-part play about the life of the virgin queen in *If You Know Not Me, You Know Nobody*, which begins with the same Marian history as that rehearsed in *Sir Thomas Wyatt*, before continuing into Elizabeth's reign until the 1590s. Heywood's is primarily a hagiographic representation of Elizabeth in trade (with Sir Thomas Gresham as the mainstay of England's international commerce at the new London Exchange) and in war (with the victory over the Spanish Armada as the pivotal encounter). In one of the earliest instances of romancing the queen, Heywood originally presents even Philip II as an attractive character. The King of Spain tries to make Elizabeth and her sister Mary friends and prevents the impending execution of Elizabeth. On one level, this may have been made possible by the peace with Spain that James effected when he came to the throne as Elizabeth's successor in 1603. On another level, however, such unusual behaviour from the enemy of Protestantism could have served to convey God's special concern for Elizabeth and the national religion she defended; as such the play may even have been critical of James' compromise policy. Heywood's diptych was to remain highly popular on the London stage until the closing of the theatres in 1642, although it was not to be in exactly the same shape. Relations with Spain deteriorated over the years, and considerable anti-Spanish revisions were undertaken in the 1630s. Heywood's play amply illustrates the use to which the memory of Elizabeth could be put; but it also underscores the sparse representation of Elizabeth as '*the child richly habited in a mantle'* in the concluding scene of Shakespeare's *Henry VIII.*[9]

As a partial consequence of their readiness to exploit Tudor history, Shakespeare's contemporaries also developed the biographical history play.[10] This genre tended to concentrate on the political life and career of a striking, often non-royal figure in sixteenth-century English history, drawing on John Foxe's *Acts and Monuments*, that immensely popular collection of lives of those who died as martyrs. The biographical, Foxean subgenre includes such plays as *Sir Thomas More* (1593) and *Thomas Lord Cromwell* (1600), as well as *Sir Thomas Wyatt*. Foxean is also Thomas Drue's *Duchess of Suffolk* (1624), dramatising the life of the Katherine of Suffolk who was forced to leave England with the accession to the throne of the Catholic Mary Tudor, and allowed to return from years of exile on the continent of Europe only when Elizabeth succeeded to the throne. In Drue's case, Tudor history really served as a veiled criticism of King James' prevaricating attitude toward his own daughter, Elizabeth Stuart, who, together with her husband, the Count Palatine, was left to her own devices amidst the political turmoil that engulfed Germany and Bohemia.[11]

With these varying biographical forms Shakespeare seems to have had little sympathy. Shakespeare had a hand in *Sir Thomas More*, but a corrective one, and *Thomas Lord Cromwell* seems to have been only spuriously attributed to him as 'W.S.' on the original 1602 title-page, Thomas Heywood and Michael Drayton being the more likely candidates for authorship. Where the Foxean history play is concerned, Shakespeare is explicit. After the protest from Sir William Brooke over the use of Oldcastle's name for Hal's drinking companion, Shakespeare changed it to Falstaff and, at the end of the second part of *Henry IV*, distanced himself from the Foxean tradition altogether, making certain that no affiliation existed between Falstaff and the Wycliffite martyr from Foxe: 'Oldcastle died a martyr, and this is not the man.'[12]

Hunter interprets the biographical history as a retreat from 'the concept of history as a matter of national success and failure'.[13] In this way, he implicitly advances a contrast between the *nation* as one of Shakespeare's main concerns, and the *individual* that appealed to a number of his contemporaries. Richard Helgerson has attractively politicised and elucidated this contrast by arguing that Shakespeare's thoughts inclined towards abstract, centralised power and empire, whereas a number of his fellow-playwrights (like those writing for Philip Henslowe), imagined the nation, their own and the nation staged, in terms of the larger community – the artisans, the merchants, womenfolk, and children – with their civic self-identity. In Helgerson's view, Shakespeare, and with him the Lord Chamberlain's Men, attempted to free themselves from such labels as 'popular', 'marginal', 'subversive', and 'folk', and the alienation of such qualities from their plays served this purpose. In this way, the new genre of the national history that Shakespeare helped to establish and focus, 'contributed at once to the consolidation of central power, to the cultural division from class to class, and to the emergence of the playwright – Shakespeare himself – as both gentleman and poet'.[14]

In contrast to the remarkable advances made in recent years in charting the writing of the English nation and of Britain, there has been a relative neglect of the continental history play, that special brand of drama about near contemporary events in Europe which was no less relevant as a constitutive factor in writing the nation. Shakespeare's history plays, of course, repeatedly take the action to France, and there is a cross-Channel location shift in *Edward III*, *Henry V*, as well as the first and third parts of *Henry VI*. Nevertheless, we hesitate to treat these plays as continental histories; the plays as developed by Shakespeare's colleagues suggest that the ultimately distinctive feature about the subgenre was not so much the change from England to another European location, as the engagement with continental historical material that had not yet shed its original political pertinence.

The earliest practitioner of the genre in England was Marlowe with *The Massacre at Paris* (1592). The play represents the aggressive Catholic force of the Pope and Spain, and portrays the French King Henry IV as a Protestant hero. To establish the connection between foreign history and domestic concerns, or in an attempt to override narrow national concerns for the benefit of European Protestantism, Marlowe deftly introduces an anonymous English agent in the final scene. He has no lines to speak, but is appointed to convey to Queen Elizabeth the dying words of Henry III of France. The dying king unambiguously extends his 'eternal love' to England and her queen, 'Whom God hath blessed for hating papistry.' Marlowe's *Massacre at Paris* was indeed, as Harry Levin has put it, 'a tale of two cities'.[15] The Dickensian allusion is further developed by Andrew Kirk, who reads into Marlowe's representation of French history a rehearsal of the threatening, other culture before securing that experience in a reassertion of English power and control (pp. 97–8). Unlike the anonymous *A Larum for London* (1599), which presents the fall of Antwerp of 1576 as a warning to London audiences to maintain a proper defence against the Spanish threat, *The Massacre at Paris* transforms England into the elect nation, predicating its political rule on the effective containment of denominational strife.

Marlowe's great successor in the field was George Chapman, the author of *Bussy d'Ambois* (1604) and its sequel *The Revenge of Bussy d'Ambois* (1610), the two-part *Conspiracy and Tragedy of Charles, Duke of Byron* (1608), as well as *The Tragedy of Chabot, Admiral of France* (1612). Kirk illustrates how the representation of Chapman's French history in the guise of neoclassical tragedy is informed by a preoccupation with alternative views of history that French historiographers were developing. In Chapman's continental histories, the linear, providential, Christian view of history endorsed by particular characters in Shakespeare's plays is supplanted by a classical view that presupposes continuing antagonism between erratic fortune and human virtue, thus rehearsing a view of history revitalised by Renaissance historians like Machiavelli in *The Prince* (1513–15) and in his *Discourses* (1513–17) on Livy's *History of Rome*.

Writing on the representation of European history on the early modern stage, J. R. Mulryne has drawn attention to differences between the cosmopolitan character of early modern English drama, and the Anglocentric brand of theatre that developed in later centuries, and has persevered. As a consequence, Mulryne observes, '[t]he theatre of England since the mid-seventeenth century has largely neglected the history of Europe'.[16] This tendency is discernible in the drama, he argues, but it is also reflected in the history of criticism of the period's literature. It is hard to substantiate the claim that such neglect of the drama's continental focus might be due to the 'continuing isolation of English academic and intellectual life' (p. 60). Nevertheless, it is good to see that a traditional study like Irving Ribner's *The English History Play in the Age of Shakespeare* (1957) has since been complemented by such eminent explorations of the multinational focus as Walter Cohen's *Drama of a Nation* (1985) and John Loftis' *Renaissance Drama in England and Spain* (1987), or Andrew Kirk's *Mirror of Confusion* (1996) about the representation of French history in English Renaissance drama, and that the Anglo-foreign stamp on the dramatic tradition is being taken ever more seriously. Increasingly, one becomes aware that, as Mulryne puts it, 'the divided national consciousness, intensely aware of a national self-identity, but aware too of a *European* context within which that identity came to express itself, nurtured a drama that was both devoted to patriotic ends . . . and was engaged imaginatively also in looking outwards to Europe' (p. 62).

In the final analysis, the perspective that Mulryne offers must bring one to the realisation that the early modern history play was an indisputably European phenomenon with multiple manifestations. The history play developed in a large number of European countries, be it as a secularised morality play or as a modernised mutation of classical tragedy, everywhere carrying its own recognisable secular, national imprint, but never ignoring foreign historical materials. Especially in those contexts where neoclassical theory with its Aristotelian unities did not stand in the way of new, meaning more flexible dramatic modes, the history play soon became an internationally oriented mouthpiece on current issues.[17] Characteristic examples of this tradition developed in Spain and the Netherlands. Both countries, whose fate was closely tied up with England's, developed a tradition of historical drama based on native as well as foreign materials.

In seventeenth-century Spain, the historical genre was marked by a conspicuous vitality, and enjoyed full royal support. Around the Madrid court, one witnesses the development of a series of plays about the country's national history, but also about contemporary European history. The latter was a near equivalent to the continental histories of the English tradition, the main difference being that the Spanish court genre emerged directly out of the nation's own immediate war effort on behalf of Roman Catholicism and the protection of its endangered power base in northern Europe. Lope de Vega's history plays – *The Spaniards in Flanders, The Attack upon Maastricht by the Count of Parma* – have a direct bearing on the prevailing troubles in the Netherlands. But there is also an interest in other Hispano-European history (Lope's *Charles the Fifth in France* and *The Tragedy of Don Sebastian*), and in the representation of expansionist policies in more distant territories, as rehearsed in Lope de Vega's *Brazil Regained* (1625). One of Pedro Calderón de la Barca's notable contributions to the genre is *The Siege of Breda*, an offshoot of the protracted hostilities between Spain and the Low Countries, celebrating the siege of the Dutch town of Breda which the Spanish had terminated in 1625.

Interestingly, of course, England and the English monarchy also featured on the Spanish stage. Calderón's first performed play, *Love, Honour and Power* (1623), for example, stages Edward III's infatuation with the Countess of Salisbury, and depicts how the king acquires self-control before making the countess his queen.[18] This court production was designed as part of a deft Hispano-English strategy, since this play about the premarital lessons of the English monarch was especially staged to delight as well as teach Prince Charles Stuart and the Duke of Buckingham, present at the Prado in June of 1623, for the marriage negotiations over the Spanish infanta that were decisively to sour diplomatic relations between the two countries.

No less intriguing is Calderón's *Schism in England*, presenting the fateful years during the reign of Henry VIII that led to the Act of Supremacy. In this Spanish play presenting the famous events from the other end of the political and denominational spectrum, King Henry is, to a degree, a pawn of Archbishop Wolsey, whose ambition it is to become pope. Wolsey's real antagonist is the strong-willed, Spanish, Catholic Katherine of Aragon. In order to neutralise her power, Wolsey convinces the king that, having illegally married the wife of his deceased brother Arthur, he is really a bachelor, and in a position to marry her lady in waiting, the tempting, French-educated Anne Boleyn. As queen of England, Anne soon loses audience sympathy not just by disgracing Wolsey, who commits suicide, but also by poisoning

the imprisoned Katherine. It is Anne's marital infidelity with the French ambassador that leads Henry to seek her execution. Under these tragic circumstances, Henry is prepared to accept Princess Mary as his successor, if she
will promise, for the time being, to uphold his new dispensation. Although
the Princess of Wales seems to accept his conditions, the audience are left
in no doubt about her determination to violate this promise at her earliest
convenience. At this juncture, the play begins to foreshadow with hindsight
the events of the 1550s as recorded in Foxe's *Acts and Monuments* as well
as such Foxean history plays on the London stage as Dekker and Webster's
Sir Thomas Wyatt, Heywood's *If You Know Not Me*, and a host of others.
Bloody Mary's *auto da fe* is foreshadowed in her pledge to burn alive those
who fail to obey what her law teaches, but also in Henry VIII's curious advice
to her to be discreet in public:

> Be silent and dissimulate; the time
> Will come when you can carry out your zeal,
> And what is now a spark become a bonfire.[19]

It may seem odd to close the play, as Loftis argues, 'with a scene that seems
to point unhistorically to the reestablishment of Catholicism in England'.[20]
However, such curious optimism becomes understandable when one considers that the play was written during the mid-1620s. At this time, Spain
enjoyed the strong leadership of Count-Duke Olivares. During the same year
that saw the decease of *rex pacificus* James I, England and Spain drifted into
war again, and were to be at each others' throats until 1630, when an impecunious Charles I was forced to agree to a peace settlement. In 1625, Spain
could already look back with satisfaction on ending the siege of the Dutch
town of Breda (staged at court by Calderón that same year), and a year later
it successfully repulsed an English raid on Cadiz. It was in the aftermath of
the English failure at Cadiz – recounted in the anonymous London history
play of *Dick of Devonshire* (1626)[21] – that Olivares conceived the plan for
another Spanish invasion of England. Just as the writing of Shakespeare's
Henry VIII took place against the backdrop of a new Armada scare, its
Spanish counterpart was devised to create yet another.[22] The analogy here
is likely to be coincidental, but the early modern tendency among European
playwrights to rehearse the same historical themes and events is too pervasive
to warrant the neglect which this topic has suffered. A comparative study
of the international historical canon is likely to offer many new perspectives
and opportunities for contextualising the history plays of Shakespeare and
his contemporaries.

Like England, and like Spain, the Low Countries developed a tradition
of historical drama in the vernacular. The Twelve Years Truce with Spain

(1609/21) which marked an interruption of the hostilities with the Catholic enemy, as well as the latter's recognition of the northern Republic, boosted national self-awareness and led to a sharp increase of native Dutch material used for stage representation. No doubt, the Republic's newness, too, invited a type of drama which, via a safe historical detour, might engage in a debate over matters constitutional and denominational.[23] The most popular plays following in the wake of Daniel Heinsius' Latin history play on the life and death of William of Orange, entitled *Auriacus* (1602), include P. C. Hooft's *Gheraerdt van Velsen* (1613) and *Baeto, or the Dutch Descent* (1617), and Joost van den Vondel's *Gysbreght van Aemstel* (1637). The canon, however, tends to obscure the scope of the Dutch history play's political engagement in the early years of the Republic, as in the case of Vondel's *The Batavian Brothers* (1663), and two nearly contemporaneous plays on the Bartholomew Massacre, by Lambert van den Bosch (1645) and Reynier Anslo (1649). As the plays on the Bartholomew Massacre suggest, the source material for Dutch drama derived not only from the Republic's own history, but also from the annals of other countries. If the plays by Van den Bosch and Reynier Anslo reflect a politico-religious concern that resembles Marlowe's in the *Massacre at Paris*, Hans Roelandt's highly popular tragical history of 1625, dealing with the conspiracy of the Duke of Biron, echoes Chapman.

As in Spain, also in the Netherlands English chronicle material was used for dramatic purposes. In 1646, the Catholic Vondel produced his *Maria Stuart*, inviting an analogy between the fate of Charles I at the mercy of Cromwell, and that of the Scottish queen at the hands of Elizabeth I. Another example of the way in which playwrights in the young Republic sought to express their anxiety about the rather strained Anglo-Dutch relations, was Joan Dullaert's *Charles Stuart* (1649). Like *Maria Stuart* – which initially landed Vondel with a fine from the Calvinist authorities – the play about the death of Charles I was considered too volatile at first, and a potential threat to Anglo-Dutch relations. During the first Sea War against Cromwell, however, it was precisely the play's expression of sympathy for the Stuart king that secured its stage success.[24]

Also Shakespearean history was rewritten for the Netherlands' stage. In 1651 Lambert van den Bosch – author also of *The Paris Wedding* – conflated a number of historical accounts of the final stages of the Wars of the Roses, including Holinshed's *Chronicles*, Sir Thomas More's pro-Tudor life of the last son of York, Thomas Legge's Latin *Ricardus Tertius*, as well as Shakespeare's *Richard III*. It was published as *Roode en Witte Roos. Of Lankaster en Jork. Blyeindent treurspel* (1651), or, *The Red and the White Rose. Or Lancaster and York. A Tragicomedy*, to use O. J. Campbell's title for the play which he translated into English in 1919 to reveal its structural and verbal indebtedness to Shakespeare.

Like many English history plays, Lambert van den Bosch's *The Red and the White Rose* originally functioned as a covert commentary on current politics, but critics of the play, in their attempt to establish its much-cherished indebtedness to Shakespeare, have tended to ignore the play's contemporary politico-historical contexts. Closer analysis, however, reveals that both domestic and international politics of some weight lurked behind the chronicled history that Lambert van den Bosch translated and reworked into *The Red and the White Rose.*

Unlike Shakespeare, Lambert van den Bosch begins his play with the death of Edward IV and the succession of his young son as Edward V, who is extremely vulnerable to the wiles of Richard of Gloucester. The obvious question that arises is why this particular moment in the history of the Wars of the Roses should be granted such prominence. As it happens, the monarch's decease as well as the succession issue in the English history play bore some resemblance to the rather grave situation in the Republic in 1651. This was the year following the untimely death, on 6 November 1650, of Stadholder William II, prince of Orange, and the birth of his heir, the future William III of England a week later.[25] Since Prince William was still an infant, the issue was raised of a protector to the new stadholder. This temporary and alternative form of leadership was a cause of considerable concern in the Low Countries, though not for exactly the same reasons as in England after the death of Edward IV, when the future Richard III held the office. The anxiety in the Low Countries was part of what Cohen calls the persistent tug-of-war between the republican Amsterdam oligarchy on the one hand, and the house of Orange with its privileges as viceroy on the province level, on the other (pp. 95–6). On the occasion of the unexpected death of William II, and given the infancy of Prince William, the Orangeists were considering who might best act as protector, but the States saw an opportunity to declare the post of stadholder vacant altogether, thus neutralising the power of the family of Orange.[26]

In the process of cultural translation, Van den Bosch's play on the reign of Richard III obtained a distinctly national Dutch imprint in more ways than one. In the play's third act, Buckingham recommends Richard of Gloucester to the Mayor and the Council of London. In view of the French, Scottish, and Irish threats that the nation has overcome, Buckingham says:

> I advise entrusting the throne to someone else, to a man who considers alike your advantage and your good, to a man whose single might dams for us an inundation as mighty as an entire sea of wretched streams, which before we are aware of it, will overwhelm [=come up to the neck of] our leader.   (p. 114)

Just as Calderón's version of *Henry VIII* as *The Schism in England* – with its vindictive finale presaging the bloodiest period in Tudor history – gave the English Reformation an obvious Spanish slant, the historian and playwright Van den Bosch gave his period of English history a curiously Dutch bias. In describing the ideal leader in terms of a dam holding out water, he opted for what Simon Schama has identified as one of the founding metaphors of the Dutch nation.[27] Within the context of Tudor history, Van den Bosch's image of the nation inevitably recalls the famous monologue of Shakespeare's John of Gaunt in *Richard II*. There is a difference, however, between a nation considered capable of naturally withstanding the sea, and one whose best safety lies in the appointed leader. This dissimilarity brings into focus the issue of England as the 'womb of kings' producing monarchs in a natural, hereditary succession, in contrast to the rather novel political experiment in the Low Countries, referred to as the Republic.

Even though *The Red and the White Rose* uses English history to reflect on the Dutch political establishment, it also airs a number of political misgivings that directly concern the nation's nearest and dearest enemy, England. England, as it is presented in the Dutch play, is a source of embarrassment in people's eyes, even in the eyes of the English characters. As Lord Stanley puts it at the end of a sixty-line monologue trying to account for the chaos that wrecks the nation:

> [A]lthough the kingdom has found again its Lord in Edward [IV], our heads are bowed under the burden of great sins . . . we became guilty of a crime, one which forever will remain the shame and disgrace of our State, because King Richard [II], the lawful prince, was destroyed by the hand of a murderer – a crime which Pomfret must still lament – and such noble blood was spilled so wantonly. *Everyone considers it a disgrace to England, that she so easily lays hands upon her legitimate Lord.*[28]

This speech, as translated by Campbell, expresses an obvious sense of national shame over the regicide committed by the English to have Henry IV succeed Richard II. A second look at the original Dutch version of 1651, however, shows that the phrase 'legitimate Lord' should read 'legitimate *Lords*' (for 'wettige Heeren'). With a minor change from singular to plural, the situation in the play no longer refers only to Richard II; it also alludes to the very recent execution of an anointed king, Charles I, by the parliamentarians in 1649, also commemorated in Vondel's *Lucifer*, where it is feared that the Legions of Hell may be building a power base on English soil.

Read in its immediate political and historical contexts, *The Red and the White Rose*, on the domestic level, brings into focus the young Republic's misgivings about the successor to the stadholder, as well as the related anxiety over the threat posed by the anti-monarchic, Protestant faction in the cities. On the international level, the play expresses its misgivings about the Republic's English neighbours, two years after the death of Charles I, two years also into the Puritan reign of Oliver Cromwell, which severely complicated the Republic's foreign diplomatic relations. As the plot of *The Red and the White Rose* suggests, with the coronation of Henry Richmond as Henry VII at the end of the play, Lambert van den Bosch would seem to support the monarchist idea, so that behind the united colours of the red and white roses, one may begin to discern the famous family colour of Orange.

In his 1840 celebration of Shakespeare, Thomas Carlyle described the politico-cultural destiny of the playwright and his work in terms of a Shakespearean history play. Carlyle alleged that Acts of Parliament and prime ministers would never be able to unite English-speaking nations around the world. Only under Shakespearean rule could the British Empire itself produce something tantamount to a national epic, styled on the Shakespearean history play:

> Call it not fantastic, for there is much reality in it: Here, I say, is an English King, whom no time or chance, Parliament or a combination of Parliaments, can dethrone! This King Shakespeare, does not he shine, in crowned sovereignty, over us all, as the noblest, gentlest, strongest of rallying-signs; *in*destructible; really more valuable in that point of view than any other means or appliance whatsoever? We can fancy him as radiant aloft over all the Nations of Englishmen, a thousand years hence. (p. 370)

As Western Europe, during the bardolatrous nineteenth century, made Shakespeare the sovereign of its cultural commonwealth, it was only natural that his own type of history play should become the imaginative model for the future. If the Duke of Marlborough, claiming that he knew no English history but what he had learned from Shakespeare, was defining a mode of cultural memory that was backward-looking, Carlyle projected an epic expansion into the future, a Shakespearean millennium. King Shakespeare, it seems, still rules, and still rules our reading of the history play as an early modern phenomenon. As Jonathan Bate has put it: Shakespeare 'ceased to be English and became world-historical'.[29]

It is unlikely that Shakespeare's apparent monopoly on the history play would have been less prone to develop if Ben Jonson had produced more than a scene and a half of *Mortimer His Fall*, or if we still had copies of such chronicle plays, now lost, as *Godfrey of Bulloigne*, *King Stephen*, *Henry I*, *Henry II*, *The Conquest of Spain by John of Gaunt*, or the second part of *Sir John Oldcastle*. Even incomplete or lost plays represent only a fraction of the collective corpus of early modern history plays in England. It seems more likely that the vision of nation and empire in Shakespeare's history plays appealed to Romantics such as Herder, Schiller, Schlegel, and Carlyle, and caused the tetralogies to be propagated and mobilised as supporting models for a new cultural nationalism. If, via the Romantics, Shakespeare's history plays served to invent the modern nation, their almost universal appeal today need come as no surprise.

Given this curious instance of absorption of Shakespeare's histories into the English, indeed European view of nation and empire, one ought, for the purpose of a convincing reassessment of the Shakespearean genre, to be prepared to decentre not just the Shakespearean history plays, but also much of their reception history. My proposal to decentre the plays and to reconsider their afterlives is not to be interpreted as a call for a palace revolution. Instead, it is a summons for the occasional adjustment of our perspective. To decentre the bard enables one better to appreciate both the early modern English preoccupation with views of Republicanism as an alternative political model, and the staged experiments with alternatives to the providential view of politics and history. Alternatively, to decentre the Shakespearean history play may lead to a more reliable appreciation of the political themes shared by the early modern European historical canon as a whole; it may help us arrive at a reassessment of the plays in a context better attuned to the cosmopolitan traffic of ideas among nations that characterises the period that brought them forth.

NOTES

1 Hunter 1997, p. 161.
2 Helgerson 1992, p. 203.
3 On early English drama and its immediate connections with the Reformation see White 1993. On the impact of John Bale and his non-dramatic writings on the self-identity of the English nation see McEachern 1996, pp. 5–33.
4 For a later date, see Jackson 2001, and for a comparison of the sense of nationhood in both plays, see Sullivan 1998, chapter 2 ('Strange Metamorphoses: Landscape and the Nation in *Woodstock*') and chapter 3 ('Reading Shakespeare's Maps').
5 Forker 1994, pp. 17–41.
6 For a succinct and lucid introduction to the issue see Corbin and Sedge 1991.
7 Meagher 1966; on the earlier dramatic tradition of Robin Hood, see Wiles 1981.
8 See also Barton 1977, pp. 69–93.
9 *Ibid.*, 1981; see also Spikes 1977, p. 138.
10 Lindenberger underestimates the scope (Lindenberger 1975, pp. 7–8).
11 See Limon 1986.
12 See Corbin and Sedge 1991, pp. 9–10; and Helgerson 1992, p. 249.
13 Hunter 1997, p. 278.

14 Helgerson 1992, p. 245.

15 Levin 1954, p. 104.

16 Mulryne 1995, pp. 59–60.

17 For the different traditions see Loftis 1987, pp. 5–6; Lindenberger 1975, pp. 4–5. See also Cohen who further demonstrates with reference to a series of canonical plays how the neoclassical mode of tragedy and the idea of empire with its notion of centralised rule mutually supported one another, thus on many occasions impeding the development of a truly national drama (Cohen 1985, pp. 218–32).

18 The other continental European version of the play was Philip Waimer's *Elisa*, a version of *Edward III* published in Gdansk in 1591, five years before *The Reign of King Edward the Third*; see Limon 1985, p. 160 n.1.

19 Calderón 1990, lines 2880–2.

20 Loftis 1987, p. 17; for the rest of the argument in this paragraph I am also indebted to Loftis.

21 The national English defeat was eclipsed by the presentation of the heroic exploits of Richard Peeke, as recorded in his own prose account *Three to One: Being, an English–Spanish Combat Performed by a Western Gentleman of Tavistock* (1626); see Hoenselaars 1992, pp. 218–22.

22 See Loftis 1987, p. 18; *H8*, ed. Foakes 1964, p. xxxi.

23 Duits 1990, pp. 27–35.

24 Smits-Veldt 1991, pp. 112–17.

25 The stadholder was the powerful Orangist post of chief magistrate on the county or province level.

26 Lambert van den Bosch's other play about the future of the stadholderate was his tragedy about the assassination of William of Orange in 1584, entitled *William, or, Freedom Wounded* (*Wilhem of gequetste vreyheyt*, 1662). Eventually, the States General managed to secure a 'First Stadholderless Era'.

27 Schama 1987, especially chapters 1 ('Moral geography'), 2 ('Patriotic scripture'), and 4 ('The impertinence of survival').

28 Campbell 1971, pp. 103–4 (emphasis added).

29 Bate 1997, p. 337.

3

DAVID M. BERGERON

Pageants, masques, and history

Thomas Heywood, defending the theatre in his *Apology for Actors* (*c.*1612), writes that through drama everyone knows the history of England from William the Conqueror, nay even from Brutus. If not that full range, Shakespeare's history plays did nevertheless offer spectators and readers an opportunity to learn a significant part of English history. These theatre participants might expand and reinforce that knowledge through pageants and masques that constituted another major form of drama; these entertainments form the focus of this essay.

The Induction of *2 Henry IV* can serve to open this subject. According to the stage directions, Rumour enters, '*painted full of tongues*' and speaks: 'Open your ears; for which of you will stop/The vent of hearing when loud Rumour speaks?' (1–2). This Rumour spreads continual slanders, a 'pipe/Blown by surmises, Jealousy's conjectures' (15–16). But, Rumour asks, 'what need I thus/My well-known body to anatomise?' (20–1). Through false report and slander Shakespeare intends, I believe, to connect Rumour with Falstaff in this play, whose well-known body the new Henry V must finally set aside and deny. The concept and symbolic representation of Rumour or Fame Shakespeare inherited from many emblematic and iconographic traditions. Certainly masques and pageants frequently portray Fame as a character. In the *Chronicles* (1587), Holinshed, for example, writes of a pageant in the reign of Henry VIII in which Report entered, '*apparelled in crimson satin full of tongues*'.[1]

In Shakespeare's time a whole array of public spectacles might fall under the category of pageants, such as processions, tournaments, and indoor entertainments. For purposes here we can restrict the term *pageant* to apply to consciously planned dramatic entertainment of three major types. First, *progresses* or summer provincial tours of the sovereign that took place on the estates of noblemen can be designated as pageants when the occasions contained outdoor dramatic shows of a wide variety, typically spread over several days or even weeks. Queen Elizabeth's progress to Kenilworth in July

1575 prompted three weeks of shows, most based on mythology. Her trip to Elvetham in 1591 caused a special pond to be dug in order to stage the battle between the wood gods and sea gods, the Queen eventually causing peace.

When the sovereign made an official entry into a city, a *royal entry* was characterised by dramatic tableaux and special structures for dramatic performance scattered throughout the streets. On the day before her coronation in January 1559, Elizabeth made a spectacular procession through the City of London, starting at the Tower and moving westward. On various scaffolds dramatic scenes unfolded, based on allegory, national history, and Biblical history. Similarly, King James' royal entry on 15 March 1604 constituted one of the most elaborate and costly civic pageants, containing seven triumphal arches placed in the streets. These arches became the stages on which dramatic speeches and action occurred. Ben Jonson and Thomas Dekker wrote this pageant, and Thomas Middleton contributed the speech of Zeal. Stephen Harrison's *Arches of Triumph* (1604) contains engravings of the triumphal arches, the most important pictorial evidence for a civic pageant.

The *Lord Mayor's Shows* constitute the third major kind of civic pageant. These took place each 29 October at the inauguration of London's new mayor, whose guild arranged and paid for the drama. Elaborate dramatic scenes greeted the mayor as he processed through London's streets. In Thomas Middleton's *The Triumphs of Truth* (1613), for example, the mayor and spectators witnessed an ongoing allegorical battle between Truth and Error for the Mayor's allegiance. Truth wins, and Zeal sets fire to Error's chariot. Every major dramatist, except Shakespeare, wrote these mayoral pageants, Anthony Munday, Thomas Middleton, and Thomas Heywood being the most prolific.

The indoor *court masque* took place on special occasions, especially the Christmas season, before a select audience of royalty and aristocrats. Although scattered examples exist in the Tudor era, masques truly become a fixture in the Stuart court, in part because of the active interest and support of first Queen Anne and then Queen Henrietta Maria. Masques included dazzling technical effects, dance, music, and drama based chiefly on allegory, mythology, and classical traditions. Typically the masque dissolved into the audience's participation in a dance. Samuel Daniel's *The Vision of the Twelve Goddesses* (1604) was the first masque of the new Jacobean court, but Ben Jonson's *The Masque of Blackness* (1605) helped establish his long tenure as the principal writer of masques. Inigo Jones, England's most distinguished architect, assisted Jonson and others in designing the increasingly elaborate staging of the masques on which the court spent vast sums of money.

The principle of emblematic representation operates in the appearance of Rumour in Shakespeare's play and in the many symbolic and allegorical

Figure 3 The Fenchurch Arch, with the City of London carved in miniature on top.

figures in pageants and masques. Ben Jonson, in his part of the 1604 royal entry for James, enunciates this idea well. Writing about the first triumphal arch, which presents the City of London carved in miniature and is adorned with various allegorical figures, Jonson notes the mixed nature of such a representation and comments: 'the garments and ensigns deliver the nature of the person, and the word the present office. Neither was it becoming or could it stand with the dignity of these shows . . . to require a truchman [interpreter], or . . . one to write, "This is a dog" or, "This is a hare": but so to be presented as, upon the view, they might without cloud or obscurity, declare themselves to the sharp and learned.'[2] Therefore, the audience presumably recognised Rumour, '*painted full of tongues*'. Shakespeare and other dramatists, writing for the regular theatre or for the theatre of the streets or court, tapped into well-established traditions of such representation.

Thomas Nelson in the Lord Mayor's Show of 1590, a few years before *2 Henry IV*, includes Fame, who sounds her trumpet and speaks. In this spare text Nelson does not describe Fame's costume, but we can assume that the audience would recognise her. In 1612, Thomas Dekker in the Lord Mayor's Show *Troia-Nova Triumphans*, depicts the House of Fame, but says cryptically of Fame that she is 'crowned in rich attire, a trumpet in her hand, etc'.[3] In the royal entry of 1604, Dekker had been more forthcoming about Fame who occupies a chief position at the Nova Faelix Arabia arch, located at the end of Soper Lane. Dekker describes Fame: 'A woman in a watchet [light blue] robe, thickly set with open eyes and tongues, a pair of large golden wings at her back, a trumpet in her hand, a mantle of sundry colours traversing her body: all these ensigns [signs] displaying but the property of her swiftness and aptness to disperse rumours' (11, 276). Here Dekker makes the distinction between the benign Fame, who gathers important historical figures to her, and Rumour, who spreads false tales. Not everyone made such a distinction. Late in the period John Taylor, in his Lord Mayor's Show *The Triumphs of Fame and Honour* (1634) creates a Monument of Fame as the last pageant device. Fame with her silver trumpet forces Time to revive the noble memory of former London mayors.

Jonson in *The Masque of Queens* (1609) presents a House of Fame, a '*glorious and magnificent building*' which includes twelve masquers sitting upon a throne triumphal, '*erected in form of a pyramid and circled with all store of light*'.[4] Heroic Virtue, as the parent of Fame, speaks first. This throne suddenly changed, and Fame appeared, '*attired in white, with white wings, having a collar of gold about her neck and a heart hanging at it*' (lines 424–5). Jonson indicates in the text that he borrows this image from Cesare Ripa's book *Iconologia*, a popular and influential Italian emblem book. Jonson adds: '*In her right hand she bore a trumpet, in her left an olive branch, and, for her state, it was as Virgil describes her, at the full, her feet on the ground and her head in the clouds*' (426–9). Jonson gives Inigo Jones credit for the House of Fame, whose lower columns included the '*statues of the most excellent poets, as Homer, Virgil, Lucan, etc., as being the substantial supporters of Fame*' (451–2). He adds: '*Between the pillars underneath were figured land battles, sea fights, triumphs, loves, sacrifices, and all magnificent subjects of honour, in brass and heightened with silver*' (455–7). Such a scene may remind us of Shakespeare's history plays with their battles, sacrifices, and magnificent struggles about honour. Clearly,

Figure 4 The Hortus Euporiae (Garden of Plenty).

Shakespeare, the pageant writers, and Jonson all explore the rich resources of emblematic representation.

The history plays contain several processions that may remind us of royal entries, although none in the plays have conscious dramatic entertainment. *1 Henry VI* opens with the funeral procession of Henry V, complete with several dukes of the realm. Act 4 of *Henry VIII* includes the coronation procession for Anne Boleyn. In unusually full stage directions, the author specifies how the procession is to move across the stage with its ten separate parts, ranging from a *'lively flourish of trumpets'* to *'Certain ladies or countesses, with plain circlets of gold without flowers'* (4.1.36SD). The procession exits at line 55, amid running commentary by the anonymous Gentlemen. A third Gentleman enters and reports on the actual coronation, which he pronounces 'Well worth the seeing' (60).

Richard II with its inverse coronation – the deposition in Act 4 – also includes the report of the new king's passage through the city. This comes from the Duke of York in conversation with his wife in 5.2. Bullingbrook, according to York, moved through the streets 'With slow but stately pace . . . / Whilst all tongues cried, "God save thee, Bullingbrook!"' (5.2.10–11). York adds a description of the street scene:

> You would have thought the very windows spake,
> So many greedy looks of young and old
> Through casements darted their desiring eyes
> Upon his visage, and that all the walls
> With painted imagery had said at once,
> 'Jesu preserve thee! Welcome Bullingbrook!'
>
> (12–17)

York also notes Bullingbrook's modest response to the crowd's adulation. Such a report and analysis echoes those found in many accounts of royal entry pageants.

Beginning from the Tower at about two o'clock in the afternoon of 14 January 1559 with a light snow falling, Elizabeth passed through the City of London in a spectacular royal entry. A scaffold in Gracious Street contained several stages. On the lowest sat representations of Henry VII and his wife Elizabeth, Henry 'proceeding out of the house of Lancaster, was enclosed in a red rose, and th'other, which was Queen Elizabeth being heir to the house of York, enclosed with a white rose'.[5] From them a branch extended to the next stage, and it contained the representations of Henry VIII and Anne Boleyn. At the top of this scaffold a 'seat royal' contained the image of Queen Elizabeth. The whole 'pageant garnished with red roses and white' (p. 33) symbolised the union of the houses of Lancaster and York, the ultimate theme of the first group of Shakespeare's English histories. In Cornhill the Queen saw the device of 'seat of worthy governance', depicting four virtues – Pure religion, Love of subjects, Wisdom, and Justice – which trod underfoot their opposing vice. A child speaker addressed the queen and underscored the theme of this device.

The Great Conduit in Cheapside contained a pageant device of the Eight Beatitudes from St Matthew's gospel. At the Little Conduit in Cheapside the Queen encountered two opposing hills, one representing a flourishing commonwealth and the other a ruined or decayed commonwealth with appropriate symbolic figures and words. This symbolically contrasting landscape also contained between the hills a small cave from which emerged Time leading his daughter Truth who was clothed in white silk. Truth carried the Word of Truth, the English Bible, which she presented to Elizabeth, who received it graciously, promising to read daily therein. After hearing a Latin oration in St Paul's Churchyard, Elizabeth moved on to Fleet Street for the last pageant device, which contained Deborah, 'the judge and restorer of the house of Israel', apparelled in 'parliament robes, with a sceptre in her hand' (p. 53). This figure from Biblical history stands as a worthy precedent for Elizabeth. Therefore, real historical examples join symbolism and allegory to illustrate the pageant's themes in an entertainment designed to honour and instruct the sovereign.

Even more elaborate, the royal entry pageant for James in 1604 lasted some five hours while his retinue passed through the city, a city graced with seven triumphal arches on which dramatic action occurred. Dekker captures the scene thus: 'The streets seemed to be paved with men: stalls instead of rich wares were set out with children, open casements filled up with women'.[6] In a description reminiscent of York's account of Bullingbrook's procession in *Richard II*, Dekker adds: 'All glass windows [were] taken down, but in their places sparkled so many eyes that, had it not been the day, the light which reflected from them was sufficient to have made one.' Even as 'desiring eyes' looked upon Bullingbrook, Dekker says that King James 'did most graciously feed the eyes of beholders with his presence' (p. 279) in his royal entry.

The first arch, designed by Jonson and located in Fenchurch, offered on its top a carved representation of the City of London, notable for its accuracy. A silk curtain covered the arch until the King arrived. Jonson explains the meaning: 'The allegory being that those clouds were gathered upon the face of the City through their long want of his most wished sight: but now, as at the rising of the sun, all mists were dispersed and fled.'[7] The King's bright presence drove away grief over Elizabeth's death. Monarchia Britannica, a woman richly attired in cloth of gold, occupied the most exalted position on the arch; but Divine Wisdom, clothed in white and holding a dove and a serpent, carried her word, '*Per me reges regnant*' [through me kings do rule].

Italian merchants living in London prepared the second arch which presented a picture of Henry VII seated in his imperial robes to whom

King James, mounted on horseback, approaches and receives a sceptre. The founder of the Tudor line, as we would know from Shakespeare's histories, gives his blessing and kingdom to James, founder of the Stuart line. On an arch at the Royal Exchange the Dutch merchants also offered a portrait of James, accompanied by Justice and Fortitude. In a square room on the arch stood representations of the seventeen provinces of the Netherlands, and the speaker urged the king to support their cause, as had been done in Elizabeth's reign. As noted above, at the *Nova Faelix Arabia* arch Fame stood, emblematically costumed. The arch also contained a Fount of Virtue, surrounded by the Five Senses. Detraction and Oblivion slept at the bottom of the fount, attempting to suck it dry. At James' arrival, Fame sounded her trumpet and beautiful music followed, all serving to defeat the vices. At that moment the fount began to flow with milk, wine, and balm. The glorious presence of the King helped bring about this transformation.

The Garden of Plenty arch greeted the king in Cheapside (discussed below), and the New World arch stood in Fleet Street. Here a great globe, located in the middle section, dominated the arch. Dekker does not bother to describe the chief figure, Justice, since everyone would know what she looks like. Directly beneath Justice stood Fortune, her foot treading on the globe and helping to turn it with the assistance of the Four Elements. Envy lurked nearby, glancing fearfully at Virtue and at the Cardinal Virtues. The speech of Zeal, written by Thomas Middleton, emphasises how James has brought union in the kingdom, once by Brutus divided. Zeal observes that the elements respond to the peaceful presence of the king: 'Earth not devouring, Fire not defacing, / Water not drowning, and the Air not chasing'.[8] The King also becomes the embodiment of the Virtues: 'Justice in causes, Fortitude gainst foes, / Temperance in spleen, and Prudence in all those' (p. 298). The allegorical qualities represented on the arch become also the virtues of the King: allegory enfolds into political reality.

The Temple of Janus, an arch located at Temple Bar, includes dramatic action designed by Jonson. This arch mixes classical and allegorical subjects. Peace was 'the first and principal person in the temple'[9] with Plutus standing nearby. Jonson carefully provides symbolic details of all the figures. Each virtue, such as Quiet, Liberty, Safety, and Felicity, has an opposing vice underfoot. The playwright explains the 'dumb argument' of the arch: 'those golden times were returned again, wherein Peace was with us so advanced, Rest received, Liberty restored, Safety assured, and all Blessedness appearing in every of these virtues her particular triumph over her opposite evil' (p. 100). The Genius of the City returns, having first been portrayed by Jonson in the Fenchurch arch, and he engages in extensive dialogue with a Flamen [attendant priest], offering 'My city's heart which shall for ever burn / Upon this altar ...' (p. 103).

Through this extraordinary pageant the city has offered its heart to the new king by means of dramatic speech and action, emblematic representation, and moral allegory. Yet Dekker writes of a sense of loss once the pageant ended: the City 'being, like an actor on a stage, stripped out of her borrowed majesty, she resigns her former shape and title of City'.[10] One may catch a hint of York's words as he turns from his report of the happy reception of Bullingbrook to the appearance of Richard: 'As in a theatre the eyes of men / After a well-graced actor leaves the stage, / Are idly bent on him that enters next, / Thinking his prattle to be tedious' (5.2.23–6). For Dekker the City as actor must abandon its role, made possible by the presence of the monarch: 'their very presence hath power to turn a village to a city, and to make a city appear great as a kingdom'. These substantial pageants in 1604, forever captured in Harrison's engravings and in Jonson's and Dekker's dramatic texts, honour and celebrate the commonwealth and its ruler. The king graces the pageant with his presence, and the pageant symbolically ratifies his position as monarch: politics, history, and drama relentlessly intertwine.

In the 'garden scene' (3.4) of *Richard II*, Shakespeare provides a kind of tableau not unlike some pageant and masque scenes. This moment in the play does little to advance the narrative and derives from no hint in the sources. Instead, the Gardener and his assistants construct an elaborate political allegory, likening the commonwealth to a garden – a familiar metaphor. The Gardener's assistant asks why they should so carefully tend their garden when 'our sea-wallèd garden, the whole land, / Is full of weeds, her fairest flowers choked up' (43–4). The Gardener makes explicit the connection between the metaphor and the current political reality: 'Oh what pity is it / That he [Richard] had not so trimmed and dressed his land / As we this garden!' (55–7). The Queen likens the Gardener to Adam: 'What Eve, what serpent hath suggested thee / To make a second fall of cursèd man?' (75–6). This scene, sandwiched between Richard's abdication and his formal deposition, moves the play into allegory while nevertheless representing current reality.

Pageants and masques also pursue the garden metaphor. In the 1604 royal entry, after James had listened to the speech of the city's Recorder, he confronted Sylvanus, 'dressed up in green ivy, a cornet in his hand'.[11] Sylvanus addressed the king and eventually led him to the *Hortus Euporiae* [Garden of Plenty] arch at the Little Conduit in Cheapside. This arch, decorated like a summer garden, full of flowers and fruit, contains as its principal figures Peace and Plenty, who sat together, both emblematically costumed.

For good measure the Nine Muses and the Seven Liberal Arts also appear. The main speech comes from Vertumnus, the master gardener, whom Dekker describes graphically (p. 288). Peace, according to Vertumnus, offers this garden and all its inhabitants to the king, in the name of the mayor, the 'consuls and senators of this city, who carefully prune this garden, (weeding out all hurtful and idle branches that hinder the growth of the good . . .' p. 288). Like the figures in *Richard II*, these officials become the 'faithful labourers' in this piece of ground, this garden. Allegorically, governing means gardening; peace and plenty become the fruit of such gardening.

The Masque of Flowers, performed by the gentlemen of Gray's Inn at the Whitehall Banqueting House on 6 January 1614 in honour of the recent wedding of Robert Carr and Frances Howard, included an elaborate garden. The anonymous dramatist describes it: 'a garden of a glorious and strange beauty, cast into four quarters, with a cross-walk, and alleys compassing each quarter. In the middle of the cross-walk stood a goodly fountain raised on four columns of silver.'[12] A low hedge of cypress and juniper surrounded the garden, which also had knots with artificial green herbs and flowers. An arbour stood on top of a mount, and it had six double arches. 'Behind the garden, over the top of the arbour, were set artificial trees appearing like an orchard joining to the garden' (p. 168). Twelve 'garden gods' sat under the arbour. 'In the midst of them sat Primavera, at whose entreaty they descended to the stage and, marching up to the King, sang to lutes and theorboes [large double-necked lutes].' After much dancing and singing, the fourth song referred to King James and linked this whole garden device to the political world: 'This isle was Britain in times past, / But then was Britain rude and waste; / But now is Britain fit to be / A seat for Fifth Monarchy [i.e. the second coming of Christ]' (p. 170). The preceding songs focused on the flowers in this stunning garden – a fitting emblem for Britain under James' rule.

The fifth device in Dekker's 1629 Lord Mayor's Show, *London's Tempe*, included an arbour complete with trees and flowers, intimating, Dekker writes, 'that as London is the best-stored garden in the kingdom for plants, herbs, flowers, roots, and such like, so, on this day, it is the most glorious city in the Christian world'.[13] In the 1628 mayoral pageant, *Britannia's Honour*, Dekker had included 'New Troy's Tree of Honour', dominated by a representation of London 'with an ornament of steeples, towers, and turrets on her head' (p. 86). Allegorical figures, emblematically presented, sit around the tree depicting qualities that bring glory and strength to the city. In her address to the Mayor, London urges him to protect this Tree of Honour and guard it. She closes with metaphorical instruction:

> You are your sovereign's gardener; for one year,
> The plot of ground y'are trusted with, lies here,
> (A city,) and your care must all be spent
> To prune and dress the Tree of Government.
> Lop off Disorders, Factions, Mutiny . . .
>
> (p. 88)

The Gardeners from *Richard II* would understand this admonition perfectly.

In *Henry VIII* an actual masque or disguising that took place in 1527 is used when, at Cardinal Wolsey's house, '*Enter King and others as masquers, habited like shepherds, ushered by the Lord Chamberlain*' (1.4.63SD). In this entertainment Henry meets Anne Boleyn. The scene after her coronation contains Katherine's rare vision, which resembles any number of moments from court masques. As Katherine sits meditating on 'celestial harmony', sad and solemn music sounds; and 'The Vision' occurs:

> *Enter solemnly tripping one after another, six personages, clad in white robes, wearing on their heads garlands of bays, and golden vizards on their faces, branches of bays or palms in their hands. They first congee [bow] unto her, then dance; and at certain changes, the first two hold a spare garland over her head, at which the other four make reverend curtsies.* (4.2.82SD)

These figures deliver a garland to Katherine; and '*so, in their dancing, vanish, carrying the garland with them. The music continues.*' Only Katherine has seen the vision, although theatre audiences certainly do. She interprets the event as a 'blessed troop' that invites her to a banquet.

In the year of *Henry VIII*, Francis Beaumont wrote *The Masque of the Inner Temple and Gray's Inn*, performed on 20 February 1613 as part of the wedding festivities for Princess Elizabeth and Frederick Elector Palatine. Mercury causes four Naiads to arise out of fountains '*and present themselves upon the stage, attired in long habits of sea–green taffeta, with bubbles of crystal intermixed with powdering of silver . . . bluish tresses on their heads, garlands of water-lilies. They fall into a measure, dance a little, then make a stand.*'[14] Mercury then has five Hyades descend in a cloud from the fir-mament, '*apparelled in sky-coloured taffeta robes, spangled like the heaven*' (p. 137). They join the Naiads in a dance and eventually four Cupids join in as well. Appropriate costume, music, and dance characterise Katherine's vision and court masques. Shakespeare found no evidence of such a vision in historical sources; he looked at other forms of drama instead.

But pageants could also on occasion explicitly confront historical events and themes. As noted above, the 1559 royal entry contained a representation of the union of Yorkists and Lancastrians. At least two Lord Mayor's Shows represent kings with whom Shakespeare's audience would have been familiar. In Anthony Munday's *The Triumphs of Re-United Britannia* (1605), Fame ushers in a chariot that conveys seven English kings, all connected with the sponsoring Merchant Taylors' Company: Edward III, Richard II, Henry IV, Henry V, Henry VI, Edward IV, and Henry VII, omitting only Richard III. Each in turn through a speaker recounts his involvement with the guild. Edward III, for example, 'gave this charter to confirm their guild', while Richard II granted them 'power to have a livery / And hold a feast on Saint John Baptist day'.[15] Henry V proclaimed 'my war-like lord maintained / His father's love to this society'. One seat in the chariot remains unoccupied, presumably left for King James to fill. This chariot thus offers a kind of telescoped vision of most of Shakespeare's English kings. John Webster, in *Monuments of Honour* (1624), a pageant that also honours the Merchant Taylors, returns to Munday's device. Here the Chariot of Kings, drawn by four horses, bears the arms of the guild. Webster has eight kings because he includes Richard III, who, Webster says, was a bad man but a good king. The chairs of the Lancastrian kings Webster decorates with artificial red roses, and the others with white. But the 'Uniter of the division and houses, Henry the Seventh, [is adorned] both with White and Red, from whence his Royal Majesty now reigning took his motto for one piece of his coin, "*Henricus rosas regna Jacobus*" [Henry united the roses; James, the kingdoms].'[16] The figure of Edward III speaks and, noting the honour that these kings have brought to the guild, bids them: 'Let all good men this sentence oft repeat, / By unity the smallest things grow great' (p. 322). To this all the kings respond by repeating the 'sentence'. Whether standing in Shakespeare's theatre or in London's streets, one could have grasped a partial sweep of English history from Edward III through Henry VII, a seeming confirmation of Thomas Heywood's judgement.

Years before Shakespeare wrote *Richard II*, the Lord Mayor's Show of 1590 by Thomas Nelson had depicted an important event of this king's reign, which occurred before the start of Shakespeare's play: namely, the Jack Straw-Wat Tyler rebellion, part of the Peasants' Revolt of 1381. Nelson represents the three principal figures: Richard, Jack Straw, and William Walworth (the Lord Mayor who helped rescue the King). The King speaks but two lines asking for Walworth's help in quelling the uprising. The rebel Straw notes Walworth's success in thwarting their efforts: 'He being Mayor of London then, soon daunted all our pride, / He slew me first, the rest soon fled, and then like traitors died.'[17] Walworth boasts of his achievement:

> I slew Jack Straw, who sought my king's disgrace,
> And for my act reaped honours of great price,
> First knight was I of London you may read,
> And since each mayor gains knighthood by my deed.
>
> (p. 7)

This whole episode emerges from a focus on Fame who underscores the successful victory and the resulting peace, all thanks to the heroic deeds of a mayor.

Munday returns to this historical event in *Chrysanaleia: The Golden Fishing*, the Lord Mayor's Show of 1616, with dramatic effect. The dramatic and thematic centre of this pageant focuses on a Bower, shaped like an arbour, located in St Paul's churchyard. This bower has a tomb on which rests the figure of William Walworth, twice mayor in the fourteenth century. The whole conceit, Munday says, 'aimeth at that tempestuous and troublesome time of King Richard the Second . . . whose life, crown, and dignity . . . were manfully defended and preserved, by that worthy man Walworth' (Munday, p. 107). London's Genius, 'a comely youth, attired in the shape of an angel' (p. 110), arrived at the tomb and summoned Walworth forth. Genius speaks, trumpets sound; and then, according to the marginal 'stage directions', '*Here the Genius strikes on him with his wand, whereat he begins to stir and, coming off the tomb, looks strangely about him*' (p. 112). Thus resurrected, Walworth speaks, noting the guild's distinguished history and the present festivity. This pageant celebrates the 'rare deed of loyalty, / Upon the King's proud enemy' (p. 112), about which Genius speaks.

Munday continues the allusion to the Walworth story in the last device of the pageant, a chariot where sits 'the triumphing angel, who that day smote the enemy by Walworth's hand, and laid all his proud presuming in the dust' (p. 110). The show 'memorises' London's great day of deliverance on Corpus Christi day in 1381: 'a case of desperate rebellion'; 'a most base and barbarous kind of proceeding'. In addition to the angel, the chariot contains a representation of Richard seated beneath her, and numerous royal virtues, such as Truth, Virtue, Honour, Temperance, Fortitude, Zeal, beating down Treason and Mutiny. These allegorical figures, Munday writes, 'are best observed by their several emblems and properties' (p. 112). The closing speech of the pageant, given by Walworth, ties together the several devices and underscores the historical importance of Richard's rescue.

The story of Brutus, Troynovant, and the settling of England by the descendants of Aeneas runs through several civic pageants, although Shakespeare does not develop it as an issue in the histories. This story, which has no basis in historical fact, emerges out of the twelfth-century chronicles and continues largely unchallenged through the early seventeenth century. It automatically gave England a connection to the ancient world, which may account for its longevity. Some Tudor historians understood that no evidence existed to support the story; nevertheless they persisted in re-presenting the Brutus story, complete with his sons Locrine, Camber, and Albanact. An anonymous late sixteenth-century play *The Lamentable Tragedy of Locrine* dramatised the tale and its division of the kingdom. Edmund Spenser refers to it in Book II of *The Faerie Queene* at the House of Alma – one can multiply the examples.

Munday's *The Triumphs of Re-United Britannia* offers the fullest exploration of the topic in the pageants as the dramatist seeks to make a connection between Brutus and King James, an idea mentioned in passing in the 1604 royal entry. In the opening of his text, Munday attempts to trace the history of Brutus back to Noah and the Flood; he also sketches Brutus' conquest of the island and the subsequent division among his sons. A '*mount triangular*' contains in its chief place 'the shape of a fair and beautiful nymph, Britannia herself' (p. 6). Brutus, dressed like an 'adventurous warlike Troyan', sits beneath Britannia, surrounded by representations of his sons. King James' 'happy coming to the crown, England, Wales, and Scotland, by the first Brute severed and divided, is, in our second Brute, reunited and made one happy Britannia again' (p. 7). In her speech Britannia complains that she would still be known as Albion but for the conquest of Brutus, who then responds by outlining the advantages that his victory has brought: taming the wilderness, overcoming the giants in the land, and establishing Troynovant (London) on the Thames. Brutus perhaps reinforces the function of poetry and drama as vehicles of history when he credits 'rich poesie, / That does revive us to fill up these rooms / And tell our former ages' history' (p. 9). Therefore the pageant can celebrate the second Brute, James, and his union of the kingdoms, a worthy political goal that finds its roots in history.

Spectators who had seen Shakespeare's history plays performed by the Lord Chamberlain's Men / King's Men in public theatres might have recognised some of the professional actors who also performed in masques and civic pageants. Although the evidence is sketchy, scholars assume that professional actors took part in court masques, usually performing the anti-masques; otherwise, ladies and gentlemen of court acted out the roles. With civic pageants we have a bit more evidence. Records from the Merchant Taylors' Company reveal that the guild hired the children of Westminster school to perform in the Lord Mayor's Show of 1561; they presented the speeches of Orpheus, Amphion, Topas, and David. A boy of the Queen's Revels performed the role of Tamesis [Thames] at the Fenchurch arch in the 1604 royal entry, a part written by Jonson. Munday in *Camp-bell, or the*

Ironmongers Fair Field, the mayoral show for 1609, complains about child actors: 'the weak voices of so many children, which such shows as this do urgently require for personating each device, in a crowd of such noise and uncivil turmoil are not any way able to be understood' (Munday, p. 29). Munday's experience underscores a conundrum of all such street entertainment; in this case he may be responding to a complaint filed against him by the Ironmongers, who noted the children's inadequate performance.

At least four members of the King's Men can be identified for their connection with civic pageants. John Heminges, for example, helped Dekker in writing and preparing the Lord Mayor's Show of 1612, *Troia-Nova Triumphans*. Records of the Merchant Taylors reveal the nature of Heminges' involvement; he had by 1612 largely given up acting, sticking to managerial tasks for the company and ultimately assisting with the publication of Shakespeare's 1623 Folio text. In the civic pageant presented on the Thames in honour of Prince Henry's installation as Prince of Wales, *London's Love to the Royal Prince Henry* (1610), Munday writes of two of the characters: 'bestowing on them the borrowed bodies of two absolute actors, even the very best our instant time can yield' (p. 40). Munday writes accurately, for he refers to two members of the King's Men: Richard Burbage, who performed the part of Amphion speaking from a dolphin, and John Rice, who portrayed Corinea, a fair and beautiful nymph who rode on a whale. Corporation of London records confirm payment to Burbage and Rice for their participation. Burbage, the most famous actor of the period and creator of many of Shakespeare's tragic figures, moves effortlessly into a civic pageant, underscoring the value of these civic entertainments as a crucial part of the theatrical world. John Lowen, another member of the King's Men, performed the extensive role of Leofstane in Munday's 1611 Lord Mayor's Show, *Chruso-thriambos*. He took on this task, in the midst of a long professional acting career, in part because he belonged to the Goldsmiths, who produced the pageant. Guild records indicate Lowen's willingness to perform, including his intention to meet with Munday and to provide a horse for the pageant. In Leofstane, Munday means to suggest Sir Henry Fitz-Alwin, London's first Lord Mayor, thereby securing the historical significance of this dramatic action.

Like history plays, pageants and masques celebrate the glory of deeds. They do this in part by connecting with England's history through fictional representation, professional actors, and emblematic staging. A Lord Mayor's Show, royal entry, or court masque also takes place in real time with mayors and sovereigns both as honoured audience and as cause for the entertainment. At such moments, these entertainments not only reflect and represent history but also *make* history, thereby adding an extraordinary dimension to the historical characters and themes represented in the fiction.

NOTES

1 Holinshed 1808, III, 849; *2H4*, p. 60n.
2 Jonson 1925–52, VII, 91.
3 Dekker 1953–70, III, 240.
4 Jonson 1969, p. 134, lines 338, 340–1.
5 Osborn 1960, pp. 31–2.
6 Dekker 1953–70, II, 258.
7 Jonson 1925–52, VII, 90. The well-known actor Edward Alleyn performed the role of Genius Urbis at this Fenchurch arch. William Bird, of Prince Henry's Men gave the speech of Zeal at the Fleet Street arch.
8 Dekker 1953–70, II, 297.
9 Jonson 1925–52, VII, 97.
10 Dekker 1953–70, II, 301.
11 *Ibid.*, 282.
12 Spencer and Wells 1967, p. 167; this masque was edited by E. A. J. Honigmann.
13 Dekker 1953–70, IV, 110.
14 *The Masque of the Inner Temple*, ed. Philip Edwards in Spencer and Wells 1967, p. 136.
15 Bergeron 1985b, p. 12.
16 Webster 1927, III, 322.
17 Nelson 1590, p. 6.

4

DOMINIQUE GOY-BLANQUET

Elizabethan historiography and Shakespeare's sources

'*Enter Time, holding an hour-glass*',[1] to usher in a new generation. Like most of his contemporaries, Shakespeare was aware of time's destructive powers. Unlike most of them, he was also sensitive to its healing qualities. Before his own farewell to the stage, he gave a speaking part to this major actor of the human drama. Richard II played with time, and discovered too late that a king can shorten lives but not add one minute to his own, nor call back yesterday to correct fatal errors. At the end of the Plantagenet sequence Henry V, who has learnt from his predecessors' mistakes, 'weighs time to the utmost grain'.

Time as a devourer had become an obsessive theme for Renaissance authors. A desperate fight against oblivion inspired the writing strategies of the poets and dramatists, who turned to historians for materials to feed their anxieties. Their forebears, like all humble Christians, had little time for this earthly life and no great doubt of their ultimate salvation. For a majority of them, life was indeed an ordeal, a passage through a vale of tears, mercifully ended by death and the reward of eternal bliss. Their main fear was of the Devil, whose traps could lure the weak flesh to damnation. If man would but see reason, Hell was too heavy a price for any pleasures the earth could afford.

No one knows precisely where to put the end of the Middle Ages, but a revolution in thought did occur at some point, upsetting such simple calculations, and substituting one form of pessimism for another. New learning and new beliefs combined towards the end of the fifteenth century to set greater value on life in this world, while at the same time the heavenly returns of virtuous behaviour were no longer a safe bet. Luther's *De servo arbitrio* (1526) spelt the end of salvation by one's good deeds. Faith alone and God's free gift of grace could save His sinful creatures.

Both partisans and enemies of the Protestant Reformation looked for materials in the history of the Church to support their theses. In the fight for religious domination, the two parties hurled historical precedents at each other to demonstrate the priority of their doctrines, and of the texts on which they based their arguments. In England, the king's 'Great Matter' rested on the anteriority of God's decrees to any canon law or the very existence of Rome, and, in this particular case, advocated divorce as a religious duty. Henry VIII's apologists defended his most radical innovations as returns to former customs; each new turn in the royal politics was justified by documents establishing its immemorial antiquity. A triumphant Erasmus could boast he had killed four thousand enemies of Seneca, i.e. corrected four thousand errors in the great Stoic's newly edited works. He must now fence with another no less threatening enemy. His revised edition of the New Testament had been translated into German by Luther, and now the Bible was the first object of contention between their camps. All agreed on the unqualified authority of God's word, but the Scriptures circulated in so many variants, Greek, Hebrew, Latin, and now vernacular, that there was plenty of room for disagreement between experts.

Humanism[2]

For better or for worse, Greek studies were back in fashion at the turn of the century. All over Europe, scholars who had been searching out old manuscripts were now eager to share their treasures with fellow enthusiasts. As translations of exhumed masterpieces multiplied, their editors flocked to Venice, Frankfurt, Basel to form highly skilled teams with the most competent printers, and conduct learned quarrels over their choice of words, heralding the major division of the intellectual community over articles of faith.

Even before its adepts split the old Christian world between two creeds, the humanist taste for antiquity had its own drawbacks. A revered scholar like Petrarch saw little point in reading Dante or his own contemporaries if one could read the classics. The achievements of the past discouraged attempts at emulation, the pattern was lost. No budding artist could hope to reach this ideal horizon, let alone improve on it. Despite a few isolated claims that modern man was like a dwarf sitting on the shoulders of giants, able to see farther and do better, novelty seemed more a threat to memory's monuments than a promise of progress.

Along with this awesome heritage, the humanists absorbed their models' ingrained pessimism. The Greek notion of perpetual recurrence left no hope for the future: the universe ran through endless repetitive cycles, deteriorating with each new cycle as it moved further away from its initial perfection. The field of human artistry was restricted to a vain fight against erosion, poor conservative efforts to slow down the decaying process. Hebrew philosophy was the first to break this vicious circle by prophecies stressing the unique destiny of the Jewish people. Then, with the advent of Christ, the world found a new sense of direction. The Fathers of the Church postulated a beginning and an end to its history. But they showed no great interest for the progress of earthly society: happiness was just around the corner, in the next world.

Saint Augustine's *Confessions* opened the first major meditation on time, a contingency induced by Adam's fall. In *The City of God*, he unfolds the complete drama of human history,which the Christian era will bring to a close, lasting just long enough to save those destined for heavenly Jerusalem. However, this promise of ultimate redemption for the elect did not dispel the shades cast by the Greek poets. The nostalgic myth of a Golden Age would travel from Hesiod via Ovid down to Elizabethan England, insisting that innocence comes from ignorance, primitive happiness from raw simplicity. As man learns more, he grows more corrupt: the only progress is of evil. In Golding's translation of *The Metamorphoses*, one of Shakespeare's favourite books, the Four Ages of Man retrace the historical decline from an idealised golden past to the present iron age of violence, which sent the goddess Astrea flying back to heaven (*Metamorphoses* I, 103–70).

The confusion of Christian and pagan beliefs climbed to uneasy heights just as Shakespeare's histories reached the stage, when the approaching 'millennium' revived the old myths of decline with fresh apocalyptic fears. According to millennialist beliefs, after a thousand years of Christ's reign on earth, Doomsday would be near, but as systems of computation disagreed, this end was repeatedly predicted as a sure thing at the turn of successive centuries, including ours. These notions often combined with another stream of ideas, derived from Augustine's commentary on the Four Monarchies,[3] the transference of world dominion from one empire to another as the result of sin. As the Queen advanced in years, it became more likely that she would die with the century, an ominous coincidence for her anxious subjects who read symptoms of disease everywhere in nature and the commonwealth: men were smaller than they used to be, crops less abundant, money worth nothing. Even the sun was covered in spots, an ailment certainly responsible for its loss of ten summer days in the recent reform of the Julian calendar. After the fall of the Four Monarchies, Babylon, Persia, Greece, Rome, foretold by the prophet Daniel, the present age was the prelude to the end of time. All preachers agreed that the end of the world was near, though whether it would be struck down by God's vengeful fire or destroyed by its own corruption, no one knew.

The cyclical notion of time and its corollary fear of universal decay appeared under many guises, including Machiavelli's theory on the decline of human societies. *The Prince* (1513) had shaken all Europe on its moral hinges by stating that the laws of Christianity did not apply to the political sphere. If his analysis of power games did break with centuries of tradition, the Florentine's equating of change with disaster in the *Discourses* on Livy's *Decades* showed him no less convinced than contemporary humanists that past models could not be improved. His view of world history was a secularised version of the old belief in the rise and fall of the Four Monarchies. Human nature being invariable – invariably bad – civilisations began to deteriorate as soon as they reached a summit. Kingdoms were by nature condemned to increase their power, see it eroded by corruption, and die. It had been the fate of the Roman Republic, to Machiavelli the ideal state. Princes must aim at stability, and learn from the past history of empires how to delay the inevitable degradation.[4]

Renaissance England would long remain under the weight of such depressing doctrines. There is no Elizabethan theory of progress, if one excepts Bacon's trust in the advancement of learning, and Shakespeare's not entirely confident stance on the edge of a brave new world, both intimations of a radical upset in thought processes. The French school of Jean Bodin rejected the myth of the Golden age, arguing that humanity has changed since its primitive age: new laws and institutions, new customs, come into being every day. Alone of his generation, Shakespeare showed a similar awareness of historical development in *Richard II*, where the opening trial by combat, which would have been assigned to God's judgement, contrasts with the human tribunal set up by Bullingbrook. This growing sense of alienation from the past is to be measured against the hackneyed vision of the world as a stage where the same old story is played over and over again in different settings.[5] As late as 1614, Raleigh voiced a largely shared feeling that 'there is no other account to be made of this ridiculous world, than to resolve; that the change of fortune on the great theatre is but as the change of garments on the less: for when, on the one and the other, every man wears but his own skin, the players are all alike'.[6]

Censors and propagandists

The persistent idea that history repeats itself affected all areas of public debate. Augustine had set an example with his *City of God*, founding his argument for divine dominion on episodes of the Roman Empire. Preaching obedience to the powers that be, the Tudor homilists told their audiences to 'look over the chronicles of our own country, call to mind so many rebellions of old time, and some yet fresh in memory, ye shall not find that God ever prospered any rebellion against their natural and lawful prince, but contrariwise that the rebels were overthrown and slain'.[7]

History was a popular commodity when Shakespeare turned it to his own dramatic use. It had so many virtues that it could serve a large variety of interests, cure individual and collective diseases, teach lessons both spiritual and practical. Its adepts seldom failed to advertise its material benefits while claiming to serve truth only, untroubled by this patent contradiction. As F.S. Fussner puts it, 'all prefaces praised TRUTH; but nearly all texts ignored the awkward consequences'.[8] Using history to serve more rewarding masters was an old practice. The medieval annalists employed in noble houses tended to privilege the events most flattering to their patrons, or even alter facts to support partisan views. There are notorious examples of writers who changed sides several times during the Wars of the Roses, and revised their chronicles accordingly.[9] The most famous case is the figure of Richard III, on whose unlucky back successive biographers piled a hump and other unattractive features.

It is now well known that representations of the last Plantagenet were deliberately distorted by propaganda. Whatever could be urged against him, Richard's death and destitution needed special treatment if his victor was to escape the fate of former rebels. It was not enough for a conquering Richmond to inherit the Lancaster claim. His historiographers were required to trace his ascendancy back to the primitive Celtic kings, and beyond them to the first Trojan settlers. The Tudor thirst for respectability turned the quest of origins into a national pastime. Like their leaders, private men and institutions at all levels of society searched records for documents to support their claims, occasionally bending facts as the cause required. Henry VIII's apologists, for one, were so certain to work in the best interests of the common weal, that they did not scruple to invent legal precedents for the King's reforms when none could be found in the archives.[10]

These manipulators found in history a double-edged weapon, as dangerous as it was powerful. Apart from teaching lessons of perennial worth, the past could be used as a mirror to project critical reflections on present realities, 'and tax the vices of those that are yet living, in their persons that are long since dead', Raleigh explained, while advising the would-be historian not to follow truth too near the heels if he did not want his teeth struck out.[11] The decoding of transparent allusions was a pastime no writer could safely ignore. At court the analogy between past and present reigns was such common practice that Elizabeth herself is reputed to have stressed it in a retort to one of her counsellors: 'But I am Richard II. Know ye not that?' The matter was so sensitive that all the copies of John Hayward's volume on Henry IV, which dealt mostly with Richard's fall, were burnt, and Hayward sent to jail, suspected of oblique ties with Essex's rebellion.[12] After which case, instead of exercising their usual intermittent controls on printed works, the Privy

Council ruled that no book on English history could appear without express authorisation. Obviously the deposition scene in Shakespeare's play had to be suppressed to prevent further parallels. After all, Bullingbrook's revolt had succeeded, despite the preachers' claims that such attempts always failed. And the Tudors owed their possession of the crown to the very act they would so loudly condemn throughout their reigns, armed rebellion against an anointed king.

The Tudor chroniclers

Henry VII was the first English monarch who used history on a grand national scale to legitimise his accession to power, thus fully deserving to be hailed as father of Tudor historiography. His chroniclers obediently sat King Arthur along with the fabulous Brut, on a family tree inspired by Geoffrey of Monmouth's *Historia Regum Britanniae*, a founding legend which would pass for gospel truth until the end of the dynasty. However concerned by his genealogy, Henry VII probably had other more elevated designs when he asked an Italian humanist, Polydore Vergil (1470–1555), to write a full history of Britain. Vergil completed a first version around 1513. His friend and fellow humanist Thomas More (1478–1535) began a biography of Richard III at about the same time, but there is a world of difference between their treatments of history. More's irony and style thinly hide his passionate concern for the workings of tyranny. He modelled his composition on classical historians like Tacitus, but his method of inquiry is typically medieval. The *History of Richard III* is drawn from earlier accounts, including Vergil's, completed by original details. More collected all the direct testimonies he could find, usually from Richard's worst enemies, without the least effort to sift truth from prejudice. His shameless piece of hearsay, immortalised by Shakespeare's character, would defeat all scientific attempts to rehabilitate Richard for centuries.

Compared with this witty but unreliable narrator, Vergil was a genuine historian, probably the best of the century, the first to use critical judgement, compare sources, and check the veracity of facts. He was also less concerned by the recent partisan quarrels than his English colleagues – the Wars of the Roses occupy but a small section of his twenty-seven volumes. When, after twenty years of polishing, the *Anglica Historia* appeared at last in 1534, it was welcomed by a stream of anti-foreign abuse, because Vergil refuted the Trojan foundation of Britain and the authenticity of King Arthur. Nonetheless, it set the model for all the great Tudor chronicles. Edward Hall's *Union of the Two Noble and Illustre Families of York and Lancaster*, published in 1548, is to a large extent a wordy translation of Vergil's elegant

Latin, embellished with extracts from other chronicles and spiced up with his own moral commentaries.

Hall (c.1498–1547) concentrates on the century of civil wars concluded by the Tudors' advent because, he explains in a foreword, the blessings of union can only be understood against a background of division. Unlike his model, Hall is a firm Protestant, and devout admirer of Henry VIII, but he never quarrels with Vergil's opinions – he simply omits them when they disagree with his own. He is also much less rigorous, seldom embarrassed by the conflicts of sources or philosophical systems he appeals to, and frequently suits his ethics to hard facts. The two widely differing accounts of Richard III, Vergil's and Thomas More's, are reproduced verbatim in his chronicle, one after the other, without any attempt to reconcile them. It is not unusual in his pages to see Dame Fortune cycling on the Lord's mysterious highways, while he wavers between a providential and a machiavellian view of world history. Hall's politics are quite variable when it comes to supporting Lancaster or York. If there is any constancy in him, it lies in his general preference for the monarch in power, and fierce disapproval of all rebels.

The same can be said of Raphael Holinshed's *Chronicles*, whose re-edition in 1587 is often thought to have inspired the vogue of the history play. After studying at Cambridge, Holinshed (c.1529–c.1580) worked as a translator for the London publisher Reginald Wolfe, who was composing a universal history. When Wolfe died in 1570, a team of writers formed under Holinshed's direction to continue the project, but decided to restrain it to the British Isles, and published *The Chronicles of England, Scotland and Ireland* in 1577. The history of England was by Holinshed himself. He used a large variety of sources, both contemporary accounts and Renaissance narratives, paraphrasing or copying Hall, in other words Vergil, on the York and Lancaster reigns, with heavy cuts of their providential comments. He died shortly after the volume's publication, and a new team led by John Hooker started work on a second edition. This revised version, brought up to the year 1553, though still known as Holinshed's, actually owed little to him: it appeared with abundant marginal notes from its copy-editor Abraham Fleming, a Protestant priest who thus reinjected large helpings of the providence Holinshed had reduced.

The mirrors of history

Hall's monument is erected against 'Oblivion, the cankered enemy to Fame', as he explains in the Preface. It is 'memory by literature'. To the humanists of More's generation, the best achievements of worldly fame were those preserved by the art of great poets for all to emulate. The *Mirror for Magistrates*,

Shakespeare's histories, Daniel's *Civil Wars*, like other Elizabethan best-sellers derived from the chroniclers' material, all aim at this ideal synthesis of history and poetry. Designed as a sequel to Boccacio's *De Casibus* tales by a consortium of young lawyers, *The Mirror for Magistrates* (1559–87) takes an important step towards the turning of history into drama even though its simplistic views of the recent past cannot have given Shakespeare much more political insight than did Hall. In a succession of 'Tragedies' augmented with each new edition, the ghosts of English statesmen narrate the circumstances which brought them to a miserable end and advise readers against the various faults responsible for their misfortune. The usefulness of their teaching was amply confirmed by the enduring success of the *Mirror* in Elizabeth's reign. Even the detractors of poetry thought an exception should be made when it was applied to the recording of true edifying stories.

The praise of history towards the end of the sixteenth century was almost unanimous, with one notable exception. Sir Philip Sidney underlined the weaknesses of history writing, and the fact that it does not belong with poetry at all. Poetry needs no excuse from it, for it is incomparably superior, 'And even historiographers (although their lips sound of things done, and verity be written in their foreheads) have been glad to borrow both fashion and perchance weight of the poets.' His claim, a straight translation of Aristotle's argument, is well known: poetry is 'more philosophical and studiously serious'[13] than history, the main difference being that the one tells what happened, the other what could happen. Historians deal in relative truths, based on hearsay, and tied to random facts, whereas poetry has access to a higher and universal form of truth.

Sidney may have misread the first signs of the great theatrical era which was about to begin, but he pinpoints the fault line of historiography. Despite their popular success, the heroical syntheses of noble deeds and sublime verse so pleasing to readers of the *Mirror* were growing obsolete. The best Renaissance historians, Jean Bodin, followed by Camden, John Stowe and others, were increasingly anxious to delineate their field of inquiry and detach it from poetic fancies, claiming it was impossible to both instruct and delight. Invoking Thucydides as their authority, they expressed distrust for the ornaments of style, advising a rugged simplicity and correct grammar as best suited to the teaching of naked truth. Even classical devices like *prosopopoeia* – interpolated speeches put in the mouths of historical characters to expose their motives – were to be avoided. Yet these were all the matter of staged history, a sure indication that the ways of historians and poets parted at the dramatic revival of England's past. The new generation were taking a decisive turn towards modern research, just too late for Shakespeare, who would have to learn his way through the chroniclers' maze.

The tools of history

Historiography turns modern when it satisfies four types of criteria: secularisation, which sets it free from theology; experimental research, which privileges documentary evidence and comparative tests over old authorities; a sense of historical development, which invalidates the traditional analogies between past and present; and the delimitation of an area of research, distinct from philosophy or poetry, which emancipates it from the need to please and persuade. The Tudor chronicles met none of these requirements, some of which would have to wait one or two centuries more before they became normal practice.

However hard they tried to broaden the narrow perspectives of their predecessors, the Tudor chroniclers still worked with the tools, methods, and intellectual limits of the medieval annalists. Hall might well sneer at their naive superstitions and crude chains of causality, for instance when he mocked them for reading God's will in the least thunderstorm or enrolling heavenly sent doves in their camp, but he was not above such simplicity himself, and equally militant in support of his revered king. He was aware, like most Renaissance historians, that the modern world called for more elaborate systems of explanation than the mystery of God's plans for humanity, but was not mentally nor professionally armed to deal with it. The double dogma of Christian teleology and the superiority of antiquity put powerful restraints on the progress of free scientific enquiry. Even if the examination of second causes, i.e. the natural concatenation of events, allowed a more secular approach, it was still framed by Christian concepts. Admittedly, Machiavelli had divorced public from private morals, but the distinction was not yet clear to every chronicler, nor its consequences fully measured.

Apart from its religious and political aspects, the authority of tradition overruled the evidence of documents or experimental tests, and would continue to do so well into the seventeenth century, at the expense of scientists like Galileo or Descartes. The scissors-and-paste method, a patchwork akin to the copy/paste of our computers, was still the current mode of writing history. If they consulted several sources, most authors collected original details, or used conflicting accounts to enliven their narratives rather than to inform critical comparisons. The 'spade work' of modern history was not yet common practice, even with a reputed pioneer like Bacon, whose *History of Henry VII* betrays his unconcern for factual veracity.

Hall and his successors did not complain about their inadequate tools of inquiry, but obviously they found the traditional methods of writing too restrictive. Their first aim no longer being to legitimise the present regime, they were more concerned to understand the larger mechanisms of history, and extract perennial truths from an objective study of the past. The form of annals, year by year accounts without perspective, did not enable them to treat problems of causality. Hall tries to overcome this limit by anticipating the long-term effects of events like Henry VI's foolish marriage, or the murder of Duke Humphrey, both in their natural consequences and their providential punishment. He is obviously at pains to reconcile those two modes of explanation, sometimes asserting that cause entails effect without need of divine interference, but more often tempted to draw simplistic moral lessons whenever facts permit. This, however, becomes increasingly difficult within the moral anarchy of the civil wars, where crime reigns supreme and virtue is seldom if ever rewarded. Even for staunch believers, God's ways proved so bloody that it must have been hard to bless His divine providence for the happy ending of the story.

The first part of *Henry VI* conforms to Hall's simple faith in union as the key to victory. England cannot be defeated abroad by inferior enemies except when divided against itself. Soon, however, the violent upsets at home exceed the chroniclers' powers of explanation, and from play to play we find Shakespeare increasingly aware of their limits. It is plain from their accounts that the traditional power structure was totally unable to control the forces of anarchy unleashed by its central weakness, something the Tudor writers sensed when they desperately tried to plant a more stable system on legal bases, even if they lacked the concepts for an objective diagnosis. If the *Mirror* adopted Hall's short-sighted patterns unquestioningly, the young Shakespeare soon took a critical distance from his sources. In fact he used these hefty narratives much as he used various second-rate scripts for his major tragedies or comedies: with a big knife, and an eye to their dramatic potential.

Looking for Plutarch

Shakespeare must have run the whole gamut of English political philosophy when he reached the conclusion of *Henry V*. After *Richard III*, he had backed out of a dead end which led straight into the Tudors' 'mysteries of state', as Queen Elizabeth called them. The 'miraculous' compromise wrought by her grandfather Henry VII between Christian laws of charity and Machiavellian *Realpolitik* could be probed no further in her own reign; the only way to display it was to lift Harry's cloak of ceremony. If Shakespeare was to pursue independent reflection on power politics, he had to step out of a mental system where God and monarchy held the world framed. The Roman world which Elizabethans felt heirs to was both close and remote enough to provide the best stage for a new sequence of plays.

Titus Andronicus in fact owed more to Ovid and Seneca than to the historians of Rome, whose writings reached a height of popularity in the 1590s, when full translations of Tacitus and Livy appeared, along with a new edition of North's Plutarch. *The Lives of the Noble Grecians and Romans*, drawn by Thomas North from Amyot's French translation, first published in 1579, would be the main inspiration of Shakespeare's Roman plays.[14] Plutarch sketches out the destiny of the Roman Empire through full portraits of the characters who played prominent parts in its growth. His philosophy of history is deeper than that of the Tudor chroniclers, more consistent, and is guided by a sense of historical evolution which they lack. And yet, especially in Thomas North's Englishing – North turns Fortune into an all-managing Providence – this is not entirely foreign to Tudor ideology. The Roman commonwealth is repeatedly compared to a ship without a pilot. After years of civil warfare, the state of Rome so urgently requires an absolute governor that God directly interferes to prevent Brutus' victory.[15] Though a Republican at heart, Plutarch is convinced that the Empire is a foregone conclusion, and the price to pay for Caesarism proves as bloody as that for Tudor stability.

Shakespeare set a precedent, and showed a keener sense of history than his fellow writers, by following Plutarch's *Lives* rather than the more gossipy Suetonius (*c.*70–128) who was the usual source for Caesar stories. As any humanist might have told him, the young playwright probably acquired a clearer understanding of English history by reading the classics than from any contemporary writer. As with Sidney's defensive use of Aristotle, all Elizabethan topics about history were culled from the ancients, and probably saved as commonplaces in writers' notebooks for subsequent quotation, the dry remnants of a sharp intellectual debate on historiography which developed from Herodotus to Saint Augustine. In the *De oratore*, the main source of these tags, Cicero observes the progress of history since its origin, when it was a mere concoction of annals, and draws a list of its virtues, 'Witness of ages, light of truth, life of memory, mistress of life, messenger of the past', while arguing that it can only be made immortal by the orator's voice.[16] He is rightly convinced that Roman historiography will develop, as did that of the Greeks, from a concise notation of events to the most polished discourse.

Writing shortly after Cicero, Quintilian (*c.* A.D.35–100) summed up the tension between the two main drifts of historiography through antiquity in a way which still applies to the Renaissance, somewhere between poetry and oratory, something like a poem in prose: 'it is written to narrate, not to prove, and the whole work is composed not to accomplish something or use in a present fight, but for the memory of posterity and the fame of talent'.[17] From one century to the next, Greek and Latin writers thus reflect upon each other's views, measuring history against poetry or philosophy, weighing its claims at scientificity and universality, disputing its degree of truth or verisimilitude, immediate or future utility, its proper subject matter – past or present facts – and its dependence on rhetoric. The arguments set forth in their reflexive prefaces reappear on a far lower level in the Tudor chroniclers' stereotyped ones. And the old commonplace lives on well into the seventeenth century: truth is the soul, eloquence the body, of history.

Plutarch, like Thucydides before him, had criticised Herodotus for sacrificing truth to his reader's pleasure. It was Thucydides (c.455–404 B.C.) who first required the historian to examine evidence and never trust the tales of the poets. But Isocrates (c.436–338 B.C.), a pupil of the sophists, was less concerned with the establishment of facts than the selection of those fittest to persuade, and founded the notion of history as an endless source of examples. It was left to Polybius (c.210–130 B.C.), two centuries later, to revive a nobler passion for the quest of truth over the arts of rhetoric, and enumerate its practical rules, the first being inquiry from actual witnesses. In an answer to Aristotle, he places history above tragedy, because it aims at truth, where tragedy favours credibility even if it is a lie. His own object, he announces, is to discover the cause of events, and more particularly to analyse the institutions which enabled the Romans to conquer the earth. They owed much of this extraordinary success to fortune, *Tyche*, but they entirely deserved it by their own merits.

The end of the Republic raised new questions among Latin writers who, like Polybius. wondered which, Fortune or Roman *virtus*, was the first cause of Roman hegemony and its ensuing decline. The notions would reappear in the guise of Machiavelli's *fortuna* and *virtù*, the tide of history and the politician's ability to swim on it to success. For Livy (59 B.C.–A.D. 17), Republican Rome stood above the rest of the world by virtue of its heroes. He used Polybius' material, though he followed Isocrates in drawing useful lessons from Rome's high deeds and moral decadence: the historian's duty is truth, but truth needs elaborating into a literary shape to achieve its object. Rome had produced more eminent men than any other people before, but it was doomed to end by its very success. The same idea forms the core of Plutarch's lives of the heroes who played leading parts in the end of the Republic, Cato, Brutus, Antony, Cassius, Caesar, Cicero. Torn by civil strife and the extension of dominion, Rome cries out for a strong leader. Caesar's murder can only delay the inevitable. Fortune, presiding over Rome's manifest destiny, removes all further obstacles, namely Brutus' high ideals and his brother conspirators' petty ambitions. But there is tragedy in the fact that the Empire has no place for men of Brutus' stamp.

Plutarch (46–126) lived in the pacified world of Trajan, when the unity of the Mediterranean was almost completed. Prosperity was at its height, and peace likely to reign forever, but the days of the great heroes were over. His biographies of excellent men are patterns of self-knowledge and virtuous behaviour, while his awareness that the best is behind gives them a tinge of pessimism, one amply shared by his contemporary, Tacitus (*c.* 55–117), who, like Plutarch, managed to live through the despotic reign of Domitian, and was equally partial to the Republic. A former student of rhetoric, praised as an excellent orator by Pliny the Younger, Tacitus draws a vivid picture of the civil wars, bloody fights, rebellions and catastrophes of the recent reigns, and a gallery of tyrants' portraits in which Thomas More found some inspiration for his *History of Richard III*.

The 'matter of Rome' was priceless to Shakespeare's contemporaries who liked to advertise themselves as its true inheritors, whereas papist Rome had proved unworthy of its admirable forefathers. Agricola, who fought Boadicea and later became governor of Britain, was the first to circumnavigate Britain and prove that it was an island. Tacitus, his son-in-law, gathered a wealth of information on the country and its tribes at the time of the Roman conquest. Camden, who had given up myths of the monarchy's Trojan or Celtic origins, retraced these Roman vestiges to establish Britain as an imperial province, sharing in the Latin culture of the ancient world which Shakespeare addresses in *Cymbeline*: at the end of the play, the Britons have defeated the Roman army, but their king freely agrees to pay a tribute to Rome, Shakespeare's delicate way to pay old debts.

NOTES

1 Adapted from *WT*, 4.1.0SD.
2 From *Humanitas*, the Latin term used by Cicero to translate the Greek *paideia*, 'human culture'.
3 *The City of God*, xxxviii.2, xx.23.
4 *The Discourses* in Machiavelli 1950.
5 Rackin 1990, pp. 8–12, overestimates the advance of historical consciousness in her appraisal of Renaissance historiography.
6 *The History of the World*, in Raleigh 1829, Preface, p. xliii.
7 Rickey and Stroup 1968, p. 301.
8 Fussner 1970, p. 237.
9 About the chronicler John Hardyng, for instance, see Kelly 1970, pp. 39–48.
10 Zeeveld 1940, pp. 406–25.
11 Raleigh 1829, Preface p. lxiii.

12 *The First Part of the Life and Raigne of King Henrie the IIII*, published in 1599, was dedicated to the Earl of Essex. For details of the Hayward case, and its connections with Shakespeare's play, see Campbell 1947, pp. 168–93.

13 Sidney 1965, pp. 97 and 109; compare Aristotle 1920, ix, p.43.

14 North's first version reappears, completed by other authors, in 1595 and 1603. On Shakespeare's access to Roman history, see Martindale 1990, pp. 141–4.

15 Plutarch 1895–6, VI, 230.

16 'Testis temporum, lux veritatis, vita memoriae, magistra vitae, nuntia vetustatis . . . qua voce alia nisi oratoris immortaliti commendatur' (*De oratore*, II, 36).

17 *Institutio oratoria*, x, 31.

5

PHYLLIS RACKIN

Women's roles in the Elizabethan history plays

If, as many scholars believe, an early version of *2 Henry VI* was the first history play Shakespeare wrote, then he began his dramatised version of the Tudor chronicles with Margaret's arrival at the English court. Although modern readers are unlikely to think of Margaret when recalling the memorable characters Shakespeare created, she is actually the subject of the earliest surviving reference to a Shakespearean character and to Shakespeare's work as a playwright. In 1592 Robert Greene complained about 'an upstart crow, beautified with our feathers, that with his "tiger's heart wrapped in a player's hide", supposes that he is as well able to bombast out a blank verse as the best of you: and being an absolute *Johannes fac totum*, is in his own conceit the only Shake-scene in a country'.[1] Even without the epithet 'Shake-scene', the identity of the upstart crow was probably clear to Greene's original readers, because 'his tiger's heart wrapped in a player's hide' echoes the charge 'O tiger's heart wrapped in a woman's hide' (1.4.137) that York had levelled against Margaret in Shakespeare's *3 Henry VI*. Greene's allusion, along with other evidence, has led James Forse to conclude that Shakespeare himself may have performed Margaret's part,[2] but whether he did or not, it is clear that Margaret was a prominent and memorable character for Shakespeare's original audiences. She is the only character who appears in all four plays of the first 'tetralogy', and she plays a major role in shaping the course of the historical action in both *Part 2* and *Part 3* of *Henry VI*.

Even in *Part 1*, where Margaret's role is minimal, she has a prototype in another powerful French woman: Joan La Pucelle. In the represented action, Joan is the most formidable opponent the English forces confront. In the scripted performance on stage, she is the most memorable and vividly conceived of all the characters in the play. Nothing else in the entire script compares with the vivid, colloquial eloquence and irreverent wit of the speech in which Joan debunks Sir William Lucy's recitation of Talbot's heroic titles.

'But where's the great Alcides of the field', Lucy asks:

> Valiant Lord Talbot, Earl of Shrewsbury,
> Created for his rare success in arms
> Great Earl of Washford, Waterford, and Valence,
> Lord Talbot of Goodrich and Urchinfield,
> Lord Strange of Blackmere, Lord Verdon of Alton,
> Lord Cromwell of Wingfield, Lord Furnival of Sheffield,
> The thrice victorious Lord of Falconbridge,
> Knight of the noble order of Saint George,
> Worthy Saint Michael, and the Golden Fleece,
> Great Marshal to Henry the Sixth
> Of all his wars within the realm of France?
>
> (4.7.60–71)

Joan's earthy, iconoclastic rejoinder, couched in the rhythms and language of actual speech, must have had a stunning impact for playgoers accustomed to the conventional sentiments and stiff, end-stopped versification in the surrounding script:

> Here's a silly stately style indeed:
> The Turk, that two-and-fifty kingdoms hath,
> Writes not so tedious a style as this.
> Him that thou magnifie'st with all these titles
> Stinking and fly-blown lies here at our feet.
>
> (4.7.72–6)

Joan had to be killed off at the end of *1 Henry VI*, but if this was Shakespeare's first English history, he may have wanted to maintain her theatrical appeal in the subsequent plays, and Margaret may have been conceived as her substitute.[3] Whichever play came first, the two wicked French women are connected, not only by the similarity of their roles and characterisations but also by the unhistorical but emblematic scene in which Margaret is first introduced, which Shakespeare placed at the very moment when Joan is about to leave the stage of history, led off by York to captivity and the stake. The stage directions show how closely the two actions were joined:

> *Exeunt [York and Joan]*
> *Alarum. Enter* SUFFOLK *with* MARGARET *in his hand*   (5.3.44)

As Michael Hattaway observes, the spectacle of the two French women with their English captors, one pair entering the stage as the other leaves it, sends the clear visual message that Margaret will now take on Joan's role in the action.[4]

Figure 5   *H VI*, RSC 2000, with Richard Dillane as Suffolk, David Oyelow as King
Henry VI, Fiona Bell as Queen Margaret. Photograph: Manuel Harlan.

Despite the prominence of Joan and Margaret in Shakespeare's earliest history plays, it has often seemed to modern scholars that, of all the
dramatic genres that were popular on the Elizabethan stage, the English history play was the least hospitable to women. In the more celebrated plays of
Shakespeare's second 'tetralogy' – *Richard II*, the two parts of *Henry IV*, and
Henry V – the roles of women are severely limited, both in size and in scope.[5]
The places where history is made – the royal court and the field of battle –
are exclusively male preserves, and the business of the main historical plots
is conducted entirely by men. Even the Henry VI plays seem to express considerable anxiety about women's exercise of military and political power.[6]
In *1 Henry VI*, all of the female characters are French, and the Countess of
Auvergne, like Joan, is cast as a threat to the heroic Talbot. In *2 Henry VI*,
Eleanor Cobham's ambition and her involvement with witchcraft help to
destroy her noble husband; and Margaret's influence at court threatens both
her husband's royal authority and the peace of the realm. Deceptive and
malevolent, all of these women constitute powerful threats to the English
men who are the plays' protagonists.

In the case of Joan and Margaret, the women are also cast as antagonists to
the apparent purpose of the plays themselves – the preservation of England's
heroic past. Gloucester explicitly names this danger in the opening scene

of 2 *Henry VI*, when he warns the assembled English nobility about the disastrous consequences that Margaret's marriage to the young king will have:

> Fatal this marriage, cancelling your fame,
> Blotting your names from books of memory,
> Razing the characters of your renown,
> Defacing monuments of conquered France,
> Undoing all, as all had never been!
>
> (1.1.96–100)

Joan defines her own role in similar terms. At the end of her first scene in *1 Henry VI*, she identifies herself with the dispersion of the heroic legacy of Henry V:

> Assigned am I to be the English scourge . . .
> Glory is like a circle in the water,
> Which never ceaseth to enlarge itself
> Till by broad spreading, it disperse to nought;
> With Henry's death the English circle ends,
> Dispersèd are the glories it included.
> Now am I like that proud insulting ship
> Which Caesar and his fortune bare at once.
>
> (1.2.129–39)

The similarity between Joan's and Margaret's roles as opponents to the historical legacy of English glory seems to suggest that the very purpose and protocols of the English history play genre tend to cast women in antagonistic roles. The same implication can be derived from an enthusiastic celebration of the genre written by Thomas Nashe, who may have had a hand in writing *1 Henry VI*.[7] In Nashe's view, the function of these plays was the preservation of a historical legacy that was as masculine as it was English. In plays taken from 'our English Chronicles', he wrote,

> our forefathers' valiant acts (that have lain long-buried in rusty brass and worm-eaten books) are revived, and they themselves raised from the grave of oblivion and brought to plead their aged honours in open presence: than which, what can be a sharper reproof to these degenerate effeminate days of ours?

'How would it have joyed brave Talbot', Nashe continues (in an apparent reference to *1 Henry VI*), '(the terror of the French) to think that after he had lain two hundred years in his tomb, he should triumph again on the stage'.[8] It is not surprising, therefore, that the plays depict the power of warlike women such as Joan and Margaret in threatening terms.

In the later plays as well, the scripts provide explicit suggestions that the stage of English history is no place for women. In *1 Henry IV*, Hotspur, rushing off to rebellion and refusing his wife's demand to know why and where he is going, explains, 'this is no world / To play with mammets [dolls] and to tilt with lips' (2.3.85–6). In *Richard II* when the Duchess of York, desperate with concern for her son, leaves her domestic space to go to the new King Henry IV to plead for Aumerle's pardon and his life, the indecorousness of her intrusion is clearly marked in the playscript as a lowering of the dramatic genre. The episode begins with the Duchess's offstage cry, 'What ho, my liege! For God's sake let me in!' The beginning of the ensuing dialogue is worth quoting in full:

> BULLINGBROOK   What shrill-voiced suppliant makes this eager cry?
> DUCHESS   [*within*] A woman and thy aunt, great king. 'Tis I.
>   Speak with me, pity me, open the door!
>   A beggar begs that never begged before.
> BULLINGBROOK   Our scene is altered from a serious thing
>   And now changed to 'The Beggar and the King.'   (5.3.73–9)

Even if the king had not explicitly noted the generic debasement, it would be apparent in the theatre, as the dignified blank verse in which the historical business of royal courts is conducted on Shakespeare's stage gives way to doggerel rhymed couplets and the action of the scene degenerates into farce. The rhymes which begin here run for the whole of the Duchess's intrusion, for thirty-two couplets. As Andrew Gurr notes, all of the characters on stage are reduced to caricature:

> The rhymes, together with the stage actions of hammering at the door and kneeling, are characteristics which bring the scene very close to the few surviving examples of the jig or knockabout act which commonly followed the performance of a public-theatre play on the Elizabethan stage. The comic burlesque manner of the scene is unavoidable in performance.[9]

Although, as Gurr points out, all of the characters on stage are reduced to caricature, the placement of Bullingbrook's contemptuous comment associates the degeneration of the dramatic action with the Duchess's intrusion.[10]

Just as Joan and Margaret are demonised for their intrusion into the historical arenas of court and battlefield, the Duchess is ridiculed. It seems, in fact, that the more active the female characters become in Shakespeare's history plays, the more negative their characterisation. The more sympathetically depicted female characters, such as the victimised women in *Richard III* and the Duchess of Gloucester and the Queen in *Richard II*, never go to war, they play no part in the affairs of state, and they seem to spend most of their limited time on stage in tears. Helplessness seems to be an essential component of female virtue in the best-known Shakespearean history plays. History-making seems to be an exclusively masculine project.

The picture becomes more complicated, however, if we look beyond the plays that constitute the major Shakespearean canon. There is an almost complete inverse correlation between the prominence of women's roles in a history play and its place in the current Shakespearean canon.[11] In the plays of the second tetralogy, the percentage of words assigned to female characters never reaches ten per cent of the script. The second tetralogy ends, as 2 *Henry VI* begins, with the announcement of a royal wedding, but none of the four plays that comprise it features female characters in prominent roles. The women who do appear are confined to enclosed domestic settings or marginalised either in foreign countries or in the fictional, anachronistically modern world of Mistress Quickly's tavern in Eastcheap. Women are never seen in the council-chambers and battlefields where English history is made. Often designated by modern scholars as 'The Henriad' (although no one has yet ventured to describe the first tetralogy as the 'Margaretsaga'), these plays are the ones most admired by scholars and critics, and they are also most frequently produced on stage and best known by the general public. By contrast, the less admired Shakespearean history plays, such as *King John*, *Henry VIII*, and the Henry VI plays, do include female characters who intervene in the historical action. In the opening scene of *King John*, for instance, Eleanor announces that she is a 'soldier' (1.1.150), and both Eleanor and Constance play leading roles in the conflict for the English throne. However, despite the play's effectiveness on stage, it has often been dismissed by critics as poorly constructed 'hack work'.[12] In *Henry VIII*, the most sympathetically portrayed character is Queen Katherine, but although the play was popular in its own time, it has often been dismissed or ignored by subsequent critics as the incoherent product of collaborative authorship.

The responses of Shakespeare's earliest audiences may have been strikingly different from our own. In the case of *1 Henry VI*, for instance, Thomas Nashe wrote in 1592 that 'ten thousand spectators at least' had seen that play,[13] and Philip Henslowe's records of the receipts for its initial run suggest a figure closer to twenty thousand, more than all but one of the many other plays that Henslowe produced.[14] By contrast, the play is rarely performed today, and it is often dismissed either as 'immature' work or as the product of authorial collaboration.

One possible reason for the apparent difference between the responses of Shakespeare's original audiences and those of modern readers is our reliance upon printed texts. Reading a playscript tends to privilege the represented action at the expense of its theatrical presentation. As a result, it tends to discount the charismatic theatrical appeal a character can have on stage when the role that character plays in the represented action is negative. Both Joan and Margaret, for instance, have a powerful theatrical presence that challenges the dominance of the heroic English men who are featured in the represented history. In *Richard III*, although it is Richmond, rather than any of the women, who finally puts an end to Richard's bloody career, the women have far more time on stage, challenging Richard's theatrical dominance in a way that Richmond never manages to do. Moreover, it is Margaret and Joan, rather than any of the male characters in the earlier plays, who anticipate Richard's demonic energy, his transgressive, irreverent wit, and his vivid theatrical presence. The fact that all three play villainous roles in the represented action in no way diminishes the powerful appeal they possess in performance.

In considering the popularity of Shakespeare's earliest history plays when they were first performed, it is also important to remember that the paying customers in Shakespeare's playhouse included women as well as men (perhaps, in fact, more women than men). We know that in Shakespeare's London women probably outnumbered men by a proportion of thirteen to ten[15] and that women were a visible presence all over the city, where they could be seen buying and selling in the markets, assisting in household businesses, running businesses of their own, engaging in litigation on their own account, and frequenting the playhouses.[16] In Southwark, the immediate neighbourhood of the theatres, at least sixteen per cent of the households were headed by women.[17] Even if, as many modern scholars assume, male spectators in Shakespeare's time would have responded with anxious hostility to representations of women's power and autonomy, Joan's energy and her transgressive wit may have constituted a powerful attraction for many of those independent women in the audience. In fact, it may very well be that modern scholars, much more than Shakespeare's original audience, prefer the plays that minimise the roles of women and depict female characters in stereotypically 'feminine' settings. If that is the case, our negative estimation of women's roles in the Elizabethan history play may be, at least partly, an artefact of our own construction.

Finally, a very different picture of the possibilities for female roles in the Elizabethan history play emerges if we look beyond the canonical Shakespearean plays and the primary historiographic sources Shakespeare is known to have used. The anonymous play *Edward III*, for instance, suggests not only that the Elizabethan history play could stage positive images of powerful women but also that these images were already available in the historical record. Although a number of recent scholars have argued for Shakespeare's authorship, *Edward III* has yet to achieve a secure place in the Shakespearean canon. Drawing upon Froissart's *Chronicles* as well as Holinshed's and also upon Painter's *Palace of Pleasure*, *Edward III* depicts female characters who are totally different from those in the canonical Shakespearean history plays.

Courageous in war, women in *Edward III* are also models of womanly virtue. To be sure, the Countess of Salisbury's defence of Roxborough Castle and Queen Philippa's role at the battle of Newcastle have precedents in Shakespeare's Henry VI plays. Joan leads the French army to repeated victories, and Margaret is always a better soldier than her husband: Clifford, in fact, urges the King to 'depart the field' of battle, explaining that 'The Queen hath best success when you are absent' (*3H6*, 2.2.73–4). But *Edward III* is the only one of these plays in which female military achievement is never condemned and never characterised as anomalous or inappropriate.

In Shakespeare's version of the English past, the martial valour of women is a monstrous anomaly. As York tells Margaret, 'Women are soft, mild, pitiful, and flexible:/Thou stern, obdurate, flinty, rough, remorseless' (*3H6*, 1.4.141–2). Although Joan and her enemies disagree about the source of her martial prowess, they all agree that it sets her apart from other women. Joan invites the Dauphin to try her courage in combat in order to prove 'that I exceed my sex' (1.2.90). Talbot marvels that 'a woman clad in armour chaseth' his troops (1.5.3). In both cases, the only possible explanation is supernatural assistance. Joan claims it comes from 'God's Mother': 'Her aid she promised, and assured success' (1.2.78, 82). Unable to overcome Joan in single combat, Talbot concludes that she must be a witch (1.5.21), a judgement later verified when Joan's familiar spirits appear on stage and she admits that she 'was wont to feed [them] with my blood' (5.3.14).

Shakespeare's women warriors inevitably feminise the men for whom they fight, but not their enemies, even when the women are victorious. Despite his defeats at Joan's hands, Talbot remains a model of heroic masculinity, both in Shakespeare's representation and in Thomas Nashe's use of 'brave Talbot (the terror of the French)' to exemplify 'our forefathers' valiant acts', which provide a sharp 'reproof to these degenerate effeminate days of ours'.[18] The manhood of the Dauphin and the French nobles, by contrast, is always compromised by their dependence upon Joan's military leadership. After the French victory at Orleans, for instance, Alençon gloats, 'All France will be replete with mirth and joy/When they shall hear how we have played the men' (1.6.15–16). The very terms in which Alençon exults identify French manhood as play-acting. Moreover, the Dauphin immediately reminds him, ''Tis Joan, not we, by whom the day is won' (1.6.17). Similarly, although Margaret's victories over the Yorkists never compromise their masculinity, they make her a constant threat to her husband's authority, despite the fact that the cause she fights for is the survival of his dynasty.

Paradoxically, the same qualities that make Margaret 'unwomanly' also associate her with a specifically female form of wickedness. 'How ill-beseeming is it in thy sex', York protests, 'to triumph like an Amazonian trull' (*3H6, 1.4.* 113–14). Here, as in Shakespeare's emphasis on Margaret's adulterous affair with Suffolk, the masculinity of the female warrior is linked with the sexual promiscuity of the harlot. As Simon Shepherd points out, 'the connection of Amazons with lust has a long history'.[19] The same associations colour Shakespeare's characterisation of Joan, who is both the leader of the Dauphin's army and his 'trull' (2.2.27) and who claims at the end of the play to be pregnant by both Alençon and Reignier (5.4.72–78). Even in her first scene, when she challenges the Dauphin to single combat to prove that she has been empowered by the Virgin Mary, their swordfight is framed by lewd comments from the French courtiers.

In the canonical Shakespearean history plays, women are always caught in a double bind: Strong women like Joan and Margaret are unchaste and unwomanly; virtuous women, like the weeping queen in *Richard II* and the lamenting widows in *Richard III* are confined to the roles of helpless victims, powerless to affect the course of history. In these plays, female characters are confronted by a recognisably modern dilemma. They can be either womanly or warlike. They can be either virtuous or powerful. But never both.[20]

In *Edward III*, by contrast, there is no trace of the anxiety about powerful, warlike women expressed in Shakespeare's demonisation of Joan and Margaret and echoed by recent scholars who repeat it as an endlessly circulated 'truth' about Elizabethan culture. Both the Queen and the Countess are depicted as paragons of womanly virtue as well as military valour. The two, in fact, are conflated. Instead of threatening their husbands' authority, these women's martial courage supports it. There are obvious parallels between the Countess of Salisbury's resistance to the Scots King's siege and her resistance to the English King's assault on her virtue. In both cases, she heroically defends her husband's property: she defends his castle against the Scots, and she defends her chastity (and thus her husband's honour) by threatening to kill herself rather than submit to the English King. Both the Countess's body and her property necessarily belong to her husband, a point emphasised by the Scots as they debate their division of the 'spoil' they anticipate from their siege:

> DOUGLAS   My liege, I crave the lady, and no more.
> KING DAVID   Nay, soft ye, sir; first I must make my choice,
>   And first I do bespeak her for myself

DOUGLAS Why then, my liege, let me enjoy her jewels.
KING DAVID Those are her own, still liable to her,
    And who inherits her hath those withal.

$(1.2.43-7)^{21}$

The connections between the two assaults the Countess repels are established from the outset and reiterated in the ensuing scenes. Her initial speech anticipates the 'grief' of becoming 'captive to a Scot': 'either to be wooed with broad untunèd oaths, / Or forced by rough insulting barbarism' (1.2. 8–9). The literal siege of her castle becomes the metaphorical equivalent for what Lodowick calls 'A lingering English siege of peevish love' (2.1.23) and the Countess calls the 'unnatural besiege' of Edward's courtship (2.1. 413).

The summary of the story in William Painter's *Palace of Pleasure* (1575), the chief source for the episode in *Edward III*, also uses military terms to describe the Countess's resistance to the king's courtship:

> seeing her constant fort to be impregnable, after pleasant suit and mild request, attempteth by undermining to invade, and when with siege prolix, he perceiveth no ingenious device can achieve that long and painful work, he threateth might and main, dire and cruel assaults, to win and get the same.
>   (reprinted in Metz 1989, p. 108)

Finally, Painter explains, the king relents, impressed by the lady's 'womanly stoutness and courageous constancy'. Like the playwright of *Edward III*, Painter associates the Countess' exemplary chastity with the daring of a courageous warrior: She is 'the perfect figure of womanhood', because

> with a curat [cuirass] of honour and weapon of womanhood, and for all his glorious conquests, she durst by singular combat to give refusal to his face: which singular perseverance in defence of her chastity inexpugnable esclarisheth [makes clear] to the whole flock of womankind the bright beams of wisdom, virtue and honesty.
>   (Metz 1989, pp. 107–8)

To be sure, the comparison of courtship to military siege comes from the conventional repertoire of Renaissance love poets, as Edward acknowledges when he describes his courtship in the language of war:

> The quarrel that I have requires no arms
> But these of mine, and these shall meet my foe
> In a deep march of penetrable groans;
> My eyes shall be my arrows, and my sighs
> Shall serve me as the vantage of the wind,
> To whirl away my sweetest artillery.
> Ah, but alas, she wins the sun of me,

> For that is she herself, and thence it comes
> That poets term the wanton warrior blind.
>
> (2.2.61–9)

What is remarkable in *Edward III* is that this lady is a literal warrior as well as a metaphorical one, defending her husband's castle with the same resolute courage that she subsequently demonstrates in the face of the king's courtship.

An even more remarkable association of female military valour and womanly virtue appears in 4.2, when Lacy brings the King a report from England that links the Queen's military victory at Newcastle with her impending labour in giving birth:

> David of Scotland, lately up in arms,
> Thinking, belike, he soonest should prevail,
> Your highness being absent from the realm,
> Is by the fruitful service of your peers
> And painful travail of the queen herself,
> That, big with child, was every day in arms,
> Vanquished, subdued, and taken prisoner
>
> (4.2.40–6)

Lacy's description foregrounds the Queen's pregnant body, emphasising her necessary role in producing what may very well have been the chief historical legacy of her husband – his fatherhood of seven sons. Certainly, that is the way he comes to readers of Shakespeare's history plays, but it is worth noting that the same emphasis is also present in the account of Edward's reign in Holinshed's *Chronicles*. Each section of the *Chronicles* includes, immediately following the account of the death of the king whose reign it recounts, a summary of the King's achievements and character. Significantly, in the case of *Edward III*, the summary begins with a paragraph devoted to an enumeration of his progeny, which begins, 'He had issue by his wife, Queen Philip seven sons' (v, 706).

The report of Queen Philippa's pregnancy at the Battle of Newcastle, unprecedented in Holinshed's or Froissart's chronicles, seems to be the playwright's invention. Froissart's account of the battle is much more detailed than the one that appears in the play, but it makes no mention of the Queen's pregnancy. Froissart relates that the Queen was 'great with child' when she knelt weeping before her husband to plead for the lives of the burghers of Calais.[22] The playwright's transfer of her pregnancy to the Battle of Newcastle seems designed to associate her best-known role in English history, the 'fruitful service' she provided as the mother to Edward's famous seven sons, with her service to England at the battle where the Scots king was captured; and the language used in Lacy's report conflates her military triumph with her pregnancy and impending labour in childbirth. The association is most striking in the image of her armed, pregnant body, conveyed in a single line – 'That, big with child, was every day in arms' – but it is reinforced in the references to the 'fruitful service' of the peers and in the description of the Queen's own military efforts as 'painful travail'. As Melchiori notes,[23] the word 'travail', was spelled 'travell' in the first Quarto, the two words were spelled interchangeably, and, as noted in the *OED*, the term was commonly used to refer to the labour and pain of childbirth.

The military achievements of the women in *Edward III* are likely to seem exceptional to a modern reader, especially to a reader of Shakespeare's English histories. They are not unusual, however, in the context of medieval history, where, as a recent historian notes,

> The participation of armed ladies...[in battles] was considered...as fairly normal. Ordericus Vitalis mentions Helvise, countess of Evreux in the twelfth century, who rode to war with the horsemen, armed as they were and showing as much ardour as the knights, clothed in their hauberts [hauberks, long coats of mail], and the soldiers carrying spears. During the crusades women fought in the Frankish armies...Froissart described Countess Jeanne de Montfort during the Breton Succession War, 'armed all over', 'mounted on a fine courser', who 'held a sharp cutting sword upright and fought well with great courage'. At the end of the fourteenth century, Thomas III, marquis of Saluzzo, described in *Le Chevalier errant* his grandmother, Richarda Visconti, who when her husband was in prison passed her time leading in person 'la greigneure guerre du monde'. 'You ought to know that she was always well and honourably armed and had her lance carried behind her like a captain, with her helmet, and always bore her bâton in her hand to command her men, and she had her ladies and damsels organized with her in this time of need.'[24]

Women warriors are also not remarkable in *Edward III* where the king gives no indication that he finds his wife's presence on the battlefield at all extraordinary. His brief, businesslike response to Percy's account of the battle focuses instead on the Scots king's capture. 'Thanks, Percy, for thy news with all my heart', he says, 'What was he took him prisoner in the field?' (4.2.47–8). Similarly, Froissart's fourteenth-century *Chronicle* contains no indication that he or anyone else found the Queen's appearance on the battlefield exceptional. In Chapter cxxxviii, entitled 'Of the battle of Newcastle upon Tyne between the Queen of England and the King of Scots', Froissart gives the following account:

> The Queen of England, who desired to defend her country, came to Newcastle-upon-Tyne and there tarried for her men, who came daily from all parts...Then

the Scots came and lodged against them near together; then every man was set in order of battle; then the Queen came among her men and there was or-dained four battles [battalions], one to aid another . . . The Queen went from battle to battle desiring them to do their devoir to defend the honour of her lord the King of England, and, in the name of God, every man to be of good heart and courage, promising them that to her power she would remember them as well or better as though her lord the king were there personally. Then the queen departed from them, recommending them to God and to St George.   (Froissart 1901, pp. 85–6)

There is only one feature of the Queen's appearance at the battle that might have been regarded as exceptional, and that is the pregnancy that the playwright apparently invented. As Nancy Huston has suggested, 'the symbolic equivalence between childbirth and war might be said to be one of the rare constants of human culture'. Citing a wide range of folk tales, an-cient myths, and primitive rituals and taboos, Huston argues that 'the two phenomena', 'traditionally . . . perceived as mutually exclusive', are 'analo-gous and complementary'.[25] Although many cultures exclude all women from hunting and war, she points out, 'even those societies in which women are allowed to hunt systematically exclude mothers from the pursuit of big game', and cultures which exclude most women from activities that involve killing, often make an exception in the case of virgins (pp. 127–8).

Given the long history in western culture of regarding killing and birthing as mutually exclusive alternatives, their linkage in *Edward III* seems truly extraordinary. However, even the Queen's presence at the battle has seemed extraordinary to subsequent historians. The account of the battle in Holinshed's late sixteenth-century *Chronicles* is derived from Froissart[26] but it minimises the Queen's role. In this version, it is the lords who, 'perceiving the king of Scots thus boldly to invade the land . . . assembled an host of all such people as were able to bear armour' to repel the invasion. As for the Queen, the chronicler simply notes that she 'was there [i.e. at the battle-field] in person, and went from rank to rank, and encouraged her people in the best manner she could, and that done, she departed, committing them and their cause to God the giver of all victory' (II, 644). Thomas Johnes, a nineteenth-century editor of Froissart goes even further. In a footnote to Chapter CXXXVIII, he writes,

Froissart supposes that Philippa, the consort of Edward III, was their leader; and in this he has been implicitly followed by the later historians of both nations. A young and comely princess, the mother of heroes, at the head of an army in the absence of her lord, is an ornament to history: yet no English writer of considerable antiquity mentions this circumstance, which, if true . . . would not have been omitted.   (Froissart 1884, I, 178n.)

Froissart, however, was in an excellent position to know what the Queen had done. The Battle of Newcastle was fought in 1346; from 1361 to 1366, Froissart resided at the English court, serving as court chronicler and as secretary to Queen Philippa.[27]

Johnes knew about Froissart's association with Queen Philippa, which is covered in his introductory 'Memoir of the Life of Froissart'.[28] Nonetheless, from his vantage point in the nineteenth century, he found Froissart's account of her role at the Battle of Newcastle incredible. Shakespeare's York would probably have agreed. By the end of the sixteenth century, virtuous women no longer led armies: the constriction of women's roles which was to become one of the salient features of modernity was already well under way.

NOTES

1 Greene 1592, Sig. F1^r.
2 Forse 1993, pp. 98–9.
3 On the order of the Henry VI plays, see *1H6*, ed. Hattaway 1990, pp. 34–41. Joan can also be seen as the prototype for an illustrious line of witty, irreverent debunkers of traditional pieties, such as the Bastard in *King John*, Richard III, and Falstaff.
4 *Ibid.*, p. 168n.
5 Howard and Rackin 1997, pp. 23–5, 137. *Richard III* is the only exception to this pattern, but although female characters do have prominent roles on stage in that play, they are powerless to affect the course of the historical action.
6 See, for example, Bevington 1966; Gutierrez 1990; Howard and Rackin *ibid.*, pp. 43–99; Jackson 1988; Marcus 1988.
7 *2H6*, ed. Hattaway 1991, p. 60; *1H6*, ed. Hattaway 1990, p. 42.
8 Thomas Nashe, *Pierce Penniless his Supplication to the Devil*, 1592, reprinted in Chambers 1923, IV, 238–9.
9 Gurr 1984, p. 162n.
10 Hodgdon 1991, p. 139.
11 Howard and Rackin 1997, pp. 23–6, 217–18.
12 *John*, ed. Beaurline 1990, p. 1.
13 Nashe 1958, I, 212.
14 Harbage 1941, p. 49.
15 *Ibid.*, p. 76.
16 Archer 1999; Gowing 1996, Gurr 1996a, pp. 56–60.
17 Henderson 1997, p. 192.
18 Nashe 1958, I, 212.
19 Shepherd 1981, p. 16; see also Loomba 1989, p. 47 and Shapiro 1987.
20 For an expanded version of this argument, see Howard and Rackin 1997, from which most of the material in the preceding three paragraphs derives.
21 Quotations are taken from *E3*, ed. Melchiori 1998.
22 Metz 1989, p. 91; see also Holinshed 1808, II, 648, who gives essentially the same account.

23 *E3*, ed. Melchiori 1998, p. 138.
24 Contamine 1984, pp. 241–2; see also Howard and Rackin 1997, pp. 201–6.
25 Huston 1986, p. 127.
26 Marginal citations, Holinshed 1808, II, 644.
27 Metz 1989, p. 32.
28 Froissart 1884, I, xviii–xxi.

2
THE PLAYS

6

JANIS LULL

Plantagenets, Lancastrians, Yorkists, and Tudors: *1–3 Henry VI, Richard III, Edward III*

By transforming the chronicles of Tudor historians into drama, Shakespeare and his contemporaries brought English history onto the English stage. History and performance converged, attracting thousands of spectators. For the Elizabethans, history meant political history, particularly stories of kings and high officials, who were seen as embodying the health of the state. As William Baldwin put it in *The Mirror for Magistrates* (1559), 'where offices are duly ministered, it can not be chosen, but the people are good, whereof must needs follow a good common weal. For if the officers be good, the people cannot be ill. Thus the goodness or badness of any realm lieth in the goodness or badness of the rulers.'[1]

The evaluation of rulers, however, was not the only goal of sixteenth-century historiographers. They wanted to know not only whether Henry VI had been a good or bad king, but also why. What were the causes of political success and failure, and what lessons could be drawn from English political history? In these concerns, Tudor historians resembled students of history today. Where they differed was in their interest, or lack of it, in accuracy. For example, Edward Hall (1548) and Raphael Holinshed (1587), the chroniclers most used by Shakespeare, gathered their narratives of medieval English history not from primary documents or eyewitness accounts, but from earlier chronicles and literary stories. Tudor historians were generally less interested in true accounts of distant events than in using those events to point out good examples and cautionary tales. Sir Philip Sidney's assertion that literature ('poetry') was a loftier form than history relied on the perceived moral superiority of literature. The purpose of studying both history and literature was to see 'virtue exalted and vice punished', and in Sidney's view, 'that commendation is peculiar to poetry, and far off from history'.[2]

This overlap of history with literature in Shakespeare's time made history a natural subject for the stage. Neither the chroniclers nor the playwrights cared as much about the facts as they did about the possibilities. Perhaps the historical Black Prince had not been the consummate warrior sketched in *Edward III*, and perhaps aristocratic society did not really fail the child–king Henry VI in the ways shown by Shakespeare's plays. Nevertheless, an Elizabethan might have replied, it could have happened that way, and our era needs to understand and imitate – or avoid – such situations. In the course of turning chronicle into drama, the Elizabethan playwrights also attempted to satisfy contemporary interest in how virtue and vice may be seen at work in great public events.

Structures and styles in the early histories

A Tudor playwright had technical advantages over a Tudor historiographer in dealing with English history. Where Holinshed evidently felt tied to a year-by-year chronicle structure, for example, Shakespeare did not. Following the chroniclers, the playwright focused on the fifteenth century, when England had been splintered by the ruinous civil wars known as the Wars of the Roses. But unlike his sources, Shakespeare usually started in the middle of the story. Although the plays are difficult to date, the first Shakespearean drama about English history was most likely not *Edward III*, which portrays the Plantagenet ancestor of the Yorkists and the Lancastrians, nor *Richard III*, the story of the last Plantagenet king. Instead, Shakespeare probably began in the middle, with the Lancastrian Henry VI, a great-great-grandson of Edward III. Henry became king of England at nine months of age and sat uneasily on the throne until he was murdered at age fifty (1471). During the boy–king's early years, England lost Henry V's conquests in France, a defeat portrayed in *1 Henry VI*. *2 Henry VI* depicts domestic disintegration under the young King Henry, concluding with the first battle in the Wars of the Roses. *3 Henry VI* traces the other major battles in these wars, ending with the Yorkist triumph and King Henry's death. *Richard III* picks up where *3 Henry VI* leaves off, but differs from the three earlier plays by turning its chronicle material into tragedy. Finally, in a mode that might almost be called political comedy, *Edward III* looks back to fourteenth-century England. The play is not funny, but unlike any of the other early histories, it has a happy ending.

1 HENRY VI: juxtaposition and suggestion

The protagonist of the *Henry VI* plays is the reign, not the king. At first glance, this seems to contradict the Tudor axiom that 'the goodness or badness of any realm lieth in the goodness or badness of the rulers'. Yet the character of the monarch remains a central concern in these plays, even in *1 Henry VI*, where the king does not appear until Act 3. Rather than showing how historical circumstances emanate from the personality of the ruler, the *Henry VI* plays show the interdependence of character and circumstance. The guardians of Henry VI use and abuse him when they should be nurturing him, and the resulting weaknesses in Henry's character lead to near-fatal weaknesses in the English state.

The success and failure of the ruler's actions cannot serve as a structural principle for *1 Henry VI* because Henry never gets a chance to act. Instead of building a plot around the king as central character, Shakespeare reveals the emptiness at the centre of English society through a series of juxtaposed displays. The play opens with the funeral of Henry V, conducted by his brothers, Bedford and Gloucester, and his uncles, the Duke of Exeter and the Bishop of Winchester. Gloucester eulogises Henry as history's ideal monarch:

> England ne'er had a king until his time:
> Virtue he had, deserving to command;
> His brandished sword did blind men with his beams,
> His arms spread wider than a dragon's wings;
> His sparking eyes, replete with wrathful fire,
> More dazzled and drove back his enemies
> Than midday sun fierce bent against their faces.
> What should I say? His deeds exceed all speech:
> He ne'er lift up his hand but conquerèd.
>
> (1.1.8–16)

This is the sovereign and father that the country and young Henry VI have lost. The question of whether England has anyone to take his place is soon answered in the negative. Gloucester, the well-meaning Lord Protector, cannot serve as an adequate foster father for the realm or for the infant king because he cannot control his temper around other courtiers, especially the scheming Winchester. As soon as Winchester speaks, Gloucester picks a quarrel with him, and the high-flown lamentations end in wrangling. Messengers begin to arrive with news of defeat in France, the first one offering a chorus-like explanation of England's military collapse:

> No treachery, but want of men and money.
> Amongst the soldiers this is mutterèd:
> That here you maintain several factions
> And, whilst a field should be dispatched and fought,
> You are disputing of your generals.   (1.1.69–73)

Following this hint, Shakespeare generally allows his audience to infer how an event reflects on other characters and conduct in the play, using juxtaposition to imply causal connection. Spectators must make the link, for example, between the bickering of Henry's 'guardians' and the young ruler's stunted personality. Similarly, as the action switches between England and France, members of the audience must see for themselves how incidents in one location echo and explain those in the other.

The central section of *1 Henry VI*, which consists entirely of incidents that Shakespeare invented, furnishes an extended illustration of the playwright's comparative method in this play. Act 2 begins with a fictitious English victory over the French (2.1). This is followed by a courtesy call on the Countess of Auvergne by the victorious English general, Lord Talbot (2.2 and 2.3), then the 'Temple Garden' scene (2.4), which imagines the Wars of the Roses originating in a disagreement among young English law students. Finally, we witness a meeting between Richard Plantagenet, Duke of York, and his Uncle Mortimer in an English prison (2.5). These scenes move from France to England and from one group of characters to another with little overt continuity. Sometimes, as in 2.1, connections to earlier action are easy to see. Shakespeare invents a temporary English victory to parallel the French victory at Orléans, just as he earlier invented a fight between Talbot and Joan La Pucelle as representatives of the two armies (1.5). In other cases, such as the encounter between Talbot and the Countess of Auvergne, parallels may seem less immediately obvious. Yet the contest between Talbot and the Countess, like the single combat between Talbot and Joan, comments emblematically on the larger public struggles in the play. Both of these scenes suggest, for example, why the English cannot rely on the old-fashioned chivalric values embodied by Talbot. The Hundred Years War, as represented here, is not the kind of honourable test of strength in which a Talbot might be expected to triumph. Instead, it is an extension of complex psychological and political motives like those of the countess. Talbot's superior military tactics win him temporary victories at Orléans and at the Countess' castle. In the end, however, he has to depend on politicians – York (Plantagenet) and Somerset – and he suffers defeat.

2 HENRY VI: story and episode

2 Henry VI has an even more episodic structure than its predecessor, presenting a succession of striking characters who play their parts and disappear: the duchess's conjurers, Horner and Thump, the Simpcoxes, the murderers of Suffolk, Cade and his rebels. In addition to this series of episodes, however, the play also traces the fortunes of several recurring figures who gradually evolve into two factions, the Yorkists and the Lancastrians. On the Lancastrian side, only Gloucester is completely loyal to the king, while the others are held together chiefly by their conspiracy against Gloucester. The Yorkists are a smaller but more cohesive group, consisting of the Yorks themselves and the Nevilles, Salisbury and Warwick.

Many of the isolated episodes in 2 *Henry VI* involve commoners, while the more continuous story of the approaching civil war focuses on the nobility. As in *1 Henry VI*, however, episodes serve as emblems: to complete their meanings, audiences must compare such moments to other actions in the play. The behaviour of common people, for example, often echoes and comments on the behaviour of England's leaders. The trials of Saunder Simpcox and of Horner and Thump travesty aristocratic legal proceedings, with gullible King Henry unable to serve as an impartial judge. The king wills himself to believe in Simpcox's bogus 'miracle', then condemns the drunken Horner for losing an unfair fight to the sober Thump. Superficially, Henry's moral condition looks like a metaphorical inversion of Simpcox's fraud. Simpcox pretends he cannot see when he really can, whereas Henry pretends to see when he cannot. Warwick comments ironically on the king's apparent blindness to the guilt of Winchester and Suffolk: 'Who finds the heifer dead and bleeding fresh / And sees fast by a butcher with an axe, / But will suspect 'twas he that made the slaughter?' (3.2.188–90). But Henry has already used images similar to Warwick's in lamenting Gloucester's fall. The similarity between Warwick's language and the king's implies that, Henry, like Simpcox, sees perfectly well:

> And as the butcher takes away the calf
> And binds the wretch and beats it when it strains,
> Bearing it to the bloody slaughter-house,
> Even so remorseless have they borne him hence;
> And, as the dam runs lowing up and down,
> Looking the way her harmless young one went
> And can do naught but wail her darling's loss,
> Even so myself bewails good Gloucester's case
> With sad unhelpful tears and, with dimmed eyes,
> Look after him and cannot do him good;
> So mighty are his vowèd enemies.   (3.1.210–20)

The deepest flaws in Henry's leadership derive not from an inability to see, but from an inability or unwillingness to act. In a way, both Simpcox and the king shirk responsibility out of 'pure need' (2.1.156). Simpcox needs a physical means of survival, while Henry needs a psychological one. But need does not excuse Simpcox, and it cannot excuse Henry. In the second half of this play and in *3 Henry VI*, the king becomes more observer than ruler, while his subjects, with chaotic results, take matters into their own hands.

As the Duke of York's faction grows, he incites Jack Cade and his artisans to rebellion, devising for Cade a false family tree that mimics York's own claims to the throne. Yet Cade's revolt is not merely a caricature of York's sedition; it mocks all misuse of authority. At the beginning of the play, for instance, King Henry is infatuated with his new wife and impulsively confers a new title on Suffolk, who has brought Queen Margaret from France:

> Lord Marquess, kneel down:
> We here create thee the first Duke of Suffolk,
> And gird thee with the sword.   (1.1.60–2)

In Jack Cade, Shakespeare creates a parody of both Henry's mismanagement and York's self-promotion. Faced with opponents who are gentlemen, the rebel leader seeks to bring himself up to their level by knighting himself:

> MICHAEL   Fly, fly, fly! Sir Humphrey Stafford and his brother are hard by, with the king's forces.
> CADE   Stand, villain, stand, or I'll fell thee down. He shall be encountered with a man as good as himself: he is but a knight, is 'a?
> MICHAEL   No.
> CADE   To equal him, I will make myself a knight presently. [*Kneels*] Rise up, Sir John Mortimer. [*Rises*] Now have at him.   (4.2.93–100)

At the close of the play, none of England's 'rulers' has achieved a stable government, and the audience knows the war will go on.

3 HENRY VI: losers and winners

3 Henry VI presents a more continuous story line than the other two *Henry VI* plays because its major incidents all depict battles in the Wars of the Roses. Act 1 begins where *2 Henry VI* ends, after the first battle of St Albans. At the end of the act, Margaret and Clifford kill the Duke of York at the battle of Wakefield (1.4). In Act 2, Warwick describes the second battle of St Albans (2.1), and King Henry observes the battle of Towton (2.5). Henry is held prisoner in Act 3 until Warwick the 'kingmaker' changes sides, takes the crown from Edward (4.3) and restores it to Henry (4.6). Act 5 portrays the battle of Barnet, where Henry was recaptured, and the battle of Tewkesbury, where Margaret was defeated and her son Edward killed. Historically, these events took place over ten years, from 1461 to 1471, and the play is crowded with violent incidents as the balance tips back and forth. Yet Shakespeare manages to shape the narrative of these battles into a dramatic structure in which the decline of the Lancastrians is counterpoised by the rise of York's two sons, Edward and Richard.

After entailing his crown to the Duke of York and disinheriting his own son, Henry VI stands on the sidelines as battles are waged in his name. In a scene that recalls the emblematic method of *1* and *2 Henry VI* (2.5), the king laments as two soldiers drag the bodies of their enemies on stage. When the first soldier discovers he has killed his father and the second discovers he has killed his son, Henry grieves for the 'bloody times' that have engulfed them all. Like the two soldiers, however, he regards himself as a victim and not an instigator of civil war, dreading censure without admitting fault:

> SON   How will my mother, for a father's death,
> Take on with me, and ne'er be satisfied?
> FATHER   How will my wife, for slaughter of my son,
> Shed seas of tears, and ne'er be satisfied!
> KING HENRY   How will the country, for these woeful chances,
> Misthink the king and not be satisfied!   (2.5.103–8)

Henry attributes events to chance, fortune, and the will of God, never to his own will. On the other side stand the wilful Yorks, especially Richard of Gloucester. Even as he struggles to maintain his brother Edward on the throne, Richard also begins a campaign for himself:

> I can add colours to the chameleon,
> Change shapes with Proteus for advantages,
> And set the murderous Machiavel to school.
> Can I do this and cannot get a crown?
> Tut! Were it farther off, I'll pluck it down.
>
>   (3.2.191–5)

Edward is still king at the end of the play, but it is Richard and Henry who face off as the champions of two opposing responses to history: complete fatalism and complete defiance of fate. When Richard comes to kill Henry in the Tower, the king's only resistance is prophecy:

> Teeth hadst thou in thy head when thou wast born
> To signify thou cam'st to bite the world;
> And if the rest be true which I have heard,
> Thou cam'st –
> GLOUCESTER   I'll hear no more: die, prophet, in thy speech,
> *Stabs him*
> For this, amongst the rest, was I ordained.
> KING HENRY   Ay, and for much more slaughter after this,
> O God forgive my sins, and pardon thee! *Dies*
>   (5.7.53–60)

Richard admits the truth of Henry's vision, but rejects the king's submissive attitude. The heavens may rule Richard's life, but they cannot make him like it:

> Then, since the heavens have shaped my body so,
> Let hell make crook'd my mind to answer it.
> I had no father, I am like no father;

> I have no brother, I am like no brother;
> And this word 'love', which greybeards call divine,
> Be resident in men like one another
> And not in me: I am myself alone.   (5.7.79–85)

The audience knows that Richard does resemble his father and once loved him deeply, yet now he denies all influences except self. In Henry's view, the forces of history leave him no room to choose or act on his own. Richard stands for self-determination, refusing to make any concessions at all to causes not arising in his will. Henry is a good man and Richard is an evil one, but they are both extremists, and neither is fit to govern, as Shakespeare demonstrates here and in *Richard III*.

RICHARD III: the tragic pyramid

In the histories section of the First Folio, only *Richard III* is called a 'tragedy'.[3] It unites the chronicle play, which Shakespeare had been developing in the three parts of *Henry VI*, with a tragic structure showing the rise and fall of a single protagonist. For all its huge cast, *Richard III* has no subplots. Opposing groups of characters – Margaret, Richard's brothers, Elizabeth's family, the York women, the York children, courtiers such as Hastings, Stanley, Buckingham, Ratcliffe, and Catesby, and the Earl of Richmond – all are used in various combinations to advance Richard's story. This single focus gives the play a classic pyramid structure: 'rising' action to the peak of the pyramid, climax, crisis, then 'falling' action to the end.[4] Beginning with the exposition in Richard's opening soliloquy, the rising action – Richard's ascent to the throne – continues until 4.2, Richard's first entrance as king. Having achieved the crown, Richard has also reached the peak of his fortunes. Immediately, the crisis or turn occurs. The new king begins to falter, expressing an uncharacteristic lack of confidence to the puzzled Buckingham:

> Thus high, by thy advice and thy assistance,
> Is King Richard seated.
> But shall we wear these glories for a day?
> Or shall they last, and we rejoice in them?
> BUCKINGHAM   Still live they, and forever let them last.
> RICHARD   Ah, Buckingham, now do I play the touch
>   To try if thou be current gold indeed.
>   Young Edward lives; think now what I would speak.
> BUCKINGHAM   Say on, my loving lord.
> RICHARD   Why, Buckingham, I say I would be king.
> BUCKINGHAM   Why, so you are, my thrice-renownèd lord.
>   (4.2.4–14)

From this point on, Richard gradually loses his earlier ability to control his environment. He continues his murders, killing the princes and possibly Anne, but Richmond gathers strength at a distance, and Margaret scents catastrophe:

> So now prosperity begins to mellow
> And drop into the rotten mouth of death.
> Here in these confines slyly have I lurked
> To watch the waning of mine enemies.
> A dire induction am I witness to,
> And will to France, hoping the consequence
> Will prove as bitter, black, and tragical.
>
> (4.4.1–7)

Historically, Margaret left England in 1476 and died in 1482, three years before Richard's defeat at Bosworth. In her anachronistic appearance in Shakespeare's play, she predicts the main action with her curses and prophecies (1.3), then returns at the opening of 4.4 to underscore the prophecies' fulfilment. The theatrical vocabulary of Margaret's soliloquy here – words such as 'induction' and 'tragical' – calls attention to the neatness of the play's structure: not only the pyramidal shape of the action and Margaret's prophetic antagonism, but also the several paired or 'mirror' scenes that enhance the impression of destiny fulfilled. The wooing of Anne is matched and to some degree inverted by the wooing of Elizabeth (1.2 and 4.4). Clarence's dream and the murderers' debate about conscience (1.4) are matched by Richard's dream and his debate about conscience with himself (5.3). Similarly, Margaret's speech at the start of 4.4 matches and transforms Richard's famous self-introduction at the beginning of the play as it transforms his seasonal images. In Richard's soliloquy, the winter of discontent, his favourite season, gives way to a 'glorious summer' that holds no delight for him. When Margaret enters for her fourth-act speech, it is the autumn of Richard's reign, a time most congenial to her, and she watches greedily while the tyrant's overripe prosperity begins to decay. As she tells the Duchess, 'I am hungry for revenge, / And now I cloy me with beholding it' (4.4.61–2).

Shaken by the ghosts of his victims (5.3), Richard recovers the bravery he showed in *3 Henry VI* and dies fighting fiercely. The triumph of Richmond, however, seems curiously flat. The new King Henry VII says all the right things – pardoning Richard's soldiers and promising peace – but somehow he evokes no joy. It is not Richard we mourn for, exactly, but Richard's tragic defiance of his fate. As Emrys Jones points out, *Richard III* supports historical determinism from the outset, not only by dealing with events of known outcome, but also by repeatedly reminding us of what we know.[5]

Yet Richard's heroic end, like the sketchy characterisation of Richmond and the withdrawal of the women from the end of the play, allows playgoers to leave the theatre still a bit on Richard's side.

EDWARD III: parallel lives

The structure of *Edward III* involves an apparent digression (1.2 and 2.2) that superficially resembles the allegorical episodes in the first two *Henry VI* plays. On closer inspection, however, King Edward's adulterous lust for the Countess of Salisbury appears more explicitly tied to the main action of this play – Edward's triumph over the French – than are many of the interludes in the *Henry VI* series. In 2.2, Edward himself draws the moral of his infatuation: 'Shall the large limit of fair Bretagne / By me be overthrown, and shall I not / Master this little mansion of myself?' (93–5). The virtuous Countess is a symbolic obstacle thrown in the path of the king as he sets out to conquer France. It takes the Countess's threat of suicide to bring Edward out of his 'idle dream' (199), suggesting that even an English hero needs moral counsel from a 'true English lady, whom our isle / May better boast of than ever Roman might' (192–3).

Later, the king receives guidance from another woman, this time his queen. As Edward prepares to execute the sacrificial citizens of Calais, Queen Phillipe reasons with him in words reminiscent of Portia's 'mercy' speech in *The Merchant of Venice* or Isabella's in *Measure for Measure*:

> Ah, be more mild unto these yielding men!
> It is a glorious thing to stablish peace,
> And kings approach the nearest unto God
> By giving life and safety unto men:
>
> (5.1.39–42)

Again, the play makes an explicit connection between Edward's mastery of his emotions and his success as a warrior. He agrees to spare the citizens, adding that 'it shall be known that we / As well can master our affections / As conquer other by the dint of sword' (50–2).

Between these two moral moments, the king conducts both the war in France and the martial initiation of his son Edward, the Black Prince. Giving Prince Edward his first battle dress, King Edward also tries to invest him with the moral armour of self-mastery:

> Edward Plantagenet, in the name of God,
> As with this armour I impall thy breast,
> So be thy noble unrelenting heart

> Walled in with flint and matchless fortitude,
> That never base affections enter there.
>
> (3.3.179–83)

When French forces surround the prince in battle, King Edward insists that his son must fight it out alone (3.4). 'O cruel father', Audley exclaims (67), but young Edward's victory vindicates the king's judgement and wins the prince a knighthood.

A subplot focused on the French neatly parallels the efforts of the English king to master his impulses and educate his son. Charles Duke of Normandy, son to King John of France, is persuaded by the honesty of Lord Villiers to give the Earl of Salisbury safe conduct through his country. Having given his word, Charles, in turn, persuades his father:

> Upon my soul, had Edward Prince of Wales
> Engaged his word, writ down his noble hand,
> For all your knights to pass his father's land,
> The royal king, to grace his warlike son,
> Would not alone safe-conduct give to them,
> But with all bounty feasted them and theirs.
>
> (4.5.97–102)

Both the English and the French behave honourably, but the English eventually win, suggesting that fate takes Edward's side. Certainly his right to the French throne through the female line is treated less ironically in this play than are the similar claims of York in *1 Henry VI* or King Henry in *Henry V*. Even the French citizens think Edward deserves to win: 'But 'tis a rightful quarrel must prevail:/Edward is son unto our late king's sister,/Where John Valois is three degrees removed' (3.2.35–7). King John puts too much faith in his own interpretations of destiny and, like Macbeth, misconstrues prophecies that predict his defeat (4.3.74–82). The English king sees the will of heaven in his successes, although he carefully refrains from over-interpreting:

> Just-dooming heaven, whose secret providence
> To our gross judgement is inscrutable,
> How are we bound to praise thy wondrous works,
> That hast this day give way unto the right,
> And made the wicked stumble at themselves.
>
> (3.4.18–22)

Edward had become a legendary figure by Shakespeare's time, the progenitor of all subsequent Plantagenets – Lancasters and Yorks alike – and more secure on the throne than any of them. In *Edward III*, he and the Black

Prince achieve a victory in France that is clouded only by what the audience knows of later English losses.

Language

In addition to the arrangement of their scenes, the structures of Shakespeare's early history plays also depend on their formal language. The study of classical rhetoric formed the basis of Shakespeare's humanist education, and he used it more overtly at the start of his career than he did later.[6] Figures such as *anaphora* – beginning each clause in a sequence with the same word – and *epistrophe* – repeating the same word at the end of each clause – occur abundantly in the early histories. Such verbal repetitions are particularly appropriate in these works because they suggest the repeating patterns of death, sorrow, and revenge engendered by internal division and civil war.

William Shakespeare: A Textual Companion includes a chart of 'colloquialism-in-verse', tracing contractions and other abbreviated linguistic forms.[7] By these measures, *1 Henry VI* is the least colloquial of Shakespeare's plays. Not until *Richard III* do audiences hear language such as Richard's casual observation on the eve of battle, 'we must have knocks, ha, must we not?' (5.3.5). Yet all five of these plays tend to observe the conventions of formal oratory more faithfully than Shakespeare's later works. There is very little prose in the early histories, and none at all in *1 Henry VI*, *3 Henry VI* or *Edward III*. Only *2 Henry VI* contains a substantial amount of prose, because only this play has many scenes involving commoners. Ordinary people almost always speak prose in the early histories, especially when their scenes contain comic material. Aristocrats and gentlefolk speak mainly in balanced, end-stopped lines of verse, as when Henry VI stands and muses on the battle taking place before him:

> This battle fares like to the morning's war
> When dying clouds contend with growing light,
> What time the shepherd, blowing of his nails,
> Can neither call it perfect day nor night.
> Now sways it this way, like a mighty sea
> Forced by the tide to combat with the wind;
> Now sways it that way, like the selfsame sea
> Forced to retire by fury of the wind.
> (*3H6*, 2.5.1–8)

In elaborate rhetorical similes, Henry compares the civil war to the struggle of night with day and the contention of sea and wind. Pauses in thought occur at the ends of lines, which also use rhyme and repetition to enhance the impression that the king is creating an artefact in his mind, setting up an orderly construct to oppose the chaos of battle. In general, however, rhyme appears infrequently in these works. Fewer than ten per cent of the verse lines in *Richard III* are rhymed – a proportion similar to the *Henry VI* series but smaller than later history plays.[8] Rhyme is used for emphasis, as when Richard III suggests that his birth was a comfort to his mother, and she replies: 'No, by the holy rood, thou know'st it well,/Thou cam'st on earth to make the earth my hell' (4.4.166–7). A couplet often provides a sense of closure at the end of a speech or scene, as when the French citizens in *Edward III* flee the invading English forces: 'Ah, wretched France, I greatly fear thy fall:/Thy glory shaketh like a tottering wall' (3.2.75–6).

The causes of history

Like most of Shakespeare's works, these early dramas take destiny seriously as a force in human affairs. The characters must reckon not only with their own actions and the actions of those around him, but also with providence or fate. Yet the attitude of these plays toward destiny is not always easy to see. Henry VI, miseducated by his guardians, embraces a passivity which he mistakes for piety: 'To whom God will, there be the victory!' (*3H6*, 2.5.15). Far from reaping divine rewards, Henry's helplessness brings on civil war. The self-reliant Yorks, on the other hand, defy prophecy even when they believe it. Henry's resignation opens the way to faction and rebellion, while the Yorks' defiance leads to savagery.

Perhaps the best way to understand Shakespeare's use of fate in his political plays is to associate it with universal determinism, the idea that every event is part of a chain of causation stretching back to the beginning of the universe. If one could know everything, one would be able to see the inevitability of historical events.[9] This kind of determinism should be distinguished at once from the fatalism to which Henry VI subscribes. He believes he can do nothing to affect the course of events, while determinists – Edward III is one – see their actions as causes like any others. *Edward III* implies that the English win because their claims are lawful. When King John tells Prince Edward, 'Thy fortune, not thy force, hath conquered us', the prince replies, 'An argument that heaven aids the right' (4.7.10–11). This view of historical causation connects historical outcomes directly to a religious standard of virtue and vice. Yet Edward is free to choose the unlawful pursuit of the Countess of Salisbury over his just wars in France, and he nearly does.

In the *Henry VI* series, no such clear association between destiny and morality appears. The three *Henry VI* plays show the king developing from a neglected infant into an idealistic figurehead who has never exercised his putative power. Unlike the decision of Edward III to master his passions,

however, Henry's fatalism is not a choice, but simply the result of his up-
bringing. Yet it is a mistake, and England must pay for it. Civil discord arises
immediately upon the death of Henry V, in the enmity between Gloucester
and Winchester. As one partisan says, 'if we be forbidden stones, we'll fall
to it with our teeth' (*1H6*, 3.1.89–90). In *2 Henry VI*, Cade's revolt, although provoked by the Duke of York, also suggests what can happen when
the masses are left out of the political process. Failure is reciprocal, as conspiracy and rebellion weaken King Henry, and Henry's weakness encourages
disorder. *3 Henry VI* focuses on the queen and the nobles who should be England's leaders after Henry's default, revealing them instead to be absorbed
in the treachery and brutality of civil war.

Shakespeare uses the government of Henry VI to explore the causes and
the dangers of a weak monarchy. He also examines, in his portraits of the
Duke of York and his son Richard, the kind of mad ambition that leads
to tyranny. A monarchical nation must somehow avoid both paths, and
3 Henry VI offers a glimpse of a better attitude toward the causes of history
than either Henry's or the Yorks'. As Shakespeare's audience would have
known, Henry is right when he predicts great things for the young Earl of
Richmond:

> This pretty lad will prove our country's bliss.
> His looks are full of peaceful majesty,
> His head by nature framed to wear a crown,
> His hand to wield a sceptre, and himself
> Likely in time to bless a regal throne.
> Make much of him, my lords, for this is he
> Must help you more than you are hurt by me.
>
> (*3H6*, 4.6.70–6)

At the end of *Richard III*, Richmond will finally end the Wars of the Roses
by killing Richard and assuming the throne as Henry VII. Yet Somerset,
who believes King Henry's predictions for Richmond, neither defies them
nor abandons the boy to his fate:

> As Henry's late presaging prophecy
> Did glad my heart with hope of this young Richmond,
> So doth my heart misgive me, in these conflicts,
> What may befall him, to his harm and ours.
> Therefore, Lord Oxford, to prevent the worst
> Forthwith we'll send him hence to Brittany
> Till storms be past of civil enmity.   (*3H6*, 4.6.92–8)

Henry knows that destiny will be fulfilled, but refuses to serve as its active
instrument. Richard thinks that destiny will be fulfilled, but refuses to submit.

Somerset and Oxford, more prudent than either Lancaster or York, manage to resolve the paradox by walking a middle way. They take for granted a determined outcome, but precisely because they do not know everything, they assume that they must act and hope for the best.

As in *Edward III*, the world of *Richard III* appears to be governed by a providential determinism associated with right and wrong. But this is not the 'special providence' that arranges each historical event; God does not necessarily contrive or even notice the fall of every sparrow. Queen Elizabeth, for example, rails against divine indifference to the deaths of her sons: 'Wilt thou, O God, fly from such gentle lambs / And throw them in the entrails of the wolf? / When didst thou sleep when such a deed was done?' (4.4.22–4). Margaret immediately answers with another such injustice: 'When holy Harry died, and my sweet son' (4.4.25). The providence of *Richard III* is rather the grand design of human salvation and damnation. God's will is shown not by the victory of one nation or one political faction over another, but by the fate of the human soul – in this case, Richard's. He is in this sense a tragic hero, opposing the will of the universe with his own, 'all the world to nothing' (1.2.241).

In Richard's remarkable soliloquy on Bosworth eve (5.3.180-206), many critics have seen the beginnings of modern tragedy. '[D]eterminèd to prove a villain' from his first appearance (1.1.30), Richard unexpectedly confronts the possibility of repentance – 'Have mercy, Jesu!' (5.3.181) – then reaffirms his earlier course: 'Soft, I did but dream. / O coward conscience, how dost thou afflict me? (5.3.181–2). He makes this choice not from despair, but as an assertion of will. Finding no pity in himself, he will ask for none. As Robert Weimann puts it, in *Richard III* 'It is not *Schicksalsdrama*, not the inscrutable workings of the gods, that finally tips the scales of life and death but the *Charakterdrama* of an individual passion and a self-willed personality.'[10] Richard's destiny is to die and be damned. The reason that he is finally tragic rather than pathetic is that he forces his own will into the deterministic equation.

Staging the early history plays

Shakespeare's early history plays were designed to be performed in Elizabethan public amphitheatres for audiences of two or three thousand.[11] Plays produced in these large, open theatres used little pictorial scenery and only the sorts of properties the actors themselves could carry on and off the stage. Scene changes were signified not by replacing one set with another, but simply by having one group of actors leave the stage and another enter. The generalised settings and the fast-paced dialogue characteristic of Elizabethan acting allowed Shakespeare to shift rapidly between locations, as in *1 Henry VI*, for instance, without losing the attention of his audience.

It is difficult to tell which were Shakespeare's most popular history plays in the Tudor–Stuart period, although the six early editions of *Richard III* suggest that it was very well received. After the Restoration in 1660, the early histories seem to have been performed infrequently until the poet–actor Colley Cibber adapted *Richard III* in 1700. By cutting other parts, Cibber made the character of Richard even more prominent than it is in Shakespeare's version, and many noted actors used the role to establish or enhance their reputations. The *Henry VI* plays, by contrast, enjoyed relatively few productions between the Restoration and the end of the nineteenth century, and *Edward III* saw none at all.[12]

At the beginning of the twentieth century, a more scholarly approach to Elizabethan drama led to more productions of the *Henry VI* series and to an early revival of *Edward III*. It was not until midcentury, however, that the increasing use of a spare, symbolic staging more like that of the Elizabethan public theatres brought greater popularity to the chronicle plays.[13] Several twentieth-century productions cut and combined the three *Henry VI* plays into two, increasing the pace for a modern audience. Two Royal Shakespeare Company productions exemplify this technique: *The Wars of the Roses*, adapted by John Barton and directed by Peter Hall (1963), and *The Plantagenets*, a trilogy including *Richard III*, directed by Adrian Noble (1988).[14]

Along with the twentieth century's return to unlocalised staging came productions focused on the political allegory inherent in the history plays. During the Second World War, for example, the English actor Donald Wolfit incorporated his impressions of Hitler into his portrayal of Richard III.[15] A recent production of *Edward III* (1987) emphasised the development of Prince Edward into an exemplary leader.[16] Yet the absence of star parts in these plays (except for *Richard III*) continues to render them less popular as vehicles for contemporary actors, many of whom now want to capture their Shakespearean productions on film.

By and large, Shakespeare's early English histories are ensemble plays. Their effects are often achieved by indirect means, such as the juxtaposition of superficially dissimilar scenes in *1* and *2 Henry VI*, or the implied comparison between a group of women in *Richard III* and the single, aggressive male lead. A BBC video from the 1980s series captures some of this subtlety of design. Jane Howell directed the *Henry VI* sequence and *Richard III* using the same anti-realistic set throughout. Repeating roles such as Henry, Margaret, and Richard are played by the same actors, whose often restrained interpretations are reinforced by the intimacy of television. To watch all four tapes in this series certainly makes for a very long theatrical experience, but it is one in which modern sympathies clearly make contact with many of the nuances of Shakespeare's political drama.

NOTES

1 Dedication, Campbell 1938.
2 Sidney 1965, p. 111.
3 The play is titled *The Tragedy of Richard III* on its first page in the Folio. Subsequent pages carry the running title 'The Life and Death of Richard the Third'.
4 This triangular structure is sometimes called Freytag's Pyramid, after Gustav Freytag, who described it in his *Technique of the Drama*, 1863. See Freytag 1896.
5 Jones 1977, pp. 222–3.
6 On Shakespeare's education, see Baldwin 1944.
7 Wells and Taylor 1987, p. 99, pp. 102–5.
8 *Ibid.*, p. 96.
9 For a definition and discussion of universal determinism, see 'Determinism in History' in Wiener 1973, II, 18–21.
10 Weimann, 1978, p. 160. See also Rabkin 1967, p. 251: 'At this moment, crucial both in the play and in Shakespeare's career, the play turns to tragedy.'
11 See Gurr, 1992.
12 See *E3*, ed. Melchiori 1998, p. 46.
13 See *1H6*, ed. Hattaway 1990, p. 44.
14 See Barton and Hall 1970, and Noble 1989.
15 See Colley 1992, p. 168.
16 *E3*, ed. Melchiori 1998, p. 48.

7

MARIE-HÉLÈNE BESNAULT

MICHEL BITOT

Historical legacy and fiction: the poetical reinvention of King Richard III

In performance, Richard of Gloucester emerges as the complete figure of the 'chameleon' prince previously featured in *3 Henry VI* (3.2.191). This essay will argue that Shakespeare poetically reworked his sources to develop further the figure of Richard III as a degenerate monster. Richard's self-proclaimed deformity, a sign both of unnaturalness and enormity, is established at the very beginning of the play when Shakespeare's brilliant strategic placing of Richard's body and large histrionic presence emerges from its famous opening speech:

> I that am rudely stamped and want love's majesty
> To strut before a wanton ambling nymph,
> I that am curtailed of this fair proportion,
> Cheated of feature by dissembling nature,
> Deformed, unfinished, sent before my time
> Into this breathing world scarce half made up,
> And that so lamely and unfashionable
> That dogs bark at me as I halt by them,
> Why, I, in this weak piping time of peace,
> Have no delight to pass away the time,
> Unless to spy my shadow in the sun
> And descant on mine own deformity.
>
> (1.1.16–27)

'Descanting', a musical term, signifying that Richard boasts of his ability to counterpoint and discourse upon a given theme, is precisely what the play seems to beg from its critics. The exploration and the staging of physical and moral deformity, evident in the opening monologue, is a most challenging and fascinating issue. The figure of Richard, the deformed monster, one who declared that he 'should snarl, and bite, and play the dog' (*3H6*, 5.6.77), did not spring unheralded on the stage in *Richard III*, a fact of which the spectators of previous histories – *2 Henry VI* and *3 Henry VI* – would have been well aware. At a performance of the play they would easily recognise the demonic role that the tyrant had been given both by history and drama. Partly shaped by historiography and dramatic construction, predetermined by the weight of hostile Tudor history which bears 'upon his shoulders with crippling, mortal force',[1] Richard III can be seen as the ultimate *exemplum*, a political emblem for human degradation, set against the idealised regeneration, the divine purpose represented by Richmond. If we are to look for a political meaning in the play, perhaps part of the message could be that such extreme perversion in a fiction might act either to warn, or to reassure contemporary princes. Richard Marienstras goes even further, stating that 'the accession to the throne of a misshapen and criminal king in the fictional kingdom of a dramatic work, made credible by its references to history, was a means to create the archetypal figure of a fabulous and oversize tyrant, so fabulous indeed that it freed most real monarchs from the suspicion that *they* might be tyrants'.[2]

Richard's dramatic substance is a clear case of the fashioning of a deformed tyrant, largely based upon narrative material taken from historical sources, in particular Polydore Vergil's *Anglica Historia* (1534), Thomas More's *History of Richard III* (1513), *The Mirror for Magistrates* (1559–96), and the chronicles of Edward Hall (1548) and Raphael Holinshed (1587). For Polydore Vergil, whose *Anglica Historia* had been originally commissioned by Henry VII (Richmond in the play), Richard embodies the culminating example of transgression within a scheme of usurpation and betrayal, bringing about a disruption of moral and political order and final chaos. Depicting the reign of Richard III as a scene of civil war and chaos, Vergil in his moral and theological approach inspired the commentators who came after. He helped fashion the sombre portrait of a tyrant whose very bodily appearance was a reflection of the ugliness of his soul. He presented him as having 'a short and sour countenance, which seemed to savour of mischief, and utter evidently craft and deceit'.[3]

One of the most abominable crimes attributed to Richard by history – or rumour – the murder of the Princes, is treated with caution by Polydore Vergil. However, he reports on the commotion which the deed provoked in the people who 'wept everywhere, and when they could weep no more, they cried out, "Is there truly any man living so far at enmity with God?"'[4] Enmity to God, Richard as a 'scourge' – such themes will recur in various accounts offered by historians or chroniclers following Vergil. Following John Rous, Vergil pointed to the tyrant's vicious soul and bodily deformity,[5] a popular belief apparently deeply rooted in his time. Thomas More provided an even more telling physical and political portrait, a probable source of inspiration to Shakespeare:

> Richard Duke of Gloucester [...] was little of stature, evil-featured of limbs, crook-backed, the left shoulder much higher than the right, hard-favoured of visage [...] He was malicious, wrathful, and envious, and, as it is reported, his mother the Duchess had much ado in her travail, that she could not be delivered of him uncut, and that he came into the world the feet forward, as men be born outward and, as the fame ran, not untoothed...[6]

Unashamedly feeding upon 'fame', Thomas More produced a concentrated, eventful record of Richard's reign. Utilising the sources of Tudor history and myth gave Shakespeare an opportunity to refashion poetically the figure of the king become monster. Our purpose should now be to explore textually the outcome of a creative process which transformed these sometimes crude sources into the complex, repulsive, and attractive, figure that is Richard III.

Shakespeare's stage fiction, then, must have gradually fed upon history, chronicles and myth but, as is often the case with the playwright, his Richard escapes from historical boundaries, strict fact and chronology, to become a stylised, larger than life demonic figure. The universality of evil, embodied here in the monstrous king, may also have originated in readings of the Bible, such as this passage on physical blemishes in *Leviticus* (21: 18–21): 'For whosoever hath any blemish, shall not come near: as a blind man, or lame... or a man that hath... a broken-hand, or is crook-backed, or hath a blemish in his eye... he shall not press [come forward] to offer the bread of his God' (Geneva Version). The Old Testament pronouncement (clearly in opposition to the teaching of Christ) against such blemishes of the body, seen as a sign of moral deformity, was manifest in sixteenth-century behaviour in England, when cripples were jeered at or rejected as objects of scorn and repulsion.[7] The transmutation of the historical figure of King Richard III was also made possible by relics of religious medieval drama: the archetype of the tyrant in mystery plays was Herod, often represented as being plagued by various infirmities, a mirror of his crimes. Thus, in *The Chester Mystery*, Herod is made to display his moral and physical complaints:

> My legs rotten and my arms;
> That now I see of fiends swarms –
> I have done so many harms –
> From hell coming after me.

The portrait of Richard as a monster marked by the seal of evil emerges not only from his own initial presentation, and his consequent display of cruelty, but also from the testimonies of the other characters in the play. Queen Margaret's famous curse in 1.3 addresses the unnatural and ominous birth of the 'monster':

> Thou elvish-marked, abortive, rooting hog,
> Thou that was sealed in thy nativity
> The slave of nature and the son of hell.
> Thou slander of thy heavy mother's womb,
> Thou loathèd issue of thy father's loins,
> Thou rag of honour, thou detested –
>
> (1.3.226–31)

In a vein similar to Queen Margaret's own evocation, Richard's mother confirms her son's unnatural birth:

> O ill-dispersing wind of misery.
> O my accursèd womb, the bed of death.
> A cockatrice hast thou hatched to the world,
> Whose unavoided eye is murderous.
>
> (4.1.53–6)[8]

The play offers further support for the notion that Richard was marked out as an evil creature at his birth: Margaret later describes him as the issue of the 'kennel' of his mother's 'womb', 'a hell-hound', a 'dog, that had his teeth before his eyes' (4.4.47–9), a claim that is paralleled by a remark from the young Duke of York to the old Duchess upon Richard's prodigious infancy:

> YORK Marry, they say my uncle grew so fast
> That he could gnaw a crust at two hours old.
> 'Twas full two years ere I could get a tooth.
>
> (2.4.27–9)

Richard, whose unnatural, monstrous birth and childhood are repeatedly emphasised is, in the Duchess of York's words, in his 'age confirmed, proud, subtle, sly, and bloody' (4.4.172). The grown man appears through numerous physical and moral features as one close to the prodigy or monster. Ambroise Paré, who was the French King Henri II's surgeon, wrote in his treatise *Des Monstres et prodiges* (1573) that prodigies were creatures 'beyond the usual course of nature'.[9] Lady Anne's cry at 1.2.57 – 'Blush, blush, thou lump of foul deformity' – could well serve to encapsulate the mixture of fascination and horror which the monster provokes in the viewer. Richard, 'the slave of nature' according to Margaret (1.3.228), seems visually to embody the fallen nature of man, the sins of a corrupt humanity foregrounded in the emblematic body of a misshapen, self-crowned king. A twisted mind in a twisted shape, Richard, the crippled figure, has an unbalanced and unfinished body, a hump, a limp and, perhaps for purely dramatic purposes, he even acquires a withered or shortened arm by the middle of the play. Which arm, Shakespeare does not tell us, and it is left to producers to decide, but a very special emphasis is set on this infirmity because of Richard's pretended 'bewitching' that costs Hastings his head:

> RICHARD   Then be your eyes the witness of their evil.
> Look how I am bewitched. Behold, mine arm
> Is like a blasted sapling, withered up.
> And this is Edward's wife, that monstrous witch,
> Consorted with that harlot, strumpet Shore,
> That by their witchcraft thus have markèd me.
> (3.4.66–71)

So, with this spectacular finishing touch, Richard becomes the physical representation not only of a monster but of a deformed body politic; he that aims at and finally achieves primacy in the realm 'wants' his 'proper limbs' – to quote Buckingham's words out of context. Buckingham, the unconscious victim of historical and dramatic irony, thus pleads before the Mayor and Citizens:

> The noble isle doth want her proper limbs;
> Her face defaced with scars of infamy,
> Her royal stock graft with ignoble plants,
> And almost shouldered in the swallowing gulf
> Of dark forgetfulness and deep oblivion.
> (3.7.123–7)

Indeed, Richard's moral and political deformity is fully confirmed by the play's action and the various descriptions of his crimes. His own gloating over the seduction of Lady Anne offers a clear self-depiction of his devilish connections:

> What, I that killed her husband and his father,
> To take her in her heart's extremest hate . . .
> And I no friends to back my suit withal
> But the plain devil and dissembling looks?
> (1.2.234–5; 239–40)

In 4.4 Margaret describes Richard as a 'dog' set loose 'To worry lambs and lap their gentle blood' (50). The Christian connotations of 'hell' and 'lambs' evoke the Renaissance belief in physical deformity as an exterior sign of spiritual evil, as we noted previously. Man is conceived of as a microcosm of the divine system, and the perverse and morally debased are lowered to the rank of the most repulsive animals. The long list of insults and degrading terms which describe Richard's bestiality in the play might suggest a hierarchic order of the Creation, as well as a political anatomy of the kingdom. In decreasing order, Richard's bloody career is marked by a metaphoric descent in the order of creation, a degeneration from tiger[10] to hound, boar, toad, spider, and finally to monstrous cockatrice and foul lump of matter. The degenerating political bestiary, which symbolises the beast become king, signifies that bestiality rules over England, that the land has surrendered to the forces of darkness and evil, with the creeping, venomous creatures as tokens of the infernal areas of witchcraft. Richard thus appears as a political monster whose deformity, a violation of God's perfection, a perfection that should be mirrored in the king, invasively infects the land and its creatures. That Richard is considered as the one who ruins God's creation is made obvious in one of Margaret's curses to the Duchess:

> That foul defacer of God's handiwork
> That reigns in gallèd eyes of weeping souls,
> That excellent grand tyrant of the earth
> Thy womb let loose to chase us to our graves.
>   (4.4.51–4)

Consequently, such base terms as 'boar' and 'swine' occur shortly before the moment of Richard's fall expressed in Richmond's address to his army:

> The wretched, bloody, and usurping boar,
> That spoiled your summer fields and fruitful vines,
> Swills your warm blood like wash, and makes his trough
> In your embowelled bosoms, this foul swine
> Is now even in the centre of this isle . . .   (5.2.7–11)

'Swine' follows closely after 'boar', the well-known emblem of Richard. The 'boar', a loathsome symbol of savagery and demonic forces, which is also ominously present in Stanley's premonitory vision at 3.2.11 – 'He dreamt the boar had razèd off his helm' – insistently recurs later in Act 3 ('Stanley did dream the boar did rouse our helms', 3.4.81). Richard is later termed 'the most deadly boar' (4.5.2) with reference to his keeping Stanley's son in his 'sty', suggesting both beastliness and filth. The king is repeatedly associated with the pig, or 'hog', a beast that stands for impurity and lechery, as in Queen Margaret's long speech in the first act. A number of other equally repulsive creatures serve as representatives of Richard's base nature in the play, such as the 'hedgehog' (1.2.105) and the 'toad', with four occurrences in *Richard III*, along with several terms of vilification often connected to slimy, creeping, venomous or predatory creatures. This again from Lady Anne:

> More direful hap betide that hated wretch
> That makes us wretched by the death of thee
> Than I can wish to wolves, to spiders, toads,
> Or any creeping venomed thing that lives.
>
> (1.2.17–20)

A sustained string of images borrowed from animality informs the speech of Richard's enemies and victims, ranging from Queen Margaret's 'this poisonous bunch-backed [hunch-backed] toad' (1.3.246), to Elizabeth's 'That bottled spider, that foul bunch-backed toad' (4.4.81) and the Duchess of York's 'Thou toad, thou toad' (4.4.145). The toad and spider images evoke humidity and darkness, darkness being quite central to the play if one thinks of the prevalence of night scenes and, above all, of the dark deeds perpetrated in cells, prisons, and the Tower.

Having lowered himself to the status of base, creeping creatures, Richard also provokes a series of insults involving other species, namely the 'dog', the 'hound', or the 'carnal cur'. Again, it is Margaret who seems to summarise the tyrant's animality, as in her premonitory warning to Buckingham:

> O Buckingham, take heed of yonder dog.
> Look when he fawns, he bites; and when he bites,
> His venom tooth will rankle to the death.
>
> (1.3.289–91)

Thus, going further than the predetermined figure of the villain shaped by history, Shakespeare created a monstrous king whose lethal powers – almost universally recognisable – are embodied in teeth and venom, a compact of darkness and death.

The Vice heritage: the histrionics and stage managing of Richard as Vice

The famous soliloquy which opens *Richard III* has many dramatic functions. As a prologue, it provides information about the present political situation: the success of the Yorkists over the last Lancastrian king, and a link with the preceding play in the historical sequence, *3 Henry VI*. It introduces the main protagonist who stands apart from the Court festivities forging schemes to promote his own warlike, deformed self. It presents itself both as a boasting confession of Gloucester's villainous manipulation of information and of his kingly brother's fears, and as a devilish declaration of intention, 'I am determinèd to prove a villain' (30). Richard asserts his will to control his destiny by ways as crooked as his own body. This creates a supplementary awareness for the audience, who know more than the unsuspecting victims, which engenders a situation of dramatic irony. As importantly, however, this opening soliloquy establishes a mocking, flouting tone and a complicity between actor and audience that is central to the development of Richard's role.

What Thomas More calls his 'pamphlet'[11] about Richard III is ironic too, but the ironist is the author/narrator. At the beginning of Shakespeare's play, it is Richard himself who is the supreme ironist. In the preceding play, his tone, if not his intention, was different. The link between his villainy and his physical shape was accepted cynically:

> Then, since the heavens have shaped my body so,
> Let hell make crook'd my mind to answer it.
>
> (*3H6*, 5.6.78–9)

The reference to heaven and hell, redolent of medieval homiletic drama, is replaced in *Richard III* by virtuoso, gleeful self-dramatisation. A comic effect of accumulation and exaggeration, created as Richard displays his imperfections (hunch-back, shorter leg, crippled arm, facial deformity), is aggravated by a sequence of past participles and negative prefixes suggesting Nature's obstinate victimisation of the speaker: *curtailed, scarce half-made-up, cheated of feature, deformed, unfinished, unfashionable*. But far from being defeated, Richard makes self-derision as charismatic a weapon in his rapport with the audience as his playing with language: with homophony (*sun/son*) or polysemy of words (*bound, tricks, spy*), with sound effects (*now are our brows bound . . . the lascivious pleasing of a lute*), rhetorical devices (anaphoras, antitheses, conceits), and obvious divergence between signifiers and signifieds as he mocks the *glorious, victorious, merry, delightful . . .* summer of others' content, parodies epic similes (*Grim-visaged war* smoothing *his wrinkled front*), or ridicules *the sportive tricks* of former warriors in ladies' chambers. The Richard of 3 *Henry VI* claimed his kinship with the devil and boasted

> I can add colours to the chameleon,
> Change shape with Proteus for advantages,
> And set the murderous Machiavel to school.
>
> (3.2.191–3)

Long before the protagonist justifies his equivocations by claiming this ancestry, the contemporaries of Shakespeare, especially the older ones, were very likely to recognise in the hero of *Richard III* kinship with another dramatic archetype, the Vice, which was extremely popular in Interludes between 1550 and 1580:[12]

> Thus, like the formal Vice, Iniquity,
> I moralise two meanings in one word.
>
> (3.1.82–3)

It is an ancestry which Richard shares with Aaron, Don John and Iago, as far as cruel villainy is concerned, and with another egregious showman and humorist, Sir John Falstaff himself, 'that reverend Vice, that grey Iniquity' (*1H4*, 2.4.375–6), as far as seduction is concerned.

Verbal and physical dexterity, inveterate punning, abrupt changes of tempo and register ('But yet I run before my horse to the market', 1.1.161), deceit in the form of physical and moral disguise, tricks of tears and laughter, shifts from controlled rational or even solemn tones to passionate, angry or amorous expostulations, sacrilegious use of oaths and Scriptures, satire of courtiers, social climbers and tractable citizens, are all part of their common repertoire, as are misogynistic sneers, self-confidence and arrogant trust in others' gullibility. Above all, there is their common ability to step out of the action of the play, comment upon it to the audience, even organise it. Most notable are their superlative acting skills, the high entertainment value of their tricks, and the jubilation they manifest in their triumphant guiles.

In spite of the conventional allusion to an interior monologue at the end of his first soliloquy: 'Dive, thoughts, down to my soul' (1.1.41), Richard's direct address to the audience is fully attested by the orchestration of deictics (*this* and *these*) and words such as 'now', 'and now', 'therefore', 'but I', 'why I' as well as by answers to supposed questions:

> What though I killed her husband and her father?
> The readiest way to make the wench amends
> Is to become her husband and her father.
>
> (1.1.155–7)

Throughout the first half of the play, he indulges in asides that secure our connivance and create the impression that he is both in the world of the play and outside it as a dispassionate Vice-like observer. When he has achieved his improbable gulling, he makes us partake in his gleeful self-congratulation.

> What, I that killed her husband and his father,
> To take her in her heart's extremest hate,
> With curses in her mouth, tears in her eyes . . .
> And yet to win her, all the world to nothing!
> Ha! (1.2.234–6, 241–2)

Richard's laughter, which is often veiled or hidden under feigned tears or anger in the presence of his victims, is turned on for our sake, as soon as those victims leave the stage for him 'to bustle' on. He also indulges in two of the Vice's favourite activities, role-playing and stage-managing, but does so with a vengeance, out-vying his predecessors.

Richard's brilliant performance as compassionate brother, desperate lover, repentant sinner, peace-seeking subject, benevolent uncle etc. . . . traditionally served, from Burbage onwards, by the skills of supremely versatile actors, climaxes in the scenes involving Hastings and the bishop of Ely and, particularly, in those involving the Lord Mayor. In these episodes borrowed from More's narrative, the stress is no longer on the amazed disbelief and reluctance of the representatives of the people. Indeed, Shakespeare chooses to have their mute reticence reported by Buckingham rather than shown. The emphasis is placed on the elaboration and performing of the tricks used to reverse what is basically a conversion of the people by the prince into a supposed conversion of a reluctant and pious prince by the people. The result is highly theatrical and entertaining. In *3 Henry VI*, Richard had claimed: 'I am myself alone' (5.6.84). In *Richard III*, he is given a partner both in his murderous practices and in his histrionics.

Although they have helpers, Buckingham and his cousin function as a comic pair harking back to Devil and Vice but also to couples of clowns or buffoons, a tradition that is still alive. Not only do they initiate and stage-manage all the manipulations, but they vie with each other in verbal skill, histrionic body language, voice modulations and simulation of extreme emotions:

> RICHARD   Come, cousin, canst thou quake and change thy colour,
>   Murder thy breath in middle of a word,
>   And then again begin, and stop again,
>   As if thou were distraught and mad with terror?
> BUCKINGHAM   Tut, I can counterfeit the deep tragedian,
>   Speak and look back, and pry on every side,
>   Tremble and start at wagging of a straw.
>
>   (3.5.1–7)

The extravagant armour, '*rotten* [. . .] *marvellously ill-favoured*', they wear in this scene[13] is clearly, like the language they use and the craft they display, inherently theatrical. Shakespeare, indulging in world-creating games, also has them make the most of the flexibility of the Elizabethan stage and its various acting areas as they feign to be assaulted on the battlements of a castle: 'Look to the drawbridge there!' 'Look back, defend thee, here are enemies!' (3.5.15, 19) or, later, as Richard appears '*aloft*', between two clergymen, holding a prayer-book (93), while Buckingham 'make[s] a holy descant' (47) below for the benefit of the Lord Mayor and Citizens, underscoring these emblems of humble piety and Christian zeal in the devout prince (95ff), according to the plan first conceived by the one (98–100) and totally appropriated by the other (46–50). History has yielded to theatricality. But the latter is intrinsically linked with irony. The pretended humility of Richard is negated by his elevated position; the sacrilegious unbeliever is presented as an idol to be worshipped from beneath. Moreover, the scenic disposition underlines the metatheatricality of the episode and makes visually alive Thomas More's often quoted parallel between theatre and politics: 'And so they said that these matters be Kings' games, as it were stage plays, and for the more part played upon scaffolds.'[14] In modern productions, the play-within-the play effect is often enhanced by the use of curtains drawn to reveal the protagonist as supreme actor above. Sometimes his henchmen are seen to hastily put on richly embroidered church vestments over their martial outfits, which underscores the acting and stage-managing manoeuvres of would-be rulers, but plays down the satire of the collusion between Church and power. As Bernard Spivack observes, 'it is a fascination to see history give way to dramaturgy' and to watch the 'historical figure who ruled England dissolve into the theatrical figure who [had] ruled the English stage'.[15]

The Vice figure had, with stylised rhetoric, established his moral pedigree in *3 Henry VI* (3.2.182–93), and joyfully instructed the audience in the art of gulling brothers or friends into mortal enmity at the beginning of our play:

> I do the wrong, and first begin to brawl.
> The secret mischiefs that I set abroach [started]
> I lay unto the grievous charge of others.
> Clarence, who I indeed have cast in darkness,
> I do beweep to simple gulls...
> And thus I clothe my naked villainy
> With odd old ends stol'n forth of holy writ,
> And seem a saint when most I play the devil.
>
> (1.3.324–38)

Yet, as the dramatic action proceeds, he gradually dissolves into other stage archetypes such as the cunning Machiavel, the frantic Herod of *The Massacre of Innocents*, or the ruthless Senecan Tyrant and finally into a more naturalistic, hence more potentially tragic, historical character.

Senecan influence and tragic dimension of the play

Even before all of Seneca's 'Ten Tragedies' appeared in English translation in 1581 and were 'let blood line by line and page by page', according to

Thomas Nashe, to provide 'whole Hamlets, I should say handfuls of tragical speaches',[16] Seneca, a favourite school author, often translated, imitated in Italian and French drama, had influenced English dramatists who addressed tragedy. Like Thomas Kyd in *The Spanish Tragedy*, Shakespeare borrows from Seneca the use of sensational themes – the murder of a brother and of young children, one of whom is a king – elaborate imagery, stichomythia in conflictual love-bantering in the two wooing scenes, an amplification of the horror of such dramatic situations as the death of Clarence, and above all rhetorical excess in the expression of passions.

In the third scene of *Richard III* 'Old Queen Margaret' enters the stage alone in the middle of a quarrel between Richard and Queen Elizabeth, and stands on the perimeter of the action, a lonely black figure, unseen and unheard by the contenders and their allies. Her isolation is foregrounded by visual and aural contrasts, created by an appearance which usually clashes with the colourful costumes of courtiers and the generally deep voice, hoarse with vindictiveness with which she croaks out her venomous asides before, no longer able to contain her rage, she bursts into the conversation on which she had been eavesdropping. This isolation is both very theatrical and symbolic. At the end of the play it is Richard who finds himself alone. He has lost the battle which he was waging against all that Margaret stands for in the play.

The historical Margaret never returned from France after her banishment, and she died one year before King Edward IV. In *Richard III*, however, Shakespeare makes Margaret the 'counterweight to the mesmerising theatricality of Richard'.[17] Both characters have dominant personalities, are proud egotists, misusers of religion, who think of their murders as glorious deeds. Through both of them the dramatist draws historical material into the present action to highlight the guilt of future victims, including Richard himself, and justify the scourging of crimes committed against the nation. Yet, whereas Richard initiates and propels the action forward, Margaret structures it and she orchestrates it. When she appears on stage, in 1.3 and 4.4, she introduces suspensions of activity, changes of focus, of pace, and of tone. When offstage, she brings remembrance of her prophetic curses as their victims succumb to their doom. Richard and Margaret are both masters of language, but the range of emotions that the widow of Henry VI displays as she goes through imprecations, clamorous curses, and distracted lamentations, reflects a truly passionate sorrow and vengeful hatred. The skill of the great 'player' who impersonates her with piercing eyes, haggard, wild intractable face, admonishing finger and vociferous mouth,[18] is meant to create an illusion of sincerity, not to hint at controlled dissembling. The performative effect of her vehement, now doleful, now snarling, always scornful and sarcastic outcries, is underlined by Richard's attempt to avoid them (1.3.213), by Hastings' horrified 'end thy frantic curse' (247) and Buckingham's comment after her departure 'My hair doth stand on end to hear her curses' (304). Contrary to Richard's, her distracting speech is not only 'altogether joyless' (1.3.154), but heavily patterned. Her ancestry, indeed, is Senecan and tragic.

Even if her action appears to be mainly verbal and is concentrated in two scenes, Margaret's dismissal from performances utterly destroys the balance of the play. Because in an unabridged version of the play she performs the tasks set out for her by Shakespeare and one of them is to establish the tragic mode.

Although the Biblical Rachel could be considered as a Christian antecedent, Margaret's laments are more likely to evoke the bereavement of Hecuba or Andromache, wailing over the dead bodies of their husbands and sons in *The Trojans*; her ravings, more often referring to hell than to Heaven, those of Seneca's Medea, when Jason, the Greek hero whom her witchcraft had helped gain the fleece, wants to divorce her in order to marry King Kreon's daughter. Like Medea, Margaret offers no excuse to her enemies to laugh at her, and her overpowering sense of injured pride makes her hunger for revenge all the more savage (4.4.61). The relentlessness of her anathemas, her piling up of insults in alliterative sequences, rich in hissing sibilants and abrupt dentals, 'poisonous bunch-backed toad' (1.3.246), 'elvish-marked, abortive, rooting hog' (1.3.226), 'Poor painted queen, vain flourish of my fortune, / Why strew'st thou sugar on that bottled spider' (1.3.241–2), the swelling up of her animal and demonic comparisons into lengthy periods (1.3.215–31), the numerous figures of opposition and repetition that punctuate her diatribes, all contribute to this sense of a tragically patterned speech in the Senecan mode.

Senecan too is the prophetic dimension of her vengeful curses: 'And say poor Margaret was a prophetess' (1.3.301). Those upon whom Revenge falls in the course of the play acknowledge both their guilt and the efficacy of her curses:

> O Margaret, Margaret, now thy heavy curse
> Is lighted on poor Hastings' wretched head.
>
> (3.4.91–2)

As they do so, the figure of Revenge becomes a figure of Retribution, Destiny, or Fortune. When Margaret invokes Heaven it is with a diabolical spirit; the fulfilment of her predictions thus gives another allegorical dimension to her role. Divine Justice or Providence is seen to be at work.

Like Medea, Margaret is often considered to be a witch, but Richard's expostulations as he sees and hears her – 'Have done thy charm, thou hateful, withered hag' (1.3.213) – serve yet another allegorical function of Margaret. In defiance of historical accuracy, she is made to appear in all four plays of the tetralogy, which makes her instrumental in linking the plays together, but which also gives the sense that she is a figure out of time, or an embodiment of Time, 'an ageless figure of moral nemesis who brings onto the stage the entire Wars of the Roses' or a woman who has journeyed from extreme youth to extreme old age,[19] and whose memories, the longest and bitterest ones, make the spectators stand back from the present and see history as a tragic cycle. Very often in modern productions the great age that Margaret has attained and her timelessness are emphasised by the make-up and the costume the actress wears, as well as by lighting effects or even sound effects. In Robin Philips' production of the play in 1977 at Stratford Ontario, for instance, the actress playing Margaret was equipped with a hidden microphone, which made her voice echo and reverberate in the theatre like that of a stage ghost. In the time of Shakespeare, on the other hand, well-known emblems of Time, Fortune, Fate, Nemesis or Revenge could be suggested in performance by the grouping or setting apart of characters, a few props, the lighting of torches and the body-language of actors that made up recognisable visual tableaux.

Margaret is given a choric function, first as she comments on the past and present actions of others, then even more obviously, when she is joined in her lamentations and curses by Queen Elizabeth and the Duchess of York. Together, the three women, when they allow 'calamity [to] be full of words' (4.4.126), stand for all suffering women carrying the emotional weight of wars, be they dynastic or not, the pain of 'Dead life, blind sight...woe's scene, world's shame' and 'earth,/Unlawfully made drunk with innocent blood' (4.4.26–30). The relentless repetition of the identical names of their lost husbands or sons, Richard, Edward, in antithetical lines with similar openings and endings (4.4.39–46) makes their utterances sound formulaic. The scene itself, as they sit together and their 'sorrow...admit[s] society' becomes the enactment of a tragic rite. Seneca's use of a chorus standing for *vox populi* has been adapted to Shakespeare's own dramatic needs. Indeed, other characters in the play, some of them minor ones, partake of this choric function inherited from Greek and Latin drama. Some, like Lady Anne (1.2.44ff), are bereaved princesses too. But the ordinary citizens also play this role when they voice their dark forebodings (2.4), meet Buckingham's suggestions with mute fearfulness (3.7), or again when, in the person of the Scrivener (3.6.5–9), they ironically marvel at having spent eleven hours writing the indictment of a man who, although 'untainted, unexamined' was executed five hours before the work was done. Richard himself, the eponymous character, in his initial soliloquy acts as a theatrical chorus. The diversity of the uses Shakespeare makes of this function points to thematic and symbolic relevance beyond dramatic efficacy. Lamenting women in this play are always three. As a result, they can in turn signify suffering mankind, the three Furies of Greek and Roman mythology who pursue and punish the doers of unavenged crimes, or the three Fates or *Parcae* who govern human destiny. For a Christian audience, they can also evoke the three Maries at the foot of the Cross. Given the ambivalence of the play and the syncretic spirit at work in the period, they may draw from the audience moral and aesthetic as well as emotional responses.

The same applies to the eleven ghosts of Richard's victims who successively appear to him and to Richmond as they sleep, on the eve of the battle (5.3). Another Senecan feature adapted to the dramatic uses of a hybrid play, they too have a choric and tragic function, as they hammer into Richard's brain formulaic condemnations 'Let me sit heavy on thy soul tomorrow' (5.3.121, 134, 142), 'Despair, and die' (5.3.123, 129, 138, 143, 146, 151, 157, 166), before they lavish encouragement with identical incantatory force on Richmond: 'live and flourish!' (5.3.133, 141), 'Live, and beget a happy race of kings' (5.3.160). They induce 'the fairest sleep and fairest-boding dreams' (5.3.228) in the future Tudor king and the foulest nightmares in Richard. The curses and blessings of these supernatural apparitions come true at Bosworth. This makes them prophetic instruments of revenge and of divine justice. Again, theatricality vies with pathos and moral implications. For an Elizabethan audience, the final fight was most probably warfare between the forces of Evil and the forces of Good, entrenched on the two sides of the stage, as in earlier Moralities and Interludes, even if the traditional Good and Bad Angels had undergone a tragic metamorphosis. For a modern audience, the ghosts of Richard's victims, anticipating Macbeth's hallucinations, tend to appear more like a theatrical representation of Richard's bad conscience. This feeling is reinforced by his confessing:

> By the apostle Paul, shadows tonight
> Have struck more terror to the soul of Richard
> Than can the substance of ten thousand soldiers...
>
> (5.3.217–19)

In his final soliloquy, although at times his self-dramatisation is a direct appeal to audience sympathy, 'And if I die, no soul shall pity me' (204), Richard is self-absorbed. It is the dichotomy within himself that the dialogic quality of his monologue is meant to reflect; the split between his former unquestionably courageous self and the fears spoken from his still unconscious mind as he awakes from his troubled sleep; the being torn between an old self-love and a new-born self-horror and self-pity. The naturalistic, chopped, questioning syntax of the verse conveys this dichotomy:

> What? Do I fear myself? There's none else by.
> Richard loves Richard, that is, I am I.
> Is there a murderer here? No. Yes, I am.
> Then fly. What, from myself? Great reason why:
> Lest I revenge. What, myself upon myself?
> Alack, I love myself. Wherefore?   (5.3.185–91)

Richard's command of rhetoric seems to have vanished as he utters short, chaotic sentences. The acting and stage-managing powers he had so brilliantly displayed have now turned against him too as he imagines a trial of himself in the old homiletic fashion:

> My conscience hath a thousand several tongues
> And every tongue brings in a several tale,
> And every tale condemns me for a villain.
> Perjury in the highest degree,
> Murder, stern murder, in the direst degree,
> All several sins, all used in each degree,
> Throng all to th'bar, crying all 'Guilty, guilty!'
> (5.3.196–202)

At this point, Richard is no longer a gleeful dramatic archetype. Nor is he presented as the scourge of England's long accumulated sins. He has become a pathetic man who realises both his isolation from the rest of mankind and the loss of his soul: 'I shall despair. There is no creature loves me . . .' (203). We are reminded that, beyond being antagonistic to martial victory, despair was the cardinal sin for the Church, the unforgivable sin committed by Lucifer, Cain or Judas. Like Marlowe's Faustus, Richard is incapable of repentance. He even becomes an anti-Christ figure, not only through his soliloquy – Antony Hammond[20] says 'one of the most celebrated antecedents for an inner dialogue of this kind is Christ's agony in the garden of Gethsemane' – but also because the sun does not rise and shine on his newly recovered courage and on his death: 'The sun will not be seen today' (5.3.284).

A sense of tragic waste is conveyed to the audience. It seems, however, that Shakespeare refused Richard full tragic awareness and stature. Like Senecan tyrants, he is allowed to die a Stoic death:

> Slave, I have set my life upon a cast,
> And I will stand the hazard of the die.
> (5.4.9–10)

But the pangs of conscience he displays are made to sound hollow. They are not as heart-rending and lyrical as those of Faustus, Richard II or Macbeth. They are indeed mechanised by a deconstructed syntax and externalised by the recourse to ghosts who also address Richmond. Although he comes closer to tragedy than any other character in the history plays so far, and clearly dominates his play, as only Richard II and Henry V will later, Richard returns to machiavellian pronouncements, confusion, misdirection and dedication to Evil at the end when he addresses his army:

> Let not our babbling dreams affright our souls,
> For conscience is a word that cowards use,
> Devised at first to keep the strong in awe.
> Our strong arms be our conscience, swords our law!
> March on! Join bravely! Let us to't pell mell,
> If not to heaven, then hand in hand to hell.
>
> (5.3.310–15)

What he appeals to is scorn of the enemy, those 'stragglers', 'overweening rags of France', 'famished beggars', 'poor rats', 'bastard Bretons', 'heirs of shame' (5.3.329–37), and self-pride again: 'Spur your proud horses hard and ride in blood' (342). So there is some poetic justice when, fallen from his horse, he stoops howling 'A horse! A horse! My kingdom for a horse!' (5.4.7), a living medieval emblem of pride, rather than a self-fashioning and self-cancelling Renaissance tragic hero, like Thomas More himself.[21]

If there is tragedy in *Richard III*, it is rather that which has made, and will still make 'poor England weep in streams of blood' (5.5.37), in spite of the union of the white rose and the red, and before it enjoys 'smiling plenty and fair prosperous days' (5.5.34), themselves threatened by succession wars at the death of Elizabeth I. Despite its ambiguity, the play suggests that the tragedy of power is not that it is doomed to fail one day, as Richard's does, but that it is bound to crush innocent victims, like Lady Anne and the two young princes.

With *Richard III*, Shakespeare reached a stage where he could shape to his own needs all the available dramatic traditions and create an enriched, more ambiguous medium to deal with history; a medium which in its versatility can still make him everybody's contemporary in the theatre or in real life.[22]

Richard III: theatrical and filmic afterlife

The first actor to be associated with the famous title role was Richard Burbage, and the popularity of *Richard III*, its continuing appeal, was attested by a late performance in 1633, before the closing of the theatres in

1642. Interest was revived by Colley Cibber's 1700 adaptation, a shortened version which he partly rewrote and combined with fragments from the *Henry VI* plays. Cibber put Richard's deformity to the fore, giving the tyrant king a comparatively larger share in the dialogue than in the original drama. Although a number of later attempts were made at adapting *Richard III*, Colley Cibber's version valiantly pursued its career on the stage well into the nineteenth century.

The fascinating, demonic king found a new lease of life when David Garrick seized the part in 1741, a blessing for great performers, and maintained it on the stage almost without interruption between 1747 and 1776. His unprecedented triumph as Richard was followed by a line of remarkable performances as Kemble, Cooke and Kean successively took the part, each with his personal stamp and some variations upon the Cibber script. In 1821, however, Macready attempted a return to the original play, although with little success, and it was not until the 1870s that a serious revival of the Shakespearean text proved possible: Henry Irving's production kept to the text, even if it was in a shortened version, focusing again, in keeping with a long-standing tradition, upon the title role.

In the twentieth century the status of *Richard III* underwent obvious changes with a reinstatement of the original text, and even more importantly, with a move from pure acting concerns to problems of interpretation and production. The emphasis was placed on presenting the play as a case of political tyranny, along with the theatricality of the main character. The memorable Berlin production of 1920, directed by Leopold Jessner, led to fresh symbolic and political treatments of *Richard III*. Jessner, at a time of social and political upheaval in Europe, had the tyrant ascend blood-red steps for his coronation. His version not only fascinated critics in his own time, prompting a reappraisal of the play's significance, but it seems to have retained its hold on more recent productions, as shown by the use in the 1963 Peter Hall and John Barton version of a symbolism redolent of the Berlin performance. At the time of Nazi horror haunting the whole of Europe, Donald Wolfit was acclaimed in 1942 with his impersonation of a Hitler-like Richard, no doubt because terror and the havoc of war were very real things for the spectators who had, on one occasion, to run for shelter during a bomb alert. Wolfit's achievement was followed in 1944 by a memorable production by Laurence Olivier in which this actor offered a very powerful representation of Richard as a supremely cunning and devilish character. The constantly spying and preying presence of the tyrant, together with his cold-blooded ruthlessness, may have reminded Olivier's spectators that Nazi monstrosity had not yet receded. The number of modern productions attests to the continued popularity of the play, as well to a general interest in politics that derives from manifestations of dictatorship in recent decades. Among the most imaginative treatments we should mention the versions of Terry Hands (1970), Bill Alexander (1984), Adrian Noble (1989), Sam Mendes (1992), and Steven Pimlott (1996). One of the most striking productions in recent years was the much praised Bill Alexander's *Richard III*, in 1984, for the Royal Shakespeare Company, with Antony Sher in the leading role. The emphasis on the monstrous features of the tyrant was remarkable as Antony Sher, making use of a pair of crutches, hopped on four legs like a large, nightmarish insect. Although he seemed to be handicapped by some crippling disease, Sher's Richard moved about the stage with alarming speed and animality, which further manifested his spider-like appearance. Bill Alexander's production was so impressive in its bringing out this combination of abnormality and vitality that it was compared to Laurence Olivier's virtuoso creation.

Olivier himself directed a filmed version of *Richard III* in 1955. His Richard retained the cunning superiority of the role in the theatre play. However, some major cuts (Margaret's role in particular) and some adjustments were made for the film. The result, even if it often greatly departs from Shakespeare, displays some terrifying effects because of the set and its expressionist treatment of shadows. A more recent film version, released in 1995, is Richard Loncraine's *Richard III* which is based on a theatre production with Ian McKellen in the title role.[23] In the film, McKellen is once again Richard, combining features borrowed from the dictator and the gangster, and with strong links to both Nazi terrorism and British fascist movements of the 1930s. The film is often shot in and around actual buildings in London that create a milieu redolent of that era, while the text of the play is adapted to a situation suggesting a vaguely decadent totalitarian state – a familiar reference for modern picture-goers, if one thinks, for instance, of Visconti's *The Damned*.

Richard III was twice filmed on video, first in 1982 for the BBC series, by Jane Howell as director. In this production she clearly chose to depart from the Olivier filmic heritage – her Richard looked somewhat less inhuman. Another version of the play on video is Michael Bogdanov's 1990 production for the English Shakespeare Company which was taped live during performance.[24]

NOTES

1 Walker 2000, p. 35.
2 Marienstras 1995, p. 160.
3 See Vergil 1844, p. 227.
4 *Ibid.*, p. 189.

5 See Rous *et al.* 1716. Rous portrayed Richard III as an unnatural man, and apparently invented the legend of the king's being born with teeth.

6 *History of King Richard III*, in Hall 1548, fol. 1^v.

7 Greg Walker quotes Francis Bacon's 'Of Envy' and 'Of Deformity' on the effect of a twisted body, commonly thought to be a mark of ill nature and moral deformity: see Walker 2000, pp. 36–7.

8 See also the Duchess of York's accusation 'Thou cam'st on earth to make the earth my hell. / A grievous burden was thy birth to me. / Tetchy and wayward was thy infancy; / Thy schooldays frightful, desperate, wild, and furious' (4.4.167–70).

9 See Marienstras 1995, p. 156. R. Marienstras quotes from Ambroise Paré, *Des Monstres et prodiges*, ed. J. Céard (Geneva, 1971).

10 See also: 'The tiger hath now seized the gentle hind' (*R3*, 2.4.53).

11 More 1963.

12 See Happé 1966 and Debax 1987; see also Happé 1989, pp. 137–8, and Debax 1999, p. 51.

13 About the imaginary castle and the armour, we agree with Michael Hattaway's observation that 'What Shakespeare may be suggesting here in Richard's Protean manipulations is that imaginary castles are no defence against the perseverance of a Machiavel' (see Hattaway 2000, p. 201).

14 More 1963, p. 81.

15 Spivack 1958, pp. 400, 395.

16 Quoted by Cunliffe 1893, p. 2.

17 Smallwood 1986, p. 155.

18 Peggy Ashcroft and Penny Downie were among the most formidable Margarets.

19 Downie 1993.

20 See *R3*, ed. Hammond 1981, pp. 106–7.

21 See Greenblatt 1980. Greenblatt sees both More and Richard III as great improvisers, but Richard seems more or less a prisoner of the archetype of the villain.

22 See Kott 1964; compare also recent interpretations of Richard as fascistic and the demonstrations of the mothers of the disappeared in Chile, Argentina or elsewhere in our present world.

23 See Loehlin 1997.

24 See also *R3*, ed. Hankey 1981; Richmond 1989; Kennedy 1993a; Davies and Wells, 1994; *R3*, ed. Lull 1999.

8

A. J. PIESSE

King John: changing perspectives

King John is a provocatively problematic play. In terms of its provenance alone, there have been keenly debated exchanges about its genealogical relationship to its main source, with editors of scholarly editions arguing on either side for Shakespeare's play as a source for the anonymous *The Troublesome Reign of John King of England* and for the latter as a source for the former.[1] While the majority prefer to see *Troublesome Reign* as the source, and the most recent accounts of this have been quite dismissive of the opposite camp, the debate in its entirety has led to useful close readings of the anonymous play. Discussion concerning other known sources (Holinshed, Foxe, Hall) and an analogue, Radulph of Coggeshall's *English Chronicle* (written in Latin),[2] has been somewhat less heated, and there are far fewer arguments for a direct use of its other dramatic analogue, Bale's *King Johan.*[3] But there are resonances, if not replications, between Bale's and Shakespeare's plays that, if properly investigated, might reinforce some of the more recent scholarly excursions on Shakespeare's behalf, and there is a strong temptation to imagine, if not actually believe, that Shakespeare 'worked with the old play in his head, if not in his hand'.[4]

With Nathan Drake, 'we are well aware, that, to many of our readers, the chronological discussion incident to a new arrangement, will be lamented as tedious and uninteresting; the more so, as nothing absolutely certain can be expected as the result'.[5] But it is important to see that argument around primogeniture begets consequent uncertainty about the date of the composition of Shakespeare's play, which in turn sets up difficulties concerning the place of the play in the development of Shakespeare's writing of history plays, and thus throws kinks into attempts at smooth accounts of the flow of style, content, and purpose across the canon of Shakespeare's writing of history.

The fact that the play does not fall clearly into any sequence, either in terms of chronology of historical representation or in terms of compositional chronology, further exacerbates the issue of comparison and contrast across the canon. Nor does the play's performance history or its critical history show any signs of consistent attention or of a clear pattern of evolution in thinking about the play.

In terms of performance, Shakespeare's *King John* has suffered long periods of neglect, when it wasn't performed at all, and enjoyed sporadic bursts of popularity, sometimes for the most nefarious of reasons. There is no record of it having been performed in the seventeenth or early eighteenth century, and it took a less than intelligent rewriting by Colley Cibber to bring about a revival even then. Cibber extensively rewrote *King John* as *Papal Tyranny in the Reign of King John*, '...to make it more like a play than what I have found it in Shakespeare'(*sic*).[6] The surrounding controversy meant that a Covent Garden performance of *King John* 'as written by Shakspear' (*sic*)[7] in the same months – beginning February 1737 – was exceptionally well attended, and for six days the performances overlapped, so that audiences had a choice of which they would see. During the next hundred years, *King John* was played frequently and, as Eugene Waith has pointed out, during three seasons, 1760–1, 1766–7, and 1817–18, 'there were rival productions at the two royal theatres in London'.[8]

Subsequent reviews of performance create nicely a record of the preoccupations of the various ages. The earliest reviews focus on realistic representation of character, and the relation of character to genre. Thus in 1734, King John's 'turbulence and grandeur of the passions . . . inconstancy of temper . . . mixture of good and ill . . . series of misfortunes' are seen as being the elements that 'might make him very fit for a hero in a just composition'.[9] The success of productions from the late eighteenth into the early nineteenth centuries is measured to a large degree in terms of the rendition of the notoriously difficult playing of Constance, whose range of emotions 'almost overwhelms the mind that meditates its realisation, and utterly exhausts the frame which endeavours to express its agitations'.[10] The Kemble/Planche production of 1823 looked for an externalised truth to life, the set and costumes attempting a historically accurate representation: John's costume for Act 1 was even based on the effigy on his tomb in Worcester Cathedral.[11] By 1948, with the memory of war quite immediate, there is praise for Audrey Cruddas' design, with a set that was gradually dismantled to show 'the rotten state of England';[12] by the early seventies, there is another much-maligned attempt to rewrite and a wilful manifestation of the central characters as playing a series of superficial roles.[13] It is Deborah Warner's productions of 1988 and 1989 that open the play up as truly reflective. Accounts of rehearsal show her willing to see roles as being polyvalent, capable of conveying a number of meanings simultaneously. The success of the production substantiates contemporary critical positions on the play, demonstrating that it experiments with the notion of the writing of history and that

Shakespeare uses the characters to make that process of experimentation explicit.[14]

An overview of the play's critical history, similarly, reveals as much about the preoccupations of the prevailing trends as it does about the play itself: lack of Aristotelian unity (Gildon 1710);[15] a preoccupation with consistency of language and character (Malone 1790, Steevens 1793);[16] the notion that 'the interest does not sufficiently centre in any one individual of the play' (Oxberry 1819);[17] poetic imagination versus historical accuracy in representation of character (Brownwell Jameson 1832);[18] the preoccupation with the character of Constance as played by Mrs Siddons to the degree where 'it was not unusual for spectators to leave the house when her part in the tragedy of King John was over' (Campbell 1833);[19] kingliness, queenliness and Englishness (Masefield 1911, Brooke 1913);[20] the shift away from character towards politics (Charlton 1929)[21] or an intellectual view of history (Tillyard 1944),[22] and on into canonical arguments about date, sources, and the relationship of character to a particular view of history, through the work especially of Bonjour (1951), van de Water (1960) Waith (1978),[23] and Mason Vaughan (1984).[24] It is clear from the work of these last four, each of whom will figure later in this essay, that the critical problematisation of the notion of history in the second half of the twentieth century allowed a radical reconsideration of King John. It is the notion that King John is a play deliberately unstable in structure and characterisation, in keeping with a view of history as unstable, which prompted so vibrant a revival in critical interest.

This is a play that currently inspires fierce debate, about which critics, literary historians, and directors have yet to agree in even the most minimal of ways. Outside of the academy it is probably one of least well-known plays in the canon. It is also a play that, at the end of the twentieth century, has enjoyed a flurry of critical writing on its behalf. Why?

Part of the answer lies, I think, in the identification of what Harold Jenkins called 'the crucial experiment of King John'.[25] This play takes risks in a number of ways. It is clear from the range of interpretation and debate, as outlined above, that this is a play of ambivalences and contradictions. In most of the history plays, themes of masculine and feminine power, of divine and temporal rights, of speaking within one's own person or in an adopted persona emerge as the plays progress. But in King John these issues are raised immediately:

> KING JOHN Now say, Chatillon, what would France with us?
> CHATILLON Thus, after greeting, speaks the King of France
> In my behaviour to the majesty,
> The borrowed majesty, of England here.

ELEANOR   A strange beginning: 'borrowed majesty'?
KING JOHN   Silence, good mother, hear the embassy.

(1.1.1–6)

Here the central concerns are raised immediately. France disputes John's legitimacy; Chatillon speaks in his own voice but represents another; Eleanor's disruptive voice is immediately established, and her presence and readiness to interrupt suggest an unusual power relationship between herself and John.

Here too it is immediately easy to see how Shakespeare tightens, transforms, or redirects his dramatic analogues. Bale's *King Johan* begins with a clearer, but single-stranded contradistinction:

KYNGE JOHAN   To declare the powers and their force to enlarge
              The scripture of God flows in most abundance;
              And of [from] sophisters [cunning men] the cautels [tricks] to
                 discharge [destroy],
              Both Peter and Paul make plentiful utterance;
              How that all people should show their true allegiance
              To their lawful king, Christ Jesus consents,
              Who to the high powers was ever obedient.
              To show what I am I think it convenient,
              John, King of England the chronicles me call.
              My grandfather was an emperor excellent,
              My father a king by succession lineal,
              A king my brother, like as to him did fall:
              Richard Coeur-de-Lion they called him in France,
              Which had over enemies most fortunable chance.

(1. 1–14)[26]

This clearly demonstrates Bale's more narrowly focused view of the contradiction at hand, that between showing and telling, between the sign and the signifier, which will come to dominate the medium of the play. The opening of *Troublesome Reign* resonates clearly with Christian preoccupations:

QUEEN ELEANOR   Barons of England and my noble lords,
                Though God and Fortune have bereft from us
                Victorious Richard, scourge of infidels,
                And clad this land in stole of dismal hue,
                Yet give me leave to joy, and joy you all,
                That from this womb hath sprung a second hope,
                A king that may in rule and virtue both
                Succeed his brother in his empery.

(*1 Troublesome Reign*, 1–8)

Eleanor is initially declarer and informer, rather than contender, which initiates a different kind of hierarchy from the outset. The conflict between
seeming and being is also strong in *Troublesome Reign*. The initial reference
to the matter is explicit: Eleanor says, '*Omne simile non est idem*' (not
everything that is similar [looks alike] is the same);[27] and the motif of seeming is also strong in Bale, where characters take on allegorical disguises
and therefore operate in both the literal and the representational paradigm
simultaneously.[28]

The shifts in paradigm that make the character of the Bastard in
Shakespeare's *King John* so utterly unlike any other kind of character in
the canon are, I believe, an indication that Shakespeare is consciously working with a similar uneasy relationship between allegorical and individual
representation. In Shakespeare's *King John*, the dislocation between what is
being presented on the surface and what is actually driving both the plot and
also the audience's view of the play is absolutely bound up in this notion
of self-conscious mimesis. This is partly why it is so informative to observe
in detail the shift in focus in account of performance history and critical
history. Once the emphasis has moved away from the efficacy or credibility of realistic representation and into the arena of interrogating the nature
of the play – where interpretations of both structure and characters suggest a representation of complexity and discontinuity rather than a quest
for a stable centre – the extraordinary nature of the play begins to emerge.
Shakespeare's play allows an initial access to this way of thinking by concentrating on the notion of legitimacy, and by placing the most disruptive
observations, initially, at least, in the most flippant of language. We have
already seen how the opening moments of *King John* set up an interrog-
ative, interrupted discourse, and a series of contradictions. The Bastard's
decision at 1.1 to embrace an illegitimate nobility rather than a legitimate
obscurity sets up early in the action a pattern of interrogation, and it is this
that characterises the overall direction of the play. Although the problem-
atically unstable character of the Bastard has attracted the most attention
in relation to this aspect of the play, the drawing of the female characters can also be read in a way that supports such a reading. This, it seems
to me, is further evidence that Shakespeare is deliberately drawing attention both to the conventions of playing and to the conventions of writing
history.

To realise the audacity of such a movement, it is useful to glance one
more time at *Troublesome Reign*. The notion of interrogating social and
historical givens is so transgressive in that play that the Faulconbridge
character ('Philip' in this play) must envision an extraneous authority through the medium of divine inspiration. To be able to make so

revolutionary a decision, he must be seen to be entranced in a sort of divine revelation:

> ELEANOR   Philip awake, the man is in a dream.
> PHILIP   *Philippis atauis aedite Regibus.*
>   [i.e.]What say'st thou, Philip, sprung of ancient Kings?
>   *Quo me rapit tempestas?*
>   [i.e.] What wind of honour blows this fury forth?
>   Or whence proceed these fumes of majesty?
>   Methinks I hear a hollow echo sound,
>   That Philip is the son unto a king;
>   The whistling leaves upon the trembling trees
>   Whistle in consort I am Richard's son;
>   The bubbling murmur of the water's fall
>   Records '*Philippus regius filius*';
>   Birds in their flight make music with their wings,
>   Filling the air with glory of my birth:
>   Birds, bubbles, leaves, and mountains, echo, all
>   Ring in mine ears that I am Richard's son.
>   (*1 Troublesome Reign*, 240–55)

While these lines are also open to a comic interpretation (the pulling together of the various images being especially suspect in the alliterative 'bubbles') there are three significant, if possibly hubristic, resonances here. Firstly, the wind of honour is suspiciously Pentecostal, especially in the context of Eleanor's earlier Biblical references, suggesting a perceived or imagined divine appointment. Secondly, the invocation of all Nature crying out the message is also a Biblical trope, as well as a thoroughly apt apostrophe to one claiming his natural (i.e. illegitimate) birthright. Thirdly, the invocation of echoing is important, evoking as it does a resonance of truth in a Platonic other realm.

Shakespeare's Bastard, on the other hand, revels in his freedom to make a personal, unencumbered, straightforward political decision to take on a new persona, and he describes it in terms of self-consciously reconstructing his own education:

>   Now your traveller,
> He and his toothpick at my worship's mess,
> And when my knightly stomach is sufficed,
> Why then I suck my teeth and catechise
> My pickèd man of countries: 'My dear sir',
> Thus leaning on mine elbow I begin,
> 'I shall beseech you' – that is Question now,
> And then comes Answer like an Absey book:

'O sir', says Answer, 'at your best command,
At your employment, at your service, sir.'
'No, sir', says Question, 'I, sweet sir, at yours.'
And so e'er Answer knows what Question would,
Saving in dialogue of compliment,
And talking of the Alps and Apennines,
The Pyrenean and the river Po,
It draws toward supper in conclusion so.
(1.1.189–204)

The notion of being able to read oneself properly according to context is vitally important. The Bastard's explicit grasp of his situation is made clear moments later in the same speech:

For he is but a bastard to the time
That does not smack of observation,
And so am I – whether I smack or no,
And not alone in habit and device,
Exterior form, outward accoutrement,
But from the inward motion . . .
(1.1.207–12)

The Bastard's view of his own possibilities begin at the lowest point – that of giving up everything that has identified him to himself as himself and following Eleanor, an artificial arbiter of his new identity. This latter point is in itself highly significant since, in the making of history, women are traditionally the arbiters of identity and the moral guardians of the blood line, as the Bastard has already pointed out to Eleanor at 1.1.62–4.[29] The fight for legitimation does appear to be largely in women's hands for the first three acts of the play. Eleanor reminds John that his claim to the throne is not as strong as he appears to believe. Constance's fight for Arthur's rights are emotive and powerful, as attested to by the power of her character in many of the early performances and the critical focus on it in a large proportion of the critical writing.

But the treatment of this issue is complex in *King John*, where 'Shakespeare subjects the masculine voices of patriarchal authority to sceptical feminine interrogation.'[30] Eleanor and Constance each wrestle separately with the restriction of their roles. Eleanor fights cynically and in a sophisticated, knowing, almost masculine fashion, as is seen in her direct engagement with male characters, Chatillon in the opening scene and later the Bastard, for example. It is also, critically, she who ultimately persuades John to allow the match between Blanche and the Dauphin at 2.1. Anger and scorn in her role are reserved for her female opponent, Constance. Constance, on the other hand, angrily complains of the restrictions of the female role. Her very first words suggest her physical powerlessness and her readiness to use the traditional woman's role, that of urging male action on her behalf. 'O take his mother's thanks, a widow's thanks / Till your strong hand shall help to give him strength / To make a more requital of your love' (2.1.32–4) she says to Austria, explicitly reminding him that, as a widow, she has no obvious male to act for her. In her vicious exchanges with Eleanor, she is more than able to match that experienced politician, often literally word for word, as Shakespeare demonstrates through a plethora of stichomythic exchanges. Four times out of the five direct spats with Eleanor, Constance gets the last word before, between them, the men silence them. On one occasion, she is revealed to be preternaturally prophetic, as her scathing 'go to it grandam, child. / Give grandam kingdom, and it grandam will / Give it a plum, a cherry, and a fig' (2.1.160–3) is chillingly recalled in Eleanor's later words to John, 'That yon green boy shall have no sun to ripe / The bloom that promiseth a mighty fruit' (2.1.472–3). On the fifth occasion, where the French turn against the English under pressure from Rome, it is Eleanor who speaks last, but by this point, the women are no longer pitted against each other but once again relatively powerless in the larger manoeuvring of the men.

Constance's powerlessness once Arthur is temporarily unimportant is powerfully drawn. She questions the legitimacy of Philip's nobility, hissing, 'You have beguiled me with a counterfeit / Resembling majesty', becoming almost inarticulate with rage and grief – 'forsworn, forsworn' – and declaring her lack of faith in any male agent of rescue, 'A widow cries; be husband to me, God!'(3.1.99–100, 101, 108). She renders invalid Pandulph's dismissal of her grief as madness by proving her self-knowledge in traditionally acceptable female terms, her role as widow and mother: 'My name is Constance, I was Geoffrey's wife, / Young Arthur is my son, and he is lost' (3.4.46–7) and confronts the men who urge her to control herself with their inability to empathise:

> He talks to me that never had a son . . .
> Grief fills the room up of my absent child
> Lies in his bed, walks up and down with me,
> Puts on his pretty looks, repeats his words,
> Remembers me of all his gracious parts,
> Stuffs out his vacant garments with his form.
> Then have I reason to be fond of grief?
> (3.4.91, 93–8).

Fittingly famous for its lyrical beauty, this speech steers the direction of the play. Constance has responded to the male view of history and society, has proved able to align herself psychologically with perceived propriety, in rehearsing her familial position. But with this speech she powerfully evokes her personal history and provocatively invokes a female alternative: this is her history of her life with her son, and it matters more than any kind of dispassionate chronicling.

It is clear then that the complex characterisation of Constance is in itself an investigation of what history means for its women protagonists. Eleanor is a political player who is ultimately powerless in the face of the male authority of the Church. I think it no accident that Pandulph persistently refers to Mother Church, the political, historical manifestation of religion easily superseding the localised, personal aspect of maternal power; nor do I think it coincidental that John's decision to return to Rome is made in almost the same breath that he learns of his mother's death. Constance plays a proper role to begin with, finds herself betrayed, and refuses to acquiesce in this male view of history. Shakespeare's powerfully drawn picture of her private history urges the audience to consider this alternative view of succession, much as he had done in *Richard III*, where the constant rehearsal of mostly first names, by mothers, aunts, and sisters, brings home more strongly than any formal list of the dead the appalling internecine murders along Richard's route to the throne (*R3* 4.4.35–42). And the traditional representation of Blanche serves as a counterpoint to this. She is the pawn, the acquiescent victim to the Dauphin's too-perfect political rhetoric and, as the two sides she is supposed to have united go to battle again, her familial loss of self, her utter disempowerment, figured in the physical dismemberment of the male protagonists, is strongly reminiscent of that same exchange in *Richard III*:

> Which is the side that I must go withal?
> I am with both, each army hath a hand,
> And, in their rage, I having hold of both,
> They whirl asunder and dismember me.
> Husband, I cannot pray that thou mayst win;
> Uncle, I needs must pray that thou mayst lose.
> Father, I may not wish the fortune thine;
> Grandam, I will not wish thy wishes thrive.[31]
>
> (3.1.327–34)

It seems to me that it is possible, then, to read the manipulation of Eleanor, Constance, and Blanche within this wider, more disruptive context of notions of rewriting the boundaries of the history play.

In contrast to these experiments, John's inability either to act independently or to present appropriate images of either his public or his private self at crucial moments in the play is telling. His reliance on his mother's advice, on his allies, and then on the authority of the Church suggest a king fearful and uncertain of himself in both his private and his public spheres. His lack of clear self-presentation is made apparent by the response of the citizens of Angiers, who refuse to make a choice between the candidates for kingship offered to them, insisting on their acceptance of the body politic rather than the body natural:

> KING JOHN Whose party do the townsmen yet admit?
> KING PHILIP Speak, citizens, for England; who's your king?
> CITIZEN The King of England, when we know the king.
>
> (2.1.361–3)

The citizens will accept the rightful king, and at this point it is not at all clear to them who that person is, as is made clear by the almost allegorical balance of scenes in this part of the second act.

John's vacillations before the nobles and with Hubert about the death of Arthur bring this lack of clarity to crisis point. He suggests to the nobles that he is as susceptible to fate as any of them ('Think you I bear the shears of destiny? / Have I commandment on the pulse of life?' 4.2.91–2). In conversation with Hubert, the instability of John's persona is made clear. First, he laments the responsibilities of authority that render kings culpable for the over-zealous actions of their servants: 'It is the curse of kings to be attended / By slaves that take their humours for a warrant / To break within the bloody house of life' (4.2.208–10). Moments later, he dismisses the hierarchical structure, not only insisting that Hubert should take responsibility for his own actions but that he should have taken upon himself the role of advisor:

> Hadst thou but shook thy head or made a pause
> When I spake darkly what I purposèd,
> Or turned an eye of doubt upon my face
> As bid me tell my tale in express words,
> Deep shame had struck me dumb, made me break off
> And those thy fears might have wrought fears in me.
>
> (4.2.230–6)

John's earlier refusal to articulate clearly his orders regarding Arthur's fate signals exactly his personal incompleteness. Incapable of inscribing a clear version of himself, he is incapable of strong leadership. John continually seeks external legitimation, and uses that externalising to refuse responsibility. This lack of a centre, of a strong internal self, is ultimately figured in the manner of his death by poison, by corruption and dissolution from within. While death by poison is analogous to some of Shakespeare's sources, it is particularly apt here.[32]

With John so clearly lacking in both the outward and visible signs and the inward, intrinsic qualities of leadership, who might be alternative leaders? Shakespeare makes John's opponent, Arthur, young and malleable, which weakens John's position still further. In *Troublesome Reign*, Arthur is older and more politically able. Even as little more than a child in Shakespeare's play, Arthur is, within his own sphere of influence, more aware of proper public process than John, more resistant to manipulation by external forces than John (as his embarrassment at his mother's excesses demonstrates), more rhetorically able than John (as his persuasiveness with Hubert shows), and more aware of the universal nature of history.

If, as Mason Vaughan has suggested, '[John's] failure in this play stems not from defiance of the Pope but from his role in planning an innocent child's murder',[33] the status conferred on the child is obviously important. The construction of Arthur's character is another element in the legitimacy debate; whatever the arguments about the legality of John's and Arthur's claims to the throne, Arthur's innate qualities, even in extreme youth, show him to be inherently fitter than John. There are two qualities that connect Arthur firmly to the wider pattern of the play. The first connects him to his mother, and to the notion of alternative views of history. He saves himself from blinding and death by invoking personal history, reminding Hubert of the strength of their relationship and of past kindnesses:

> Have you the heart? When your head did but ache,
> I knot my handkercher about your brows
> (The best I had, a princess wrought it me)
> And I did never ask it you again;
> And with my hand at midnight held your head;
> And like the watchful minutes to the hour,
> Still and anon cheered up the heavy time,
> Saying, 'What lack you?' and 'Where lies your grief?'
>
> (4.1.41–8)

He later invokes fate and faith on his side:

> See else yourself,
> There is no malice in this burning coal;
> The breath of heaven hath blown his spirit out
> And strewn repentant ashes on his head.
>
> (4.1.107–10)

Thus, through the use of the transferred epithet of penitence, he recalls Hubert to a proper Christian perception, to a view of Hubert's own possible future should he proceed with the act. Arthur can usefully invoke history and prompt a rewriting of it by a suggestion of the future. And apparently he does this quite consciously, because at the end of the scene he explicitly announces that he has reconciled the Hubert who was acting out orders out of character to the personally true historical version of self: 'O now you look like Hubert. All this while / You were disguisèd' (4.1.125–6). In the perceptions of Arthur, a momentarily possible saviour of the kingdom, there is a temporary rapprochement between personal history and the broader notion of seeming and proper integrity. There is a momentary glimpse that the problematic elements of the play as a whole might potentially have been resolved in this figure and that his death indeed is the vital moment in the undoing of John. This is underpinned by the second connection, a single line that reveals Arthur's implicit understanding of the extent of John's unfitness. As he attempts to leap to safety but falls instead to death, he cries 'O me, my uncle's spirit is in these stones' (4.3.9). The king *is* England; instead of the nurturing, nourishing, fertile land so frequently invoked in the history plays, England is death-dealing stones. Arthur pronounces with his last breath his intrinsic grasp of universal significance.

Where Arthur draws attention to the potential process of history, to the possibility of a reconciliation of alternative views, accounts of the Bastard at the end of the twentieth century argued for his being a figure who tests out a series of perspectives. The Bastard sees 'with complete realism';[34] he is 'an amalgam of character and commentator';[35] he is a 'ficelle', a thread joining a disjointed play, playing Vice-like in comic, revelatory opposition to the tragic hero;[36] he is a chorus figure, 'outside the structure of the play as he is outside it historically'.[37]

It is true, as van de Water insists, that the figure of the Bastard changes rather than develops. It is also true that there is a sense of adapting into certain situations in a way that John seems unable to do. It is also true that the Bastard performs an opposite notion of legitimacy to the one that John fails to execute. Marsha Robinson has argued that in *King John* Shakespeare aims to 'dramatize the process by which historical experience is translated into historiographical meaning', a movement that 'exposes the disparity between the events of history and their conventional representations'.[38] By constructing an eccentric central figure, and by making the obvious central figure centreless, Shakespeare continually and consistently draws attention to point of view in a way that a simple chorus figure cannot. The Bastard, the illegitimate, the unfathered, the maternally adopted, the figure whose blood allegiance is uncertain, ultimately has the task of legitimating process in this play. He is initially brought into events by a figure who is herself unconventional (Eleanor); he is relied upon by the figure who should be most certain of his own legitimacy (John). This doubly unstable figure is active and effective both within the process of the play – that part which is aligned with history – and with external commentary on it – that part which is aligned with historiography. History is presented in order to interrogate it, its players, and its means of representation. For this reason the historical analogue *Troublesome Reign* is half-acknowledged, but used as a point of departure. Further, the Bastard reconfigures the notion of the choric figure, the means by which history is interrogated, by refusing to be a stable commentator. If the character of the commentary changes with the changing of the times, then historiography is as unstable as history. The Bastard then is a genuinely ambivalent construction, a figure whose function as character and chorus is unstable, figuring both the cracking open of the notion of character in a history play and also the notion of the representation of history itself. Shakespeare is apparently nervous about the possibility of certainty in an individual perspective. In a play that works hard to establish personality traits within typical roles, it is appropriate to experiment with the tensions within individual omniscience. The Bastard is explicitly used as a signifier of tension between form and content, as demonstrated in speeches like the one at 5.1:

> Be great in act, as you have been in thought.
> Let not the world see fear and sad distrust
> Govern the motion of a kingly eye.
> Be stirring as the time, fight fire with fire,
> Threaten the threat'ner . . .
>
> (5.1.45–9)

The Bastard is here closer to describing himself than he is to describing John. He urges a proper response, as figured in the repetitive language. The only other speeches like this come from Pandulph, who speaks with the impenetrable orderliness of the Church, immovable in his faith that the invocation of historical obedience will result in an unquestioning restoration of order. But the Bastard's speech in the same register serves only to demonstrate the dislocation between a vision of right kingship and the present reality. The witty fool (witness the Bastard's early speeches and his taunting of Austria) capable of natural tenderness (witness his response to his natural mother) and a degree of self-knowledge lacking in the majority of his counterparts ('If ever I remember to be holy', he says (3.3.15), immediately after promising to pray for his grandmother), slips on the role of choric alarm ('England now is left / To tug and scamble . . .' (4.3.145–6)) of the recognition of universality ('How easy dost thou take all England up' (4.3.142)) and relinquishes it all when his purpose is achieved.

David Scott Kastan has described the Bastard as 'an outsider who has no legitimate relationship to the past'.[39] Legitimised socially by Eleanor's 'irreverent, witty' voice,[40] relying on her accuracy of recognition, he in turn becomes the irreverent, witty commentator in a newly legitimised view of history. Prompted by the alternative views of history provided by Eleanor, Constance and Arthur, the various voices of the Bastard interrogate the legitimacy of the historical medium in which he has been drawn.

NOTES

I would like to record my thanks to Patrick Prendergast for his invaluable assistance in the writing of this essay.

1 Honigmann 1987.
2 The most straightforward way of consulting the relevant part of these sources and analogues is by using Bullough 1957–73, IV, 1–151. All subsequent quotations from *Troublesome Reign* are modernised from this work.
3 See Morey 1994.
4 Richard Grant White, cit. Candido 1996, p. 178. This volume has proved invaluable in the preparation of this essay, and I gratefully acknowledge its use. In this particular case, Candido is reprinting excerpts from Richard Grant White's 1859 edition of *King John*. White has dismissed Bale as a source and is referring to *Troublesome Reign* with this quotation.
5 Nathan Drake, cit. Candido 1996, p. 56. Candido is quoting from Drake's *Shakespeare and His Times* (1817).
6 Colley Cibber, *The Dramatic Works*, 5 vols., (New York, 1966), V, 242, cit. Cousin 1994, p. 4.
7 Cousin, *ibid.*, p. 5.
8 Waith 1978, p. 193; both Waith and Cousin 1994 give thoughtful detailed accounts of productions, with illustrations and photographs. Cousin in addition gives a detailed account of Cibber's rewriting, pp. 3–11.
9 Lewis Theobald, *The Works of Shakespeare*, 7 vols. (London, 1733), III, 167, cit. Candido 1996, p. 2; Waith, *ibid.*, p. 194.
10 Waith, *ibid.*, p. 198.
11 Cousin 1994, pp. 28–32.
12 *Ibid.*, p. 50.
13 This is John Barton's production at Stratford in 1974 and London 1975 (see *ibid.*, pp. 64–83).
14 See Waith 1978, van de Water 1960, and Vaughan 1984.
15 Cit. Candido 1996, p. 1.
16 *Ibid.*, pp. 31–41 and pp. 45–49 respectively.
17 *Ibid.*, pp. 62–3.
18 *Ibid.*, pp. 75–81.
19 *Ibid.*, p. 83.
20 *Ibid.*, pp. 351–4 and 353–61 respectively.
21 Cit. Jenkins 1953, p. 6.
22 Tillyard 1944, cit. Burden 1985, p. 1.

23 Waith 1978, pp. 209–11.
24 Vaughan 1984, pp. 408–9, 415–19.
25 Jenkins 1953, p. 6.
26 All quotations from *King Johan* are from Happé 1979.
27 Latin is used only four times in the play, once to demonstrate the Romishness of the friar and the nun. On each of the other three occasions, it is used as an intensifier, to draw attention to a universally important moment.
28 Happé 1979, p. 53.
29 For a detailed account of this notion throughout Shakespeare's history plays, see Rackin 1990.
30 *Ibid.*, p. 79.
31 I think it interesting that Eleanor is included in this list of political players. There are no females in other such lists in Shakespeare.
32 See Morey 1994 for a detailed account of the poisoning, with a reproduction of the woodcuts from Foxe's *Actes and Monuments*, 1596.
33 Vaughan 1984, p. 415.
34 Knights 1959, p. 38, cit. Waith 1978, p. 200.
35 Leggatt 1977, p.16, cit. Vaughan 1984, p. 414.
36 Van de Water 1960, pp. 141–6.
37 Campbell 1947, p. 166, cit. van de Water, *ibid.*, p. 145.
38 Robinson 1989, p. 30.
39 *Ibid.*, p. 35.
40 Rackin 1990, p. 178.

9

ROBYN BOLAM

Richard II: Shakespeare and the languages of the stage

Richard II is a *tour de force* in verse with every character speaking poetry from beginning to end, but the play has many languages: its poetry is only one of them. Believed to have been written in 1595, *Richard II* is poised mid-way through the decade in which Shakespeare rewrote English history for the years 1398 to 1485. This play, whose second Quarto (1598) was the first of his published play–texts to have Shakespeare's name on its title-page, is also a key text for exploring his development as a writer. In 1679, thinking particularly of York's speech in 5.2 (lines 23–40), Dryden suggested that Shakespeare was able to 'infuse a natural passion into the mind', the implication being that he operated at a level deeper than the superficial 'noise' of bombastic poetry.[1] Following the recognition of dramatic (as opposed to purely verbal) imagery in the early 1950s, in 1966 John Russell Brown stressed that understanding Richard's character involved more than merely analysing what he said: the importance of audiences being able to reach thoughts beyond words and read a subtext from them was seen as crucial to the 'stage reality' of Richard himself. For Russell Brown, Richard's silences and 'his last unthinking, physical reactions' were also part of languages that needed to be read.[2]

Today we no longer focus solely on Richard. An audience is alerted to the existence of a subtext from the first scene and, for the rest of the play, watches character after character trying to read it and play their parts within it. We witness the way blame for Gloucester's murder moves through indirections, steadily closer to the king, Bullingbrook's denial of ambition and the contradictions of his actions, the conflicting dramatic portrayals of Richard's relationship with Bushy, Bagot, and Greene, Richard's ambiguous relationship with his queen and her perspective on events, the nature of Aumerle's loyalty to Richard, Exton's attempt to read the thoughts behind Bullingbrook's fatal line (5.4.2) and Bullingbrook's response to his deed. All of these make it necessary for an audience to adjust their impressions and understanding of characters and events constantly. In *Richard II* what is unsaid is often as significant as the poetic language which plays off visually on-stage against the languages of action, gesture, spectacle, and symbolic representation to create a drama that is also *about* language – its power and its weaknesses.

Identity, politics, and verbal versatility

Jane Donawerth identified *Richard II* as the play containing the highest proportion of key words concerning language (particularly relating to oral speech) of all Shakespeare's plays. Some of her examples (speak(s), speech(es), language(s), word(s), name(s), voice(s), tongue(s), mouth(s), throat(s), ear(s), breath, air, airy, pen, paper(s), ink, and parchment) are more significant than others.[3] Names, their multiplicity, instability, and crucial relationship with identity are prominently placed from the play's first lines. Shakespeare's main source, the second edition of Raphael Holinshed's *Chronicles of England, Scotland and Ireland* (1587), supplied him with 'Henry, Duke of Hereford', who later became 'Duke of Lancaster', but Shakespeare, like Samuel Daniel, whose poem *The First Four Books of the Civil Wars between the two Houses of Lancaster and York* (1595) is another possible source for the play, preferred the name 'Bullingbrook' for Richard's rival. ('Bolingbroke' only became the norm in the eighteenth century.) This has been upheld in the New Cambridge edition. It takes us back to the ambiguities the name contains: 'bulling' could mean 'to deceive' or, more likely in relation to water, 'to boil' or bubble up from its source.[4] Bullingbrook, as a newly emerging, active source of water (with a possible subtext of deceit) provides Shakespeare with the beginnings of an elaborate pattern of water imagery,[5] associated with the character who quenches a king whose badge depicted the sun partly obscured by cloud, a king who identified with 'glistering Phaëton' (3.3.178), handsome and vain, destroyed by Jupiter when he lost control of the horses drawing the sun's chariot and almost destroyed the earth.

A character's right to speak is explored from the first scene – not only his right to speak out against perceived injustice (Bullingbrook, Mowbray, Gaunt) – but also, after Mowbray's exile abroad, his right to be able to express himself in daily communication with others who speak the same language (1.3.154–73). Yet, as those who are left in England show, communication is fraught with restrictions and misunderstanding, even in a common tongue. Momentous actions are set in motion by the smallest breath needed to utter words. Richard talks himself out of his kingship:

> What must the king do now? Must he submit?
> The king shall do it. Must he be deposed?
> The king shall be contented. Must he lose
> The name of king? A God's name let it go.
>
> (3.3.143–6)

In a sense he already has, if we remember Gaunt's words 'Landlord of England art thou now, not king, / Thy state of law is bondslave to the law' (2.1.113–14). The implication is that Richard enslaves himself as well as his people by talking and acting as if their interests are unimportant.[6] He goes against the principles of the commonwealth in making unjust demands of his subjects, particularly through taxation, and though he has 'quite lost their hearts', they appear to be suffering in relative silence (2.1.246–50). Yet the most powerful voice in the play is the one we never really hear – that of the commons.

Anticipating the Induction to 2 *Henry IV*, it is the rumour that Richard is dead, passed from mouth to mouth, which causes thousands of fighting men to desert the king for Bullingbrook (3.1.73–4) and encourages thousands more – young, old, male and female – to join with Bullingbrook's army (3.2.112–20). In 4.1 it is the voice of the commons, recalled by Northumberland: 'May it please you, lords, to grant the commons' suit?' which triggers Bullingbrook's command 'Fetch hither Richard, that in common view / He may surrender. So we shall proceed / Without suspicion' (154–7). Behind the voice of the new king is the voice of the people.

At this point in the play we are also reminded that *Richard II* is the Shakespearean text most associated with the political power of words in the theatre – and the difficulties involved in determining such influence. All the printed versions published in Elizabeth I's lifetime are believed, by many critics, to have been subject to press or government censorship:[7] 4.1, the most politically subversive scene in the play, in which Richard is deposed, exists in them without lines 154–317, now considered the play's climax. Elizabeth died in 1603 and there is no way of ascertaining whether the full version of this scene, which only appeared in print from the fourth Quarto (1608) onwards, had been presented on the stage from the play's first performance. The shortened text breaks off at the point where Richard's loyal supporter, the Bishop of Carlisle, is arrested for treason, and omits the lengthy, largely psychological struggle between Richard and Bullingbrook, once the king has been summoned. These lines contain the greatest mystery of the drama: why did he resign the crown in such a manner? They also dramatise the way in which it physically changes hands, revealing insights into both Richard and Bullingbrook's characters, as well as giving the Earl of Northumberland a significant role as Bullingbrook's spokesman.

Without these lines the Abbot of Westminster's 'A woeful pageant have we here beheld' (320) refers immediately back to the arrest of the Bishop of Carlisle after he has announced Thomas Mowbray's death, York has brought news that Richard 'with willing soul' adopts Bullingbrook as his heir, Bullingbrook is declared the new king (4.1.108–12), and Carlisle has

Figure 6   Richard Pasco as Richard II and Ian Richardson as Bullingbrook (disguised as the Groom in 5.5) in John Barton's RSC production of *Richard II*, 1973. Photograph: Donald Cooper.

denounced him as 'a foul traitor', and delivered a prophecy of civil war. In the longer version of the scene, the 'woeful pageant' is not the spectre of England as a field of blood and 'dead men's skulls' (144) conjured up by Carlisle, but the sight the audience has just witnessed, of an anointed king relinquishing his crown in humiliating circumstances.

One of the reasons this scene has received so much attention is due to the play's identification with the drama that the Earl of Essex's supporters asked Shakespeare's Company to perform at the Globe on the eve of their rebellion in February 1601. Elizabeth's comment, in August 1601, to William Lambarde, the Keeper of the Records at the Tower of London: 'I am Richard II, know ye not that?',[8] coupled with her bitter reaction to the play's popularity, have fuelled critical debate. Why she identified so strongly with Richard is not absolutely clear. What they had most notably in common was childlessness – and in her case, being a woman, unwed, and older – the lack of an heir meant pressure to name a successor and abdicate. There was also a shared guilt at being implicated in the murder of a family member, believed to have been involved in treasonous activities. In 1587, eight years before *Richard II* was written, Elizabeth finally signed cousin Mary Queen of Scots' death warrant. Richard's implication in his uncle's murder abroad poses an uneasy question from the play's beginning. It is this question which lurks beneath the initial confrontation of Mowbray and Bullingbrook and surfaces again in Bagot's and Fitzwater's accusations of Aumerle, just before Richard's deposition in 4.1. The sources show Gloucester as a potential threat and offer some political justification, should Richard have done the deed – but Shakespeare does not put this in his play. Intriguingly, Essex was descended from the same Duke of Gloucester – so Elizabeth's much quoted line, like Shakespeare's play, raises all manner of possibilities.[9] At the time, playwright, actors, and theatre emerged surprisingly unscathed. As the coup was unsuccessful, this might imply that the drama was not considered effectual – or it could mean that those who requested it to be performed were not aware of the different ways in which it could be 'read' by the audience.

Instabilities of text, meaning, and genre are all essential to *Richard II*. Entitled a tragedy in its first printed versions (the five 1597–1615 Quarto editions), the play appears as a historical chronicle ('The Life and Death of Richard the Second') in the 1623 First Folio.[10] More recently it has even been called a 'Lamentable comedy'.[11] John Halverson focuses on it as 'a study of absurdity: rhetorical, historical and political': his analysis of Richard's language demonstrates a breakdown of the eloquence usually attributed to him, into what are seen as outbursts of absurd rhetoric from 3.2 onwards, which prompts a radical reassessment of Richard's verse in relation to his psychological state.

Holinshed portrays Richard as a wasteful, ambitious man who indulged in luxury and bodily pleasures, but Shakespeare's play introduces us to a king who indulges primarily in the luxury of eloquent words from the beginning of the dispute between Bullingbrook and Mowbray, which also has its farcical moments. Although Mowbray scornfully rejects what he calls 'a woman's war' of words (1.1.48), Richard refuses to allow action, so words are the first weapons in the duel and an audience has to gauge the strength of their verbal blows from the poetry they speak. Bullingbrook lapses into partial rhyme as he turns to address his opponent (lines 35–6), and into full-blown couplets as his temper mounts and his repeated accusation of 'traitor' leads to a plea to Richard to authorise the settlement of the matter through battle. Couplets for Bullingbrook, here, show passion breaking through control. When Mowbray replies he is also calm initially and speaks in blank verse, but a similar partial rhyme appears at lines 60–1 – when he spits at Bullingbrook and calls him 'a slanderous coward and a villain' – though he quickly recovers himself to protest his own innocence. A full couplet at lines 82–3 is used to emphasise this: 'And when I mount, alive may I not light / If I be traitor or unjustly fight.' It is not until the scene's eighty-fourth line that Richard demands to know exactly what Bullingbrook's accusation is. This suggests that not only is he happy to indulge in words himself, but that he allows them to do the same to waste time for a purpose. When Bullingbrook eventually voices his main charge – that Mowbray plotted and carried out the murder of Gloucester – an audience may suspect a game of 'call-my-bluff' between him and his sovereign. Having brought it out into the open, he closes his cry for 'justice and rough chastisement' with a closing couplet at 107–8: 'And by the glorious worth of my descent, / This arm shall do it, or this life be spent', in which he counters Mowbray's previous rhymed lines (82–3) and his mounting (of a horse to engage in 'knightly trial' to defend his honour) with his own 'descent' from the royal blood of Edward III which cries out for him to 'do it', i.e. revenge his uncle's death.

In the middle of Mowbray's answer to Bullingbrook's charges, concerning Gloucester he insists: 'I slew him not, but to my own disgrace / Neglected my sworn duty in that case' (1.1.133–4). Dangerous words: the couplet emphasises an important ambiguity and indicates the king's involvement in the murder. From the end of Mowbray's speech to the end of the scene, couplets dominate in every character's lines. They begin as an indicator of control in Richard, signal strong passion in both Bullingbrook and Mowbray, draw attention to the existence of a subtext concerning a royal murder, and finally show Richard struggling to remain in command but, at the end of the first scene, already being forced to compromise.

The nature of the verse in *Richard II* is not aligned uniformly with seriousness or levity in its content, nor is it allocated to characters according to their social station. In 5.1 Richard parts movingly from his queen with a stichomythic exchange of rhyme, while in 5.3 Bullingbrook, now king, is drawn into exchanges of increasingly comic couplets with York and his duchess.[12] Blank verse is equally versatile: gardener, servant, and groom speak varieties of it – the former politically symbolic, the latter clumsily banal – and in between is Gaunt's most famous speech, packed with *sententiae* and rhetorical devices (2.1.31–68), and Richard's moving soliloquy at 5.5.1–66 that has helped his reputation as actor–king to grow to that of poet.

Often cut from performances, 5.3 is not the isolated comic instance we are sometimes led to suppose. However much our readings of the whole text may lead us to stress its serious nature, Halverson has a point concerning the way that performances, which add gesture and visual display to verbal language, continue to find humour to exploit. This can be bitter or uneasy, and is often created by allowing an absurd perspective to be revealed at unlikely moments. Even at the dramatic climax in 4.1, at the moment one king surrenders his rule to another, in performance the protagonists are often unsettlingly close to staging 'a comic tug-of-war with the crown'.[13]

Beyond words: the play in performance

Richard II is a play which generates questions. Trying to find answers makes it a challenging text in performance and may explain its continued popularity in the theatre. Textual instability can be a positive force on the stage as each director cuts, interprets, and shapes the material anew. In the last thirty years *Richard II* has inspired a number of controversial productions which have polarised audiences. John Barton's 1973 RSC production, heavily influenced by Ernst Kantorowicz's *The King's Two Bodies*, not only emphasised the enforced division of public and private selves within the king, but also stressed a tragic affinity between Bullingbrook and Richard through Richard Pasco and Ian Richardson alternating the protagonist's roles at each performance.[14] In 1995, Deborah Warner cast Fiona Shaw as Richard opposite David Threlfall's Bullingbrook at the National Theatre. Finding his queen's affectionate attentions tedious, Shaw's king was in love with his cousin, provoking an emotionally heightened playing out of the shifts in the balance of power.[15]

In March 2000, when two new performances of Richard II opened, the affinities between the protagonists were less to do with their private selves. Sam West played Richard to David Troughton's Bullingbrook for the RSC at The Other Place in Stratford-upon-Avon, while Ralph Fiennes and Linus Roache out-faced each other in the Almeida Theatre Company's production at Gainsborough Studios, near the site of the Theatre, the playhouse for which *Richard II* was written to be enacted by the Lord Chamberlain's Men. Roache's Bullingbrook was in control of his emotions and expressed them for political effect, but Fiennes' Richard succumbed to his need to

Figure 7 Samuel West as Richard II, RSC 2000. Photograph: Donald Cooper.

play to the audience of the moment – a haughty, slightly bored public pose shifting to one of childish recklessness in more private scenes. He was a player king who assumed that centre stage was his by divine right: both men were part of a medieval pageant. Coleridge called this play a 'history of the human mind, when reduced to ease its anguish with words instead of action, and the necessary feeling of weakness which such a state produces'[16] and Steven Pimlott's white box of a set at Stratford immediately took the audience into an internal world, as did this Richard's unexpected opening lines:

> I have been studying how I may compare
> This prison where I live unto the world,
> And for because the world is populous
> And here is not a creature but myself
> I cannot do it. Yet I'll hammer't out.
>
> (5.5.1–5)

Prefacing the start of Act 1 with the beginning of the play's final act was Pimlott's first move in a sequence of inserted rearrangements which placed the focus on states of mind and a many-sided tragedy, rather than the portrayal of medieval history. Later, the same lines were given to Queen Isabel (Catherine Walker), the phrase 'I'll hammer't out', to Bullingbrook in an out-of-text confrontation with Richard, and finally he spoke them in their entirety, creating symmetry and a disturbing coda, after the text's last line.

On a sparsely propertied set, which bridged the modern and medieval worlds, Sam West conveyed a sense of boy-king come of age, a young man who took the crown for granted because he had known it since childhood. He sported an easily removable gold circlet, as if to demonstrate to court and audience that he had reduced the heavy weight of monarchy to something more manageable for everyday use. A rigid, military man, Troughton's Bullingbrook looked foolish when Richard teased him with the ceremonial crown in 4.1.181 ('Here, cousin, seize the crown'), forcing him, eventually, to snatch it clumsily and become an uneasy possessor from that moment. This was not the lightweight diadem Richard had worn up to that point, but a large, jewel-encrusted crown representing the full responsibility of monarchy. It was a painful fit, far heavier than Bullingbrook appeared to have expected, and looked silly atop his military uniform – yet he felt the need to wear it.

In Jonathan Kent's Almeida production, traditional costumes, a turfed stage, and a sinisterly cracked old wall, evoked a chilly medieval world, complete with choral chanting. Yet, possibly because grass was always underfoot, the performance focused on the earth very little though, symbolically, this is one of the play's most powerful images. In Pimlott's set (designed by Sue Willmington) a grave-sized heap of earth occupied a prominent position stage-right throughout the play. The Duchess of Gloucester lay grieving over it in 1.2; Bullingbrook took a handful of it with him into exile and came back to return it to the mound. Richard ran his fingers through the earth, passed it through his diadem, and fell down to embrace it on his return from Ireland. It became a garden in 3.4 in which the gardener planted flowers, which the queen tore up and left lying across it like a grave bouquet. Richard deconsecrated himself over it, leaving a white rose for his sceptre, a garland for his crown, and covered all with the flag of St George. In the later, formal deposition scene, it supported both throne and crown. Mimicking this plot of earth, stage-left, was a coffin-shaped wooden box which held the weapons for the duel, represented the looking glass, became an upright coffin-cum-torture chamber for Richard in prison, then his coffin, and finally both throne and crown were mounted on it as Bullingbrook took possession of them.

Of the two productions, Kent's was initially more visually striking, but ultimately less symbolic and thought-provoking. It helped its audience to come closer to the play's historical context, but did not challenge an audience's preconceptions. Partly because of Fiennes' stage presence, and partly because of the nature of the set, costumes, props, and elaborate ceremonial entrances, this became a wide-screen theatre in a vast warehouse which had once been Hitchcock's film studio. We are used to seeing *Richard II* as ceremonial in language and stage presence, but Pimlott forced his audience to look beneath the layers of ceremony and discover something less attractive. Like Barton before him, Pimlott expected an audience to need help in interpreting the ideas behind the text and drew attention to an additional voice in the drama – that of the director and production team. Barton chose to give verbal images concrete expression on stage – a progression of hobby horses, from brightly coloured ceremonial mounts to a crude wooden image of Barbary taken to Richard's prison – a snowman, a bowl of earth, and a skull. In Pimlott's production both verbal images and named props were transformed: instead of traditional spears (1.3.119) Bullingbrook and Mowbray were presented with axes to fight their duel. This might have been seen as a tactical decision of Richard's to shock them into reconciliation but was, instead, purely the product of a discussion between actors and director to find a way of thrusting the audience into an awareness of the brutality behind medieval chivalric ceremony. Though not specified in the text – historically, as tournaments became tame entertainment, knights also fought in less formal feats of arms – 'with dagger and axe as well as lance and sword'.[17] The directorial voice would have sounded more clearly had a former suggestion to substitute chain-saws been taken up![18] This particular moment is also a reminder that, in the theatre, a prior knowledge of the text can be a disadvantage. For full dramatic effect a director needs to assume that an audience does not expect Richard to halt the proceedings. Some knowledge we need, some we are better without. How much did Shakespeare expect his audience to have?

Historical and creative contexts

In the historical story told by the eight plays, which comprise Shakespeare's two tetralogies, he began towards the end. *Richard II*, focusing on the last two years of the king's twenty-two-year reign (1398–9), chronologically gives us the beginning of the whole story. It is the play in which the seedlings of disruption, that later grow into the Wars of the Roses, first take root. In the Epilogue to *Henry V* (1599), the Chorus' words tell us that Shakespeare has filled the final gap in the cycle with that play. He began his apprentice-ship with *Henry VI* (*c*.1589–92), and dramatised the establishment of the Tudor dynasty as the end of the chronological sequence, as early as 1593. He did not cast a Tudor as the ultimate hero; instead, he gave the role to a Plantagenet. The 'star of England' who 'most greatly lived' is identified by the Chorus, as Henry V, the warrior king who united England and won France, achieving 'the world's best garden', which he passed on to be lost after his death. *Henry V* is the climax of all eight plays. The Chorus' speech, with its references to the playwright's task of 'confining mighty men' in 'little room' and 'small time', with its allusion to a king who is England's greatest star, achieving 'the world's best garden', helps us to understand some of the main constituents of *Richard II*. They are at its heart, reworked and reassessed – most significantly, the image of the garden.

For his Epilogue to *Henry V*, Shakespeare selected from and rearranged the Duke of Burgundy's earlier words in 5.2.(31–7). Later in that speech Burgundy laments that, because of an absence of peace, 'all [France's] husbandry doth lie on heaps, / Corrupting in it own fertility' (39–40); instead of producing wine to cheer, France's vines die through lack of pruning, her hedges grow wildly, her land lies uncultivated, nothing grows but weeds – and the degeneration of the land is matched by that of the people (38–62). A solution follows when, extending the analogy of the garden, the King of France gives Henry his daughter in marriage, instructing him to raise 'Issue to me' from 'her blood' and 'Plant neighbourhood and Christian-like accord' in the 'sweet bosoms' of both their countries (311–18). The tetralogy ends when fertility and peace are associated with an ordered garden, which exists on both sides of the channel. It begins in *Richard II* with John of Gaunt's famous impassioned lament for the England he remembers as a second paradise:

> This royal throne of kings, this sceptred isle,
> This earth of majesty, this seat of Mars,
> This other Eden, demi-paradise.
>
> (2.1.40–2)

Gaunt recalls a national garden, which is a natural fortress and home to Mars, god of war. It is: 'This precious stone set in the silver sea' (46), 'This land of such dear souls, this dear, dear land' (57). He describes the country itself as 'This nurse, this teeming womb of royal kings' (51), but in *Henry V* it is Peace who is France's 'Dear nurse of arts, plenties and joyful births' (5.2.35) according to the Duke of Burgundy. In Gaunt's idealistic vision his 'other Eden' is founded on English military strength and valour, particularly in the Crusades, and he feels it keenly

> That England that was wont to conquer others
> Hath made a shameful conquest of itself.
>
> (2.1.65–6)

Graham Holderness argues that Christian kingship was united with chivalry in the image of the Crusade and that Gaunt is looking back to a time before there was conflict between the king and his lords who, at the beginning of the play, use the ancient chivalric code to challenge his power over them.[19] This counters the view, in older criticism such as that of E. M. W. Tillyard,[20] that the monarchy was identified with chivalric ritual and feudalism, and it is borne out by Nigel Saul's study of Richard II and chivalric kingship.[21] Historically, Richard II is recorded as entering the lists only once and, as tournaments were a means of integrating monarch and noble subjects (because in a joust they met as equals), this has a bearing on the play. The language of chivalry stressed equality and brotherhood. The historical Richard, like Shakespeare's character, avoided combat, preferring to observe rather than take part. Yet his nobles supported chivalric honour and chose to battle rather than to talk, as the throwing down of gauges demonstrates to an extreme in 4.1. Bullingbrook sympathised: Richard did not. In his reign, peace was seen as an opportunity for the king to squander time and money on dishonourable activities:

> NORTHUMBERLAND Wars hath not wasted it, for warred he hath not,
> But basely yielded upon compromise
> That which his ancestors achieved with blows.
> More hath he spent in peace than they in wars. (2.1.252–5)

The Crusades represented meritorious warfare, seemingly justified by religious motivation, and the contrast between the positive peace sought by
a defeated France and Gaunt's view of England in which peace signals dishonour, shows the shift that takes place from the first to the last play in the
tetralogy. Gaunt looks back to the days of Edward III and beyond him to
the best known Crusader of all, Richard the Lionheart. But in *Richard II*,
as in the plays which follow, this legacy becomes an ironic one. Richard,
at his deposition, toys with the substitution of sceptre for a holy pilgrim or
'palmer's' staff,²² yet the only pilgrimage on which he embarks is a personal
and metaphorical one at his death. At the end of the play, after Richard's
murder, Bullingbrook identifies with Pilate when he expresses his resolution
to journey to the Holy Land to 'wash this blood off from my guilty hand'
(5.6.50) but, throughout both parts of *Henry IV* the insurgency his own
actions inspired prevents him from achieving his ambition, and he dies in
the Jerusalem Chamber at Whitehall, mocked by his failure.

Richard II is, in many ways, a play about failure – balanced by *Henry V*,
a drama of success. Gaunt, transformed by Shakespeare into a sympathetic,
patriotic, prophet, gives the play two of its major symbolic structural frames –
the Crusade, based on chivalric honour, representing unity between king and
subject, and the garden paradise – both are evoked as lost glories. Gaunt is a
sympathetic figure in the play, not just because he is old, grieving, and finally,
dying, but also because he has the greater good of the country at heart and
dares to speak out at the last, risking a traitor's death, for Richard's irritation
with his uncle takes him as far as:

> Wert thou not brother to great Edward's son
> This tongue that runs so roundly in thy head
> Should run thy head from thy unreverent shoulders.
>
> (2.1.121–3)

In Gaunt's rejoinder he accuses Richard of having already murdered one of
his father's brothers, Woodstock, and scorns being made an exception:

> Join with the present sickness that I have
> And thy unkindness be like crooked age
> To crop at once a too long withered flower.
>
> (2.1.132–4)

The garden in which he is now a 'too long withered flower' is that planted
by Gaunt's father, Edward III, handed on to his son, Edward, the Black
Prince, and is now in the hands of his son, Richard (his queen's 'fair rose'
5.1.8), who became king as a child but, despite two marriages, is childless.
Elizabethan audiences and readers would know that, although he dies in

despair in the play, it was Gaunt who, through his first marriage to Blanche of Lancaster, produced Bullingbrook, later Henry IV, from whom Henry V and VI descended – and, through his third marriage to Catherine Swynford, was the great-grandfather of Margaret Beaufort, wife to Edmund Tudor, and mother of Henry VII.

Gaunt dies as a grieving father, denied 'The pleasure that some fathers feed upon . . . I mean my children's looks' (2.1.79–80) and it is Richard who has caused this by exiling his son to safeguard his own position. Gaunt grieves for the barren garden he believes England has become, not only through the exile of Bullingbrook, but also because of Richard's debasement of land ownership by seizing it for his own use – and his selling the right to tax to those whose behaviour he then had no means of controlling. Gaunt's words evoke the fertile garden of a second Eden, only to show how it has been transformed into a barren, leased-out land that has become Richard's deathbed (line 95). Earlier, speaking of his own death, Gaunt called the grave a 'hollow womb' that 'inherits naught but bones' (2.1.83) – an expression that would have been keenly felt by the ageing, childless Elizabeth at an unstable time in her reign.

The historical Richard married his second queen when she was seven years old: she was eleven at the time of the play. Yet, like Samuel Daniel, Shakespeare gave her the voice of an adult woman. Stanza 97 of Daniel's poem chimes with Shakespeare's focus on the lack of actual children. When his queen visited Richard in his confinement, they were both 'big with sorrow, and both great with woe / In labour with what was not to be borne.' Daniel's stanza concludes:

> This mighty burthen wherewithal they go
> Dies undelivered, perishes unborn;
> Sorrow makes silence her best orator
> Where words may make it less not show it more.[23]

In 2.2.65, auguring Richard's later quip that Bullingbrook is old enough to be his heir (3.3.204), the queen tells Green that Bullingbrook is her sorrow's 'dismal heir', born from her soul out of her grief: she is a 'gasping new-delivered mother' of woe. At the beginning of 5.5 Richard proposes that his female brain and his male soul will 'beget' discontented thoughts to people his empty prison world until he is finally 'eased / with being nothing' (40–1). They give birth only in metaphor – and to their own destructive forces. Yet *Richard II* is also about the positive creative recycling of words and the generation of new dramatic language which both reaches back to Shakespeare's earlier works and anticipates future plays. The works (apart from other histories) most likely to be closest to the composition time of *Richard II* are

Romeo and Juliet, *A Midsummer Night's Dream*, and some of the *Sonnets*. Like *Romeo and Juliet*, but in very different ways, *Richard II* experiments with tragedy. The word games and lyrical poetry of these works also have striking counterparts in the play, but it is an amalgamation of creative interplay with his own works and with those of Christopher Marlowe that is most intriguing.

Both Charles R. Forker and Meredith Skura[24] have recently reassessed the mutual influence of Marlowe and Shakespeare evident in the play. Richard's lines in the mirror scene (4.1.275–319) famously contain an echo of Faustus' words to Helen of Troy in Marlowe's *Doctor Faustus*. This is a Helen conjured by Mephostophiles, rather than the woman herself – a deceptive image which is strangely in tune with Richard's perception of his own face in the glass. Forker suggests that Richard's next speech is related to the Marlowe play most often associated with *Richard II* – *Edward II*, specifically Edward's lines: 'But what are kings when regiment is gone / But perfect shadows in a sunshine day?' Where the associations begin and end is harder to judge than he implies, as this speech of Edward's also relates to Richard's musings on his private cares and griefs in 4.1.181–8, 190–8, and the strongest association with the 'perfect shadow in a sunshine day' would seem to be, not 4.1.293, but 4.1.219–20, when Richard declares bitterly: 'God save King Henry, unkinged Richard says, / And send him many years of sunshine days.' Exploring the nature of the mutations these images undergo helps to differentiate between the two kings. Forker also traces the inspiration for Marlowe's speech back to an earlier play by Shakespeare – *3 Henry VI*.

In *3 Henry VI* 4.3, when Edward IV tells Warwick that he will always be king in his own mind, despite his deposition, Warwick replies, as he removes the crown, 'Then, for his mind, be Edward England's king, / But Henry now shall wear the English crown / And be true king indeed: thou but the shadow' (48–50). In reworking this idea in *Richard II*, Shakespeare may (not for the first time)[25] have looked back to his own *3 Henry VI* – or, more likely, since the influence of *Edward II* is apparent in *Romeo and Juliet* as well as in his histories – he may have done so with an awareness of what Marlowe had already created out of the image. Shakespeare's borrowing from his own earlier work is done through the lens of its partial transformation, in the meantime, by Marlowe.

Richard II also anticipates future plays. The symbolic gardeners of 3.4 are transformed into the equally unlikely fisherman with political opinions in 2.1 of *Pericles* – but, most notably, there are strong links between *Richard II* and another tragedy of a king swayed by flatterers, who talks himself into an abdication, who has a Fool rather than having to play the part for himself as Richard does, whose kingdom is driven into civil war, and who dies after a brave fight in prison. More nobly than Richard, Lear kills Cordelia's murderer; he is not struggling for his own life. When he requests a looking glass it is to see whether she is alive, not narcissistically to examine his own face for signs of change. Lear's is the greater tragedy because his self-knowledge is more completely and more painfully achieved, yet there is evidence to suggest that, partly through his apparent interest in the anonymous tragicomedy, *King Leir* (published in 1605, but likely to have been enacted at the Rose in April 1594 and earlier), Shakespeare was moving towards its creation from the time he was writing his first histories. Like King Lear, Richard II sets historical chronicle against personal tragedy, but against a subtext of irresolution and future disharmony. In 5.5 of *Richard II* 'sweet music' is sour and maddens; it does not speak the language of restoration and reconciliation as it does at the end of *Lear*. Even at his end, to Richard, love is 'a strange brooch in this all-hating world' – an optional adornment: to Lear it is something worth dying for. Above all, *Richard II*, a play about the power, danger, and ultimately, the inadequacy of the word, marks a significant movement towards *King Lear*, the play in which Shakespeare most effectively dramatises the strength of silence.[26]

NOTES

1 Dryden 1912, p. 143.
2 Brown 1973, pp. 93–4.
3 Donawerth 1984, p. 141.
4 *OED* bulling vbl. sb. 3 and 4.
5 Liebler 1992, p. 236.
6 See Hamilton 1983.
7 See Clare 1990, pp. 47–51 and Clegg 1997.
8 Nichols 1823, III, 552.
9 Albright 1927, p. 695; see also Healy 1998, pp. 17–30.
10 See Hattaway in this volume, pp. 1–2.
11 Halverson 1994, p. 357.
12 In *The True Chronicle Historie of King Leir* (Anon), lines 2315–55 (Bullough 1957–73, VII, 393–4) are comparable in the use of couplets and repetitious kneeling and rising, though the reconciliation is not comic as in *Richard II*, 5.3; see Pearson 1982.
13 Halverson 1994, p. 357.
14 See Barton *et al.* 1990, pp. 19–56.
15 The production (with Richard Bremmer replacing Threlfall) was later filmed for BBC2 (broadcast 22 March 1997); see Rutter 1997.
16 Coleridge 1930, II, 232.
17 Saul 1999, p. 11.
18 From a conversation with David Troughton at the Shakespeare Institute, Stratford-upon-Avon, 4 August 2000.
19 Holderness 1981.

20 Tillyard 1944.
21 Saul 1999.
22 See *2H6*, 5.1.96–8.
23 Samuel Daniel, *The First Fowre Bookes of the Civile Wars Between the Two Houses of Lancaster and Yorke*, in Bullough 1957–73, III, 452.
24 Forker 1996 and Skura 1997.
25 See note 22.
26 Further to the significance of absence, 'Nothing' is a pregnant word in both plays. Both Isabel in *R2* (2.2.34–40) and Cordelia in *Lear* demonstrate how wrong Lear's phrase, 'Nothing will come of nothing' (1.1.90), could be.

10

JAMES C. BULMAN

Henry IV, Parts 1 and 2

i

The two parts of *Henry IV* dramatise Prince Hal's coming of age amidst the political unrest following his father's usurpation of the throne of Richard II. The consequences of that usurpation weigh heavily upon King Henry: civil broils prolonged by those lords who helped him to the crown and now feel abandoned by him; fear of a rival claimant, Edmund Mortimer, whom Richard designated his heir; and an acute awareness that by killing Richard, he has violated – and made impossible to assume for himself – the divine right of kings. Such obstacles help to explain why his son Hal chooses to idle away his time in a tavern rather than at court. But Hal must learn to surmount them if he is to succeed his father, and in the royal narrative of *Henry IV*, which chronicles his progress from the taverns of Eastcheap to his coronation at Westminster, he does so: he defeats the rebels, transforms himself from wastrel to responsible heir, and strives to prove that linear succession can serve as a legitimate alternative to divine right.[1] In dramatising his success, the two *Henry IV* plays offer a comic view of fifteenth-century history. Yet they also address political and social issues pertinent to Elizabethan England, and their popularity for Shakespeare's audiences no doubt resulted in part from their use of the past to comment on the present.

Part 1 (1596–7), with its focus on a centralised monarchy attempting to bind together diverse geographical territories, languages, and cultures, dramatises the wresting of a nation–state from the feudal grip of powerfully independent warlords, particularly some from the North, who had been emboldened to challenge the authority of the king.[2] The depiction of Henry IV as an early modern monarch is, of course, anachronistic, for the emergence of England as a nation–state was a sixteenth-century phenomenon forged by Henry VIII and crowned by Elizabeth's skill at manipulating her opponents and consolidating power. Indeed, one model for the rebellion in *1 Henry IV* may have been an attempt by Northern Catholic lords in 1569 to advance the cause of Mary, Queen of Scots against Elizabeth – an uprising instigated by descendants of the Northumberland Percies who continued to prize feudal loyalties over fealty to a single monarch.[3] In *1 Henry IV*, Shakespeare traces the origins of centralised government to the strategies of a wily ruler and his son who, like Elizabeth, was aware of the importance of public self-fashioning. Hal's justification of his idleness and promise of reformation during his first soliloquy broadcast his Tudor spirit of calculation: 'So when this loose behaviour I throw off, / And pay the debt I never promised', he strategizes, 'My reformation, glitt'ring o'er my fault, / Shall show more goodly, and attract more eyes / Than that which hath no foil to set it off' (1.2.168–75).

In opposition to such calculation, the figure of Hotspur is pivotal. Often in performance a romantic figure, impulsive and valiant, young Henry Percy embodies all that is glorious about feudal chivalry – its code of honour, its passion for heroic achievement in arms, its emphasis on loyalty to self and family over state – which had to be tamed in the process of centralising authority. Nostalgia for chivalric ideals led paradoxically to a cult of medievalism in Elizabeth's court, though the chivalry practised there was more political and symbolic than real: tournaments and pageants appropriated only the *forms* of a bygone culture, not its ethos, and courtiers were cast as medieval knights who worshipped their queen as a lady of romance and fought on her behalf.[4] For Elizabethans, Hotspur's zealous adherence to individual will was an attractive anachronism. He exercises that will by refusing to hand over his prisoners to King Henry, knowing that unless he holds a bargaining chip, Henry will never ransom Mortimer from the Welsh. When pressed, however, Hotspur tells Henry that the reason he denied him the prisoners is that he was maddened by the effete hauteur of Henry's envoy, who came 'perfumed like a milliner', took snuff from a pouncet box, and, 'as the soldiers bore dead bodies by ... called them untaught knaves, unmannerly, / To bring a slovenly unhandsome corpse / Betwixt the wind and his nobility' (1.3.35–44). Hotspur's peevish account illustrates what makes him so delightfully blunt a character; yet it also impugns courtly values and, by extension, Henry himself.

More dangerous to Henry is Hotspur's angry assertion of feudal rights against the law of the land. Disregarding allegiance to anyone but himself, he rants in a language at once heroic and comically egotistical, setting himself up against a monarch whom he regards not as the sun – a traditional image of kingship – but as the moon, a wan reflection of the legitimate king whom Henry deposed. 'By heaven, methinks it were an easy leap / To pluck bright honour from the pale-faced moon', he vaunts, 'So he that doth redeem her thence might wear / Without corrival all her dignities' (199–200, 204–5).

The nakedness of his ambition is palpable. Through him, Shakespeare voices a feudalism that still threatened the stability of Elizabeth's reign; for even within her court there were dissidents such as the Earl of Essex and his circle who embraced personal honour and lineage above nationalism, valued bravery and military prowess for its own sake, and asserted political autonomy.[5] Much as Elizabeth favoured Essex, King Henry envies Hotspur and wishes that his own son were imbued with such chivalric ambition; yet he knows that the intrinsic honour of such a warrior, valuable if circumscribed by the court, will be dangerous if channelled by those who wish to subvert Henry's rule. Indeed, Northumberland and Westmoreland, politicians as astute as Henry himself, also know Hotspur's worth and use him as their chief weapon of war; but fearing his irascible nature, they dismiss him from any discussion of policy. Indeed, when Hotspur is left to his own devices at the Welsh court, he does nearly irreparable damage to the rebel cause by insulting Owen Glendower.

Prince Hal must defeat Hotspur if he is to inherit a secure kingship from his father. Shakespeare alters his sources to make Hal and Hotspur the same age – the historic Hotspur was closer to the age of Henry – so that their eventual confrontation will be dramatically more compelling. But Hal's greater challenge will be to spurn those tavern companions with whom he has chosen to revel; for Shakespeare devoted his most creative energy to dramatising the temptations of the tavern world, and Hal, like audiences everywhere, understandably is drawn more to that world than he is to the court. Taverns were upscale alehouses visited by anyone who wished to drink liberally and publicly: here, the criminal underworld could hobnob with the nobility, and it is not surprising that Hal, seeking freedom from the restraints of Westminster, joined a 'family of vagrancy' in a tavern often identified as the Boar's Head.[6] This alternative to the court – a place of festivity and holiday release – is presided over by Jack Falstaff, the most seductive character Shakespeare ever drew. Fat, old, dissipated, and given to lying, Falstaff is a knight – *Sir John* – who, like many on the fringes of Elizabeth's court, is impecunious and preys on others. He embodies the spirit of hedonism, and his days are numbered by pleasures of the flesh, as Hal attests: 'Unless hours were cups of sack, and minutes capons, and clocks the tongues of bawds ... I see no reason why thou shouldst be so superfluous to demand the time of the day' (1.2.5–9).

Originally Falstaff was called Sir John Oldcastle, the name of a Lollard leader who was martyred for his Protestant beliefs during the reign of Henry V and who figured as one of Prince Hal's companions in Shakespeare's source play, *The Famous Victories of Henry the Fifth*. Censorship probably forced Shakespeare to change the name: a descendant of Oldcastle's widow was

Figure 8   Richard Burton as Hal holding the crown above his sleeping father, RSC, 1951.
Photograph: Angus McBean. (See *2H4*, 4.2.)

Lord Chamberlain when the two parts of *Henry IV* were licensed for performance by the Master of the Revels, who served under him; and any implied
defamation of his ancestor would have been sufficient cause to scuttle the use
of his name. Vestiges of Oldcastle, however, remain in the speech headings
of quarto editions, in Hal's reference to Falstaff as 'my old lad of the castle'
(1.2.34), and in the Epilogue to *Part 2*, which assures us that 'Oldcastle
died martyr, and this is not the man' (24–5).[7] What Shakespeare may have
had in mind by naming his fat knight after a proto-puritan martyr is un-
clear, apart from the ironies apparent in Falstaff's riotous living and in his
occasional uttering of a puritan oath for comic effect; but recent critical

controversy surrounding the Oxford editors' decision to revert to 'Oldcastle' has been sufficient to revive interest in Falstaff's historical reception and to encourage speculation that, in him, Shakespeare contributed to the political satire against puritans 'as grotesque individuals living in carnivalesque communities'.[3] Other sources for Falstaff have been less hotly contested. The figure of the *miles gloriosus* (braggart knight) from Roman comedy probably served as a model for Falstaff's increasingly inflated lies about his exploits at Gad's Hill; the Vice of the medieval Morality plays underlies his gregarious promotion of lewd behaviours in the Prince; and the tradition of electing a Lord of Misrule to displace legitimate authority during the Christmas revels in London doubtless allowed Shakespeare's audiences to link Falstaff to native holiday customs. None of these sources, however, can account for the larger-than-life comic resourcefulness of a man who, as an Elizabethan clown, has the privilege of addressing the audience directly and offering commentary that often subverts the royal narrative.[9]

Part 1 is a play structured on dramatic oppositions – tavern versus court, mock king versus legitimate king, wayward prince versus chivalric warrior – which frequently are more apparent than real and, in the end, collapse into similitude. If Hotspur is a rival for Hal, then Falstaff represents a kind of surrogate father for him, a rival to the King for paternal authority. That rivalry is established quickly in the first tavern scene, when Falstaff asks whether Hal, when he is king, will metamorphose those who steal purses by night ('thieves of the day's beauty') into something more courtly: 'Diana's foresters, gentlemen of the shade, minions of the moon' (1.2.20–2). The question is crucial; for if Hal promises to legitimate Falstaff as his chief counsellor, he'll be enthroning disorder and riot – something he cannot afford to do – and displacing his royal father. Yet, as a thief, Falstaff is no worse than the man who now occupies the throne; for, as the imagery repeatedly reminds us, the occupant seized the throne through usurpation and thereby stole rights from the divinely anointed monarch, much as the moon steals light from the sun. Falstaff is thus akin to Henry in fashioning for himself a position of power based on theft. Only Hal, who will inherit the kingship through legitimate succession, may have the authority to reclaim some of that light as rightly his.

All this suggests that kingship depends for its authority not on God, but on performance. After the violation of sacramental and inherited kingship by Henry, the office itself has become secular: anyone who performs kingship can lay claim to it. As Machiavelli observed in *The Prince*, and as Elizabethan practice confirmed, political power is secured by theatrical illusion – a populace can best be controlled by dissimulation, image-making, and role-play.[10] In the great tavern scene at 2.4, Hal and Falstaff engage in just this form of

Figure 9   Desmond Barrit as Falstaff, Benjamin Whitrow as Shallow, and Peter Copley as Silence in Michael Attenborough's production of *2 Henry IV*, RSC 2000. Photograph: Malcolm Davis.

theatre. Hal has been summoned to his father to account for his prodigality, and Falstaff encourages him to practise an answer. The stage is set for a comic enactment of kingship: Hal will play himself before the tavern public, and Falstaff will take the role of father–king, the very substitution to which he has aspired all along. Donning a cushion for a crown, holding a dagger as a sceptre, and using a joint-stool as his throne, he proceeds in wittily self-serving speeches to advise the Prince to trust no one but Falstaff: 'If that man should be lewdly given, he deceiveth me, for, Harry, I see virtue in his looks … Him keep with, the rest banish' (351–5). When Falstaff adopts a more parental tone, however, and chides his son as a 'naughty varlet' (355), the Prince demands that they switch roles: 'Dost thou speak like a king? Do thou stand for me, and I'll play my father' (357–8). The moment is rife with metaphoric riches: playing, standing for, and speaking like a king are theatrical terms which reveal regal imposture. 'Depose me?' Falstaff cries incredulously (359); but as we have seen, deposition is as easy as removing a crown – Henry has demanded Richard's public abdication at Westminster, as if such a show could undo the sacred rites of kingship, and the same ritual is comically reenacted here.

Hal and Falstaff change places, but Falstaff, insisting that kingship owes everything to performance, protests: 'If thou dost it half so gravely, so majestically, both in word and matter, hang me up by the heels for a rabbit-sucker, or a poulter's hare' (359–61). In the role of his father – a rehearsal for kingship – Hal proceeds to disparage Falstaff as a Manningtree ox, a Vice, an Iniquity, a Father Ruffian, a Vanity, and a white-bearded Satan – insults drawn largely from Morality play tradition. Falstaff, playing to the crowd, pleads for himself as a microcosm of humanity – 'Banish plump Jack, and banish all the world' (397–8); and in a line which may be as serious as playful, Hal assures him, 'I do, I will' (399). This of course anticipates the rejection of Falstaff in *Part* 2; but at the moment, it demonstrates Hal's capacity to forsake old allegiances with each new role and harks back to his promise of a glittering – and theatrical – reformation. History plays, simply by representing kingship on the public stage, stripped it of its sacred aura and thereby altered the spectator–subjects' relations to royalty.[11] In this tavern scene, Shakespeare goes even further to expose the workings of royal self-fashioning and to suggest that kingship, once regarded as sacramental, now amounts to no more than good acting.

Hal's tavern rehearsal pays rich dividends when he is reprimanded by his father at court, for he is prepared to defend himself not with denials, but with contrition. As Henry enumerates the follies of Hal's wild youth which chroniclers had made legendary, he betrays a surprising lack of insight into both his son and himself.[12] Drawing an analogy between the situation in Richard's court and his own, he suggests that Hal is behaving much as Richard once did, and that Hotspur, with whom Henry identifies, stands to reap the benefits of Hal's profligacy. Henry appears to have no idea how different his political opportunism is from Hotspur's feudal nobility, nor how different his son is from the 'skipping King' (3.2.60). Indeed, though Henry is ignorant of it, Hal has patterned his behaviour on that of his father, carefully calculating the moment to seize what he never asked for. Henry's account of his strategy for winning popular support in Richard's court bears an ironic resemblance to Hal's promise to garner public acclaim by imitating the sun: 'By being seldom seen, I could not stir / But like a comet I was wondered at', Henry admits; 'And then I stole all courtesy from heaven / And dressed myself in such humility / That I did pluck allegiance from men's hearts' (46–52). The King here provides his son with an object lesson in Machiavellian policy.

Hal, however, is astute enough not to point out his father's misperception. Instead, he vows to reform himself in the mould of Hotspur, adopting the language of chivalric heroism to convince Henry of his sincerity: 'I will redeem all this on Percy's head, / And in the closing of some glorious day / Be bold to tell you that I am your son' (132–4). He invokes images of medieval warfare: he will 'wear a garment all of blood' and 'stain [his] favours in a bloody mask' (135–6); and as his vaunt grows more hyperbolic, culminating in a vow to 'tear the reckoning' from Hotspur's heart, only the vocabulary of the marketplace betrays his true intent – to use this 'reckoning' as a means to achieve political legitimacy: 'Percy is but my *factor*, good my lord, / To *engross up* glorious deeds on my behalf, / And I will call him to so *strict* account / That he shall render every glory up' (147–50, italics mine).[13] Hal does not come by legitimacy through blood or lineage; rather, like new-made gentry in Elizabethan England who bought their coats of arms, he must *earn* it.[14]

Whether or not Hal believes in the chivalric ethos he here espouses, Henry is convinced of his son's loyalty – and that, after all, is the point. Hal's success in fashioning a heroic image for himself is confirmed by Vernon's report that 'I saw young Harry … Rise from the ground like feathered Mercury' (4.1.104–6); and when Worcester comes from the rebel camp to make terms, Hal magnanimously offers to settle the war in a single combat with Hotspur. The King steadfastly affirms his belief in his son – 'And, Prince of Wales, so dare we venture thee' (5.1.101) – yet there is no further mention of Hal's offer, leading one to suspect that this show of chivalry may have been more rhetorical than real. The distrust on both sides, furthermore, leads rebel and royal alike to lie, feign, and counterfeit. Worcester does not credit the King's promise to redress the rebels' grievances, fearing with good cause that Hotspur will be forgiven and the others put to death: thus he lies when he returns to camp and reports that the King has bid them do battle. For his part, in an attempt to confuse the enemy and to better protect his royal person, 'the King hath many marching in his coats' (5.3.25) – a strategy common in Elizabethan warfare. Nothing dramatises more visibly that the ethos of medieval warfare is gone for good than this royal subterfuge. To put a pragmatic gloss on the new spirit of self-interest, Shakespeare allows Falstaff to reduce honour to its essentials: 'What is honour? A word … Who hath it? He that died a' Wednesday' (5.1.132–4). Falstaff's dissident observation casts chivalry as a 'sentimental extravagance' in which the nobility may indulge but which common soldiers such as his own 'commodity of warm slaves' (4.2.16) cannot afford.[15]

At the battle of Shrewsbury, Shakespeare holds chivalry and pragmatism in a fine tension. When Hal meets Hotspur for a single fight which resembles the ritualised combat of neochivalric Elizabethan tournaments, he outdoes him in prowess, winning those 'proud titles' which have been the source of Hotspur's honour (5.4.78). In so doing, Hal symbolically appropriates 'honour' for a new nationalism: chivalry is thus contained within a political context that eschews heroic individualism. When Hal turns from Hotspur's corpse, however, he finds Falstaff lying as if dead. In a stage allegory reminiscent of Morality plays, Hal, a princely Everyman, stands between the paragon of chivalric virtue he has just overcome and the proponent of self-interest, deception and pragmatism which he also has shown himself adept at practising. He appears ready to fulfil his destiny – and please his father – by claiming victory over Hotspurious feudalism and Falstavian excess together. Yet Falstaff, in the most daring counterfeit of all, rises from the ground where he has feigned death, stabs Hotspur in the groin, and carries him off as if the prize were his. Hal faces a dilemma: whether to insist on the honour rightly his and expose Falstaff as a liar, or to protect Falstaff to his own detriment. With scant hesitation, he complies with Falstaff's deception: '[I]f a lie may do thee grace, / I'll gild it with the happiest terms I have' (5.4.148–9). The play thus achieves a morally complex and tentative resolution. On the one hand, Hal's defeat of Hotspur signals his assumption of royal responsibility and ensures reconciliation with his father; on the other, his protection of Falstaff intimates his potential for regression and a profound ambivalence about the role he is destined to play. Formally, the play fulfils our expectations of Hal's reformation; morally, it remains on the fence.

ii

The inclusion of so much official history in *Part 1* means that very little of the royal narrative is left for *Part 2* (1597–8). The only significant events left to be dramatised are the King's death and Hal's accession. The rest of the play occupies itself with politically lesser stuff – the prelates' rebellion – which is meant to follow hard on the rebels' defeat at Shrewsbury:[16] historically of no great importance, it acts as filler before the conclusion of the royal *Bildungsroman* in Acts 4 and 5. This imbalance of historical matter between the two parts of *Henry IV* raises the question of whether they were originally planned as one. Did Shakespeare plot out one long history play along the lines of his source, *Famous Victories,* but find himself with too much material and therefore divide the play in two? Did Falstaff achieve such huge proportions during composition that Shakespeare chose to curtail the royal narrative in *Part 1* in order to allow his comic powers free rein? And if so, did he, at the time, plan *Part 2* as a sequel or simply proceed with *Part 1* as an autonomous work – a play which easily stands alone – and begin work on *Part 2* only when the popularity of *Part 1* prompted him to satisfy the public with another Falstaff play?[17]

Whatever the process (and it is impossible to discover), if one looks at *Part 2* largely as an extension of the royal narrative of *Part 1*, it is a disappointment. Structurally it echoes the earlier play: tavern scenes are juxtaposed with scenes of political rebellion, Falstaff is tricked by Hal and Poins in a 'big' tavern scene, the royal father and son have a scene of confrontation and reconciliation, the rebels are defeated, and the Prince acquits himself, redeeming time when men think least he will. Compared in this way, *Part 2* often is disparaged as a pale imitation of its greater first half, lacking in narrative drive, its comedy less exuberant, with Falstaff grown old and cynical, the King sick, and Hal, who appears to have lapsed after his reformation at Shrewsbury, bored as he awaits his father's death. This way of regarding the play, however, ignores its substantially different qualities, for, unlike those sequels that strive to repeat the successful formula of an original (as Marlowe had done in the second part of *Tamburlaine*), *2 Henry IV* has a darker tone and more ambitious aims. It is as much the obverse of *Part 1* as its sequel.[18] Its originality resides in the casual, digressive, almost ramshackle way in which it casts a wide net over England, gathering in social groups whose unwritten histories rival in importance, even supersede, the official history which concludes with Hal's accession.

Shakespeare takes risks in *Part 2*. Most strikingly, he displaces the royal narrative by relegating the King and Prince to the margins for much of the play. Hal's first scene, which doesn't come until 2.2, affords him little to do other than lament his own lapse, and his late arrival at the tavern to trick Falstaff (2.4) is of little consequence. Henry doesn't appear until 3.1; and even then, his scene does not so much advance the plot as establish that he is unwell: 'Uneasy lies the head that wears a crown' (31). This scene, furthermore, was omitted for some unknown reason from the first issue of the Quarto: clearly it was written not of dramatic necessity, but because without it, Henry wouldn't appear until his deathbed scene in Act 4. A king and prince whose political conflicts were at the centre of *Part 1*, therefore, have been marginalised; and for three acts, the political focus is trained on the rebels. There is little faith among them. The allegorical figure of Rumour, in a robe '*painted full of tongues*' (Induction) opens the play by warning that no news should be trusted; and this is borne out in the ensuing scene when Northumberland hears contradictory reports that his son Hotspur has won the field at Shrewsbury or has died there. False expectation among the rebels works its mischief further when the Archbishop miscalculates the size of the opposing forces (1.3) and again when Northumberland is persuaded by his wife and Lady Percy to flee rather than bring reinforcements to the rebel army: 'O fly to Scotland, / Till that the nobles and the armed commons / Have of their puissance made a little taste' (2.3.50–2). There is no pretence to chivalric honour in this camp, none of the nobility embodied in Hotspur: it is a world of reduced heroism. Machiavelli wins the day, too, when Prince John outsmarts the rebels with a ruse at Gaultree Forest. He succeeds because the rebel leaders – particularly the Archbishop, who tries to put a moral gloss on political action – momentarily lower their guard and choose to believe the

Prince's promise that their griefs will be redressed. Once they are tricked into discharging their army, John is free to arrest them for high treason without fear of reprisal. This way of quashing the rebellion is dramatically daring: it denies audiences the thrill of an onstage battle such as Shrewsbury and frustrates their desire to witness individual heroism in a noble cause. The victor is he for whom policy is the chiefest virtue. The Gaultree episode thus offers a view of history as radically contingent and amoral: it is devoid of the chivalric ethos which, albeit compromised, informed the military conflict in *Part 1*.

Shakespeare carefully keeps the King and Hal out of this episode. Although they may be tainted as the beneficiaries of John's policy, they are not its instruments nor its authors: the King has appeared only once before news of Gaultree is brought to him, and the Prince has been wasting his time with Poins. When they meet, however, their interaction is politically and emotionally charged. Hal, attending on his sleeping father, thinks him dead and takes the crown with him into the next chamber. The King, who wakes to find the crown missing, summons Hal to scold him for his impatience. Where, during their confrontation in *Part 1*, Hal was able to redeem himself by appropriating the chivalric diction of Hotspur, here the stakes are higher: the King is on his deathbed, Hal has in his hands the evidence of a patricidal wish, and this will be their final interview. The King's accusations sting: 'Harry the fifth is crowned, up, Vanity, / Down, royal state, all you sage counsellors, hence! / And to the English court assemble now / From every region, apes of idleness!' (4.2.248–51). Hal weeps at the rebuke and with apparently unfeigned emotion seeks to prove his loyalty and love; but as he does so, he recounts a speech which bears little resemblance to what he actually has said just moments earlier. Then, his words to his sleeping father were sober and politically aware: 'My due from thee is this imperial crown / Which, as immediate from thy place and blood, / Derives itself to me' (171–3). Now his remembered apostrophe to the crown is far more histrionic and self-justifying: 'I spake unto the crown as having sense, / And thus upbraided it: 'The care on thee depending / Hath fed upon the body of my father; / Therefore thou best of gold art worst of gold' (286–9). Hal's memory of what he said, which continues for several more lines, amounts to a theatrical fiction intended to exculpate him – the sort of revisionism at which Hal repeatedly proves himself skilled. It is sufficient, however, to win his father's trust. In his dying speech, the King gives Hal a lesson in policy, rehearsing the devious methods by which he came to power and urging him, as a means of diverting rebellion on his accession, 'to busy giddy minds / With foreign quarrels' (341–2), a strategy which Hal, on the evidence of the play's concluding lines, chooses to adopt. The King and his son are more honest with each other in this scene than in its counterpart in *Part 1*, yet they share a sense of political calculation which allows the upshot of their conversation – Hal's determination to keep the crown – to beg the question of legitimacy: 'You won it, wore it, kept it, gave it me: / Then plain and right must my possession be' (348–9). This couplet occludes the sin of regicide that accompanied Henry's occupation of the throne and thus permits Hal to substitute linear succession for divine right.

If Shakespeare's strategy in *Part 2* was to displace the royal narrative by foregrounding an ill-starred rebellion, his most daring gambit was to give Falstaff his own scenes to bustle in, unimpeded by the burden of Hal's protection or the demands of chronicle history. He created for Falstaff a world rich in the quotidian life of Elizabethan subcultures and populated by figures far more imaginatively drawn than any in *Part 1*. Falstaff dominates this world; and since his role is so big, it isn't surprising that *Part 2* has often been called *Falstaff* in performance: in so far as the play has achieved popularity, it is because audiences have paid to see *him*.[19] In his scenes Shakespeare dramatises a social history of the *other* England – its taverns, brothels, and farms – which rivals the official history in importance and surpasses it in the sheer energy and copiousness of its detail.

Falstaff in *Part 2* is – despite the plays' ostensible temporal continuity – an older, more diseased, and more corrupt figure than he was in *Part 1*. He thrives on the reputation for valour falsely won at Shrewsbury and therefore is determined to cut a figure in the world. Indeed, his opening speech wryly acknowledges the reputation he has earned among theatre audiences as well as his contemporaries: 'the brain of this foolish compounded clay-man is not able to invent anything that intends to laughter more than I invent, or is invented on me; I am not only witty in myself, but the cause that wit is in other men' (1.2 4–7). Falstaff's complaints about his gout, his tailor, and his consumptive purse establish key motifs for the official history as well: age, disease, and consumption, both moral and physical, plague the King and Northumberland alike. The thread connecting Falstaff most securely to the royal narrative, however, is his pairing with the Lord Chief Justice, a scrupulously virtuous man who, according to legend, once had Hal jailed for boxing him in the ear. The Lord Chief Justice has summoned Falstaff for the robbery at Gad's Hill, but the honours Falstaff won at Shrewsbury now incline the Lord Chief Justice to drop the charges. In a sense, these two old men offer competing centres of authority for England and for Prince Hal. Perhaps because they both recognise this, the animosity between them is palpable; and though audiences of course know that Hal, when he is king, will embrace the Lord Chief Justice as his chief adviser as surely as he will reject Falstaff, their joy lies in watching Falstaff attempt to outwit him and presumptuously beg him for a thousand pounds to furnish his next expedition.

The figures who frequent the tavern represent Shakespeare's most explicit foray into the material world of Elizabethan 'low' culture. Some who appeared in *Part 1*, such as Mistress Quickly and Bardolph, are more fully fleshed and idiosyncratic in *Part 2* – she in her determination that her neighbours respect her as a gentlewoman and her tavern as a respectable house, he in his caricature as a flaming-nosed alcoholic who serves as Falstaff's lackey. Mistress Quickly's role is significantly different from what it was in the earlier play, more deeply immersed in the social matrix of Elizabethan London. Managing a tavern was one of the few avenues for women of low degree to achieve economic independence and social recognition, and Mistress Quickly is acutely aware of her position.[20] A widow of a certain age, she has lived in hope for the past twenty years that Falstaff would marry her, and thus gentle her condition; and although she attempts to have him arrested for non-payment of his tavern debt – a debt which substitutes for his failure to honour his promise of marriage – her affection for him eventually prompts her, in a comic about-face, to agree to lend him another ten pounds. Her memory of Falstaff's proposal is marked by details of her material surroundings – he was sitting in her 'Dolphin chamber' by a 'sea-coal fire' and swore 'upon a parcel-gilt goblet' (2.1.67–8). The list of goods she must pawn in order to pay for his new wardrobe betokens a culture of getting and spending remarkably Elizabethan in temper: plate and tapestries, glasses for drinking, and German hunting scenes painted in distemper for wall-hangings. Furthermore, Mistress Quickly is given an idiosyncratic way of speaking through which she unwittingly reveals her sexual history with Falstaff and punctures her pretence to respectability. Her account of Falstaff's stabbing her 'most beastly' in her own house illustrates how *double entendres* tell all: he foins so lustfully 'if his weapon be out', she says, that he threatens anyone within reach (10–13): he is thus, in her malapropian terms (which have come to be called Quicklyisms), a 'honeyseed' (homicide), a 'man-queller, and a woman-queller' (39–40). And since her 'case' – a slang term for a vagina – is 'so openly known to the world', she instructs the officers to 'let him be brought to his answer' (22–3). Such bawdy innuendo creates a comic subtext of Falstaff's sexual prowess and her own promiscuity of which she remains blithely unconscious. Her character is both defined and undone by her absurdly original speech.

Other denizens of the tavern are newly created for *Part 2*. Doll Tearsheet, the 'parish heifer' (2.2.120) whose drunken debauchery with Falstaff suggests that Mistress Quickly does indeed run a brothel, operates on the lowest rung of the social ladder. Apparently not jealous of Falstaff's affection for a younger woman, Mistress Quickly brings Doll to him for a last night of merriment before he goes off to war: their salacious banter is all of sexual combat, venereal disease, and the consumption of Bordeaux. They are soon joined by the Ancient Pistol, a scurrilous rogue with whom Doll has had rough dealings and who attempts to brawl with her until Falstaff, in his one act of bravery, intervenes on her behalf. Pistol is a *miles gloriosus* of Jonsonian excesses: the language he uses, scraps and orts from heroic plays of an earlier generation, inflates him with comic bravado and, at the same time, recalls those hyperbolic sentiments which once invoked a world of greatness not unlike that imagined by Hotspur, but which now sound ludicrously out-of-date. 'Shall pack-horses / And hollow pampered jades of Asia, / Which cannot go but thirty mile a day, / Compare with Caesars, and with Cannibals, / And Troyant Greeks?' he rants (2.4.130–4), nonsensically echoing great speeches in *Tamburlaine*, the play whose two-part structure underlies that of *Henry IV*. As a parody of what has happened to English chivalry during an age of political self-interest, Pistol, whose most valiant act is 'tearing a poor whore's ruff in a bawdy-house' (112–13), stands as the *reductio ad absurdum*.

The rich variety of idioms in *Part 2*, whereby socially marginalised characters reveal differences in region, degree, and occupation, dramatises an expansion of the cultural boundaries of nationhood unattempted in Shakespeare's earlier history plays. In *Part 1* Hal, who boasts that he 'can drink with any tinker in his own language' (2.4.15–16), implies that learning the vernacular will be essential if he intends to govern an emerging English nation, though he doesn't show much linguistic virtuosity beyond thieves' cant.[21] In *Part 2*, the importance of a vernacular education is made explicit: 'The prince but studies his companions / Like a strange tongue, wherein, to gain the language, / 'Tis needful that the most immodest word / Be looked upon and learnt' (4.2.68–71).[22] In the distinctive idioms of Hal's companions – Bardolph, Doll, Pistol, Mistress Quickly, and above all, Falstaff – Shakespeare provides alternatives to the official speech of the court; and in keeping with his decision to displace the royal narrative, he moves them from the margins to the centre.

No one handles language with more brio than Falstaff. He is a master of wordplay, equally adept at the bawdy pun in the tavern and the political *bon mot* with the Lord Chief Justice. Where Mistress Quickly's *double entendres* are comic because unconscious, Falstaff's puns amuse because they are so calculatedly self-serving. His quibbles on military service enhance his claim to sexual potency with Doll – 'to come off the breach with his pike bent bravely; and to surgery bravely; to venture upon the charged chambers bravely' (2.4.41–3) – just as his ribald play on Pistol's name ('pizzle' as penis) denigrates the frail virtue of Mistress Quickly: 'Pistol, I charge you with a cup of sack: do you discharge upon mine hostess . . . She is pistol-proof, sir: you shall not hardly offend her' (89–92). Puns, in fact, announce Falstaff's strategy for survival early in the play, when, in cursing his big toe – 'A pox of this gout, or a gout of this pox' (1.2.191) – he vows to turn his diseases to commodity. To work his way around the Lord Chief Justice, he confesses that he suffers from 'the disease of not listening' (96–7) and repeatedly puns about his own girth. When the Chief Justice tells him that he lives 'in great infamy', Falstaff replies, 'He that buckles himself in my belt cannot live in less' (109–10); and here begins a string of puns about wishing his 'waste' (waist) slenderer (111–13), burning as long as a wassail candle whose 'wax' (growth) proves his worth (125–6), and following the prince not as his 'ill angel' (counterfeit gold coin), but as genuine currency, for an 'ill angel is light, but I hope he that looks upon me will take me without weighing' (130–2). Such wordplay disarms the opposition. It demonstrates Falstaff's virtuosity in turning ironic self-deprecation to advantage and colours his rapaciousness with apparently benign humour.

Falstaff manipulates others more cynically when he stops in Gloucestershire at the estate of Robert Shallow to recruit soldiers for the wars.[23] The rural Gloucestershire scenes depict a world unlike any other in Shakespeare, where Silence and Shallow, two country justices, nostalgically recall their days at the Inns of Court fifty years earlier, lament the passing of old friends, and bid Falstaff, who was known to them then as page to Thomas Mowbray, to join them in eating 'last year's pippin of [Shallow's] own graffing' (5.3.2). To this idyllic world Falstaff brings the predatory ethos of an 'old pike' (3.2.267). Where in *Part 1* he admits to having recruited 'slaves as ragged as Lazarus in the painted cloth' (4.2.21–2) because others more ablebodied had 'bought out their services' (28), in *Part 2* Shakespeare *dramatises* that process. Those called for service are yeomen and householders who have no appetite for war. Boasting rustic charactonyms such as Mouldy and Bullcalf, they make cowardly excuses to avoid being 'pricked' – one has 'a whoreson cold' (3.2.151); another a wife who 'will be undone now for one to do her husbandry' (93) – and Falstaff has great fun playing on their names, their occupations, and their excuses.[24] But when the ablest recruits bribe Bardolph to let them go, Falstaff makes do, over Shallow's objection, with a ragtag assembly of wraiths: 'give me the spare men, and spare me the great ones' (220). Falstaff here is guilty of the same corrupt practices that brought shame to Elizabethan commanders whose abuses were catalogued in military conduct books. Although levying men for service had become so difficult by the late sixteenth century that soldiers were recruited from prisons or by means of the press-gang, corruption among recruiters was never condoned, and Falstaff's behaviour, however comic, is morally censurable.[25]

The rural domain of Silence and Shallow is therefore not an idealised garden, but a fallen world. Despite Shakespeare's characteristically generous view of the human condition – a generosity which permits the women's tailor Feeble to step forward as the one recruit willing to give his life for his country, or Shallow, even as he contemplates death, to reveal an undimmed interest in the price of bullocks at Stamford fair – he nevertheless uses Falstaff to cast a cold eye on the vanity of human wishes. The two justices, far from embodying civic virtue, are vain and self-deluding: when Shallow reminisces about his wild carousing and sexual exploits at the Inns of Court, Falstaff exposes the folly of memory – 'Lord, how subject we old men are to this vice of lying!' (246) – and etches for the audience an indelible portrait of a fool. Furthermore, when Falstaff returns from Gaultree to bilk Shallow of a thousand pounds, one needn't view Shallow as an innocent victim, for with that money he hopes to buy favour at court when Falstaff's minion comes to power. His aspirations are as vainglorious as Falstaff's; his bribery as bald. Even Shallow's man Davy betrays a corrupt sense of justice when he asks Shallow decide a lawsuit in favour of a friend: 'if I cannot once or twice in a quarter bear out a knave against an honest man, I have little credit with your worship' (5.1.38–40). The dishonour of the country justices stands in marked contrast to the integrity of the Lord Chief Justice, who acts on his belief that true justice is blind to political persuasion, bribes, and threats. No matter how comically poignant these Gloucestershire scenes are, they depict an unweeded garden.

Through its degeneracy, this 'other' world of England prepares us for Hal's rejection of Falstaff, whose delight in news that the King is dead and assumption of royal privilege cannot be condoned:

> Master Shallow, my Lord Shallow, be what thou wilt: I am fortune's steward . . .
> I know the young king is sick for me. Let us take any man's horses, the laws of
> England are at my commandment. Blessed are they that have been my friends,
> and woe to my Lord Chief Justice! (5.3.106–13)

Morally, the audience knows that Falstaff should not be permitted to come within the circle of Henry V's court and that Shallow by rights should lose his thousand pounds. Hal of course must banish plump Jack – as he has promised to do in *Part 1* – and retain the Lord Chief Justice if he is to gain credibility as king. Falstaff's public interruption of the coronation procession to claim Hal as his own 'sweet boy' (5.5.39) is presumptuous, and Hal's rejection of him, while harsh, is political necessity: 'I know thee not, old man. Fall to thy prayers' (43). But as centuries of audiences would attest, such 'necessity' is dramatically unsavoury, for Hal appears in his coronation as the impersonal manifestation of state will, and Falstaff, the all-too-human victim of a callous political system. It was he, after all, who in soliloquy aptly characterised Prince John as cold-blooded but held out some hope that Hal, because he drinks 'good store of fertile sherris' (4.1.468–9), might put a more humane face on government. Here, Hal becomes as 'sober-blooded' (436) as his brother; and when he warns Falstaff that 'the grave doth gape / For thee thrice wider than for other men' (5.5.49–50), he recalls the feigned death of Falstaff at Shrewsbury, over whose corpse he delivered an affectionate epitaph: 'Death hath not struck so fat a deer today' (5.4.106). Here, he speaks no epitaph, and his allusion to Falstaff's size is cruel. Critics concede that Falstaff's punishment could have been worse, for Hal grants him an allowance sufficient to live on and holds out the possibility of advancement if Falstaff reforms. But that is not the *dramatic* impression one is left with. In the new government's attempt to clean up the stews, Doll and Mistress Quickly are brutally arrested; and although Falstaff deludes himself, or attempts to delude others, that he 'shall be sent for soon at night' (5.5.83), the Lord Chief Justice commits him and his companions to the Fleet. Policy inevitably wins out over humanity.[26]

2 *Henry IV*, therefore, is an independent work which, while it brings to closure the royal narrative of Hal's growth to kingship, is concerned primarily with other things. It is less about chronicle history than about the more encompassing 'state' of Elizabethan England – the whores, drunks, false captains, country gentlemen, yeomen, and women's tailors who populate the world *outside* the court and whose histories had never been recorded. At the centre of these alternative histories is not the King nor Hal, but a fat knight who embodies a license and vitality that are crushed by the apparatus of state – an apparatus which, if a force of historical inevitability, nevertheless is at odds with both human compassion and theatrical pleasure. In all but the most militant productions, the state does not win the audience's sympathy. Falstaff does.

NOTES

1 See Hattaway, p. 9 in this volume.

2 A. R. Humphreys discusses the play as a dramatisation of emerging nationhood (*1H4*, ed. Humphreys 1960, pp. xxi–xxii); see also Helgerson 1992. On the ways in which Shakespeare's history plays address Elizabethans' interest in recovering their nation's past, see Holderness 1985 and Rackin 1990.

3 James 1986, pp. 270–307 provides a detailed account of the Northern Rising of 1569; see also Campbell, 1947, pp. 231–4.

4 Helgerson 1992, p. 50; see also Yates 1975, pp. 88–111, and Strong 1977.

5 James 1986, pp. 437–9; see also McCoy 1989.

6 Clark 1983, pp. 111–15, discusses the alehouse as a permissive site where all classes could converge for public drinking. Shakespeare collapses under one roof an alehouse and a tavern, which offered wine: usually identified as the Boar's Head, Mistress Quickly's tavern may allude to a historical tavern of that name (there were six by that name in London) which served as a playing space for actors long before there were public theatres: see Gurr 1992, p. 117.

7 Barbara Hodgdon provides a concise account of the Oldcastle controversy in Hodgdon 1997, pp. 349–91. For the Oxford editors' justification of their reversion to Oldcastle, see Taylor 1985, pp. 95–100, and David Scott Kastan's judicious rebuttal (Kastan 1999).

8 Poole 1995; see also Holderness 1985, pp. 107–12.

9 The identification of Falstaff with the Lord of Misrule was made by Barber 1959. On the radical potential of the Elizabethan clown to alter playgoers' perspectives, see Weimann 1978, and Bristol 1985. Wiles 1987, pp. 116–35, argues the likelihood that Falstaff was written for Will Kemp, the actor who played clown roles in the comedies. See also Helgerson 1992, pp. 220–8.

10 Greenblatt 1980, pp. 162–3.

11 See Kastan 1986; also Howard 1994 and Montrose 1996.

12 Many chroniclers – Stow, Camden, Speed, Holinshed – invented tales of Hal's madcap youth to mask evidence of a strong political antagonism between father and son which led the Privy Council, staunch supporter of the Prince, to seek the King's abdication, and as a consequence led Henry, fearing armed rebellion, to dismiss Hal and his friends from all state offices: see McFarlane 1972, pp. 92–3, 121–3. Shakespeare domesticates the tension between them: a father's disappointment in his son's prodigal ways, after all, was safer subject-matter than a king's fear of the prince's political ambition.

13 Cohen 1985, p. 80.

14 Rackin 1990, pp. 77–8.

15 Hodgdon 1997, p. 334. On the language of counterfeiting, translating and cozening, see Parker 1996, pp. 157–64.

16 The prelates' rebellion occurred in May 1405, nearly two years after the battle of Shrewsbury was fought on 21 July 1403.

17 *Part 1*'s popularity is confirmed by the publication of seven Quarto editions prior to the First Folio. The relationship of the two plays to one another and the process of their composition have been widely, but never conclusively, debated. To survey all sides, see Tillyard 1944; Wilson 1945; David 1953 ; Jenkins 1956; and introductions to two recent editions: *2H4*, ed. Melchiori 1989, and *2H4* ed. Weis 1998.

18 This is the position taken in *2H4*, ed. Davison 1977.

19 For a provocative account of the fortunes of Falstaff in the play's performance history, see Hodgdon 1993 and Hodgdon 1991, pp. 151–84.

20 On stereotypes of the entrepreneurial alewife, see Clark 1983, pp. 111–15. Jean E. Howard and Phyllis Rackin discuss Mistress Quickly as an anarchic figure, and the sexualising and criminalising of her which coincide with her economic prosperity, in Howard and Rackin, 1997, pp. 176–85.

21 Hodgdon 1997, pp. 210–11 cites Thomas Dekker's *Lantern and Candlelight* as a guide to the hierarchy of London's vagrant population, and reprints his first

chapter, 'Of Canting', 250–5, as a context in which to read the colloquialisms, 'strange tongues' and 'gross terms' used by the lowlifes in *1H4*.

22 See Mullaney 1988, pp. 76–82.

23 That Falstaff should pass through Gloucestershire on his way to meet Prince John in Yorkshire makes little geographical sense and possibly is evidence that Shakespeare originally intended the Gloucestershire scenes to precede and follow the battle of Shrewsbury in an earlier draft of *Henry IV*.

24 Anne Barton discusses Falstaff's attempt to dehumanise the recruits through wordplay, which she calls a 'callous and unimaginative cratylism' (Barton 1990, pp. 108–101.

25 See Fortescue 1916, pp. 112–26. Among contemporary observers, Barnaby Rich asserts in *Pathway to Military Practice* (1587) that captains were often incompetent and corrupt, negligent of their men and provisions, cowardly and undisciplined, and, at worst, thieving murderers; and Thomas Nashe, in *Pierce Pennilesse* (1592), ranks captains among those who devote themselves to pleasure – gaming, drinking, and whoring.

26 Stephen Greenblatt argues that the state is preserved in *2H4* through a series of squalid betrayals, of which Hal's rejection of Falstaff is the final and definitive one, and that characters such as Falstaff who have appeared to undermine state authority turn out to be its props (Greenblatt 1985, pp. 18–47).

11

PAMELA MASON

Henry V: 'the quick forge and working house of thought'

Discussion of *Henry V* is too often concerned solely with the character of its eponymous hero. Buoyed by the rich psychology of the resembling contrasts that infuse pairs of characters in *1* and *2 Henry IV*, critics may be disappointed by the transmutation from prince to king. Una Ellis-Fermor declares 'it is in vain that we look for the personality of Henry behind the king, there is nothing else there',[1] and she concludes that Henry has become 'a dead man walking'.[2] Evaluation of Henry becomes inextricably entangled with unease about definitions of the heroic and disquiet about patriotic fervour. Michael Billington's assumption that 'We see more productions of *Titus Andronicus* than of *Henry V* these days' because the 'latter's undeniable patriotism'[3] embarrasses us may reflect how *Henry V* has been misrepresented in recent years. Although discussion of character and of the military ethic have dominated the critical debate,[4] the antipathy that the play can prompt may stem from a mistaken assumption about its focus. The priority in *Henry V* is not with exploring character but rather in the play's profound consideration of the theatrical construct. Shakespeare's investment in his choric architecture insists upon an intellectual engagement with the process whereby a creative partnership can be forged between stage and audience. The speech which opens *Henry V* presents in the form of an uncompromising direct address to its audience Shakespeare's dramatic manifesto.

Although what the Chorus says is initially expressed as an emotional evocation with an intensity of suppressed feeling bursting forth, it becomes essentially a rational appeal for the audience to recognise the context in which the actors function. The representational aspects of performance are reiterated in:

> A kingdom for a stage, princes to act
> And monarchs to behold the swelling scene!
> (1.Chorus.3–4)[5]

and the sense of role-playing is explicitly emphasised through a sequence of similes. There is a tentative quality in the repeated use of 'should' and in the way in which the Chorus apologises for his presumption. The series of antitheses also make clear the presumption of the actors in tackling such an enormous task with such meagre resources. The reference to the makeshift structure of the theatre ('scaffold') glances at the transience of life itself and the use of 'cockpit' points to the practicality of the building they are inhabiting through its reminder of the dual use of many theatres. The actor's place at the hub of the experience is emphatically asserted by the reference to 'this wooden O' and the Chorus might also be said to be alluding tantalisingly to the excitement of the empty space of the stage. After another apology, the image of 'O', nought or 'cipher', is extended intellectually as again the actor adopts a self-deprecating attitude. However, within the description of his fellows as 'flat unraised spirits' there is an implicit promise that they might be raised, particularly if they are infused with the inspirational power invoked in the opening lines. Again the Chorus insists upon the scale of the actors' temerity ('ciphers to this great accompt') before introducing the notion of partnership in a relationship that is characterised by work rather than play. There will be later injunctions to 'Grapple your minds' (3.Chorus.18) and 'Work, work your thoughts' (3.Chorus.25), culminating in a precise definition of the imagination as 'the quick forge and working house of thought' (5.Chorus.23) which will be necessary if the creative process is to be realised.

The opening speech also offers a series of albeit gentle imperatives addressed to the audience – 'Suppose . . .', 'Piece out . . .', 'make . . .', and 'Think . . .' – before the ultimate necessity of:

> For 'tis your thoughts that now must deck our kings

The climactic sense of the interdependence of 'your' and 'our' confirms the sense of duality already established through alliteration, rhythmic structure and such patterning as 'we talk . . . you see . . .'. That the act of communication is essentially reciprocal is signalled by the earth 'receiving' the imaginary horses' hooves. The actor's role depends upon the participation of an audience and the Chorus politely asks ('Admit me . . .') that he might be allowed to fulfil his essential function. He appears 'prologue-like', reminding us of the impersonation that has been promised of 'the warlike Harry, like himself' and prefiguring the clash between Henry and Williams:

> —It was ourself thou didst abuse.
> —Your majesty came not like yourself.
> (4.8.49–50)

The Chorus concludes by stressing the sense of theatrical presentation and defining the dual responsibilities of the audience:

> Admit me Chorus to this history;
> Who prologue-like your humble patience pray,
> Gently to hear, kindly to judge, our play.
>
> (1.Chorus.32–4)

Having established the nature of his theatrical contract the Chorus' direct access to the audience enables him to perform a range of roles. He is far more than a narrator, for he is the audience's mentor alerting those in the Globe to engage with the essence of the theatrical experience. Above all they must recognise their roles in the creative process. Location is established on the bare wooden stage through the illusion created by the power of language, but an audience has to be prepared to be carried away by the experience:

> and the scene
> Is now transported, gentles, to Southampton.
> There is the playhouse now, there must you sit,
> And thence to France shall we convey you safe
> And bring you back, charming the narrow seas
> To give you gentle pass; for, if we may,
> We'll not offend one stomach with our play.
>
> (2.Chorus.34–40)

With the humorous reassurance that calm seas will be provided for the voyage (to avoid seasickness!), a literal sense of the journey that the audience will make is linked with the playwright's desire to please. The Chorus' power to shift location is exploited, and later he creates a visual, aural and tactile sense of stillness and darkness through the evocative power of words:

> Now entertain conjecture of a time
> When creeping murmur and the poring dark
> Fills the wide vessel of the universe.
>
> (4.Chorus.1–3)

As he continues an audience can share something of the tension that derives from the proximity of the contrasting camps:

> That the fixed sentinels almost receive
> The secret whispers of each other's watch.
>
> (4.Chorus.6–7)

and the whole scene is shrouded in darkness as 'Fire answers fire'. There is more here than word-painting, for the Chorus takes us into the minds and consciousness of the 'poor condemned English' who:

> Like sacrifices, by their watchful fires
> Sit patiently, and inly ruminate
> The morning's danger; and their gesture sad,
> Investing lank-lean cheeks and war-worn coats,
> Presenteth them unto the gazing moon
> So many horrid ghosts.   (4.Chorus.23–8)

The Chorus at the beginning of Act 5 manages an important transition by compressing a large expanse of time and offering, on this occasion, not a foretaste of scenes to come but a vivid account of events following the victory. Crucially, the Chorus acknowledges his role as a narrator who recounts events for those who 'have not read the story' (5.Chorus.1). He reaffirms the theatrical frame and offers excuse:

> Of time, of numbers, and due course of things,
> Which cannot in their huge and proper life
> Be here presented.   (5.Chorus.4–6)

After he acknowledges his role in collapsing time:

> myself have played
> The interim, by remembering you 'tis past
> (5.Chorus.42–3)

his final words draw an interesting distinction between the different kinds of theatrical experience the play has offered:

> Then brook abridgement, and your eyes advance,
> After your thoughts, straight back again to France.
> (5.Chorus.44–5)

In no other play does Shakespeare invest so much in a structure that powerfully serves to engage his audience in intellectual consideration of the experience in which they are involved. The regular interruptions deny organic development to the drama and require an audience to step back from emotional involvement to gain a perspective upon character and event. The experience of *Henry V* in performance is a process in which its audience is invited, even urged, to think, judge, and assess. The perspective continually shifts and, although Henry dominates the dialogue through the weight of his part, the Chorus is a worthy antagonist who effectively competes for the hearts and minds of the audience. His incisive interruptions ensure that the participation insisted upon in the opening speech is sustained throughout the play to define the audience's role as an active one. Fundamentally, an audience needs to engage with the debate promoted by the interplay between the Chorus and the intervening scenes. The mesh of choric commentary ensures that the King himself is contained within a tight structure: any consideration of character is disciplined by the pattern of the play's analytical discourse. However, in performance, the text is habitually cut and reshaped in an insistent attempt to defy and subvert a carefully crafted structure. Theatre practitioners are too often anxious to make the play conform to a more conventional structure. But Shakespeare's text requires an audience to produce its own synthesis. The vigorous, energetic debates which rage around Henry's scenes construct a fretwork of memory, reflection, and thematic parallel which consistently limit his domination over what, only very superficially, would seem to be his play. This may account for the 'coldness' that Traversi identifies in a play which he concludes is a 'balanced, sober study'.[6]

Henry may instruct 'every man' to 'task his thought' towards the French campaign but outside the court the proposed invasion is viewed with more pragmatic honesty framed by the mundane colloquialisms of petty rivalry. The antagonism between Nym and Pistol arises from an act of usurpation in their own domestic sphere and it claims priority over national issues. Pistol has married Mistress Quickly despite her being 'troth-plight' to Nym, who 'dare not fight', but he will 'hold out [his] iron'. These men are unmoved by patriotic fervour. In their world the fact that 'knives have edges' simply serves to enable Nym to threaten Pistol: 'I will cut thy throat one time or another.' In response Pistol anticipates the cry of his French prisoner '*Couple a gorge!*' These men's knives are 'to cut one another's throats', but the entrance of the Boy interrupts their war:

> Mine host Pistol, you must come to my master – and you, Hostess: he is very
> sick, and would to bed. Good Bardolph, put thy face between his sheets, and
> do the office of a warming pan, Faith he's very ill.   (2.1.78–81)

The Boy's 'master' is not named, for the assumption is that those on stage and Shakespeare's audience share a sense of deprivation. The scene revives memories of the Eastcheap encounters in the *Henry IV* plays and the notable absentee here is the unnamed Falstaff. As the Hostess goes to tend him, she attributes responsibility unequivocally, for 'the King hath killed his heart' (2.1.84).

The wrangling between Nym and Pistol subsides. A recognition of their common cause and of the commercial opportunities offered by war is resonantly announced in verse:

> And friendship shall combine, and brotherhood.
> I'll live by Nym, and Nym shall live by me.

Is not this just? For I shall sutler be
Unto the camp, and profits will accrue.
(2.1.104–7)

While they may be able to dispel differences, believing that 'friendship shall combine', the reiteration of Falstaff's frailty prompts Nym to offer his censure of the King: 'The King hath run bad humours on the knight, that's the even of it.' They all feel Henry has treated his old friend badly, and although Nym asserts 'The King is a good king' his resigned after-thought 'but it must be as it may' drains conviction from his words. Not once in this scene is Falstaff named, for his identity is secure and the audience share in his friends' concern for his welfare. The extent of the King's responsibility will have to be debated more fully later.

As the Hostess, Pistol, Nym, and Bardolph leave to 'condole the knight', Bedford enters talking of 'trust' and 'traitors'. Undoubtedly the revelation of the treachery of Cambridge, Scroop, and Grey which follows is coloured by the previous scene. Henry's anger at his friends' betrayal is set within a context which invokes memories of his rejection of Falstaff. The willingness of Henry's friends to 'sell' him 'for a foreign purse' also echoes Pistol's determination that 'profits shall accrue' from this enterprise of war. The earlier insistence upon the financial imperative and Nym's repeated concern with his 'eight shillings' forge a link across the hierarchy of degree with those anxious to get their hands on 'the gold of France'. The apparent moral certainty surrounding issues of loyalty and betrayal has been blurred and an audience might once more find Henry's rallying couplet not wholly convincing:

Cheerly to sea! The signs of war advance!
No King of England if not King of France!
(2.2.192–3)

Pistol's parallel rallying cry early in the following scene tightens the structural patterning. His words cannot be contained within the tidiness of a rhymed couplet and Falstaff's death once again deflates the preceding rhetoric. Henry's actions are, in what is now a familiar way, both defined and confined:

Bardolph, be blithe! Nym, rouse thy vaunting veins!
Boy, bristle thy courage up! For Falstaff, he is dead . . .
(2.3.4–5)

Falstaff's former companions have no stomach for the enterprise to come. The grief at Falstaff's death sets a sombre tone for a scene that resonates through the ages as the men who are going to war take leave of their women. Pistol's words of advice to the Hostess offer commentary upon much that has gone before:

> Trust none:
> For oaths are straws, men's faiths are wafer-cakes,
> And Holdfast is the only dog, my duck.
>
> (2.3.47–9)

Shakespeare is giving voice to the perspective of the ordinary man and he employs the theatrical vitality of established characters to ensure that Henry will have to work hard to rally support. The tone is resolutely unsentimental as Pistol continues:

> Yoke-fellows in arms,
> Let us to France, like horse-leeches, my boys,
> To suck, to suck, the very blood to suck!
>
> (2.3.51–3)

Quite crucially, the whole sequence provides an ironic counterpoint to the Chorus' assertion that:

> The French, advised by good intelligence
> Of this most dreadful preparation,
> Shake in their fear . . .   (2.12–14)

One of the many achievements of the English Shakespeare Company's 1986 presentation of *The Henrys* was the determination to 'cope' with the Chorus' 'manifold' ironies. Michael Bogdanov and Michael Pennington devised a solution to this particular movement in the play which proved controversial:

It seems tradition has not changed much. The English invade the Continent much like the marauding Celts of old. Imperialism encourages jingoism. So the Falklands. So Agincourt. 'Fuck the Frogs.' The banner hung out by the send-off crowd at Southampton in our production of *Henry V* grew out of the desire to bridge nearly six hundred years of this same bigoted xenophobic patriotism. As Pistol *et al.* turn at the end of the farewell to Mistress Quickly, punch the air to a chorus of ' 'ere we go, 'ere we go, 'ere we go', 'Jerusalem' swells. The last night of the Proms, the troops getting the blessing at Portsmouth, football fury, all combined in my mind to produce this image . . . Some spectators found the moment offensive, others misunderstood, most applauded. A letter from a member of the public: 'The use of the word was offensive and the term "Frogs" hardly helps promote racial harmony and dispel old prejudices. I was ashamed to be English.' Precisely. The case rests.[7]

This sequence had the effect also of allowing the French to enter the play on a note of unquestionable moral superiority. With cool disdain the French King remarked, 'Thus come the English...' The audience laughter which greeted the line was at the expense of the English, not the French, and ensured a better balance between the rival courts than is usual. In complicating the audience's perspective, the production recognised that the play resists simplistic oppositions.

Rather than offer polarised debate, Shakespeare's preference is to exploit groups of three characters. The trios of 'Pistol, Nym, and Bardolph' and 'Cambridge, Scroop, and Grey' are recalled when, on the night before Agincourt, the Folio stage direction instructs: *Enter three soldiers, John Bates, Alexander Court, and Michael Williams.* These men are not known to the audience, but naming them reveals a concern to individualise them, if only in the writing. For in the theatre it is only John Bates whose name we learn but the stage direction's indication of different characters is reflected in their words. The audience is offered a choice of 'Everyman' representatives as Shakespeare promotes opportunities through casting to encompass a range of age, background, attitude, and experience.

The Chorus' words have closed down the theatrical space for this scene so that there is an intense engagement with the quiet, intimate voicing of 'cold fear'. The entrance of the disguised Henry gives the audience a complex perspective. As the soldiers face the prospect of combat they are not bolstered with any secure sense of 'right and conscience'. They are frightened and are ready to voice the cynicism they feel about regal responsibility and the realities of negotiation. The privileged knowledge of spectators secures an affinity with Henry but Shakespeare provides access for the common man to enter the debate and confront the King. There is a powerful case to answer:

> But if the cause be not good, the King himself hath a heavy reckoning to make, when all those legs, and arms, and heads, chopped off in a battle, shall join together at the latter day, and cry all, 'We died at such a place'; some swearing, some crying for a surgeon, some upon their wives left poor behind them, some upon the debts they owe, some upon their children rawly left. I am afeard there are few die well that die in a battle; how can they charitably dispose of anything when blood is their argument? Now, if these men do not die well, it will be a black matter for the King that led them to it, who to disobey were against all proportion of subjection. (4.1.130–42)

Williams is not convinced by the arguments he hears, nor does he find the reassurances satisfactory. He challenges Henry:

> Let it be a quarrel between us, if you live.
> (4.1.200)

Their exchange of gloves is a time-honoured ritual, declaring a formal challenge, with Williams as the people's champion. However, Henry's promise to wear Williams' glove in his 'bonnet' and Williams' reciprocal action also suggest something of a camaraderie which provides the basis of Williams' powerful defence of his presumption when Henry later reveals himself. When Henry declares 'It was ourself thou didst abuse' Williams' response provides a sharp riposte and explicit exposure of the common humanity which lies beneath the 'ceremony' of kingship:

> Your majesty came not like yourself: you appeared to me but as a common man – witness the night, your garments, your lowliness; and what your highness suffered under that shape, I beseech you take it for your own fault, and not mine; for had you been as I took you for, I made no offence: therefore, I beseech your highness, pardon me. (4.8.50–6)

Williams' words also offer retrospective commentary upon Hal's earlier double-dealing in Eastcheap and judgement of such duplicity. His words hit home. Henry replies not to Williams but to Exeter and not in prose but in verse. As the King instructs Exeter to 'Give him the crowns' he is not simply paying Williams off but is also reciprocating in offering to share with him the trappings of 'ceremony'.

The debate concerning the ethics of war is intensified through Shakespeare's use of the 'poys'. Violence against children will always engender a vehement condemnation of the perpetrators, but such is the emotional immediacy of its impact and so unqualified are the judgements it provokes that it needs to be used with caution and subtlety. Shakespeare uses it sparingly in his plays, but his restraint is frequently negated by choices made in performance. Shakespeare's use of the killing of the boys is much more vigorous and more objectively challenging than most productions of *Henry V* allow. A combination of selective editing of the text and manipulative insertion of invented business subverts a sequence carefully crafted by Shakespeare to expose in a balanced way the brutal reality of war. He presents the absurdity of the notions that war can be made more acceptable by having 'codes' or that it is only foreigners who break them. Shakespeare characteristically prompts reasoned reflection upon the issues rather than offers gruesome spectacle to provoke the emotions. He had done the same earlier when dealing with the hanging of Bardolph. The text of *Henry V* does not distract an audience by showing Bardolph being hanged (or garrotted) on stage. The decision that Kenneth Branagh makes in his film of *Henry V* (1989) to show the hanging is an example of the director's determination to emphasise the personal cost for Henry. A similar determination would seem to have shaped Branagh's decision to invent a sequence dealing with the French troops' killing of the boys while removing all references to Henry's killing of the French prisoners.

Shakespeare's text presents a challenging and complex sequence which forces an audience to confront the uncompromising nature of the fiercely pragmatic decisions faced by both sides in war. Henry responds to the 'new alarum' signalling that the French 'have reinforced their scattered men' by issuing the command:

> Then every soldier kill his prisoners!
> Give the word through.
>
> (4.6.37–8)

Immediately Fluellen announces:

> Kill the poys and the luggage? 'Tis expressly against the law of arms; 'tis as arrant a piece of knavery, mark you now, as can be offert – in your conscience now. Is it not?
> (4.7.1–4)

One 'piece of arrant knavery' is being juxtaposed with another. Killing the prisoners is 'against the law of arms' but tough circumstances demand tough decisions. Both sides are breaking the rules but, through Gower, Shakespeare also exposes the pressure that there is to tailor history to suit one's audience. Gower provides an astute rewriting of the sequence of events:

> 'Tis certain there's not a boy left alive, and the cowardly rascals that ran from the battle ha' done this slaughter. Besides, they have burnt and carried away all that was in the King's tent, wherefore the King most worthily hath caused every soldier to cut his prisoner's throat. O, 'tis a gallant King! (4.7.5–10)

In the exchange which follows Gower does his best to sustain that image of the 'gallant king', but his assertion that Henry 'never killed any of his friends' prompts an audience to think of Bardolph. Fluellen revives the earlier history of the 'fat knight . . . full of jests' whom it falls to Gower to name as 'Sir John Falstaff'. The scene which Shakespeare creates here is not one littered with the poignant sight of the bodies of small, huddled, murdered boys. It is rather one littered with the jagged fragments of Henry's past which have snagged Gower's attempts to weave a pleasing tapestry of history. Henry now offers his own press release. He moves from the emotional confession that 'I was not angry since I came to France' to words which offer his troops licence for bloody revenge:

> Besides, we'll cut the throats of those we have . . . (4.7.61)

Neither Henry here nor Gower earlier acknowledges Henry's first order to kill the prisoners.

It is perhaps inevitable that, in 1944 with the French as allies, Olivier in his film should have felt it appropriate to omit all reference to the killing of the prisoners, but it is more surprising that Branagh could not accommodate these lines. In his introduction to the published screenplay he contrasts his 'darker, harsher'[8] interpretation with the pageantry of Olivier's film and makes much of the fact that he includes 'significant scenes'[9] that Olivier had excluded. He makes no reference to his decision to cut this episode.

Branagh's film 'includes' the following sequence. The description is from the *Screenplay*:

> We see the boy running, carrying a pennant through the fighting soldiers back towards the camp . . . A group of French horsemen ride towards him . . . alarums are sounded from the direction of the camp. Then the terrified screaming of children . . . Henry struggles through the water, the last of the battle still going on around him. He runs as fast as his blood-stained and exhausted body can manage, towards the camp.
>
> As Gower and Fluellen arrive, the scale of the carnage is obvious. Every English boy has been killed. Fluellen and Gower walk among the pitiful pile of corpses as the rest of the English army principals arrive to be greeted by the same dreadful sight. Fluellen kneels down beside the body of the dead Boy . . . Fluellen breaks down in tears and, crossing himself, leans his head on the Boy's outstretched arm . . . Henry arrives . . . In despair he turns his back on the scene to deliver a great howl of rage against the French.
>
> > I was not angry since I came to France
> > Until this instant.[10]

These are the only words Henry speaks (of his eleven line speech). He turns then to drag Montjoy off his horse. A little later to the swelling notes of the *Non nobis* we have:

> . . . we remain with Henry and the dead Boy as he walks slowly and painfully through the carnage . . . He gently lays the Boy down, kisses him gently on the head . . . [11]

Shakespeare's text is richly complex and, far from exploiting the emotional and sentimental impact of the killing of the boys, he has crafted a sequence which challenges and disturbs its audience. The Boy's choric role is established from his first appearance when, as a serious messenger warning of Falstaff's imminent death, he cuts through the in-fighting and squabbling in Eastcheap. Later in the play his two soliloquies offer both perspective and reflection. He challenges emotional complacency and intellectual laziness. Both speeches of direct address display the Boy's clarity of vision about his elders and betters. His words complicate our attitude towards Bardolph,

Pistol and Nym. Indeed, his words prevent a sentimental response to these characters:

> As young as I am, I have observed these three swashers. I am boy to them all three, but al they three, though they would serve me, could not be man to me; for indeed three such antics do not amount to a man. For Bardolph, he is white-livered and red-faced . . . For Pistol, he hath a killing tongue, and a quiet sword . . . For Nym, he hath heard that men of few words are the best men; and therefore he scorns to say his prayers, lest 'a should be thought a coward; but his few bad words are matched with as few good deeds . . . They will steal anything and call it purchase . . . They would have me as familiar with men's pockets as their gloves or their handkerchers: which makes much against my manhood . . . I must leave them, and seek some better service. Their villainy goes against my weak stomach, and therefore I must cast it up.   (3.2.28–53)

In Act 4 we see the Boy act as interpreter in Pistol's confrontation with a French soldier. The Boy can speak French and in crossing the barriers of language he provides an alter ego for Katherine. The link prompts a reflection upon issues of class in the disparity between the opportunities offered to a boy or a Princess. His role as interpreter also forges an important link between the women and the children in the way the play considers the consequences of war. Pistol is initially determined to 'cut his [prisoner's] throat' but agrees to a ransom of 'two hundred crowns'. His French victim's conclusion that Pistol is therefore 'the most brave, valorous, and thrice-worthy signieur of England' provides an ironic foreshadowing of Henry's wooing of Katherine.

The Boy's soliloquy with which the scene ends invites an audience to note the terrible inappropriateness of the position of a child in war, a child who has a risky, dangerous job to do because there are not enough 'men':

> I must stay with the lackeys, with the luggage of our camp. The French might have good prey of us, if he knew of it, for there is none to guard it but boys.
>
> (4.4.73–5)

Just over one hundred lines later his death is announced as part of the killing of the 'poys'. It is not shown. An audience is invited to grieve for youth, not for one boy. The 'boy' who was their spokesman functions as an emblem for the universal child who will never grow up; his potential, of which there is considerable evidence, will never be realised.

War is traditionally sober about women and children and yet Shakespeare's use of both in this play does not seem to have permeated much of the critical writing. Interest in the 'boys' is in terms of Henry's military tactics, and from Sidney Lee's complaint that 'women play in it the slenderest part'[12] critical blindness concerning the women seems to prevail. However, not only does the Hostess figure strongly but there are also the three French women. Katherine,

Alice, and Queen Isabel make significant contributions to the play's debate. Katherine's potential as political pawn is signalled in the Chorus to Act 3:

> the [French] King doth offer him
> Katherine his daughter, and with her, to dowry,
> Some petty and unprofitable dukedoms.
>
> (3.Chorus.29–32)

This provides an urgency to her English lesson (3.4) as does the scene of threat to the Governor of Harfleur which immediately precedes it. The juxtaposition of the two scenes alerts us to recognise the serious dimension beneath the apparent comic gloss. Far from Katherine's scene providing 'the greatest possible contrast to the strained brutality of Henry's threats to Harfleur',[13] we can understand that Katherine might understandably prefer an arranged marriage to the English king rather than risk becoming a participant in the scenario he has just outlined:

> look to see
> The blind and bloody soldier with foul hand
> Defile the locks of your shrill-shrieking daughters
>
> (3.3.33–5)

Henry has consistently used the threat of attacks upon women as an integral component of his campaign. In the first scene he warned that the humiliation of the Dauphin's gift of tennis balls would 'mock' from their husbands 'many a thousand widows' and would 'Mock mothers from their sons'(1.2.285,287). Exeter tells the French King that 'hungry war' will cause 'the widows' tears, the orphans' cries...the prived maidens' groans' (2.4.106–7). Katherine's lesson recognises both her female vulnerability and that as a Princess she is a valuable commodity for negotiation. Her struggles with the language demonstrate a dehumanising fragmentation of self in the listing of hand, fingers, nails, elbow, neck, chin, foot. The dissection of her body echoes the 'fleshed soldier', 'bloody hand', 'foul hand', and 'reverend heads' which have punctuated Henry's speech to the Governor of Harfleur in the preceding scene. The *double entendre* of 'count' has been robbed of any innocent humour by the 'hot and forcing violation' Henry threatened to 'pure maidens'. The text offers no 'gown' to clothe her nakedness. Her words also anticipate Williams' terrified vision of 'all those legs, and arms, and heads, chopped off in a battle' (4.1.131–2).

All three French women participate in the play's last scene which has sometimes been dismissed as a disappointing, romantic conclusion. Often judged as 'humorous love-making' it has excited parallels with Petruchio's wooing of his Kate.[14] Henry's awkwardness is felt to provide a gently amusing foil to Katherine's shyness. However, far from being a 'brisk and joyous wooing'[15] it is a very long scene infused with the cost of war and a fierce political imperative. As with other areas of this play, performance has distorted Shakespeare's text through cutting and reshaping not only to edit Henry's verbosity but even to exclude Queen Isabel. In the stage tableau the trio of women gives physical form to the scene's opposition between a male and female discourse. Henry acknowledges the Queen and Katherine in his opening speech but terming them 'sister' and 'cousin' appropriates them to his 'side' of any dispute. To the King's three lines Isabel has nine. Explicitly she looks Henry in the eye to urge that his 'murdering basilisks' and the erstwhile 'venom of such looks' will 'change' to 'love'. Burgundy takes from her his cue to argue the need for an insistently feminine and vulnerable peace ('naked, poor and mangled . . . dear nurse of arts') to 'put up her lovely visage'. Henry resists both appeals. His language makes peace a cold and factual object 'you would the peace . . . you must buy the peace'. As the assembly divides for political negotiation it is Isabel's own decision that she should go and it is she who gives Katherine 'leave' to stay. Her conviction that 'a woman's voice may do some good' will be demonstrated in the parallel sequences which follow. After what are clearly protracted negotiations, the French King will return to signal his consent and in Henry's concurrent scene enacted on stage the two women will present more resistance than the English King might have expected.

Henry defines Katherine as his 'capital demand' but his assumption that his appropriation will be unchallenged has not reckoned with the women's voices. Alice is a buffer between Henry and his prize. She provides space for Katherine, gives her time to think, and ensures a divided focus of attack for Henry. Working together, the women wrongfoot him. He is forced to speak their language and in doing so draws a parallel with his earlier campaign, 'It is as easy for me, Kate, to conquer the kingdom as to speak so much more French.' He is forced to work harder than he would seem to have anticipated and indeed the length of the scene forces him to invest more in this enterprise than he suggested initially. His approach has no structure. His prose is verbose and inelegant as he struggles to deal with female discourse of disarming directness. By forcing him to translate her words Katherine ensures he confesses his undistinguished past. It is Henry's voice which speaks 'the tongues of men are full of deceits' and Katherine's question, 'Is it possible that I should love de *ennemi* of *France*?' forces him into a frank admission of the reality of his invasion and occupation of her country.

Isabel's words frame the sequence. Her prayer expresses the hope that a harmonious marriage will parallel a long-lasting peace between the two countries. Following the affirmation of her solemn plea through the choric

'Amen' Henry's words seem anti-climactic. His repeated concern with oath-taking lacks conviction and his jingly rhyming couplet offers an uncertain conclusion. The Chorus has the last word in the play and reaffirms his authority.

The play's epilogue forsakes the flexibility and fluidity of organic blank verse for the formal, patterned structure of a sonnet. The Chorus' words once again confine Henry by making it clear how 'mighty men' are constrained by history and the limitations of the stage. Although the Chorus remains apologetic about the limitations of the theatrical space ('In little room ...') he gives priority to the 'rough and all-unable pen' with which 'our bending author hath pursued the story'. The creative process whereby the text necessarily precedes the performance urges an audience to detach itself from involvement with the 'mighty men'. The perspective is lengthened further as Shakespeare looks forward historically and back theatrically to remind his audience of what they know (through his own plays) happened next. The lines strike an uncompromisingly solemn note as the savagery of subsequent events is presented:

> Henry the Sixth, in infant bands crowned King
> Of France and England, did this King succeed,
> Whose state so many had the managing
> That they lost France, and made his England bleed
>
> (Epilogue.9–12)

At the moment of celebrating England's most famous victory Shakespeare ensures that his audience remembers the transience of such success. In a final rhetorical twist the Chorus acknowledges the common currency of theatrical experience. Shakespeare gives priority to his own history as a dramatist to remind those watching of the popular success of his *Henry VI* plays:

> Which oft our stage hath shown; and, for their sake,
> In your fair minds let this acceptance take.
>
> (Epilogue.13–14)

The ultimate appeal is for judgement within a theatrical context. What we have experienced is to be judged as a play, in relation to other plays.

The particularity of Shakespeare's point of reference in these lines is frequently lost. For, even if audiences today hear the play's final lines spoken, it is simply not true that the stage 'oft hath shown' the *Henry VI* plays. More usually the play's conclusion will be shaped to celebrate the agreed marriage between Kate and Henry where the convention being drawn upon is that of a Shakespearean comedy. The play thereby becomes more comfortable and infinitely less subtle. In his film Olivier keeps just six and a half lines of the closing sonnet appropriately acknowledging that invoking Henry VI will strike no chord of theatrical memory in most of his audience. However, he does succeed in reaffirming the crucial importance of the audience in the process of theatrical chemistry through his return to the frame of his Globe performance. After having been crowned, Henry and Katherine join hands and move to the upstage thrones:

> HENRY V turns round on reaching the throne. He is wearing the crude Globe Theatre make-up.
>
> Applause is heard as we pan to show a BOY made-up as KATHARINE.
>
> Track back from KING HENRY and the BOY playing KATHARINE to reveal the stage of the Globe Theatre.
>
> CHORUS enters and pulls the curtain across.[16]

The theatrical self-consciousness of the make-up worn both by Henry and his boy-actor bride ensures that the film audience in 1944 register, just as Shakespeare's own audience would have done, that the experience has been a fiction constructed through participatory illusion. Olivier's device as a means of accommodating the play's exploration of the theatrical process is a striking, yet under-rated, feature of his film. Throughout *Henry V* Shakespeare insists upon the recognition that the 'flat, unraised spirits' on the unworthy scaffold have had life breathed into them by the collective imaginative energy of an audience not at play but at work in the 'quick forge and working house of thought' that is theatre.

NOTES

1 Ellis-Fermor 1964, p. 45.
2 *Ibid.*, p. 47.
3 Michael Billington, *Guardian*, 12 May 1994.
4 Traditionally discussion has focused upon the character of Henry. A useful survey of earlier criticism of the play is given in Jorgenson 1947. In his later survey Edward Berry describes *Henry V* as 'by far the most controversial of the histories' and he offers a clear account of the polarised views (Berry 1986, p. 255).
5 All quotations have been taken from *H5*, ed. Humphreys 1968.
6 Traversi 1958, p. 198.
7 Bogdanov and Pennington 1990, p. 48.
8 Branagh 1989, p. 9.
9 *Ibid.*, p. 12.
10 *Ibid.*, p. 108.
11 *Ibid.*, p. 114.
12 Lee 1900, p. 12.
13 *H5*, ed. Taylor 1982, p. 70.
14 Stríbrný 1964, p. 96.
15 *H5*, ed. Walter 1954, p. xxxi.
16 Olivier 1984, pp. 90–1.

12

R O B E R T S. M I O L A

Shakespeare's ancient Rome: difference and identity

John Heminges and Henry Condell, Shakespeare's fellow actors and the compilers of the first collection of his plays in the First Folio (1623), would have been surprised at critical reaction to their organisation of the volume. Gathering plays about England under the rubric of History and plays about Rome under the rubric of Tragedy, they could have intended no serious generic distinction. In the parlance of the time the terms overlapped and interpenetrated. Both histories and tragedies related stories of past 'contentions' as well as the lives and deaths of famous figures. The 1594 Quarto of 2 *Henry VI* featured the 'Contention' between the houses of York and Lancaster as well as the 'tragical end of the proud Cardinal of Winchester'; similarly, the Quartos of *Richard II* (1597) and *Richard III* (1597) both offered 'Tragedy' to their readers on the title-pages. *Titus Andronicus* appeared in the Stationers' Register, the official record book of the London company of Stationers (booksellers and printers), as 'a Noble Roman History'; the 1594 Quarto, however, advertised the play as *The Most Lamentable Roman Tragedy of Titus Andronicus*. In its table of contents the First Folio identified one Roman tragedy as 'The Life and Death of Julius Caesar' and three English histories (*King John*, *Richard II*, and *Richard III*) with the same life-and-death formula. Another English history appeared in the Folio as a tragedy but in Quarto (1608) as the *True Chronicle History of the Life and Death of King Lear*.

What is more, the Roman tragedies and English histories exhibit the same kinds of actions and concerns: both depict councils, battles, rebellions, invasions, and crises in government. Both examine the nature of sovereignty, tyranny, patriotism, imperialism, and honour. Both explore the shifting relationships between the public and private selves, between rhetoric and reality, between war and peace. English and Roman citizens live in a tense, conflicted present, shaped by the pressures of a mythic past and by those of a destined future. The English remember the Plantagenet dynasty and the legendary Richard I (1189–99), Cœur de Lion, as well as the Lancastrian patriarch

Edward III and his seven sons. Each play recalls the battles and figures from its more immediate past. Carlisle prophesies the Wars of the Roses following the deposition of Richard II (*Richard II*, 4.1.137ff.); Cranmer foresees the dawning of the glorious Elizabethan age at the end of *Henry VIII* (5.5.16ff.). Romans look to their mythical ancestors Aeneas and Lucius Junius Brutus, expeller of the Tarquins; those in the Empire recall the age of Cato and stern republican virtue. Like Carlisle, Antony predicts 'domestic fury and fierce civil strife' (*Julius Caesar*, 3.1.263). And like Cranmer, Menenius predicts the glorious future; the course of the Roman state 'will on / The way it takes, cracking ten thousands curbs . . . asunder' (*Cor.*, 1.1.55–7).

In Shakespeare's English and Roman worlds women voice important insights that go unheeded. Katherine comments in *Henry V*, where rhetoric sometimes substitutes for reality, '*Les langues des hommes sont pleines de tromperies*', 'The tongues of men are full of deceits' (5.2.117–18, 119–20). In *Julius Caesar* Calpurnia cuts through conflicting perceptions of Caesar to deliver a devastating character summary in one line: 'Your wisdom is consumed in confidence' (2.2.49). Both English and Roman women often oppose the tragic march of history and all its destruction. In *1 Henry IV* Kate comically represents the civilised values of hearth and home that Hotspur rejects. The weeping women of *Richard III*, Yorkists and Lancastrians, register the devastation of the wars in terms personal and familiar. Lavinia, likewise, wanders through *Titus Andronicus* as a victim of Gothic and Roman barbarity, finally stabbed by her own father, the *paterfamilias*. Playful and indulgent, Cleopatra mocks the austere values of *Romanitas* – Stoic fortitude, self-sacrifice, military honour, and constancy. Even a woman who celebrates the male warrior code of honour, Volumnia, halts her son's invasion of Rome in *Coriolanus*.

But though the genres of English history and Roman tragedy share fundamental similarities, Shakespeare depicts Rome as different, as a strange world apart. His Roman vision largely derives from a Greek historian, Plutarch, as he appears in the racy and colloquial translation of Sir Thomas North (1579). From Plutarch, Livy, and many other sources, remarkably combined and transformed, Shakespeare imagines a Rome characterised by the spectacle of violence, by bloodshed, mutilation, and murder. Paradoxically, this brutal place also distinguishes itself in the civilised arts of language, particularly the practice of oratory and rhetoric. The city functions as a world, complete with its own history and codes of honour and constancy, but it also struggles with the larger world outside its walls. The plays reveal Roman politics in action and examine the torturous progress of Roman history. *Roma* is *alia*, 'other', strange and alien, but it is also *eadem*, 'the same', local and familiar, bearing resonant similarities to the world of Early Modern England.

Figure 10   Toby Stephens as Coriolanus, Caroline Blakiston as Volumnia, directed by David
Thacker, Barbican Theatre 1995. Photograph Alastair Muir.

In Shakespeare's ancient Rome original audiences could see strangers and
themselves.

The spectacle of violence

Violence sickens and enthrals throughout Shakespeare's Roman works. The
narrative poem, *The Rape of Lucrece*, features rape and suicide. The conspirators in *Julius Caesar* wash their hands and swords in the slain dictator's
blood. Antony resolves to win battle, or to bathe his 'dying honour in the
blood / Shall make it live again' (4.2.7–8); he later appears with Scarus, who
exhibits his wounds and jests about their shape. Coriolanus returns from
battle covered in blood, 'as he were flayed' (1.6.22); his shed blood and

scars qualify him to stand for the consulship, to wear the white robe and exhibit his wounds in the marketplace. Blood assumes a mystical quality in these plays as Romans spill, bathe, and revel in it.

Titus Andronicus represents Shakespeare's most graphic depiction of Roman violence. Early critics found the play gruesome and repulsive.[1] As in the other works, Romans here prove their *Romanitas* by spilling the blood of their enemies. The soldier Titus returns to Rome, weary but triumphant. His son Lucius demands a living sacrifice from the enemy Goth:

> Give us the proudest prisoner of the Goths,
> That we may hew his limbs, and on a pile
> *Ad manes fratrum* sacrifice his flesh
>
> (1.1.96–8)

Shakespeare invents here a non-historical Roman ritual of blood. Helpless Goths, Alarbus' brothers, comment tellingly on what such blood rituals say about civilised Rome:

> CHIRON   Was never Scythia half so barbarous!
> DEMETRIUS   Oppose not Scythia to ambitious Rome.
>
> (1.1.131–2)

Lucius and the remaining brothers exult in the slaughter, probably returning to the stage with bloody swords (142). After the Goths take their revenge by raping and mutilating Lavinia, Titus' daughter, the Andronici commit themselves to more revenge on their enemies, either to 'see their blood or die with this reproach' (4.1.94). Titus cuts the throats of Demetrius and Chiron on stage; he tells Lavinia to catch the blood in a basin:

> Receive the blood, and when that they are dead
> Let me go grind their bones to powder small,
> And with this hateful liquor temper it,
> And in that paste let their vile heads be baked.
>
> (5.2.197–200)

Titus serves the remains of her sons to Tamora in a ghastly Thyestean banquet.

A society that thrives on such violence and bloodshed must ultimately turn on itself. Soon after he has Alarbus killed, Titus stabs his own son for blocking him: 'Barr'st me my way in Rome?' [*Strikes him*] (1.1.291). Titus *Pius*, unlike the Virgilian prototype, *pius* Aeneas, here rages in *impius furor* against his own family. Later, trying to save the lives of other sons falsely condemned, Titus assents to Aaron's request and has his own hand chopped off on stage. In a final moment of bizarre paternal care, Titus stabs

Lavinia: 'Die, die, Lavinia, and thy shame with thee, / And with thy shame thy father's sorrow die' (5.3.45–6). Here the Roman shame/fame ethic requires expiation of a crime by demanding more blood, not that of Alarbus, but that of the victim, Lavinia. The murder of these two innocents frames the play and depicts Roman honour as barbaric and insatiable.

This self-destructive Roman ethos and its bloodlust leads naturally to suicide in Shakespeare's ancient Rome. Romans often assert their *virtu* by taking their own lives. Self-immolation asserts the self's *imperium*, its power over fortune and disgrace. Cassius makes good his initial promise, 'Cassius from bondage will deliver Cassius' (1.3.90), and kills himself to avoid defeat; Brutus expresses his admiration for Cassius, 'the last of all the Romans' (5.3.99). Brutus likewise offers to commit suicide during the course of the action, once 'when it shall please my country to need my death' (3.2.39), and again when he resolves not to go bound into Rome because he 'bears too great a mind' (5.1.112) for such dishonour. Likewise refusing the ignominy of public defeat and the triumph, 'his face subdued / To penetrative shame' (*Ant.*, 4.14.74–5), Antony falls on his sword; he supplies his own eulogy, 'a Roman by a Roman / Valiantly vanquished' (4.15.59–60). Women in Shakespeare's Rome also take their own lives. To avoid shame after rape, Lucrece stabs herself; her blood 'bubbling from her breast, it doth divide / In two slow rivers' (1737–8). Portia commits suicide by swallowing coals. Refusing to be led in triumph to the 'shouting varletry' (5.2.55) of Rome, resolving to do 'what's brave, what's noble . . . after the high Roman fashion' (4.15.91–2), the Egyptian Cleopatra also commits suicide.

The impulse to kill oneself to assert one's honour, so consistently present in Shakespeare's Rome as to be a characteristic signature, displays qualifying ironies in every case. Self-destruction in Shakespeare's Rome never appears simply as proof of a sovereign and invincible self, as the ultimate act of courage and constancy. Admitting that his sight was ever thick, Cassius misinterprets the outcome of a battle and Titinius' fate and then kills himself; an onlooker comments, 'Mistrust of good success hath done this deed' (5.3.66). Dying, Cassius proclaims Caesar's ultimate victory, not his own: 'Caesar, thou art revenged / Even with the sword that killed thee' (5.3.45–6). The dying Brutus too pays tribute to the conquering Caesar: 'Caesar, now be still, / I killed not thee with half so good a will' (5.5.50–1). His final words suggest regret for past mistakes. Antony dies in error of another sort, victimised by the false report of Cleopatra's death. Another Brutus comments on Lucrece's noble gesture: 'Thy wretched wife mistook the matter so / To slay herself, that should have slain her foe' (1826–7). In her last appearance (2.4), Portia appears nervous and frightened; Brutus later reports that she 'fell distract / And, her attendants absent, swallowed fire' (4.3.155–6). This suicide betokens collapse more than command. And Cleopatra dies in most un-Roman fashion, staging a highly eroticised and theatrical scene complete with luxurious costume, poisonous asps, and magnificent rhetoric.

The spectacle of such bloodshed and death defines Shakespeare's ancient Romans as other, as deeply alien and strange. But Roman violence had other significations for original audiences, imaging forth as well familiar political and religious conflicts. David Kaula has well demonstrated, for example, that *Julius Caesar* reflects contemporary religious disputes over popish ceremonies, papal authority, reliquary veneration, and the Eucharist.[2] The line between antiquity and modernity shifts constantly in the Rome of *Titus Andronicus* as well, as Julie Taymor well illustrates in the atemporal juxtapositions of her 2000 film, *Titus*. In Shakespeare's play an invading Goth stops to 'gaze upon a ruinous monastery', fixing his eye upon the 'wasted building' (5.1.21–3). Ancient Rome here changes into the familiar landscape of Reformation England.[3] Aaron demands that Lucius take an oath:

> I know thou art religious,
> And hast a thing within thee callèd conscience,
> With twenty popish tricks and ceremonies
> Which I have seen thee careful to observe,
> Therefore I urge thy oath.   (5.1.74–8)

Aaron here appears as a reformer, scorning Roman Catholic tricks and ceremonies, echoing, in fact, Article Nineteen of the original Protestant Thirty-Nine. By the time of the play 'ceremony' could, in Reformation discourse, denote the superstitious beliefs and practices of Catholics. Mocking his conscience, demanding an oath from the 'popish' Roman Lucius, Aaron enacts another cultural paradigm from the later wars of religion. Throughout the period reformist authorities required oaths of allegiance and Catholics, after the famous refusals of John Fisher and Thomas More, struggled with their consciences and divided loyalties.

The barbarous action of Shakespeare's Rome, its display of mutilation and murder, also evokes the contemporary culture of martyrdom. Lucius asks Lavinia, 'Speak, gentle sister, who hath martyred thee?' (3.1.81). Titus notes sadly that Lavinia has no 'tongue to tell me who hath martyred thee' (3.1.107), but he later interprets 'all her martyred signs' (3.2.36). Capturing Chiron and Demetrius, he says: 'Hark, wretches, how I mean to martyr you' (5.2.180). The making, interpreting, and telling of martyrs occupied Protestants and Catholics alike in Shakespeare's England. Copies of John Foxe's book of *Acts and Monuments*, which recounted gruesome tales of Catholic persecution, were on display in many Anglican churches. On the other side, the Catholic Philip Howard, Earl of Arundel, suffered dismemberment and torture eerily reminiscent of the atrocities here staged. The horrific public executions of Catholics like Edmund Campion, disembowelled and quartered in 1581, terrified and inspired others, who kept such tales alive in talk and print. The Elizabethan culture of martyrdom finds in ancient Roman barbarity its own religious practices and discourses.

Finally, the display of *disjecta membra* in the play, the cut-off tongues, heads, and hands, mimics the contemporary controversy over venerating relics. Article Twenty-Two of the Protestant Thirty-Nine, of course, had pointedly prohibited the invocation of saints and the adoration of images such as relics. In his Convocation Sermon (1536) Hugh Latimer likewise warned against 'juggling deceits', the veneration of Saint's relics that are actually pig bones, the vain pilgrimages to St Blaise's heart at Malvern and to St Algar's bones. Cranmer's chaplain, Thomas Becon, contrasted the Biblical prohibition against images (*Exod.* 20) with the encouragement of Antichrist,

> Antichrist also diggeth out of the ground to old rotten bones or relics of saints, translateth them, incloseth them in gold, keepeth them in precious shrines and costly clausures, and setteth them forth to the people to be kissed and worshipped.[4]

In *Titus Andronicus* Aaron again plays contemptuous reformer to gullible and superstitious Catholics. After having cut off Titus' hand, Aaron scornfully sends it back to him along with the heads of the two sons it was supposed to have saved. Aaron here cruelly empties the body parts of meaning, emphatically denying their symbolic or salvific power. The hand and heads on stage, however, galvanise the religious energy of the oppressed and become the centre of a religious ritual:

> The vow is made. Come, brother, take a head,
> And in this hand the other will I bear;
> And Lavinia, thou shalt be employed in these arms;
> Bear thou my hand, sweet wench, between thy teeth.
> (3.1.278–81)

The Andronici reinvest the discarded relics with meaning; they take up the hand and heads as signs of their belief, love, suffering, and identity, and pursue revenge. Original audiences who watched the spectacle of violence in Shakespeare's ancient Rome also found there surprising images of their own culture and religious conflicts.

Oratory and rhetoric

Shakespeare's Rome originated in Latin exercises and texts. In Elizabethan grammar school students parsed, read, memorised, composed, and versified Latin six days a week throughout the long school year. Lily's *Grammar*, which supplies a snippet of Horace in *Titus Andronicus* (4.2.21–2), supplied basic morphology and simple *sententiae*. Students progressed to Caesar, Cicero, Ovid, Virgil, Sallust, Quintilian, and Renaissance Latinists like Erasmus and Susenbrotus. They mastered texts, imitated forms like epistles, declamations, and *controversiae*, and invented rhetorical figures. Such training characterised Romans as people who practised the ancient arts of oratory and rhetoric. In Shakespeare's first Roman work, *The Rape of Lucrece* (1593–4), the narrator expatiates and embroiders in leisurely fashion while Lucrece laments in mannered apostrophes to Night, Opportunity, and Time. The Romans in the plays constantly make speeches, declaim, argue, praise, censure, persuade, and cajole.

No Roman work of Shakespeare displays more brilliantly the Roman arts of oratory and rhetoric than *Julius Caesar*. The famous forum scene, greatly expanded from Plutarch, follows Marullus' opening rebuke of the people and Cassius' persuasions, and precedes the quarrel between Brutus and Cassius and Antony's eulogy. The scene features Brutus' defence of the murder:

> not that I loved Caesar less, but that I loved Rome more. Had you rather Caesar were living, and die all slaves, than that Caesar were dead, to live all freemen? As Caesar loved me, I weep for him; as he was fortunate, I rejoice at it; as he was valiant, I honour him; but, as he was ambitious, I slew him. (3.2.19–23)

Here Brutus speaks a measured prose, constructed of repetitions, balanced clauses, and answering phrases. His careful style simulates the order and logic of rational argument. Antony, in contrast, speaks in a florid, emotive, 'Asiatic' rhetoric:

> He [Caesar] hath brought many captives home to Rome,
> Whose ransoms did the general coffers fill;
> Did this in Caesar seem ambitious?
> When that the poor have cried, Caesar hath wept:
> Ambition should be made of sterner stuff;
> Yet Brutus says he was ambitious,
> And Brutus is an honourable man. (3.2.80–6)

The blank verse, punctuated by questions and exclamations, repeats the refrain, 'Brutus is an honourable man', until it grows in ironic potency. Antony completes the performance with appropriate gestures and stage actions – the pause for composure, the display of Caesar's bloody corpse, the reading of the will. His masterful oration sets the crowd aflame with fury and indignation: 'All: Revenge! About! Seek! Burn! Fire! Kill! / Slay! Let not a traitor live!' (195–6).

Shakespeare's Rome recurrently features such confrontations between an orator and a crowd. Titus settles the succession question early in *Titus Andronicus*. Menenius quells the plebeian revolt in *Coriolanus* with the fable of the belly. Coriolanus spectacularly fails to master the art of speaking 'mildly' (3.2.145) to the citizens, lapsing instead into the rhetoric of the battlefield – proud, contemptuous, defiant; consequently, he earns their hatred instead of their love. Brutus, Antony, and these Romans well demonstrate that Roman *eloquentia* varies from orator to orator as well as from play to play. Yet there are some stylistic features of speech in *Julius Caesar* that resonate throughout Shakespeare's Rome. Like Antony, other Romans invoke abstract virtues like 'honour' and 'constancy'. Brutus loves 'the name of honour' more than he fears death (1.2.89); here honour is both a public and private virtue, military valour and private rectitude. Honour is the subject of Cassius' story (1.2.92), namely the tale of Caesar's rise and the disgrace it signifies for Rome: 'Age, thou art shamed!' (150). The assassination appears as an enterprise of 'honourable dangerous consequence' (1.3.124), requiring no other oath but an honourable Roman's word, 'honesty to honesty engaged' (2.1.127). Strato says that Brutus only overcame himself 'And no man else hath honour by his death' (5.5.57). Octavius allows Brutus' body to lie in his own tent, 'Most like a soldier, ordered honourably' (5.5.79). Constancy, composed of steadfastness, perseverance, and self-sacrifice, appears too as a characteristically Roman virtue. The constant Roman lives a life lived according to reasonable, virtuous principles, proof against the blows of change and fortune. Brutus exhorts the conspirators to conduct themselves as 'Roman actors do, / With untired spirits and formal constancy' (2.1.226–7). Portia wounds her thigh as proof of her 'constancy' (2.1.299); she later begs the virtue itself for strength, 'O constancy, be strong upon my side' (2.4.6). Brutus calms Cassius' fears with a curt command, 'Cassius, be constant' (3.1.22). Caesar refuses to repeal Publius Cimber's sentence of banishment with a ringing declaration:

> But I am constant as the northern star,
> Of whose true-fixed and resting quality
> There is no fellow in the firmament.
>
> (3.1.60–2)

Sensing the end, Cassius resolves 'to meet all perils very constantly' (5.1.91).

Appealing to other virtuous abstractions as well (nobility, worthiness, majesty), such Roman rhetoric clashes with Roman reality. The bloody murder of Caesar, often staged as a brutal series of stabbings, confounds the conspirators' high-minded formulations. Though he tries to live and die by a code of honour, Brutus illustrates how confusing and contradictory its demands can be. Caesar is a friend, Brutus admits, whose affections have never 'swayed / More than his reason' (2.1.20–1). Yet, Brutus feels an obligation to protect Rome, to overlook 'personal cause' for 'the general' (11–12). Can Brutus, or any honourable Roman, be entirely free from 'personal cause', or entirely untainted by pride and envy? Constancy likewise appears as an ideal potentially vicious as well as virtuous. Portia's devotion to constancy results directly in her self-mutilation and suicide. Caesar's boast of superhuman constancy smacks of stubbornness and megalomania. Ironies beset Roman devotion to such ideals in other plays as well. Aufidius' praise of Coriolanus' 'constant temper' (5.2.88) rings ironically since that Roman soldier refuses to stand, stands, refuses to stand, and stands again for the consulship. He rejects then yields to embassies from Rome, and acts as Aufidius' mortal enemy, then friend, then enemy at last.

Speakers of Roman rhetoric, moreover, delight in the sound of their own names. Characters in *Julius Caesar* continually refer to themselves in the third person, leaving first-person pronouns to serve lesser beings. Caesar addresses the soothsayer, 'Speak, Caesar is turned to hear' (1.2.17). He protests his fearlessness to Antony, 'for always I am Caesar' (1.2.212). Even at home with his wife he employs the imperial style of self-reference: 'Caesar shall forth' (2.2.10). This stylistic feature conflates the public and private selves, or rather subsumes the private identity into public persona. In this Rome the sounding of one's own name conjures into existence an ideal self whom all auditors must recognise and whom the namer himself must constantly strive to become. Like Caesar, ironically, Brutus also speaks of himself in the third person, here refusing to live under the domination of one man, Caesar:

> Brutus had rather be a villager
> Than to repute himself a son of Rome
> Under these hard conditions as this time
> Is like to lay upon us.   (1.2.172–5)

Later, he implores the gods to dash him with thunderbolts, 'When Marcus Brutus grows so covetous' as Cassius (4.3.79). Such self-naming implies the existence of ironic parallels between those mighty opposites, Caesar and Brutus. Cassius had suggested as much in his earlier exhortation:

> Brutus and Caesar: what should be in that 'Caesar'?
> Why should that name be sounded more than yours?

> Write them together, yours is as fair a name;
> Sound them, it doth become the mouth as well;
> Weigh them, it is as heavy; conjure with 'em,
> 'Brutus' will start a spirit as soon as 'Caesar'.
>
> (1.2.142–7)

Nomen equals *omen*, name equals destiny. Neither name has any claim to superiority, hence neither man has any claim to superiority; if Caesar predominates, Brutus can too. Cassius goes on to remind Brutus of his namesake, his ancestor Lucius Junius Brutus, who once expelled the Tarquin kings from Rome:

> There was a Brutus once that would have brooked
> Th'eternal devil to keep his state in Rome
> As easily as a king.   (1.2.159–61)

To decide the course of Roman history Brutus need only be Brutus, genealogically speaking; he need only live up to his name.

Manifold ironies attend this Roman habit of onomastic self-creation as various namings unsettle and disturb. After the assassination and Brutus' forum speech, the crowd cries out:

> 3 PLEBEIAN   Let him be Caesar.
> 4 PLEBEIAN   Caesar's better parts
>   Shall be crowned in Brutus.   (3.2.43–4)

The people here wholly ignore the political meaning of the assassination, the defence of republican liberty, and identify Brutus as Caesar. And, as the play goes on, Brutus sounds increasingly like the Caesar he slew:

> There is no terror, Cassius, in your threats,
> For I am armed so strong in honesty
> That they pass by me as the idle wind,
> Which I respect not.   (4.3.66–9)

Cinna, moreover, dies futilely proclaiming himself the poet, not the conspirator, tragically misidentified because of his name (3.3). Witlessly repeating himself, Young Cato proclaims himself 'the son of Marcus Cato, ho!' (5.4.4, 6), just before he is killed on stage. Lucilius identifies himself as Brutus, 'And I am Brutus, Marcus Brutus, I' (5.4.7), and then gets captured and exposed. Throughout the second half of the play, the name of Caesar lives on as Julius Caesar's grand-nephew and adopted son, Octavius Caesar rises to replace him actually and onomastically. The killing of Caesar only brings out the Caesar in other men. Similar ironies qualify Roman self-namers and their struggles in other plays. The Roman warrior Caius Martius wins the honorific agnomen 'Coriolanus' for his heroism at Corioles then, exiled, loses all name:

> 'Coriolanus'
> He would not answer to; forbade all names.
> He was a kind of nothing, titleless,
> Till he had forged himself a name o'th'fire
> Of burning Rome.   (5.1.11–15)

His mother Volumnia dissuades him from revenge on Rome by asserting that his name would then remain 'to th'ensuing age abhorred' (5.3.148).

Crafting Roman oratory and rhetoric, then, Shakespeare creates ancient Rome as a world apart. Paradoxically, however, the language of this ancient Rome also contains discourses familiar, even vital, to early modern audiences. Like the earlier *Richard II*, *Julius Caesar* dramatises the contemporary debate on tyrannicide which long engaged the best political minds in England and on the Continent.[5] This debate argued and reargued the central questions of the play: how to tell a tyrant from a just king; whence the real power in the state; what difference between vicious murderers and heroic republicans; how and when to justify assassination. These questions resound throughout the play, even in common conversation:

> 1 PLEBEIAN   This Caesar was a tyrant.
> 3 PLEBEIAN   Nay, that's certain.
>   (3.2.61)

This identification of Caesar as a tyrant echoes others – Cassius' exhortations (1.3.92, 99, 103), Brutus' reference to 'high-sighted tyranny' (2.1.118), and in the conspirators' triumphant cry after the assassination, 'Liberty! Freedom! Tyranny is dead!' (3.1.78).

But is Caesar a tyrant? Renaissance theorists agreed that one could qualify as a tyrant in entrance, *ex defectu tituli*, 'by a defect of title', in other words by an usurpation of power. Cassius characterises Caesar as this type of tyrant, breaking with republican traditions, illicitly arrogating power to himself, now 'prodigious grown' (1.3.77). But Cassius, by his own admission in soliloquy, wants to seduce Brutus into the conspiracy, to wring him from his honourable mettle. And twice we hear that the Senate plans to crown Caesar in the Capitol on the Ides of March (1.3.85–8; 2.2.93–4). One could also prove oneself a tyrant in practice, *de parte exercitii*, 'from the part of exercise', in other words by the proud or wilful abuse of power. Shakespeare's Caesar certainly shows *superbia*, an arrogant, overweening pride, and wilfulness. After refusing to go to the Senate, he responds to Decius' request for a reason: 'The cause is in my will. I will not come: / That is enough to satisfy the Senate' (2.2.71–2). But Caesar also yields to Decius' persuasions and shows generosity. He bequeaths considerable wealth and possessions to the people. And, in a revealing divergence from Plutarch where Caesar cannot read Artemidorus' warning about the conspiracy because of the crowd, Shakespeare's Caesar refuses the petition because it concerns him: 'What touches us ourself shall be last served' (3.1.8). Fluent in the contemporary discourse concerning tyrannicide Shakespeare shapes Plutarchan materials into a taut and ambivalent drama. The Romans on stage here enact current political controversies and embody contemporary struggles.

Urbs et mundus: city and world

Shakespeare constructs a distinct topography for Rome, resonant with symbolic features and localities. The city walls define Rome as a discrete space of political institution, religious ritual, social tradition, and ethical value; they protect the *urbs* from the barbarians without. The storied Tiber river runs through the city, irrigating Caesar's orchards, providing fertility and life. The Tarpeian rock, place of execution, looms threateningly for criminals. The Capitol stands at the centre of Rome's political life, more a symbol of *imperium sine fine* (*Aeneid*, 1.279), 'power without end', than a precise place or institution experiencing changes and redefinition through the ages. So too the Senate, Shakespeare's august, rhetorical, and fractious equivalent to the House of Lords, embattled both by an unruly populace and by great soldiers like Titus, Caesar, Antony, and Coriolanus. There are private spaces too, homes where wives, particularly, live and struggle. At home are Lucrece, Portia, and Calpurnia, who tells Caesar of her nightmare and begs him to stay inside. In *Coriolanus* Virgilia knits at home with her mother-in-law, raises the child, and waits for her warrior husband to return. The people, meanwhile, walk the wide streets, gather, and talk. They repair to the Forum, which Shakespeare conceived of as a marketplace, where ideals as well as goods could be traded, bought, and sold. There Antony wins the crowd to rebellion; there the tribunes discredit Coriolanus.

Leaving Rome, Coriolanus defiantly proclaims, 'There is a world elsewhere' (3.3.143). Perhaps so, but not for him. Wholly unable to live outside city walls, Coriolanus must return to Rome as its destroyer rather than its saviour. Rome exerts an irresistible, magnetic pull upon Shakespeare's Romans, always summoning them not just to a place but to an ideal mythical city. This mythical city makes harsh and relentless demands of its inhabitants. Cassius recalls Aeneas, for example, and then chides Brutus: 'When could they say, till now, that talked of Rome, / That her wide walks encompassed but one man?' (1.2.154–5). Here the city, concretely figured in 'her wide walks', becomes metaphor and myth, a place that summons the degenerate present to former glory. Octavius, similarly, reproaches Antony for abandoning Roman ideals and past traditions. Both urge fellow Romans to assume their true identity as citizens of the proud and eternal city.

Shakespeare's Rome, both the actual and mythical *urbs*, often opposes the outlying *mundus* or wild world without. Imagery in *The Rape of Lucrece* portrays Tarquin as a predatory animal and as a hostile invader of the city. Rome struggles against the Goths in *Titus Andronicus*, the Volscians in *Coriolanus*, and the British in *Cymbeline*, Shakespeare's last Roman play. The struggle between *urbs* and *mundus* defines much of the action of *Antony and Cleopatra*, which panoramically stages the conflict through forty-two scenes and the far-flung quarters of the world. The action veers back and forth across the Mediterranean between the poles of Rome and Egypt, moving also to Pompey's camp in Messina, Sicily (2.1), to the area around Misenum in Southern Italy (2.6), to Pompey's galley on the sea (2.7), to the Middle East (3.1), to Athens (3.4, 3.5), to Actium and the environs in Western Greece (3.7–10), to Caesar's camp (4.1) and Antony's (4.5), and to battlefields (4.7–8, 10–12). We hear a Miltonic catalogue of exotic names and places; for war with Caesar Antony assembles

> Bocchus, the King of Libya; Archelaus,
> Of Cappadocia; Philadelphos, King
> Of Paphlagonia; the Thracian king, Adallas;
> King Manchus of Arabia; King of Pont;
> Herod of Jewry; Mithridates, King
> Of Comagene; Polemon and Amyntas,
> The Kings of Mede and Lycaonia.
>
> (3.6.71–7)

And from Tarentum and Brundisium in Southern Italy, Antony marvels, Caesar cuts through the Ionian (here, Adriatic) sea to conquer Toryne (3.7.20–3). Testing the boundaries of the audience imagination and of theatrical representation, Shakespeare in this play stages a grandly epical, global conflict.

At the centre of the conflict is the struggle between Rome and Egypt. Antony's 'captain's heart, / Which in the scuffles of great fights hath burst' (1.1.6–7) is now vanquished by Cleopatra. Philo announces in the opening lines of the play that Antony serves 'a gipsy's lust' (10). Antony enters with Cleopatra in glorious procession, declaring 'There's not a minute of our lives should stretch / Without some pleasure now' (1.1.48–9). By contrast, Octavius Caesar embodies the austere virtues of *Romanitas*, discipline, valour, constancy. He makes his first appearance reading dispatches, curling his lip in contempt at Antony. He 'fishes, drinks, and wastes / The lamps of night in revel' (1.4.4–5). In place of the 'lascivious wassails' (57) and luxurious banquets, Octavius fondly remembers Antony dieting on the heroic Roman soldier's fare – puddle slime and horse piss: 'Thou didst drink / The stale of horses and the gilded puddle / Which beasts would cough at' (62–4). The oppositions in locality betoken oppositions in values. Rome, dominated by men, appears as a daylight world of conquest, rationality, and self-sacrifice. Egypt, dominated by women, appears as a night-time world of love, fantasy, and self-indulgence.

But such distinctions in Shakespeare are rarely absolute. The course of the action qualifies the dichotomy between Rome and Egypt, offering curious angles of perspective on the eternal city. Caesar ruthlessly discards Lepidus and laughs at Antony's challenge to combat; he seeks to magnify his own glory by leading Cleopatra in triumph. The disenfranchised Roman Pompey, who, like Caesar, bears the name of his great predecessor, challenges Caesar's power; he bears witness to the past political struggle and murder upon which the current regime rests. In one of Shakespeare's revealing departures from Plutarch, a Roman officer Ventidius refuses to accept hard-earned glory for his victory over the Parthians because he fears the envy and reprisal of his commander Antony (3.1). Such moments expose a core of self-interest and braggadocio in the ethic of Roman honour. And perhaps its hollowness. Teasing Antony, Cleopatra mocks Roman honour as mere show: 'Good, now, play one scene / Of excellent dissembling, and let it look / Like perfect honour' (1.3.78–80). And, as the play goes on, spectators may well succumb to the allure of Egypt and its captivating queen, who commands the stage with vitality, passion, and eloquence. John Dryden called his revision of this play *All for Love or The World Well Lost* (1678).

The alien landscape of Rome in *Antony and Cleopatra*, like those of the other Roman works, offered glimpses of contemporary realities. The Roman Octavius Caesar presented an image of royal power that James I appropriated and cultivated for himself. Believing in his absolute, divinely appointed right to rule, James adopted Caesar as his pagan predecessor and model. James' coronation medal depicted him in a laurel wreath with the motto, 'Caesar the heir of the Caesars'. Banners proclaimed him *Augustus Novus*. The iconography of royal pageantry further asserted the identification. In his 1604 ceremonial entrance to London James processed through seven arches of triumph. No less a poet than Ben Jonson prophesied that the lasting glory of James would parallel that of 'Augustus' state'.[6] This rhetoric of political ideology had another, more specific application for first audiences. In

Shakespeare's play Caesar prophetically envisioned himself as founder of the *Pax Augusta*, which encompassed Asia, Europe, and Africa:

> The time of universal peace is near.
> Prove this a prosp'rous day, the three-nooked world
> Shall bear the olive freely.   (4.6.5–7)

James likewise saw himself as inaugurating the *Pax Britannica*, bringing into one harmonious concord England, Scotland, and Wales. This project, particularly the unification with his native Scotland, occupied James and Parliament during the time of Shakespeare's play.

Though James envisioned himself as Augustus, others may have perceived him as more Egyptian than Roman. His court abounded in sexual passions and illicit affairs, to which gossipy 'secret histories' and responsible accounts all give witness. Married to Anne of Denmark, James himself had several male lovers. In Whitehall as in Alexandria, a heady mix of sex, power, and money excited and intoxicated. The entertainments lavished upon Christian IV of Denmark during his four-week visit in the summer of 1606 perhaps inspired some scenes of the play. That riotous celebration, H. Neville Davies has noted, also featured all-night revelry, prodigious drinking, and feasts aboard ship (see *Ant.*, 2.7). Such prodigality was typical of the notoriously extravagant king. The apocryphal story circulated that an exasperated royal treasurer heaped up money in a room so that James, marvelling while passing by, asked whose it was. 'Yours, before you gave it away', the treasurer replied.[7] Accounts of royal excess must have evoked the same vicarious thrill (and disapproval?) experienced by the Romans who question Enobarbus about Egyptian banqueting:

MAECENAS   You stayed well by't in Egypt.
ENOBARBUS   Ay, sir, we did sleep day out of countenance, and made the
night light with drinking.
MAECENAS   Eight wild boars roasted whole at a breakfast, and but twelve
persons there. Is this true?
ENOBARBUS   This was but as a fly by an eagle. We had much more
monstrous matter of feast, which worthily deserved noting.

                              (2.2.188–94)

The alien worlds of Rome and Egypt in Shakespeare's play presented a royal sovereignty and style familiar to its original audiences.

Politics and history

Each of Shakespeare's Roman works dramatises a pivotal moment in Roman history. *The Rape of Lucrece* (1593–4) depicts the expulsion of the Tarquins in 496 B.C. and the beginning of the Republic. *Coriolanus* (1608) recounts the establishment of the tribunacy in 494 B.C. and the new order of mixed rule in the next generation. *Julius Caesar* (1599) portrays Caesar's assassination in 44 B.C. and the battle of Philippi (42 B.C.), thus showing the end of the Republic and the beginning of Empire. *Antony and Cleopatra* (1606–7) continues the story through the rise and fall of the second triumvirate, the battle of Actium (31 B.C.), and the deaths of the principals. *Titus Andronicus* (1589–92) features battles with the Goths and the dissolution of Empire in the fourth century A.D. *Cymbeline* (1608–10) records the clash between ancient Rome and modern Britain in the reign of Augustus, as well as the westward movement of Empire and later dominance of a new Christian world.

Throughout Shakespeare's Rome politics and political institutions figure centrally. Rome bequeathed to early modern Europe a conception of civil organisation as well as basic structures of government. Its complicated and evolving system for exercising power, ensuring representation, resolving conflict, and administering justice lived on, transformed, in England and the Continent. Contemporary interest in Roman politics and government appears especially in *Coriolanus*, which features insurrection, the newly established representative government, the processes of Roman campaigning and election, and Roman civil officers – consuls, tribunes, censors, aediles. The play takes a dark view of the Roman achievement. Here political institutions strain, adapt, and ultimately fail to meet the needs of the commonwealth. Patricians and plebeians struggle against each other, each group serving its own interests.

Coriolanus opens with an insurrection. Shakespeare alters Plutarch's account, wherein war veterans have been impoverished by greedy usurers, to present a class conflict over grain. The patricians have 'storehouses crammed' (1.1.66); the plebeians starve. The Senate, the rebels charge, merely serves the rich supporting usurers and enacting 'piercing statutes daily to chain up and restrain the poor' (68–9). Menenius calms the crowd by comparing the Senate to the belly, which seems inactive but which actually nourishes the entire body. The fable defuses the crisis but does not resolve the conflict. And, moreover, the senators consistently fail to live up to Menenius' claims for them. They exist safely within city walls, absent from the battlefields where warriors like Coriolanus, Titus Lartius, and Cominius carve out Roman victories. The Senate never invests Coriolanus with the consulship after he wins the people's approval and watches helplessly while the crowd changes its mind (3.1). All the 'nobles in great earnestness' (4.6.60) go to the Senate House when they hear of the imminent invasion; but they only sit and worry while individuals like Menenius and Volumnia take concrete action. Shadowy, feckless, and old, the Senate represents patrician power in decline.

The plebeians, by contrast, rise in power, despite the quelled insurrection. The play depicts the establishment of the tribunacy, the office of the people. The newly created tribunes oversee the *Comitia tributa*, a voting assembly organised by tribes:

> SICINIUS Have you a catalogue
> Of all the voices that we have procured
> Set down by th' poll?
> AEDILE   I have; 'tis ready.
> SICINIUS Have you collected them by tribes?
> (3.3.9–12)

Though this body took tribal, rather than individual, voices or votes, the play here records the transfer of power to the people. Early in the play, Shakespeare depicts the class conflict that engendered this political innovation and that will continue through much of its action. After the revolt, Menenius asks what concessions the people have won from the Senate. Coriolanus replies:

> Five tribunes to defend their vulgar wisdoms,
> Of their own choice. One's Junius Brutus,
> Sicinius Velutus, and I know not. 'Sdeath,
> The rabble should have first unroofed the city
> Ere so prevailed with me! It will in time
> Win upon power and throw forth greater themes
> For insurrection's arguing.   (1.1.198–204)

Haughtily scorning the common 'rabble' and their 'vulgar wisdoms', the patrician sees the new office as dangerous and destructive. The tribunes in this play confirm such fear as they prove to be devious and untrustworthy. They plot conspiratorially and manipulate the citizens; they stage the confrontations with Coriolanus, goading him to anger; they succeed in banishing the best defender of the city. Such actions imperil the republic. When Coriolanus returns for revenge, the tribunes are as weak and helpless as the senators. They do not even accept responsibility for their actions, for the 'trembling' (4.6.124) they have brought upon Rome. Sicinius and Brutus merely protest weakly, 'Say not we brought it' (125).

Plebeians and patricians clash in the exercise of another political process, the public election to consul. Coriolanus grudgingly agrees to wear the white gown and submit himself to public examination in order to gain their voice, or approval. For him, however, this voice issues from the 'stinking breaths' of the 'mutable, rank-scented meinie' (2.1.290; 3.1.67). The people are mere rabble, intrinsically inferior to him and his fellow aristocrats; in his view, plebeian 'crows' threaten to peck at patrician 'eagles' (3.1.140). Unlike his Plutarchan counterpart, Coriolanus refuses to submit to custom and show his wounds. The people initially approve him but then, spurred by the hostile tribunes, change their minds: 'He's not confirmed. We may deny him yet' (2.3.195). Challenged later in a second interview and banished (3.3), he turns on them with savage scorn:

> You common cry of curs, whose breath I hate
> As reek o'th'rotten fens, whose loves I prize
> As the dead carcasses of unburied men
> That do corrupt my air, I banish you.
>
> (3.3.128–31)

Banishing the city, however, Coriolanus cuts himself off from kin and from civilised humanity, 'as if a man were author of himself' (5.3.36). The political process of the election reveals the worst aspects of both patricians and plebeians. Coriolanus embodies an arrogance and hauteur that unfit him for political life. Reverence for his own extraordinary self makes him scorn the ordinary man whom he, as consul, would serve. He cannot live within city walls or without them. The people show dangerous fickleness and volatility. Easily swayed by demagogues, they lack political judgement and constancy. Like the crowd in *Julius Caesar*, they turn on their former favourite with frightening rapidity and ferocity. Variously self-interested, senators, tribunes, patricians, and commoners all prove incapable of prudent action and just government.

As ever, original audiences may well have seen local reference in Shakespeare's depiction of ancient Rome. The opening insurrection replays in Roman dress the Midlands uprisings of 1607–8.[8] In several counties surrounding Stratford-upon-Avon people rioted to protest rising food prices and the increasingly severe Poor Laws Statutes. The audience could easily have understood the First Citizen's complaint about statutes that oppress the poor (1.1.68–9). Like the aggrieved and starving plebeians in the play, the ill-organised and ill-equipped peasants in England protested the hoarding of grain and the laws that ignored the poor to make the rich richer. R. B. Parker observes that the phrasing of complaint in the play, particularly the plebeians' paradoxical resolve 'to die than to famish' (1.1.3), appears also in a Warwickshire petition (*c.*1607); moreover, Roman arguments and images, particularly those of cannibalism, idle bellies, and cormorants, echo contemporary protests.[9] Like their ancient counterparts, the English authorities effectively put down the rebellions. The peasants did, however, win some concessions, though not, of course, the establishment of popular representation analogous to that represented by the tribunacy. The Privy Council eventually recognised the severity of the problem, declared an amnesty for the surviving rebels, and reaffirmed existing laws against enclosures and hoardings.

The larger power struggle between patrician and plebeians also had contemporary application and analogue. In 1598 James articulated his absolutist doctrine of monarchy in *The True Law of Free Monarchs*, and upon his accession in 1603, entered into continuous debate with the House of Commons about royal prerogatives and popular rights. In 1605, while arguing that the crown had the right to purchase goods below market rates, James, who disliked staging himself in public performances for commoners, disparaged his opponents as 'some tribunes of the people, whose mouths could not be stopped'.[10] James' habit of identifying his reign with imperial sway naturally prompted identification of opponents as tribunes here and elsewhere. And like Coriolanus, many English aristocrats insisted on their innate superiority to the masses. These groups debated the issue of representation and the processes of appointment and election, with all the attendant questions concerning the rights and responsibilities of the electorate. The play reflects contemporary tensions between classes and theories of rule as it depicts opposing claims and competing centres of authority.

The political conflicts of Shakespeare's *Coriolanus* and other Roman works transcend their Roman origins and settings. Human societies, including Shakespeare's own, always debate the nature of sovereignty and representation. Nobles elsewhere clash with commoners; many great soldiers, like Titus Andronicus and Coriolanus, struggle to move from 'th'casque to th'cushion' (4.7.43), from warrior to politician. The ordinary, hard-working, and fairminded citizen has often become fickle and dangerous in a crowd. The politics of *Coriolanus* have seemed particularly relevant to audiences in modern times, as two events in its history well witness. A production by René-Louis Piachaud at the Comédie Française in 1933–4 provoked fascist and royalist riots. The German glorification of Coriolanus in school editions as a figure of Adolf Hitler, a superman about to lead his country to a healthier society, prompted American authorities to ban the play during the early years of its occupation after the Second World War.[11]

Rome cast a deep spell on early modern Europe, striking into wonder many later artists and thinkers, who agreed with Martial's terse praise: *Terrarum dea gentiumque Roma/cui par est nihil et nihil secundum* (*Epigrams*, 12.8.1–2), 'Rome, goddess of nations and races, who has no equal or second.' Shakespeare's depictions of the ancient city ally him locally with fellow dramatists like Thomas Lodge, Ben Jonson, and the authors of the forty-three Roman plays that survive from 1497 to 1651.[12] Imagining Rome, Shakespeare also joins the larger humanist project of recovering antiquity that once upon a time gave the age its name – the Renaissance. In his six Roman works, the playwright follows the early lead of Italians like Petrarch, who wrote Latin letters to Cicero and other Romans, and Machiavelli, who wrote discourses on Livy to apply ancient principles to contemporary politics. In France Rabelais had Ponocrates instruct the young giant Gargantua in the classical languages and authors; Montaigne lived in daily imaginary conversation with Roman poets, philosophers, and politicians; Du Bellay contemplated the ruins of Rome in his *Antiquitez*. While illustrating both the splendour and vanity of earthly glory, Rome afforded later generations practical lessons in the arts and sciences, in art, architecture, history, politics, and literature. Shakespeare shares the humanists' double vision of that incomparable ancient city as both a world apart and, in some true sense, home.

NOTES

1 For a sampling see Kolin 1995, pp. 3ff.
2 Kaula 1982, pp. 197–214.
3 Jonathan Bate argues the point differently (*Tit.*, ed. Bate 1995); I am indebted to him (pp. 23–4) for the reference below to the Earl of Arundel.
4 See Rogers 1854, pp. 223, 225; Latimer 1968, pp. 23–5; Becon 1844, p. 521.
5 See Miola 1985.
6 See Davies 1985; Kernan 1995, pp. 106–31.
7 Ashton 1969, pp. 68–9.
8 See Pettet 1950; Zeeveld 1962.
9 Parker 1994, pp. 35–7.
10 See Miller 1992; *Cor.*, ed. Parker 1994, pp. 38–41; *Cor.*, ed. Bliss 2000, pp. 17–40.
11 *Cor.*, ed. Brockbank 1976, pp. 84–6.
12 See Ronan 1995.

13

R.A. FOAKES

Shakespeare's other historical plays

Shakespeare's plays on the reigns of English monarchs from King John to Henry V, together with his later groups of plays on ancient Rome, constitute what most of us think of as his history plays. A number of his other mature works have some connection with history and, though they do not form a group either in date of composition or in relation to one another, they illustrate Shakespeare's developing concern with the nature of history and the issues it raises.[1] I want to focus on two matters which came, I believe, to trouble him deeply, and provoked his most serious investigations of the processes by which we understand the past. The first of these matters may be briefly defined as the relation between history and myth. In the English history plays Shakespeare recreated Richard III cheerfully as the Yorkist monster we all love to hate, who prepared the way for the Tudor succession idealised in Queen Elizabeth. Also in the 1590s he established Henry V as a great, heroic English king whose glorious victories over the French might foreshadow later glorious victories over a Spanish enemy. It has become commonplace to stress the qualifications, even contradictions, in Shakespeare's portrayal of Henry, whose 'largess universal, like the sun' (Chorus, Act 4) and religious scruples (4.1) hardly square with his threats to destroy Harfleur (3.4) and orders to kill the French prisoners (4.6); yet after all such anxieties are taken into account, including Falstaff's send-up of heroic posturing and honour, the Henriad sequence remains to a significant degree a celebration of English history with a strong propagandist element appropriate to a decade when the country seemed to be under threat from the dominant power in Europe, Spain.

After the death of Philip II of Spain in 1596 this threat diminished, and Shakespeare soon turned away from English history to write in other dramatic modes. Beginning with *Julius Caesar* he probed more deeply into the relation of myth to history. Caesar is depicted as someone who has already become a myth in his lifetime, embodied in his name, and Shakespeare explores the predicament of Brutus as one who fails to discriminate, thinking he can destroy the myth by murdering the man. The relation of myth to history is an issue investigated in more depth in the first of the plays that stand outside the main historical sequences, *Troilus and Cressida*. Written around 1602–3, at the very end of the long reign of Elizabeth, this play may reflect Shakespeare's awareness of the decline of the virgin queen, who had consciously encouraged writers and artists to create an image of her as an icon, an embodiment of unchanging beauty and chastity. She too tried to establish herself as mythical. In this play Shakespeare explores the gap between myth and actuality most powerfully in relation to the Trojan war, in an action that continually contrasts the heroic legend of great warriors battling over the most beautiful woman in the world with the petty and often contemptible nature of their daily occupations. After creating his English histories for the popular theatre Shakespeare seems in *Troilus and Cressida* to be writing for himself in a work that may not during his lifetime have been 'staled with the stage', as the foreword to the first edition of 1609 puts it. It represents the dramatist's most considered response to war and heroism at a time when he was also perhaps contemplating *Othello*; but instead of celebrating the 'pride, pomp and circumstance of glorious war' (Othello's words at 3.3.354), *Troilus and Cressida* shows how war exposes the hollowness of heroic posings and ends in mere butchery.

Two council scenes, one in the Greek camp, and one in Troy, reveal the contradictions between the actions of men who speak as if they know they are legendary heroes, and the political or moral ideals expressed in their grandiloquent words. The first of these scenes contains the famous speech by Ulysses on the need for order, proportion and hierarchy as the only alternative to chaos: 'Take but degree away, untune that string, / And hark what discord follows' (1.3.109–10); but when the Greek leaders seek to restore some order by persuading the sulking Achilles to fight, they agree to play a cheap trick upon him by pretending to elevate Ajax above him in heroic stature – so much for 'degree'! The Trojan leaders debate whether to accept the offer of Nestor to end the war by returning Helen, stolen from Menelaus by Paris, to the Greeks. Paris and Troilus argue for keeping her on the grounds that

> She is a theme of honour and renown,
> A spur to valiant and magnanimous deeds,
> Whose present courage may beat down our foes,
> And fame in time to come canonize us.
>
> (2.2.199–202)

Paris is right to the extent that 'fame' has indeed immortalised the heroes of the Trojan war as mythical figures, but his reasoning cannot be accepted as a defence of rape. Hector knows this, having pointed out that

> these moral laws
> Of nature and of nations speak aloud
> To have her back returned; thus to persist
> In doing wrong extenuates not wrong,
> But makes it much more heavy.
>
> (2.2.184–8)

Hector nevertheless proposes to keep Helen for the sake of 'promised glory' on the battlefield, and for the sake of the 'cause', the war on which their 'dignities' depend. Abstract principles are thus jettisoned by the Greeks when they clash with the practical expediencies of human relationships; and the Trojans abandon the principles enunciated so clearly by Hector, preferring to seek honour and renown by continuing the war.

War is business or sport for men, while women in the male-dominated world of the play are mere chattels or currency. Helen has been stolen in retaliation for the capture of Hesione by the Greeks, and her personal feelings are not an issue. Just as the moral and political ideals of the Greeks and Trojans are contradicted by their actions, so the relationship of Troilus and Cressida that gives the play its title is bedevilled by contradictions: Troilus seeks to seduce Cressida, to possess her like a merchant seizing a pearl (1.1.96) while expecting an eternal constancy on her part (3.2.156). When Cressida is taken by force from Troy and handed over to the Greeks in exchange for the captured Trojan Antenor, her feelings are not considered. Her situation parallels that of Helen, and to the Greek and Trojan warriors she is an article for barter. It is a surprise only to Troilus that she adapts to life in the Greek camp by becoming the mistress of Diomedes. The ideal of constancy and purity in love is rendered impossible by the exigencies of war: 'The bitter disposition of the time / Will have it so', says Paris (4.1.50–1) about the transfer of Cressida, but the war and its bitter disposition have been created by the very men who blame the time. The heroes end up fighting for personal revenge, Achilles for the death of Patroclus, Troilus for the loss of Cressida to Diomedes, and only Hector has some larger sense of duty to King Priam and Troy; significantly, he is the only character shown with a wife, Andromache. Yet in the conditions of war, which require him to lead the Trojans in battle, his very virtues become vices, as Troilus tells him, 'Brother, you have a vice of mercy in you' (5.3.37). Hector spares Achilles when they first meet on the battlefield, only to be struck down by Achilles' Myrmidons when he is unarmed.

The cynical and reductive observer, Thersites, for whom 'all the argument is a whore and a cuckold' (2.3.69), scores points by his mockery, but is contemptible at the same time, for, as he shows in his 'prayers' at the beginning of 2.3, he is motivated by 'devil Envy', whose pleasures derive from watching the miseries and follies of others acted out. He is there in part to prevent our sharing his point of view. The ideals generated by love and war are fine and noble, but belong to myth, in which Helen survives as the most beautiful woman, and Achilles and Hector as the greatest of heroes. What Shakespeare does in this play is invent a history of day-to-day practicalities and reinscribe it upon the myth of the Trojan war. The result is his most devastating critique of war, and also a powerful dramatisation of the inevitable gaps between historical and mythical versions of the same events. *Troilus and Cressida* appears to have no direct connection with current events in Shakespeare's England, although some would link the portrayal of Achilles to the Earl of Essex,[2] whose failure as a military commander led to his execution in 1601; the play may also distantly reflect the final years of Elizabeth, when the gap between the idealised, goddess-like and for ever young Virgin Queen, and the aged and decaying woman lent a special anxiety to the problem of the succession. In *King Lear* and *Macbeth*, written soon after the new monarch, James I, came to the throne, Shakespeare returned to Holinshed and British history, and both plays show a consciousness of the contemporary political situation. Shakespeare was by now a sharer in the Globe theatre and a member of a company of actors which had been taken into the patronage of James as the King's Men. He always seems conscious of the new dispensation of King James when he turns to British history in his later plays.

Shakespeare found the story of King Lear in Holinshed's *Chronicles*, in which early British history is built on the legend of Brutus, who was said to have escaped from Troy, sailed to the west, and founded 'Brutain'. King Lear reigned some time later, about 800 B.C., according to Holinshed, and the Quarto of Shakespeare's play published in 1608 has a title-page calling it *HIS True Chronicle History of the Life and Death of King LEAR and his Three Daughters*. Shakespeare allows his legendary king some appeals to classical deities like Apollo and Jupiter, but avoids any indication of historical time, so that the play floats free, and can apply to any period. He was in some degree responding to the new regime in England, with a king on the throne whose political stance was very different from that of Elizabeth. James took pride in his motto '*Beati pacifici*', blessed are the peacemakers, so that old-style history plays celebrating wars and conquests fell out of vogue. Shakespeare deftly exploits some analogies with James, who, like Lear, had three children, two sons, and a daughter. Prince Henry, the eldest, included amongst his titles Duke of Cornwall, while Prince Charles was also Duke of Albany, and these are the anachronistic titles of Lear's sons-in-law. James liked to claim godlike status, and spectators at the play might have seen a link between the authoritarian Lear, with his love of hunting and bursts of anger, and James. How then could the play have been performed at court in 1606? It seems likely that Shakespeare knew how James had advised his son and heir, Prince Henry, not to divide his kingdoms: his book of advice to Prince Henry, *Basilikon Doron*, published in Edinburgh in 1599 and in London in 1603, shows James drawing lessons from the story of Brutus, who had three sons according to Holinshed:

> And in case it please God to provide you with all these three kingdoms, make your eldest son Isaac, leaving him all your kingdoms . . . Otherways, by dividing your kingdoms, ye shall leave the seed of division and discord among your posterity, as befell to this isle by the division and assignments thereof to the three sons of Brutus: Locrine, Albanact, and Camber.[3]

James warns explicitly against the division of the kingdom that sets in motion the frictions that lead to the ultimate civil war and its attendant horrors in *King Lear*. Lear has no male heir, so that dividing the kingdom between his daughters seems a plausible option, but the action of the play shows how it turns daughters against their father, sisters against sister, and father against son (Gloucester against Edgar). Lear's act is so disruptive that only invasion by an enemy force led by his own child Cordelia, now Queen of France, can set things right and protect the old king her father. The play, in other words, offers a dramatised lesson on the theme of James' advice to his son, and this may be how the King interpreted it. As lesson and as mythical history the play could survive his scrutiny and have contemporary relevance. At a deeper level the play deals with the potential for cruelty in human beings, with the vulnerability of old age to suffering, with poverty, with goodness, loyalty, and sacrifice, and it exposes the great to 'feel what wretches feel' in the process of discovering the need for humility. In his skilful treatment of a legendary reign, Shakespeare avoids any reference to period, and scatters anachronisms, allusions to works of his own time such as the Bible and Montaigne's essays, invents characters named after Saxon kings or saints (Edgar, Edmund), and makes social criticisms that apply to his own and any period, especially in the voices of the Fool and Edgar playing Poor Tom. The casting out from society of Lear and Gloucester, both reduced to beggary, reflects anxieties about the poor and homeless that are as appropriate now as at any time; and the play's interrogation of authority and justice retains its powerful urgency: a dog is still obeyed in office, and justice may still be perverted by corruption (4.5.151–2). I think the anchoring of Shakespeare's tragedy in historical legend based on Holinshed in some sense authenticates a dramatic action that is unlocalised in time and that seems capable in any age of both a local and a universal relevance.

Macbeth (1606) has still closer links with James I, the first Scottish king of England and author of *Demonology* (1597), a treatise in which he proclaimed his belief that the Devil may teach ignorant and superstitious women his arts and enable them as witches to practise mischief. Shakespeare converted Holinshed's 'Weird Sisters', 'the goddesses of destiny', or 'fairies', into strangely terrifying creatures, bearded like old witches, certainly of the devil's party, and practising black arts such as Agnes Sampson confessed (after being tortured) to using in an attempt to harm James I, or James VI of Scotland as he then was, in 1591. An account was available in a little book, *News from Scotland* (1591). Shakespeare altered Holinshed's version of eleventh-century history by blackening Macbeth, who, had hopes of the crown after Duncan's death according to the traditional law of tanistry by which it passed to the 'next of blood'.[4] Duncan scuppered these hopes by nominating Malcolm as his successor, so provoking Macbeth, with the support of Banquo and other friends, to murder him, and afterwards, according to Holinshed, Macbeth ruled well for ten years. Only then did fear about his own successor drive him to seek the death of Banquo. Shakespeare gives the virtuous Banquo a 'royalty of nature' (Macbeth's words, 3.1.51), and makes him an appropriate ancestor for King James, who prided himself on his descent from the line of Scottish monarchs shown as apparitions by the Witches to Macbeth in 4.1. So if he saw it, James would have appreciated the play as history, especially as Shakespeare added references to the English King Edward the Confessor (3.6.27; 4.3.140–61) as Macbeth's contemporary, and one who was said to possess a 'healing benediction', a power to cure scrofula by touching sufferers. Touching for the 'King's evil' was still practised by King James.

For most of the audience, however, I suspect that the play has always seemed more mythical than historical. The sensational opening scene in which the Witches know where they will meet Macbeth, establishes at once a sense of supernatural intervention. They do not control Macbeth, who is driven to seek the crown by ambition and the pressure of his wife, developed from a mere sketch in Holinshed. Yet their impact is out of proportion to their limited presence in the play, since their 'supernatural soliciting' extends to the apparitions that haunt Macbeth, the air-drawn dagger, the Ghost of Banquo; to the strange appearances they conjure up in Act 4; even perhaps to the mysterious third murderer of Banquo who completes a trio matching the trio of Witches. If they prompt Macbeth initially by naming him Thane of Cawdor before he himself has heard the news, he instigates the murders of Duncan and Banquo, and seeks to identify himself with the powers of evil, to become one of 'night's black agents' (3.2.53) like the Weird Sisters. In so doing he becomes an agent of destruction, a tyrant who lays waste to Scotland, a quasi-mythical figure, the devil that provokes Macduff to cry:

> Not in the legions
> Of horrid hell can come a devil more damned
> In evils to top Macbeth.   (4.3.55–7)

Duncan had greeted the victorious Macbeth in 1.4 by saying, 'I have begun to plant thee, and will labour / To make thee full of growing', but we see Macbeth wither himself ('my way of life / Is fallen into the sere, the yellow leaf', 5.3.22–3), and turn Scotland into a wasteland. When Malcolm orders his soldiers to cut branches from trees at Dunsinane and create a moving forest, this stage image not only marks the end for Macbeth, but also the return of fertility to the country.

The King's Men began to perform at their new indoor theatre at Blackfriars from about 1609, probably to a more courtly audience than that at the Globe. Shakespeare's late plays are overtly theatrical, seem partly designed for such an audience, and make much use of spectacle and dance, reflecting perhaps the popularity of masques at the royal court. He still kept his Holinshed by him, however, and *Cymbeline* (?1610) takes off from the chronicler's account of ancient Britain, which is a mixture of myth and history. Cymbeline (Cunobellus) reigned when Augustus was Emperor in Rome, and during the period when Christ was born, though no mention is made of this event in the play. The main action of the play is either invented by Shakespeare or derived from a novella by Boccaccio and other sources, and the historical framework remains puzzling. According to the chronicles, the association between Rome and Britain goes back to the legendary Brutus, who established Troynovant on the Thames, and was descended from Aeneas who founded Rome. Some generations later Mulmutius, son of Cloton, King of Cornwall, became the first King of Britain, and in 72 B.C. King Lud rebuilt Troynovant as Lud's town, later corrupted to London. The one historical event that frames the play is the refusal by Cymbeline to pay tribute to Rome (in Holinshed it is his son Guiderius who denies Rome). Past history is recalled in a central scene, 3.1, when Caius Lucius, the Roman ambassador, Cymbeline, the Queen, and Cloten, speak of Julius Caesar's conquest of Britain, of the prowess of Cassibelan, who 'Made Lud's town with rejoicing fires bright' (32) but in the end submitted to Caesar, and of the establishment of laws by Mulmutius. Lud's town is mentioned several times, and the play ends with Romans and Britons marching off to the temple of Jupiter in the town. The point of introducing these historical references has been much debated.

Cymbeline and his family challenge the Romans, and refuse to submit. The action of the play has the Roman forces invading from France (Gallia) and rather oddly landing at Milford Haven, where Lucius accepts Imogen (or Innogen, the name of the wife of Brutus) instantly as his page, anticipating the general reconciliation that takes place after the British forces, or more accurately three men, Belarius and Cymbeline's two sons, defeat the Romans. In spite of his victory, Cymbeline promises to pay the tribute as usual in the interests of peace. In seeking to make topical sense of the historical references in the play, critics have noted two facts that seem important: first, that there is no reason for Romans to sail from France to England by way of Milford Haven unless it is an allusion to Henry Richmond, who landed at Milford Haven to establish the Tudor dynasty as Henry VII, with whom James I liked to boast his connection; and second, that James prided himself on his abilities as a peacemaker, so that the end of the play might be seen as a compliment to him. *Cymbeline* is the only play in which the term 'Briton' occurs, seventeen times (in addition to 'Britain', twenty-seven, and British, two), and perhaps there is a connection not only with the descent the Tudors liked to claim from ancient British dynasties going back to Brute, who brought his pedigree from Jupiter, according to William Warner in *Albion's England* (1586),[5] but also with the attempt made by James to effect a union between the kingdoms of Scotland and England – James was proclaimed 'King of Great Britain' in 1604. But such allusions seem peripheral to the main action of the play, and Cymbeline is merely sketched as a king who is blind to the iniquities of his evil wife, so that Shakespeare would not have wished to give possible offence by hinting at any analogy with James and Queen Anne. It seems rather that the dramatist was playing wittily with surprise effects, appropriate to romance, that might draw sudden recognition and momentary applause – such, for example, may be the discovery midway through the play that Cymbeline has not only a fine daughter, but two noble sons who have been raised in a cave in Wales (James had two sons and a daughter); or having the Romans arrive at Milford; or the descent of Jupiter as protective deity to bring about the revival, to make Britain fortunate, of the 'stately cedar' (5.4.439);[6] or the sudden reconciliation between the Britons and Romans at the end. Shakespeare, I think, found a new way to exploit history as myth in this play.

The Quarto of *King Lear* claims to offer a 'true chronicle history'. What value did the word 'true' have in advertising? Shakespeare may not have had anything to do with this title-page, but he did become increasingly interested in the relation between history and truth. In his early histories he never hesitated to alter narratives in the chronicles for dramatic effect, even in plays on comparatively recent history, which suggests he could assume that most of his audience would not have a detailed knowledge of the history of England. He altered chronology, created characters, invented meetings that never happened, introduced anachronisms, and dramatised history as dependent on character and the whims and decisions of individuals. Is there then a dramatic 'truth' distinct from historical truth in these plays, and what is the relation between them? It is not an issue Shakespeare explored until later in his career. It could be that the closer association of his company with the court as the King's Men, and a felt need to provide some complimentary references to James in his drama triggered Shakespeare's interest in this matter. James may have seen in *King Lear* the expression of a truth about what he believed would be the inevitable consequence of a division of a kingdom between children, that is to say, civil strife. *Macbeth* offers more direct reference to James, not only in relation to his succession in Scotland, but in its reflections on tyranny, one of the concerns in his many writings. In his advice to his son, *Basilikon Doron*, he condemned the 'usurping tyrant' with his 'ambitious pretences' who thinks himself 'never sure but by the dissension and factions among his people', in contrast to a good king, who works entirely to maintain through good laws the welfare and peace of his country:

> For a good king (after a happy and famous reign) dieth in peace, lamented by his subjects, and admired by his neighbours; and leaving a reverent renown behind him in earth, obtaineth the crown of eternal felicity in heaven ... Where, by the contrary, a tyrant's miserable and infamous life, armeth in the end his own subjects to become his bourreaux [i.e., hangmen].[7]

Shakespeare could have had this passage in mind in composing his Scottish play, which again presents the horrors of civil war.

Both plays use quasi-mythical history to convey, amongst other things, what James regarded as political 'truth', though at the same time *Macbeth* is also concerned with equivocation, with the problem of knowing what to believe, as Macbeth learns at last to 'doubt th'equivocation of the fiend / That lies like truth' (5.5.42). The self-conscious playing with history and fiction in *Cymbeline* follows from this, and when Shakespeare returned in *Henry VIII* (1613) to a play on English history, his self-consciousness about dealing with history is shown at once in the subtitle, 'All is True', and by the speaker of the Prologue, who assures the audience they will be seeing only what is true, 'The very persons of our noble story / As they were living'. The claim is an intriguing one, for Henry VIII had long become, in effect, a legendary figure. Visual evidence about earlier kings is scanty, but Henry brought Hans Holbein and other artists to his court, and his image became familiar, not least because of the representations of Henry as defender and head of the Protestant church in printed works such as the Great Bible of 1540, and in John Foxe's *Acts and Monuments* or Book of Martyrs. From 1570 Bibles and Foxe's book were placed in churches and other public institutions to propagate in the reign of Elizabeth a version of history that represented England as a nation of the elect.[8] The 1610 edition of Foxe retains a print of Henry from the 1570 edition, showing him enthroned with his foot on Pope Clement VII under the title, 'The Pope suppressed by K. Henry the eight', with Archbishop Cranmer handing the king a copy of the Great Bible he sponsored. Shakespeare, working with his colleague John Fletcher, used Foxe for his account of Cranmer in the last act of the play.

A cartoon survives of Holbein's great fresco of Henry VIII and his family painted for his palace at Whitehall, a building destroyed in the late seventeenth century. The Holbein image of an ageing Henry with his broad bulk and almost square, bloated face, remains familiar, and was used in a woodcut on the title-page of Samuel Rowley's play celebrating his military campaigns and foreign ambitions, *When you see me, you know me*, written for Prince Henry's men in 1605, reissued 1613. The extent to which Henry's image had become fixed is shown in the reworking of an allegorical painting of the Tudor succession Queen Elizabeth presented to Sir Francis Walsingham in 1572. This was published in the form of an engraving by William Rogers about 1595, and in it Elizabeth's costume has been updated, but Henry's remains unchanged in what had become by this time the accepted image of the King. In the verses printed beneath Henry he is mythologised as a warrior hero:

> Behold the figure of a royal king
> One whom sweet victory ever did attend:
> From every part where he his power did bring,
> He homeward brought the conquest in the end.

Shakespeare's company may have used the traditional image in staging *Henry VIII*, but the play also challenges that image. The play presents an apparently youthful Henry (even though he has been married to Katherine for more than twenty years, 2.4.34), no warrior, but a king finding his way as a politician, and still reliant on the counsel of Cardinal Wolsey.

Sir Henry Wotton, who reported the burning of the Globe Theatre at a performance of the play in 1613, said it was 'set forth with many extra-ordinary circumstances of pomp and majesty, even to the matting of the stage . . . sufficient in truth to make greatness familiar, if not ridiculous'.[9] These 'circumstances' included the trial of Katherine, the coronation procession for Anne Boleyn, and the christening of the infant Elizabeth, later to be queen. The play, however, is much more than a historical pageant, for it presents an ambivalent protagonist in Henry, and constantly questions the nature of historical truth. If the staging seemed to Wotton to imitate real

Figure 11 'The Tudor Succession' (1572), attributed to Lucas de Heere and given by Elizabeth to Walsingham. The painting shows Henry VIII in state, with Mary and Philip of Spain accompanied by War on his right, while to his left Edward VI kneels and Queen Elizabeth is accompanied by a figure representing Peace.

majesty, the text never allows us to think we can be sure of what is true or real; throughout, as Gordon McMullan has shown, it sustains 'a sense of radical uncertainty', which points up the irony of the subtitle, 'All is True'.[10] The costumes are those of court authority and may imitate real majesty, but the vision of the king is limited by his dependency on others for information, until, after the fall of Wolsey, he at last begins to take direct note of what his council is doing when he defends Cranmer. Historical events are rearranged for what I take to be the play's larger purpose; it deals in the rumours, backbiting, and plotting that take place in the corridors of power, and offers shifting perspectives that never allow us to be sure of the truth about political events. The Prologue speaks of 'our chosen truth', a phrase that not only points to the difference claimed from other plays on the reign of Henry, but also to the construction of a dramatic 'truth' by selection of the events portrayed.

Anyone familiar with the details of the reign of Henry VIII could see that the play does not represent with historical accuracy the events 'chosen'. Chronology is radically altered, as in linking in time the trial of Buckingham (2.1; 1521) with the masque at which Henry, in the play, encounters Anne

Figure 12   William Rogers, 'The Family of Henry VIII' (c.1590–1595), based on the painting (figure 11). The costume of Henry remains fixed, while that of Elizabeth is updated to current fashions; the inscription sets out the popular idea of Henry as a warrior king, a reformation hero.

Boleyn (1.4; 1527); in bringing forward Henry's marriage to Anne Boleyn (1533) to make it take place before the fall of Cardinal Wolsey (1529); and in making the death of Katherine (1536) precede the birth of Elizabeth (1533). Where it suits their purpose the dramatist(s) transfer incidents from narratives unrelated to the story told in the play. So Wolsey's downfall is brought about in the play by his mistake in placing an inventory of his wealth in papers of state sent to the king (3.2.121); this mistake Holinshed reports was made in fact by Bishop Ruthall of Durham in papers sent to Wolsey, and led to the disgrace and death of the bishop. The citation of Archbishop Cranmer is brought forward in the play to precede the baptism of Elizabeth in 1533; in fact it took place perhaps as late as 1544, long after the death of Cromwell, who defends Cranmer in Act 5. To what extent would Shakespeare's audience have noticed such discrepancies and transferences? There is no way of knowing, but the play seems designed to challenge the idea that historical truth can be known. Shakespeare here teases his audience with a sequence of conflicting perspectives, showing what Annabel Patterson has called an 'urbane skepticism'[11] that disallows the certainty of knowledge.

'History', as the play presents it, is dramatised as a changing pattern of viewpoints out of which no clear 'truth' emerges about any person or incident. The opening scene brings reports about the Field of the Cloth of Gold, the famous meeting between Henry and Francis I of France, a memorable occasion of dazzling splendour in Norfolk's opinion, but a mere vanity that bankrupted many, according to Buckingham, in their extravagant spending on rich clothes. The charges brought against Buckingham by his surveyor in the next scene may be false, as Katherine believes, or may be true, as his peers decide in finding him guilty of treason. Buckingham is convinced that Cardinal Wolsey is 'corrupt and treasonous' (1.1.156), and it may be that Wolsey engineered Buckingham's fall, but we cannot be sure that he isn't guilty as charged, especially as he seems to know that his surveyor has evidence that will condemn him (1.1.222). The varying accounts, contradictory as they appear, all may contain a 'truth'. So it is with the trial of Katherine. Henry's motives in seeking a divorce are mixed; he needs a male heir and has succumbed to the beauty of Anne Boleyn, yet his scruple about the legality of his marriage to Katherine may be genuine (2.4.168–73). Two gentlemen who discuss the matter in 2.1 think Wolsey responsible for promoting the divorce, as does Katherine (2.4.76–7), but Henry says his conscience was stirred by a question raised about the possible illegitimacy of his daughter Mary in connection with the marriage proposed between her and the Duke of Orleans. Henry's affection and consideration for Katherine seem genuine, but we surely feel the law fails to do her the 'right and justice' (2.4.11) she seeks; no one blames the King, but it is clear he wants to be rid of her.

It turns out that Wolsey in fact tried to prevent the divorce in order to prevent Henry from marrying Anne (3.2.33–6). Though Henry's limitations and manipulation of the 'truth' are exposed in the matter of the trial and divorce, a benefit accrues in that he learns to distrust the Cardinal, whose treachery is at last revealed. At a crucial point in the action Wolsey hopes Henry will always yoke together his 'doing well' with his 'well saying' at the very moment when Henry has discovered the gap between the Cardinal's words and his deeds:

> KING   'Tis well said again,
> And 'tis a kind of good deed to say well,
> And yet words are no deeds. My father loved you,
> He said he did, and with his deed did crown
> His word upon you.   (3.2.152–6)

The play is much concerned with the discrepancies between what people say and what they do, and with the problem of assessing the truth of any words. Henry's blind trust in a servant inherited from his father may in part excuse some of his actions, and his growth in understanding here can be set against the pathos of the divorce and death of Katherine. Henry then intervenes directly to support Archbishop Cranmer when the Council conspires against him. Yet are the Bishop of Winchester's accusations against Cranmer, which he calls 'the plain truth' (5.2.105), entirely without foundation? We cannot be sure, and they are not refuted in the play. Henry uses his authority to enforce a reconciliation, which we may hope, but cannot be sure, shows the 'true heart' of both Cranmer and Gardiner (5.2.204, 207).

History is here shown in conflicting voices, in deeds concealed under fine words, and words that cannot be trusted to convey the truth. Yet something positive grows out of the confusion, in spite of the fall of Buckingham and the divorce and death of Katherine. Indeed, it is Katherine who suggests a generous way of understanding history. On learning of the death of Wolsey, she breaks into a denunciation of him as a proud, ambitious intriguer, a liar and equivocator; but her physician Griffith counters with an alternative view, praising him as a great scholar, wise and eloquent, and a princely benefactor. Although these accounts are contradictory, they could both be true, for they are not mutually exclusive, and Katherine learns to see another kind of truth here:

> Whom I most hated living, thou hast made me,
> With thy religious truth and modesty,
> Now in his ashes honour: peace be with him.
>
> (4.2.73–5)

The idea of 'religious truth' suggests a charitable interpretation of people and events, which allows for a mixture of good and evil, for words and deeds failing to match, and for a recognition that in most circumstances the truth is at best problematic.

Cranmer claims that his vision of the future with which the play ends is true: 'the words I utter / Let none think flattery, for they'll find 'em truth' (5.4.15–16). I think they may be seen as expressing a 'religious truth' such as Katherine approved, as he looks to what for the audience was the immediate past and the present, in the succession of the infant Elizabeth to the throne (eliding the reigns of Edward VI and Mary), followed by James I. Henry's main motive for divorcing Katherine was her failure to produce a male heir (2.4.184–96), but this is forgotten in Cranmer's celebration of the reign of Elizabeth, as his prophecy 'constructs the theatrical illusion of a non-problematic – and patriarchally sponsored – genealogy that, however James privately felt about Henry's memory, was politically useful to the first Stuart King of England'.[12] Cranmer's benign version of history was appropriate in 1613 when later Princess Elizabeth was married to Prince Frederick, the

Elector Palatine, but the audience had lived through the last years of Queen Elizabeth's reign with all the anxiety about the succession, and, after ten years with James on the throne, may well have had reservations about his 'honour and the greatness of his name' (5.4.51). The play they saw had shown them that truth is never simple, but Cranmer's vision, which tends to convert history into myth, charitably overrides the deceptions, injustice, and suffering dramatised in the action.

NOTES

1 The introductions to the following recent editions provide informed discussion of the relation of *Troilus and Cressida*, *King Lear*, *Macbeth*, and *Henry VIII* to history: *Tro.*, ed. Bevington 1998; *Mac.*, ed. Braunmuller 1997; *Lear*, ed. Foakes 1997; *H8*, ed. McMullan 2000.
2 *Tro.*, ed. Bevington 1998, pp. 11–16.
3 Modernised from King James 1994, p. 42.
4 See *Mac.*, ed. Braunmuller, 1997, p. 16.
5 Warner 1586, ; II.xiii.63.
6 Is this James as King? He is imaged as a 'mountain cedar' at *H8*, 5.4.53.
7 Moderised from King James 1994, p. 21.
8 See Collinson 2000b, p. 34.
9 *H8*, ed. Margeson 1990, p. 1.
10 McMullan 1995, pp. 29–30.
11 Patterson 1996, p. 163.
12 Kreps 1999, p. 182.

14

STUART HAMPTON-REEVES

Theatrical afterlives

Tetralogy thinking

In its Summer 2000 programme, the Royal Shakespeare Company announced the staging of Shakespeare's two tetralogies as a cycle called *This England*. The programme made a distinctive break with the past by conceding that the plays were 'originally conceived by Shakespeare at different times and written in non-chronological order', but, in order to preserve the integrity of the history play cycle, the programme went on to argue that the separate plays together 'form a collage of one man's insight into England's history'. No one authorial vision, or even one directorial vision, would dominate this cycle, and the plays were to be staged in all the different theatre spaces of the Royal Shakespeare Theatre. As a self-styled 'national' theatre, the RSC was swimming with the currents of the time, matching national devolution with a form of artistic devolution in which its various, disparate spaces were reconstellated as an architectural metaphor of the United Kingdom, with unity is sustained only through the acknowledgement of difference. In this way, the *This England* cycle both accepted that the plays are not a unified, complete work *and* presented an authorial, legitimate way of seeing the plays as a set of works on a shared theme.

I wanted to begin here, because it is my intention in this essay to trace the theatrical afterlives of the history plays principally through their coperformance as history play cycles. The millennial cycle is a possible *telos* for this history, as its rationale is an attempt to reconcile two traditions in performance history: one which sees the history plays as episodes in a larger, national epic; and another which plays against the totalising notions of 'tetralogy thinking', stressing the differences inherent in each play. Yet both traditions see value in playing the history plays together, whether they imagine that a history play constitutes a total, unified vision, or whether, through arbitrary juxtaposition of separate plays, epic themes emerge. There is, besides, a sense in which the history plays only started to be performed as *history* plays once they began to be seen as works which are part of a wider narrative, which represent and speak to notions of historicity and even national consciousness.

The practice of playing the history plays together is, by and large, a modern one. Up until the late nineteenth century, history plays were frequently performed, but often in much altered forms, and often as either tragedies or comedies, in which 'history', as the subject of performance, was either played down, or meant little more than historical authenticity in set design and costume. The two most consistently popular plays in the eighteenth and nineteenth centuries were *Richard III* and *Henry IV*, but their popularity was almost entirely due to the attraction of characters like Richard and Falstaff. The fictional and fictionalising elements of Shakespeare's historiography were foregrounded by performances which emphasised the psychological melodrama of Richard's character (as Garrick and later Kean did), or Falstaff's clownish upstaging of history. When history did appear, it was in the form of historical pageant. In particular, *Henry VIII* afforded theatre practitioners an opportunity for elaborate, historical spectacles, as Sir William Davenant realised in his famous Restoration productions. By the nineteenth century, the fashion for spectacles which were historically authentic often displaced the text of the plays, whose long running time was unsuited to a theatre which had to make complex adjustments to the stage between each spectacle. For example, Charles Kean's production of *Henry V* at the Princess's Theatre in 1859 was over four hours long despite extensive cuts to the script.[1]

However, towards the end of the eighteenth century, writers such as Coleridge and Schiller began to speculate about the theatrical possibilities afforded by what appeared to them to be a coherent, unified, and significant national epic. This laid the intellectual basis for playing the plays together, but what made such an conception viable, however, was a gradual move away from the spectacular, actor–manager paradigm towards modern theatrical techniques, such as ensemble companies, the rise of the director and the development of new theatre spaces. Since 1864, the date of the first known production of a history play cycle, the performance of the history plays as *history* plays – that is to say, where 'history' is the centre of the performance, rather than one or two main characters – has been influenced and shaped by cycle productions, the contexts in which they emerge, and the kind of cultural statements which they have made. In this limited sense, then, the theatrical afterlives of the history plays do indeed begin when they appear in the theatre not as single works, but as episodes in a larger, meta-narrative, in which history and nation are the main subjects of performance, rather than a notable battle, a famous king or a humorous clown.

In *Shakespeare's Elizabethan History Plays* (1944), which remains the exemplary exegesis of tetralogy thinking, E. M. W. Tillyard argues that there is an 'unnamed protagonist' in the history plays, a main character who is not acted by any single actor, but emerges out of the totality of characters, events, and language of the history plays. Tillyard named this character 'England', but in the productions discussed here, his unnamed protagonist has many different names and many different identities.[2] Such totalising strategies characterise tetralogy thinking, which presumes that the characters, episodes and themes of individual plays are always subordinate to an overarching, binding artistic idea. The act of naming this unnamed protagonist is frequently implicated in issues of national and cultural politics. Formations of national ideologies and cultural identity themselves involve totalising narratives, teleological histories, and binding, overarching concepts, in which the individual is subsumed within a larger, collective consciousness. In the theatre, tetralogy thinking has frequently echoed these ideologies, so that the plays can be, for some, a mainly patriotic celebration of national culture, for others, an affirmation of the need for order, and for others a way of exploring the sinister, oppressive mechanisms of power in society.

Early historical cycles

Though Heminges and Condell, the editors of Shakespeare's 'First Folio' complete works (1623), chose to publish the history plays in the chronological order of their narrative, nothing that we know of the playing practices of the Elizabethan playhouses suggests that they were ever performed in that order, so the notion of a history play cycle is strictly speaking anachronistic. Even so, the episodic nature of the history plays meant that they were always able to be reconfigured to serve different ends. Even before the First Folio was printed, there appears to have existed a manuscript written for private performance, which compiled episodes from the two parts of *Henry IV* into one play (this is known as the Dering ms., after its owner Sir Edward Dering).[3] In 1817, Edmund Kean had James Merivale conflate much of the first tetralogy to make a 'new' Shakespeare play called *Richard, Duke of York*, though Kean was motivated more by the prospect of creating a new star part for the theatre than he was in any form of tetralogy thinking.[4] In 1810, Coleridge had an idea for an annual Christmas festival of history plays, which he believed would be a 'fine national custom' that would counter the 'mock cosmopolitanism which under a positive term really implies nothing but a negation of, or indifference to, the particular love of our country.'[5] Though Coleridge's idea never came to anything, he was far-sighted in realising the important role that a history play cycle could have in national culture. It was not in England, however, but in Germany, that Shakespeare's history plays were first played together in the sequence suggested by Heminges and Condell.

In 1864, Franz von Dingelstedt produced all eight 'Wars of the Roses' plays at the Weimar Court Theatre as part of the celebrations of the ter-centenary of Shakespeare's birth. Dingelstedt anticipated the major cycles of the mid-twentieth century by treating the plays as a single, artistically unified work, with political, contemporary relevance, adapting and adding to the plays where necessary, and eschewing an emphasis on star parts for a putative form of ensemble playing and directorial theatre. Simon Williams claims that the cycle was 'one of the most important events of the nineteenth-century German theatre, comparable in stature to Wagner's *Ring* cycle'.[6] The comparison which Williams draws with Wagner's *Ring* cycle is an apposite one, as Dingelstedt was famous for his productions of Wagner's operas, and his history play cycle was conceived as a Shakespearean production which would aspire to the epic theatrical spectacle and cultural significance of the *Ring* cycle. The supposed inner unity of the eight plays had long been sus-pected by German romantics, and Dingelstedt was initially inspired by a comment by Schiller to Goethe that the theatrical performance of the his-tory plays as a single work 'could mark the start of a new epoch'.[7] Like Schiller, Dingelstedt regarded the history plays as a single, five-act narrative but nevertheless made extensive changes to the plays, particularly the early history plays. Some of these changes were necessitated by practical and politi-cal pressures (Joan La Pucelle was cut entirely, due to the political sensitivity of her character) but many of them were designed to make Shakespeare's texts conform to Dingelstedt's classical sense of dramatic form.[8]

The cycle brought the plays together with a controlling, political vision of history which was rooted in a notion of the parallels between the civil wars of old England and the current state of the German Reich, which Dingelst-edt made explicit in an interpolated prologue.[9] The history plays illustrated the responsibilities of the political class to its people, and in performance celebrated the brotherhood of the German Reich. In some respects this was a highly nationalist production, but Dingelstedt's basic theme was a political one, that injustice leads inevitably to disunity and the horrors of civil war. Subsequently, history play cycles were frequently staged in Germany, with up to forty cycles being produced in Germany up to 1914.[10] England was slow to respond to this theatrical appropriation of Shakespeare's national epic, and when it did, its cycles were, initially at least, looser and more *ad hoc* works than Dingelstedt's, caught on the cusp of modernity and the waning Victorianism of the Edwardian years.

In 1902, Frank Benson directed the first British history play cycle for the annual Shakespeare festival at the Shakespeare Memorial Theatre in Stratford-upon-Avon. The Historical Cycle (or, as it was dubbed locally, the 'Week of Kings') combined cultural ambition, contemporary performance methods, and textual authenticity. The event was significant enough to draw a national audience to a festival that had, up to that point, been largely a provincial affair. Unlike Dingelstedt, Benson did not see the history plays as an opportunity for political or social commentary and, though Benson's company made some superficial gestures towards the innovative methods of Dinglestedt and, later, the Meininger company, in many respects their Week of Kings was marked by a persistent, residual Victorianism.[11] The cycle deliberately eschewed any sense of a continuing cycle narrative by beginning with *King John* and leaving out critical plays like *1 Henry IV* and *3 Henry VI*. The result was an uneasy compromise between treating the history plays as individual works and treating them as parts of a larger whole.

Benson mounted another 'Week of Kings' in 1906 which focused on the two tetralogies and so developed a more coherent narrative. A character called Lord Essex (played by Arthur Machen) was invented to take on some of the roles of the minor nobles, providing continuity across the cycle, whilst the staging of all three *Henry VI* plays in sequence was a major theatrical event, which helped to force a reassessment of these early history plays' theatrical and artistic strengths. The *Henry VI* plays also gave Benson a political theme for his cycle. Benson's own 'Notes on the Production of *Henry VI*' stresses 'how during the death and the ruin of so many nobles and gentry, the Commons of England were growing in power and importance and laying the foundation of the English empire'.[12] For Benson and his company, then, the history plays were primarily political allegories of the rise of the Protestant, parliamentary empire that they lived in. This was as political as Benson got, however, and he was more interested in the opportunities that the plays presented for dramatic and spectacular battle scenes.

History play cycles continued after the First World War. In England, Robert Atkins (at the Old Vic) and Nugent Monck (at Maddermarket, Norwich) both staged history play cycles as part of large-scale projects to stage the whole Shakespearean canon. Though in some way very conservative productions, the work of Atkins and Monck nevertheless represented the wholesale incorporation of Shakespeare's complete works into mainstream theatrical culture, and adumbrated the more sensitive rediscoveries of his more obscure works – including the *Henry VI* plays – later in the century. In 1927, Dr Saladin Schmitt staged an important cycle at the municipal theatre in Bochum, Germany[13] and in 1938, Orson Welles premiered an ambitious conflation of the second tetralogy at the Colonial Theatre in Boston called *Five Kings*. *Five Kings* presented on a revolving stage scenes as montages and episodes in which individual characters were subsumed in the march of history. Orson Welles was excited by the opportunities the plays gave to speak to the contemporary experience of war, and drew explicit parallels between Shakespeare's battlefields and the battlefields of modern Europe. Welles was the first director since Dingelstedt to realise the potential of the plays to speak to contemporary concerns. Only a few years after Welles, Bertolt Brecht went even further and recast *Richard III* as a parable of the rise of fascism in his *The Resistible Rise of Arturo Ui*. Welles and Brecht anticipated the contemporary themes which would dominate late twentieth-century history play cycles, and both were influential when their ideas were replayed in a postwar context. The Berliner Ensemble's international tour of *Arturo Ui* in 1956 stimulated interest in Brecht's methods and techniques in British theatre, whilst Orson Welles' film of *Five Kings*, called *Chimes at Midnight*, was similarly influential in re-thinking the nature of the Shakespearean history play.

Postwar histories

Whereas history play performance had, prior to 1939, been by and large an antiquarian pursuit of the 'complete' Shakespeare, after the war the plays took on new meanings for a generation facing the aftermath of world war on the one hand, and the failure of the great early twentieth-century ideologies on the other. For thirty years at least British and European productions of the history plays bore the marks of the Second World War in varying degrees. In Britain, national service continued for more than a decade, so that the 'angry young man' generation developed its anti-establishment attitude through a semi-militarised youth, which provided a new, different context for the performance of battle-scenes and wars. From the 1940s the history plays took on a new role, as epic texts through which the nature of national self, and the direct experience of history, could be examined. In 1944, E. M. W. Tillyard's *Shakespeare's Elizabethan History Plays* had presented a coherent interpretation of the history plays as a patriotic celebration of nationhood, with a political role in the sustaining of the Tudor myth. Tillyard's work made a huge impact at the time, though many of its assumptions have since been questioned. However, the number of history play productions which followed in the 1940s and 1950s are partly due to the way Tillyard's tetralogy thinking gripped postwar imaginations. Tillyard was the first critic, but not the last, to give a full, scholarly reading of the history plays as a unified, single work. In 1965, the Polish critic Jan Kott's *Shakespeare Our*

Contemporary began with a chapter on Shakespeare's history plays which gave a modernist spin to Tillyard's reading. Kott interpreted the plays as studies in power politics, in which 'history' emerges as a dark, oppressive, intractable, and inhuman force. Productions in the 1960s developed Kott's thesis into an anti-establishment critique, as dramatic meditations on the nature of history became, by deduction, meditations on the relationship between rulers and ruled. Politics, which had once been the great emancipator, was increasingly seen as a kind of power game which could only produce disasters like the Second World War. The theatrical afterlives of the history plays were in varying degrees infected by the polarities of tetralogy thinking which Kott and Tillyard charted.

In the same year that Tillyard's theories were published, Laurence Olivier filmed and released *Henry V* which brought a Technicolor, Hollywood aesthetic to the performance of English history. Filmed during the war, Olivier deliberately pitched the film as a form of cultural propaganda for a beleaguered and war-weary nation. The film has been repeatedly criticised for its triumphal and uncritical vision of Henry as the great English warrior–king. However, the film should be understood as one part of a series of history productions which Olivier acted in from 1944 to 1946, which, whilst not strictly speaking a history play cycle, nevertheless constituted a cultural response to the war and its aftermath through the performance of four of Shakespeare's history plays: the film *Henry V*, *Richard III* (1944) and the two parts of *Henry IV* (1945). The performance of Shakespeare's history plays was a way of using the theatre to assert the continuation of English history in the face of the catastrophe of war and attempted invasion.[14] However, a more ambiguous representation of English history could be felt in the postwar histories. In John Burrell's 1945 production of the two parts of *Henry IV* at the Old Vic, Olivier played Hotspur to Ralph Richardson's Hal, an interesting turn from hero to anti-hero. The production sounded a subtle, war-weary note when Falstaff's recruits were heard marching off-stage, tiredly mumbling a weary version of 'Greensleeves'.[15] English culture sounded tired, its meaning somehow forgotten in the midst of battle. Subsequent productions in England and Germany over the next twenty years explored increasingly dark and problematic representations of nation, war, and politics, often using Olivier's histories as a starting point, and frequently also as a point of departure.

The most significant of these early postwar productions was Antony Quayle's second tetralogy cycle at Stratford's Shakespeare Memorial Theatre in 1951. The production was mounted for the Festival of Britain, which was meant to remotivate a nation tired of war and rations and remind the nation of its own heritage and identity in postwar, postimperial Britain. This was the first time that the history plays had been revived in this way since Benson, but the cycle marked a significant advance on these earlier cycles. Whereas Benson had put together an *ad hoc* programme based on what he knew and what he could learn, Quayle believed that the plays had an 'inner unity and a dramatic progression'[16] which justified staging them together, with one company, in order to bring out the underlying narrative patterns of Shakespeare's work. The productions returned to the original Elizabethan stage spaces for which the plays were written for inspiration. Tanya Moiseiwitsch's stage was a wooden, tiered pavilion which had the feel of an Elizabethan theatre and anticipated the mock-Elizabethan theatre which Moiseiwitsch constructed for the Stratford Ontario festival in 1953. This was enhanced by billowing curtains at the top and sides which worked to blur the frame of the proscenium arch, as if the Shakespearean inauthenticity of the Victorian architecture of the stage was being shamefully hidden from view. Yet, as Dennis Kennedy notes, what Moiseiwitsch achieved was more in the nature of a picture of an Elizabethan stage, not the thing itself.[17] The result, then, was an uneasy compromise between the inauthentic structures of the traditional theatre and the more 'authentic' Shakespearean spaces. This particular staging of the histories has been highly influential in the British theatre, however. The Birmingham Repertory productions of the *Henry VI* plays, which provided a neighbourly continuation of Quayle's project, utilised a stage space that was recognisably similar to the Stratford histories, whilst both productions underpinned the BBC's *Age of Kings* series in 1960, which staged the entire cycle in ten-hour-long instalments. Tyrone Guthrie's *Richard III* (with Alec Guinness as the lead role), which was the opening production of the Stratford, Ontario festival in Canada, made full use of Moiseiwitsch's Elizabethan stage, which was taken by some reviewers as the main star of the show. By returning to the plays' theatrical origins, and fulfilling the epic cycle dreamt of by Coleridge, Quayle was also, perhaps, inviting a national reflection on cultural origins relevant to a period of postwar austerity and an atmosphere of wanting to 'start again', a general sense of a need to build something new which Quayle described as a 'surge of post-war energy and idealism'.[18] The production was not wholly idealist, however. Richard Burton's performance of Henry explored the character's insecurities and self-doubt, his disaffected masculinity foreshadowing the redundant heroism of Burton's later performance of Jimmy Porter in *Look Back in Anger* (1956). Burton's Henry was a darker, more remote figure than Olivier's warrior–king. Quayle saw this aspect of Hal as inevitably rising from the innovation of staging the plays together: Falstaff's comic persona (played by Quayle himself), for example, was given added tragic depth by his final rejection, which emphasised Henry's increasing isolation. Though it would be wrong to characterise the Stratford histories as dark or anti-patriotic, they did open up darker, problematic subtexts, at the same time as rescuing the histories from a sentimental tradition and paving the way for the more politically engaged productions of the 1960s.

With Douglas Seale's first tetralogy,[19] Guthrie's *Richard III* and the BBC's *Age of Kings* cycle, one period in postwar history play cycles came to a conclusion, but in 1963, Peter Hall produced his own version of the first tetralogy with John Barton for the Royal Shakespeare Company, and added the second tetralogy the following year, producing the first full 'historical cycle' with one company, in one theatre, since the turn of the century. The cycle, called *The Wars of the Roses*, was the definitive RSC production of the 1960s, combining an ensemble ethic, a Brechtian aesthetic, radical leanings and a sense of national culture which helped to define Shakespearean perfor-mance for a decade. The script for the first tetralogy was even displayed in the British Museum, with John Barton's red pen altering, adapting and adding to Shakespeare's work like a corrective schoolmaster. The directors initially positioned themselves against the 1950s cycles, which they characterised as confusing, out-moded and unengaging but, like Quayle, Hall and Barton were self-consciously working within a postwar milieu, in which 'politics' and 'history', to many people, were inevitably implicated in the crisis of war and its aftermath. They sought to draw out homologies with the present-day crisis of English nationalism by identifying power and politics as the main agencies of disorder. In his introduction to the published script of *The Wars of the Roses*, Hall explained that one of his central preoccupations was 'the dilemma of power', which he expressed as the question 'Can a man be 'good' and politic? Do you have to be a bad man to make a good king?'[20] *The Wars of the Roses* made an allegory of modernity out of the materials of chronicle history, so that *Richard II*, which Hall's design notes referred to as the 'garden of England', represented preindustrial England, and *Richard III*, described by Hall simply as 'the bunker', dressed the actors in black leather armour in a deliberate echo of fascism.

Through the course of the seven plays (*Henry VI* was reduced and rewrit-ten by Barton as two plays), the stage was drained of its colours as the politi-cal failures of the ruling classes lead to a progressive, darkening modernity.[21] John Barton's script narrowed the focus of the plays to centre upon the workings of history as a grand narrative force, and John Bury's set was constructed as a giant steel cage, materialising these forces upon the stage as an oppressive trap for its participants. History was both the centre of the production, its 'main protagonist',[22] and its surface, its body and its soul, leaving the human subject to the desolate battleground constituted by its *mise-en-scène*. Yet this dark vision of English history was off-set by the cycle's ending. Barton's rewriting of *Richard III* developed the sense of closure by adding the marriage of the two houses, a scene which Shakespeare curiously misses out. At the very end, the need for order is affirmed out of pragmatic necessity: explaining this, Hall wrote that 'history is a constant tragic pressure on all human beings and unless they govern themselves and their institutions pragmatically, there is a perpetual natural tendency to return to chaos'.[23] Despite its radical style, the cycle finally affirmed the need for governing institutions as a bulwark against the chaos represented by fascism and by Richard Gloucester.

Hall's European, radical stylings provoked several notable European productions of history play cycles which similarly used the plays to engage with historical consciousness after the war. However, where *The Wars of the Roses* finally emphasised the pragmatic necessity of political order, productions in Europe were more sceptical about the possibilities offered by politics. Giorgio Strehler's *Il gioce dei potenti* (1965) (usually translated as *Power Games* or *The Game of the Mighty*) was a free adaptation in Italian of the first tetralogy and, as the title implies, the political analysis explored by Hall and Barton in the history plays was foregrounded. Strehler was sympathetic to the existential vision that Hall and Barton brought to the history plays, and in his hands they became performances of 'the anguish, the void, the nothingness surrounding man' which 'could be overcome through an act of artistic affirmation...'. The production was, said Strehler, 'born as a drama of rupture, modern, contemporary'.[24] The Italian context lent the postwar connotations suggested by narratives of political corruption, civil war, and the rise of fascism more immediate and problematic resonance, as they did also in Peter Palitzsch's *Der Rosenkrieg* (1967). The production's dramaturg, Jörg Wehmeier, arranged an eight-hour production in two parts called *Henry VI* and *Edward IV*, with the opening monologue of *Richard III* providing a climactic moment marking the unexplored threat of totalitarianism. Where Strehler stressed the modernity of his histories, Palitzsch followed his mentor Brecht by stressing the pastness of history, arguing that only by establishing historical distance can meaningful contemporary relevance be achieved.[25] The adaptation's main innovation was to adjust the characterisation of some of the more sympathetic characters in order to remove any sense of heroism in the play-world; Gloucester no longer had unselfish motives and Talbot was a cowardly, brutal butcher.[26] This was, again, a very Brechtian move, which privileged dialectical and social history as a process of class struggle and demystified Olivier's heroic stereotype as a part of the fictions generated by the ideologies of power.[27] For Palitzsch and Strehler, history was a fatal mechanism, a game played by the powerful which produces nothing but self-destructive wars, in which ordinary people are swept up by unstoppable historical forces.[28]

Alternative histories

The next major European cycle marked a departure from post-war cycles, and helped to transform the theatrical possibilities for Shakespeare's history plays. Terry Hands directed the two tetralogies at the RSC over five years, producing the *Henriad* in 1975, the *Henry VI* plays in 1977, with *Richard II* and *Richard III* completing the cycle in 1980. Alan Howard played the lead role in all eight plays, playing five Shakespearean kings in five years. The productions were a self-conscious challenge to the monumental histories of the 1960s. History was represented on a stage (designed by Farrah) which had been stripped to reveal the wood and brickwork of the theatre. Yet, against this anti-illusionist backdrop, battles were performed with unsentimental realism: history was encountered raw and unmediated. *Henry V* opened with the startling, counter-intuitive image of Henry and his court dressed in casual, modern clothes. As the scene developed, the characters changed into period dress, as if to stress the theatricality of history. In fact, Hands used costume through the *Henriad* to make aesthetic points about history and national identity. For example, in *Henry V* the French were 'trapped' (as Sally Beauman puts it) in beautiful, gold armour so that 'they died visibly imprisoned in the symbol of a way of life and set of assumptions that they – unlike the English – had been unable to escape.'[29] This rhymed ironically with the climax of 2 *Henry IV*, when the new king appeared onstage in a coronation costume which completely encased him from head to foot in gold armour. Even his face was covered in a moulded, gold mask and he moved slowly and mechanically, as if the event of becoming King had dehumanised Hal.

Henry V, then, was very much at the centre of Hands' approach to the history plays and, following Olivier's film, perhaps reflected the critical importance of the play to issues of national culture. *Henry V* was revived the following season alongside the *Henry VI* plays, constructing a new tetralogy beginning with Agincourt and ending with civil war. So, where the first season had begun with a heroic Henry V, and then explored his rise to power retrospectively and critically, the second season looked in the other direction, at the unravelling of English society after Henry's death. The *Henry VIs* were a bleak coda to the 1975 histories, in which England was presented in shades of disillusionment and anger, which concluded with the unresolved final scene of 3 *Henry VI*. After Edward IV's closing speech, musicians started to play the only tune they knew, which was militaristic and bombastic; then Edward signalled a change of tune and the musicians started to play a dance tune, but the court could not remember the steps. It was a powerful image of a nation which had lost or forgotten a great part of its culture, which was struggling to find a lost cultural identity that was only dimly remembered.

'History', then, was approached in terms of the dialectic between culture and power. Rejecting the monolithic histories of the 1960s, Hands explored the social textures of history and the relationship of individuals to history. For example, in 2 *Henry VI*, the commoners were separated from the nobles by a rope which was later used by Jack Cade to hang the clerk of Chatham, appropriating a symbol of division and repression to a violent revolution. The influence of Hands' socialisation of history was apparent in Robert Sturua's carnivalesque *Richard III* for the Georgian National Theatre in Tbilisi (1979), which was also performed at the Edinburgh Festival, and Dominic Llorca's 1978 adaptation of the first tetralogy, *Kings, ou les adieux à Shakespeare* at the Maison des arts André Malraux, Créteil. Both productions went further than Hands in sounding the cyclical, seasonal rhythms of Shakespeare's history plays, and both were strongly influenced by Mikhail Bakhtin's study of renaissance folk culture, which provided a quite different view of communal consciousness to the ideologies of power analysed by Kott and Tillyard.[30] Sturua's production invoked the grotesque paintings of Hieronymus Bosch, whilst Richard (played as a vampiric Lord of Misrule by Ramaz Chkhikvadze) was followed through the production by a figure in white, who emerged at the end as Richmond to kill the tyrant king.[31] Llorca's production presented the first tetralogy in spectacular and highly realistic panoramic vistas of sixteenth-century peasant life, and the titles of each part revealed the seasonal pattern Llorca saw in Shakespeare's histories: '*Le printemps*', '*L'été*', '*L'automne*' and '*L'hiver*'.[32]

Adrian Noble's first tetralogy cycle *The Plantagenets* (1988) also explored a Bakhtinian version of history, with Saunders Simpcox played as a large, jolly man brought on a cart, as an image of abundance and fecundity. *The Plantagenets* stressed the presence of magic and prophecy in the history plays, playing up on the inherent strangeness of the worlds Shakespeare depicted. Here, history play performance moved the furthest away from a contemporary sense of history, choosing instead to locate the plays within the popular traditions of performance, prophecy, and magic, simultaneously opening up the history plays to a popular audience, and remystifying their study of power politics.

The English Shakespeare Company's *Henriad* and *Wars of the Roses* cycles, which toured internationally between 1986 and 1989, used an eclectic mix of historical periods to construct a stylised representation of history on the stage, in which modern punks interacted with Victorian generals, soldiers from the two world wars, nineteenth-century peasants and medieval knights, as if all the past performances of the histories were brought together in an anarchic and often satirical pastiche of Shakespearean history. If the productions following the RSC histories of the 1970s had moved away from political interpretation, the director Michael Bogdanov firmly situated the performance of Shakespeare's history plays in the cultural politics of the present. In *Henry V*, Bogdanov's mix of postmodern pastiche and political satire found its most resonant and controversial images, and this production proved to be the definitive ESC production, and the artistic centre of the cycle. Bogdanov's *Henry V* was avowedly anti-Thatcherite and took on two of Thatcherism's icons with a pseudo-patriotic appropriation of 'Shakespeare' and allusions to the Falklands Crisis.

The Falklands Crisis had been approached in a similar way in Adrian Noble's *Henry V* earlier in the 1980s. Noble's treatment of history was dark but sought to preserve Shakespeare as a privileged text, emphasising the continuing importance of tradition as a bulwark against the modernity represented by Thatcherism – a theme that Noble extended considerably in his 1988 adaptation, *The Plantagenets*. Bogdanov's *Henry V* focused instead on Henry V's use of war as a political device for the manipulation of the working class. The tabloid mentality of the Falklands was invoked by a stunning set-piece in which the English army, played as a gang of football hooligans and lager-louts dressed in Falklands-style combats, filled the stage, chanting 'Fuck the Frogs!' against a rock soundtrack, and dressed the set with a huge banner with the same xenophobic expression emblazoned in graffiti. Invoking a modern history of productions of *Henry V* which either embraced or critiqued the Olivier *Henry V*, Bogdanov seemed to be suggesting that the play had become a caricature, a cliché, whose only remaining theatrical possibility was as viscous, hugely entertaining political satire.

The ESC histories were indebted to a much earlier production, Joan Littlewood's conflation of the *Henry IV* plays, which were performed at the Edinburgh Festival Assembly Hall in 1964. Littlewood followed Welles in using the conflation to foreground the Boar Tavern subplot. By revoicing history in this way, Littlewood claimed that she was being true to the eclectic, maverick, diverse constituency of Shakespeare's company. In this spirit, Littlewood used a mixture of historical costumes and regional dialects, breaking down the monolithic, nationalising and alienating concept of history which underwrote *The Wars of the Roses* by asserting difference – period, accent, class – as a historical principle. In this way, history was recovered for those outside history: Littlewood in effect turned away from 'royal'

Shakespeare to a conception of Shakespeare as a popular dramatist, alert to the silent voices of history.

A notable feature of both productions was their emphasis on a variety of regional dialects as a form of political recuperation of both Shakespeare and English history. For Littlewood, the use of regional accents was a challenge to the RSC's monumental representation of history: playing the *Henry IV* plays in various accents was not only 'authentically' English but, the production claimed, authentically Shakespearean. For Bogdanov, the modern, standard way of speaking Shakespeare is a 'dreadful tradition' in which the 'richness and texture' of the 'variety of extraordinary accents' that the plays were first performed in are homogenised and made to serve dominant cultural formations.[33] Both productions adumbrated Northern Broadside's influential *Richard III* (1993) with Barrie Rutter playing the king in the dialects and idioms of northern working-class culture.[34] In all three cases, the regionalising of Shakespearean performance was seen as both a challenge to conventional, metropolitan voicings of Shakespeare and English history and as a recuperation of the diversity of Elizabethan accents.

Following the work of the English Shakespeare Company and Northern Broadsides, various forms of fragmentation, pastiche and reappropriation have characterised the Anglo-American performance of Shakespearean history. *Henry VI: The Edged Sword* and *Black Storm*, directed by Karin Coonrod at the Joseph Papp Public Theatre, New York Shakespeare Festival in 1997, used cross-gendered doubling to subvert and even parody the plays (for example, Lady Bona was extremely large and had a huge, bushy beard). Warwick was played by an African-American, Fanni Green, who also doubled as Eleanor, whilst the Duke of Somerset was doubled with Joan. According to Nina da Vinci Nichols, the performance was 'about the eclipse of our own historical consciousness', echoing Frederick Jameson's complaint that postmodern society has lost its sense of historicity, and fulfilling Jan Kott's prediction that, without the absolute of history, tragedy becomes grotesque and absurd.[35] Cross-gendering was also at the centre of the most controversial production of a history play in 1990s Britain, the National Theatre's *Richard II*, directed by Deborah Warner, with Fiona Shaw as the king. The production began with an apparent dismantling of the set as the audience entered, as if the traditional modes of performing English history were being taken apart and discarded. Unlike Coonrod's *Henry VI*s, Warner and Shaw were determined that their experiment should not be seen as a gimmick, and rejected any notion of a feminist appropriation of history as *passé*. Shaw told Carol Chillington Rutter that what mattered to her was 'that a woman was playing the king and refusing to play by "boys"' rules': the object of the production was, says Rutter, not to regender the role of Richard but to put another spin on what it means to be a player-king.[36] There has also been a revival of interest in *King John* as two productions in Britain invited a reappraisal of its theatrical possibilities. In 2001, Northern Broadsides toured the play with *Merry Wives*, directed by Barrie Rutter and Conrad Nelson; whilst a few months later, Gregory Doran produced an acclaimed *King John* for the RSC in the Swan, which had only recently been vacated by Michael Boyd's *Henry VI* trilogy. In his review in *The Guardian* (30 May 2001), Michael Billington commented that '*King John* has suddenly moved from unloved orphan to teacher's pet' and went on to praise the sharp, cynical portrayal of power politics in both productions. Both Rutter and Doran also emphasised the play's comic dimension: Guy Henry's lanky John lent an element of physical comedy to the performance of sovereignty, whilst Rutter's Pandulph owed more than a little to Falstaff. In the run up to a controversial general election, the recovery of *King John* as black political satire was a timely reinvention of the relationship between Shakespeare's history plays and contemporary political discourse.

If, as some have argued, post-modernity does indeed represent the 'end of history', then what can 'history' mean in the theatrical performance of Shakespeare's history plays? The RSC's fragmented *This England* cycle is perhaps one answer to this question. Another, more deliberately ironic 'end of history' was marked by the Globe Theatre in London, which opened its Bankside reconstruction of an Elizabethan playhouse in 1997 with a mock-Elizabethan production of *Henry V*, retitled *The Life of Henry the Fift*. The unfamiliar, anachronistic title was only one part of a wholesale attempt to recapture an authentic Elizabethan performance. The actors wore Tudor dress, and musical interludes and aftershow jigs lent the occasion extra 'authenticity', so that the whole performance was not so much a theatrical afterlife as a triumphant, slightly tongue-in-cheek theatrical homecoming. It was a national, cultural event, as if *Henry V* had never played anywhere else, or on any other stage. However, this negation of history was a highly artificial one: the programme contained stills of Olivier's film, and the performance was directed by Olivier's son, Richard Olivier so that, even in its homecoming, Shakespeare's penultimate history play was haunted by its afterlife.

NOTES

1 Loehlin 1996, p. 18.
2 Tillyard 1944, p. 160.
3 *1H4*, ed. Weil and Weil 1997, p. 42.
4 See Myers 1996, pp. 95–107.
5 Hawkes 1969, p. 242.
6 Williams 1990, p. 154.

7 Quoted by Sarlos 1964, p. 121. I am grateful to Anne Wichmann for the translation.

8 *Ibid.*, p. 121.

9 *Ibid.*, p. 122.

10 According to Hortmann 1998, p. 94.

11 Beauman 1982, p. 28.

12 Quoted in Sprague 1964, p. 112.

13 The festival and this cycle are described in full in Hortmann 1998, pp. 93ff.

14 McMillin 1991, p. 15.

15 *Ibid.*, p. 20.

16 Beauman 1982, p. 205.

17 Kennedy 1993a, pp. 156–7.

18 Beauman 1982, p. 170.

19 *1H6*, ed. Hattaway 1990, pp. 44–5; *2H6*, ed. Hattaway 1991 pp. 48–9; *3H6*, ed. Hattaway 1993, pp. 39–40.

20 Barton and Hall 1970, p. xii.

21 *Ibid.*, p. 267.

22 Hodgdon 1972, p. 175.

23 Barton and Hall 1970, pp. xii–xiii.

24 Quoted by Kennedy 1993a, pp. 217–18.

25 Innes 1979, p. 142.

26 Hortmann 1998, p. 229.

27 Palitzch's Kottian vision of power politics was shared by Dürrenmatt's contemporaneous and influential production of *King John* (1968).

28 Hortmann 1998, p. 227.

29 Beauman 1982, p. 328.

30 Bakhtin 1984.

31 This production is discussed at length in Stříbrný 2000, pp. 121–2.

32 See *3H6*, ed. Hattaway 1993, p. 47.

33 These quotations are from an interview by Christopher McCullough, published as 'Michael Bogdanov' in Holderness 1988, p. 93.

34 See Peter Holland's insightful review: Holland 1994, pp. 185–7.

35 Nichols 1997, pp. 10–12.

36 Rutter 1997, pp. 315–16.

3

REFERENCE MATERIAL

PRINCIPAL AND RECURRENT CHARACTERS IN THE ENGLISH HISTORIES

This is a list of the most important figures in the English history plays, designed particularly to help readers trace those that reappear in subsequent plays. They are listed according to the highest rank they achieved in the plays: thus Richard, Duke of Gloucester, appears as Richard III. Not all of the details or events mentioned below were dramatised by Shakespeare.

QUEEN ANNE [*R3*] (1456–1485) Lady Anne Neville, younger daughter of Warwick 'the king-maker' and betrothed to the Edward Prince of Wales who appears in *3H6*. (It is not certain, as Shakespeare implies, that they were married before his death.) She became the wife of Richard of Gloucester, later Richard III, in 1474.

QUEEN ANNE [*H8*] (1507–1536) Anne Boleyn, Maid of Honour to Katherine of Aragon, was second queen of Henry VIII, and mother of Elizabeth. After the birth of her child she was accused of adultery by the king and ultimately executed.

ARTHUR, DUKE OF BRITTANY [*John*] (1187–1203) Posthumous son of Geoffrey, third son of Henry II and Constance, daughter of Conan le Petit; declared heir to the throne by his uncle Richard I.

DUKE OF AUMERLE [*R2, H5*] (see Edward of Norwich, Duke of York).

DUKE OF AUSTRIA [*John*] A conflation of Duke Leopold who imprisoned Richard Lionheart and held him for ransom (1192) and Viscount Limoges from whose crossbow a bolt killed the king.

LORD BARDOLPH [*2H4*] (1368–1408) Having supported the Percies during Richard II's reign, he reverted to his allegiance with them and was killed at Bramham Moor.

BARDOLPH [*1-2 H4, H5*] A fictional follower of Falstaff.

DUKE OF BEDFORD [*1H6*] (see Prince John of Lancaster).

DUKE OF BUCKINGHAM [*R3*] (1454?–1483) Henry Stafford, second Duke of Buckingham and married to Catherine Woodville, sister of Queen Elizabeth. Joined Richard of Gloucester, acted as great chamberlain at his coronation. After turning against him he was captured and executed.

DUKE OF BUCKINGHAM [*H8*] (1478–1521) Third Duke of Buckingham and eldest son of Henry Stafford. Privy Councillor 1509, but executed after trumped-up charges were brought against him by Henry VIII.

JACK CADE [*2H6*] Like 'Jack Straw', the name might be folkloric; Holinshed reports that some called him John Mend-all (1808, p. 220) and that Polychronicon said he was an Irishman.

EARL OF CAMBRIDGE [*H5*] (?–1415) Second son of Edmund of Langley, Duke of York; married Anne Mortimer, plotted to place his wife's brother Edmund Earl of March on the throne. Attainted and executed by Henry V.

CATHERINE OF ARRAGON [*H8*] (1485–1536) Youngest child of Ferdinand and Isabella of Spain. Married to Arthur, Prince of Wales, 1501. Married to Prince Henry (later Henry VIII), five years her junior, 1509. After her divorce in 1531 moved about England against her will (she refused to accept the Act of Succession 1534) until her death.

CATHERINE OF VALOIS [*H5*] (1401–1437). Youngest daughter of Charles VI of France. Married Henry V at Troyes in 1420 and crowned queen in 1421. Her eldest son by her second husband, Edmund Tudor, was the father of Henry VII.

KING CHARLES VI [*H5*] (1368–1422) Son of Charles V. His daughter Isabelle married Richard II in 1396, and his youngest daughter Catherine married Henry V. After the defeat at Agincourt in 1415 he lived 'in a state of great neglect' (Thomson, 1951, p. 124).

KING CHARLES VII [*1H6*] (1403–1461) As Dauphin (heir apparent) succeeded his father Charles VI of France as Charles VII in 1422 although he was not crowned at Rheims until 1429.

GEORGE DUKE OF CLARENCE [*3H6-R3*] (1449–1478) Sixth son of York, born in Dublin while his father was Lord Lieutenant of Ireland. Edward IV created him Duke of Clarence (1461). Assisted Warwick restore Henry VI. Deserted to Edward at Coventry and fought with him at Barnet and Tewkesbury. Quarrelled violently with his brother Richard over latter's desire to marry Anne Neville. In *R3* 1.4 Shakespeare portrays the rumoured manner of his death, in a butt of malmsey.

THOMAS DUKE OF CLARENCE [*2H4, H5*] (1388?–1421) Second son of Henry IV. Fought and eventually killed in France at Beaugé where he was attempting to emulate his brother Henry V's victory at Agincourt.

LORD CLIFFORD [*2H6*] (1414–1455) Thomas, twelfth Baron Clifford, of Clifford Castle in Herefordshire. His father was killed while fighting for Henry V at Meaux and he himself served with distinction under Bedford in France. One of the most loyal supporters of Henry VI, and killed while fighting for him at the first Battle of St Albans. The chroniclers call him John.

YOUNG CLIFFORD [*2-3H6*] (1435–1461) John, thirteenth Baron Clifford, son of the above and, like his father, a determined foe of the Duke of York. He survived the second Battle of St Albans but was killed at Ferrybridge on the eve of the Battle of Towton.

CONSTANCE [*John*] (?–1201) Daughter and heiress of Conan le Petit, count of Britanny. Her first husband was Geoffrey, third son of Henry II, to whom she bore Arthur posthumously.

ARCHBISHOP CRANMER [*H8*] (1489–1556) Archbishop of Canterbury who supported Henry VIII's divorce from Katherine of Aragon. One of the council who governed during the minority of Edward VI and supervised the production of the first prayer-book. Burned at the stake under Mary Tudor.

DAUPHIN [*1H6*] see King Charles VII.

KING DAVID II OF SCOTLAND [*E3*] (1318–1371) Succeeded Robert Bruce and married Joan, sister of Edward III of England. Defeated and captured at the battle of Neville's Cross (1346).

KING EDWARD III [*E3*] (1312–1377) Oldest child of Edward II, husband of Philippa of Hainault, and father of seven sons. Defeated the French at the battle of Crécy and gained sovereignty over large parts of France. The Lancastrians descended from his fourth son, John of Gaunt, and the Yorkists from his fifth, Edmund Langley.

KING EDWARD IV [2-3H6, R3] (1442–1483) Son of Richard Duke of York and his wife Cicely Neville. Born at Rouen, he was attainted as a Yorkist in 1459. Defeated Henry VI's forces at Northampton in 1460 and proclaimed King Edward IV in 1461. Privately married Elizabeth Woodville, widow of Sir John Grey in 1464. Defeated at Edgecote in 1469, fled to Holland, but in 1471 returned and captured Henry VI who had just been reinstalled as king; slew Warwick at Barnet, captured Queen Margaret at Tewkesbury and slew her son immediately after the battle.

KING EDWARD V [3H6-R3] (1470–1483) Eldest son of Edward IV and Elizabeth Woodville, created Prince of Wales in 1471. His father entrusted him to a Council of Control. Succeeded to the throne in 1483 and reigned as Edward V for two months. Sent to the Tower by Gloucester along with his brother where the two boys were murdered – by order of Gloucester, according to Sir Thomas More.

EDWARD, PRINCE OF WALES (The Black Prince) [E3] (1330–1376) Son of Edward III and father of Richard II. His name derived from the black armour he wore while fighting in France.

EDWARD, PRINCE OF WALES [3H6] (1453–1471) Only son of Henry VI and Margaret. Present at the second battle of St Albans, 1461 and knighted that year. Supported by Louis XI and René of Lorraine. Betrothed to Warwick's younger daughter Anne Neville. Defeated at Tewkesbury and murdered by the Yorkists.

QUEEN ELEANOR [John] (1122?–1204) Duchess of Aquitaine, Queen of France by marriage to Louis VII (1137) from whom she was divorced; married Henry II of England (1152). Mother to King John and grandmother to Prince Arthur.

QUEEN ELIZABETH [3H6-R3] (1437?–1492) Daughter of Sir Richard Woodville, later Earl Rivers, by Jacquetta of Luxembourg, widow of John, Duke of Bedford. She married Sir John Grey who was killed at St Albans in 1461. Secretly married Edward IV in 1464 and was crowned in 1465. The advancement of her relatives alienated her from the court of

Richard III and she was not better treated by her son-in-law Henry VII. Died at Bermondsey Abbey.

DUKE OF EXETER [*H5*, *1H6*] (d. 1427), Thomas Beaufort, youngest son of Henry IV's father John of Gaunt by his mistress Catherine Swynford who later became his third wife. (John of Gaunt was the fourth son of Edward III.)

DUKE OF EXETER [*3H6*] (?–1473) Henry Holland, son of John Holland Earl of Huntingdon. (Thomas Beaufort, the 'Exeter' of *1H6*, left no issue.) Although the brother-in-law of Edward IV, he supported the Lancastrians, and was left for dead at Barnet. He recovered, only to be attainted by Edward IV. He died in poverty.

SIR JOHN FALSTAFF [*1-2H4*] A fictional character, descended from the Vice of the morality plays and the *miles gloriosus* of classical drama. Traces in the text of *1H4* indicate that originally he was called [Sir John] Oldcastle, a historical figure who died in 1417 (see Taylor 1985). Oldcastle, later Lord Cobham, was probably a friend of the historical Prince Hal, was declared a heretic for his Wycliffite beliefs, and was eventually executed, later to be designated a blessed martyr by Bale and Foxe. Oldcastle has a minor role in the anonymous *Famous Victories of Henry V* (1586) and a play of 1599 bears his name.

SIR JOHN FASTOLF [*1H6*] (1378?–1459) a Norfolk landowner who distinguished himself at Agincourt and subsequently held high offices in France. However, the Tudor chroniclers and Shakespeare followed a tradition which branded him as a coward at the battle of Patay. Throughout the Folio text of *1H6* and in all editions of the play before that of Theobald he is called 'Falstaffe', because, no doubt, of scribal or compositorial confusion with the famous character in *1* and *2H4*.

DUCHESS OF GLOUCESTER [*2H6*] (?–1454) Eleanor Cobham, third daughter of Sir Reginald Cobham of Sterborough Surrey, first the mistress then wife of Gloucester whom she married in 1428. Her ambition caused her downfall, and she is said to have died in Peel Castle.

DUKE OF GLOUCESTER [*2H4*, *H5*, *1-2H6*] (1391–1447) Humphrey of Lancaster, youngest son of Henry IV. At his brother Henry V's death he claimed the regency, but had to defer to Bedford and accept the title 'Protector of England' which he held from 1427 to 1429. He was the constant enemy of his uncle, Bishop of Winchester. After a relationship with the Lady Jaquet, wife of John of Brabant, he married Eleanor Cobham.

LORD HASTINGS [*3H6-R3*] Sir William Hastings (1430?–1483), Sheriff of Leicestershire and Warwickshire, made a peer by Edward after his coronation in 1461. He opposed the queen's brother Lord Rivers and, without a trial, was beheaded by Richard of Gloucester.

KING HENRY III [*John*] (1207–1272) Oldest son of King John and his second wife; appears in *John* as Prince Henry. Succeeded to the crown at the age of nine.

KING HENRY IV [*R2, 1-2H4*] (1367–1413) The oldest surviving son of John of Gaunt, the fourth son of Edward III. He was called Bullingbrook after the castle of Bullingbrook, near Spilsby in Lincolnshire, and also Henry of Lancaster after his mother, Blanche of Lancaster. Created Duke of Hereford in 1397. His right to succeed Richard on grounds of heredity was invalid as Edmund de Mortimer (1391–1425), fifth Earl of March, descended from Lionel Duke of Clarence, the third son of Gaunt, had been recognised as his heir-presumptive by Richard II even though he was only a child when the latter died.

KING HENRY V [*1-2H4, H5*] (1387–1422) Prince Hal was the oldest son of Henry IV and born at Monmouth. Contemporaries offer no witness to the wild youth Shakespeare depicts. He revived the claim of his great-grandfather Edward III to the French throne by virtue of their descent from Isabel, wife to Edward II and daughter of Philip IV of France. The Salic law forbade the succession of a woman to the French throne. Married Catherine of France in 1420.

KING HENRY VI [*1-3H6*] (1421–1471) Son of Henry V whom he succeeded when nine months old. He was deposed in 1461 by Edward IV and restored in 1470.

KING HENRY VII [*3H6-R3*] (1457–1509) Henry, Earl of Richmond, son of Edmund Tudor, Earl of Richmond, and Margaret Beaufort, the great-grand-daughter of John of Gaunt. He was brought up in Wales. In 1470, during the brief restoration of Henry VI, he is reported to have been presented to the king (see *3H6*, 4.6). He had to take refuge in France when Edward IV was restored, and remained there until 1485 when he landed in England and defeated Richard III as Bosworth. He married Elizabeth of York, daughter of Edward IV, in 1486, thus uniting the white rose with the red.

KING HENRY VIII [*H8*] (1491–1547) Son of Henry VII. Met François I of France at the Field of the Cloth of Gold in 1520. Began negotiations with the Pope in 1527 for divorce from his first wife Katherine of Aragon, widow of his older brother Prince Arthur. Their daughter, later Mary Tudor, was born in 1516. Secretly married Anne Boleyn who was crowned Queen of England in 1533. Their daughter, later Elizabeth I, was born in 1533.

HOTSPUR [*1-2H4*] (1364–1403) Sir Henry Percy, oldest son of the first Earl of Northumberland. Helped place Henry IV on the throne and helped defeat the Scots at Humbledon Hill in 1402. Annoyed by being forbidden to ransom his brother-in-law Sir Edmund de Mortimer. Killed at the Battle of Shrewsbury but probably not by Prince Hal.

ISABELLA OF FRANCE (*R2*) [1389–1409] Daughter of Charles VI and Isabelle of Bavaria (1370–1435: she appears in *H5*) and second wife of Richard II; Queen of England. Allowed to return to France after her husband's death where she married Charles of Angloulême but died in childbirth.

JOAN LA PUCELLE [*1H6*] (1412–1431) Jeanne d'Arc, born at Domrémy and saviour of the French, for whom she raised the siege of Orléans, won the battle of Patay, and had Charles crowned at Rheims. After being abandoned by those for whom she had served as a champion, she fell into the hands of the Burgundians who sold her to the English. She was declared a heretic and burned alive at Rouen.

KING JOHN [*John*] (1167?–1216) Youngest son of Henry II; nicknamed 'Lackland', contested the throne with his brother King Richard I (the Lionheart). His defiance of Pope Innocent III over the appointment of the Archbishop of Canterbury, Stephen Langton, later made him a champion in the eyes of Protestants. Despite papal support he had to agree to demands of his barons at Runnymede in 1215 (the signing of Magna Carta).

PRINCE JOHN OF LANCASTER [*1-2H4*, *1H6*] (1389–1435) Third son of Henry IV, became Duke of Bedford in 1414, fought under Henry V (although he does not appear in *H5*). Regent of France, he relieved Orléans in 1429 and arranged for the execution of Joan la Pucelle at Rouen in 1431.

KING JOHN II OF FRANCE ('le bon' de Valois) [*E3*] (1319–1404) In the play there are events that took place during the reign of his father Philip VI.

DUKE OF LANCASTER [*R2*] (1340–1399) John of Gaunt was the fourth son of Edward III and born at Ghent. He first wife was Blanche of Lancaster and, having succeeded to her estates, he was made Duke in 1362.

KING LEWIS [*3H6*] (1423–1483) Louis XI, son of Charles VII (who appears as the Dauphin in *1H6*) and Marie of Anjou (the aunt of Queen Margaret). In 1436 married the daughter of James I of Scotland, Margaret, and then, after her death, Charlotte of Savoy. Succeeded to the throne in 1461.

QUEEN MARGARET [*1-3 H6*, *R3*] (1430–1482) Daughter of Reignier of Anjou, who married Henry VI by proxy at Nancy in 1445, Suffolk standing as proxy for the king. She courted unpopularity by allying herself with Suffolk and then Somerset, both of whom were held responsible for the loss of territories in France – a league that York was able to exploit.

MONTAGUE [*3H6*] John Neville (?–1471) third son of the Richard Neville, Earl of Salisbury who appears in *2H6*. He was brother to Warwick and nephew to York. Defeated the Lancastrians at Hexham in 1464 but after a dispute over the estates and earldom of Northumberland fought on the Lancastrian side at Barnet where he was killed.

SIR EDMUND MORTIMER [*1H4*] (1376–1409?) Second son of Edmund Mortimer, third Earl of March. Associated with his brother-in-law Hotspur. Edmund Mortimer, fifth Earl of March (see below), was his nephew.

SIR EDMUND MORTIMER [*1H6*] (1391–1425) Fifth Earl of March, who had been recognised as his heir by Richard II. He was uncle to Richard Plantagenet, Duke of York (see below). Some editors have argued that Shakespeare confused him with his uncle, Sir Edmund Mortimer (see above). The author did, however, attribute to him some of the misfortunes of his cousin Sir John Mortimer who was executed in 1424.

DUKE OF NORFOLK [*R3*] (1430?–1485) John Howard, first Duke of Norfolk. Supported both Edward IV and Richard III and killed at Bosworth.

DUKE OF NORFOLK [*H8*] A conflation of Thomas Howard, Earl of Surrey and second Duke of Norfolk (1443–1524), his son, the third Duke of the same name (1473–1554). In *R3* Thomas Howard appears as Earl of Surrey.

THOMAS MOWBRAY, DUKE OF NORFOLK [*R2*] (1366?–1399) Assisted in negotiations for Richard II's marriage to Isabella of France. Arrested and held Thomas of Woodstock, Duke of Gloucester in Calais where the latter died in mysterious circumstances. Sent into exile by Richard II, he died in Venice.

EARL OF NORTHUMBERLAND [*R2*, *1-2H4*] (1342–1408) Henry Percy, the first Earl, Earl-Marshal under Richard II but joined Bullingbrook when he landed in Yorkshire. Conspired with Owen Glendower and Edmund Mortimer against Henry IV but was killed on Bramham Moor. He was father to Hotspur.

EARL OF NORTHUMBERLAND [*3H6*] (1421–1461) Henry Percy, the third Earl, grandson of Hotspur and son of the Henry Percy whose death is reported in 1.1.4–9. He was knighted as a child in 1426 along with the infant Henry VI; he attended the parliament in Coventry where the Yorkist leaders were attainted; slain at Towton.

EARL OF OXFORD [*3H6*, *R3*] (1443–1513) John de Vere, the thirteenth Earl. Helped to restore Henry VI but imprisoned in Hammes Castle near Calais. Joined Richmond and fought at Bosworth.

NYM [*1-2H4*, *H5*] Follower of Falstaff.

CARDINAL PANDULPH [*John*] A combination of several papal emissaries sent to England by Innocent III. Pandulf was born in Pisa, and first came to England in 1211. Supported John at Runnymede against the barons and made Bishop of Norwich where he was buried in 1226.

PETO [*1-2H4*] Follower of Falstaff.

KING PHILIP II [*John*] (1165–1223) 'Philip Augustus', King of France, who accompanied Richard I on his crusade.

PHILIP THE BASTARD (FALCONBRIDGE) [*John*] Not really a historical character but suggested by a mention in Holinshed of 'Philip, bastard son to King Richard'.

PHILIPPA [*E3*] (1314?–1369) Wife of Edward III and mother of his twelve children. Was with him at the battle of Neville's Cross and the siege of Calais. The chronicler Froissart became her clerk.

PISTOL [*2H4, H5*] Falstaff's fictional ensign or ancient (both words have the same source): a standard-bearer (equivalent to a sublieutenant) whose name suggests his nature.

EDWARD POINS [*1-2H4*] Called Ned and Yedward, a fictional boon companion of Prince Hal.

KING RICHARD II [*R2*] (1367–1400) Younger son of Edward, Prince of Wales, and grandson of Edward III. Born at Bordeaux. Put down the Wat Tyler Rebellion (1381). Married Anne of Bohemia (1382). For years contested John of Gaunt for power, and made his uncle Thomas of Woodstock Duke of Gloucester play him off against Lancaster. Lost popularity after Anne's death by his second marriage to Isabella, daughter of Charles VI of France. Gloucester died in suspicious circumstances at Calais which gave Gaunt's son Henry the cue to accuse Thomas Mowbray Duke of Norfolk of treasonable designs. After Henry IV's succession, Richard was at first lodged at Leeds Castle in Kent and then sent to Pontefract where he was murdered by friends of Henry IV. He died childless.

KING RICHARD III [*2-3H6, R3*] (1452–1485) Eleventh child of Richard Duke of York, born at Fotheringay Castle. Created Duke of Gloucester 1461, accompanied his brother into exile but commanded the vanguard at Barnet and Tewkesbury. Murdered Henry VI and contrived to have himself proclaimed King in 1483. His nickname 'Crouchback' derived from a real but possibly minor deformity: More reports that his left shoulder was higher than his right.

EARL RIVERS [*3H6-R3*] (1442?–1483) Anthony Woodville, brother to Elizabeth, became the second Earl in 1469. He helped Edward IV at Barnet, and in 1473 became Chief Butler of England. He was suspected of treason by Gloucester, the Protector after Edward's death, and was beheaded, probably without trial at Pontefract.

EARL OF RUTLAND [*3H6*] (1443–1460) Edmund Earl of Rutland, second son of York, although treated in the play as the youngest of the family.

COUNTESS OF SALISBURY [*E3*] Wife of Sir William Montacute. The play reflects the confusion of the chroniclers over her identity (see *E3*, ed. Melchiori 1998, p. 186).

EARL OF SALISBURY [*E3*] (1301–1344) Sir William de Montacute (Montague), created first Earl of Salisbury in 1337. In the play he outlives his death and plays the role of Sir Walter de Manny who lived until 1372 (see Melchiori 1998, pp. 208–9). The Salisbury title was transferred to the Neville family when Anne Montague married.

EARL OF SALISBURY [*1H6*] (1388–1428) Thomas de Montacute or Montague, fourth Earl of Salisbury, had been one of Henry V's most able leaders and, with Talbot, one of the foremost English soldiers in France after Henry's death. He besieged Orléans in 1428 and died of injuries received from a cannon ball at Tourelles.

EARL OF SALISBURY [*2H6*] (1400–1460) Richard Neville was the first Earl of Salisbury. In 1431 he joined Henry VI in France and later was connected with the Beauforts in opposition to York. He persuaded York to lay down his arms at Dartford in 1452 but supported his claim to the protectorship in 1453 when Henry became insane, but after his recovery allied himself with the Yorkists, being one of the chief commanders at the first Battle of St Albans. After York was slain at Wakefield in 1460 Salisbury was wounded, imprisoned, and then beheaded at Pontefract.

DUKE OF SOMERSET [*1-2H6*] A conflation of two historical personages: John Beaufort, first Duke of Somerset (1403–1444) – who was 'alive' at the time of *1H6*, 2.4 which alludes to the death of Mortimer in 1425 and draws upon an account of a quarrel in 1435 between York and John Beaufort whom Holinshed and Hall wrongly call Edmund. This was his younger brother Edmund Beaufort, second Duke of Somerset (1406–1455), who was openly accused of treason by their antagonist Richard Plantagenet, Duke of York in 1452.

DUKE OF SOMERSET [*3H6*] As in *1* and *2H6*, Shakespeare seems to have deliberately conflated two members of this family: Henry Beaufort (1436–1464) the third Duke, son of the Edmund Beaufort whose head is thrown down by Gloucester at 1.1.16, and his younger brother Edmund Beaufort (1438–1471) the fourth Duke. Henry Beaufort was made Captain of Calais by Queen Margaret in 1459. By 1462 he was in favour with Edward IV but he rejoined Margaret at Hexham where, after the Lancastrian defeat, he was executed. Edmund was brought up in France, returning to England after Warwick's defection. He fought at Barnet but was taken prisoner at Tewkesbury and beheaded by order of Edward IV.

EARL OF SURREY [*R3*] See Duke of Norfolk.

DUKE OF SUFFOLK [*1-2H6*] (1396–1450) William de La Pole, fourth Earl then Marquis and finally Duke of Suffolk (1448), had served with success in France. He married the widowed Countess of Salisbury and emerged as an advocate of peace with France in opposition to Humphrey Duke of Gloucester who, after Bedford's death, led the war party. He had arranged the marriage of Henry with Margaret of Anjou, but the sexual intimacy between him and the Queen has no basis in the chronicles.

LORD TALBOT [*1H6*] (1388?–1453) First Earl of Shrewsbury and the most brilliant soldier of his day. He was captured at the Battle of Patay and imprisoned for two years until 1431. He took Bordeaux but was defeated and slain at Castillon.

EARL OF WARWICK [*E3*] (died 1401) Thomas de Beauchamp fought in the French and Scottish campaigns. Imprisoned for opposing Richard II but freed by Bullingbrook.

EARL OF WARWICK [*1H6*] A conflation of two personages: Richard de Beauchamp, Earl of Warwick (1382–1439) – who had accompanied Henry V to France, was present at the funeral of Henry V in 1422 and charged with the education of the infant Henry VI in 1428, and who was dead (by the time of the truce signed at Tours) – and his son-in-law Richard Neville, Earl of Warwick (1428–1471), known as the 'Kingmaker'.

EARL OF WARWICK [*2H6*] (1428–1471) A conflation of two personages The 'Warwick' of *1H6* was largely Richard de Beauchamp. The 'kingmaker' was Richard Neville, son of the Earl of Salisbury; he succeeded in 1449 to the title and estates of Richard de Beauchamp whose daughter Anne he had married. He supported York and distinguished himself at the first Battle of St Albans and won the battle of Northampton in 1460, taking King Henry prisoner. At Wakefield, however, the Lancastrians regained their ascendancy in 1460 when York and Warwick's father Salisbury were killed. Warwick escaped, helped proclaim Edward king, and defeated the Lancastrians at Towton in 1461. Defection to the Lancastrians was caused by his annoyance at Edward's marriage with Elizabeth Woodville.

Withdrew from the court but returned to be reconciled with Margaret whose young son Edward was betrothed to his daughter Anne. In 1470 Henry VI was proclaimed king again and Warwick was made protector with Clarence. In 1471 killed at Barnet.

EARL OF WESTMORLAND [*1-2H4, H5*] (1364–1425) Ralph, sixth Baron Neville of Raby and created first Earl of Westmorland by Richard II. Supported Bullingbrook. His despondency on the eve of Agincourt (*H5*, 4.3.16–18) has no good historical warrant. 'He had 23 children by his two wives, and he devoted himself to found the fortunes of his sons by rich marriages' (Thomson 1951, p. 304).

EARL OF WESTMORLAND [*3H6*] (?–1484) Ralph Neville, second Earl of Westmorland, who married Hotspur's daughter Elizabeth, the widow of John Clifford. In fact it was his younger brother John who fought for the Lancastrians, but Holinshed and Hall mistakenly have him slain at Towton.

CARDINAL OF WINCHESTER [*1-2H6*] (d. 1447) Henry Beaufort, the second of Gaunt's illegitimate sons; Chancellor on the accession of Henry V and named guardian of Henry VI. He was made a Cardinal in 1426 by Pope Martin V, and led the opposition to Gloucester.

CARDINAL WOLSEY [*H8*] (1475?–1530) Said to be a butcher's son from Ipswich, appointed by Henry VII to be Dean of Lincoln and rose to be Archbishop of York and made Cardinal by Leo X in 1515. Until the time of the divorce of Katherine of Aragon, the second most powerful man in England. Deprived of the Great Seal in 1529 and died in Leicester on his way to stand trial for high treason.

DUCHESS OF YORK [*3H6, R3*] (?–1495) Cicely Neville, daughter of Ralph Neville, married Richard Plantagenet in 1438; mother of Edward IV, Richard III, and the Earl of Clarence.

DUKE OF YORK [*R2*] (1341–1402) Edmund of Langley, fifth son of Edward III, first Duke of York. Fought in France and Spain with the Black Prince and, under Richard II, transferred his allegiance to Henry of Lancaster.

DUKE OF YORK [*R2, H5*] (1373?–1415) Edward of Norwich, second Duke of York and eldest son of Edmund of Langley. Under Richard II created Earl of Rutland in 1390 and later rewarded with the Duchy of Albemarle

(Aumerle). There is little reliable evidence that he was involved in the conspiracy against Richard II of Christmas 1399. Succeeded his father in 1402 and, after falling out of favour under Henry IV, died in glory at Agincourt.

DUKE OF YORK [*1-3H6*] Richard Plantagenet (1411–1460), third Duke of York, descended through his mother from the Mortimer line, which derived from Lionel Duke of Clarence, third son of Edward III. His father, who was descended from Edmund of Langley, fifth son of Edward III and first Duke of York, had been executed in 1415 for conspiring against Henry V.

DUKE OF YORK [*R3*] (1472–83?) Richard Duke of York, younger son of Edward IV and Queen Elizabeth. Married to Anne, daughter of the fourth Duke of Norfolk. With his brother died at the Tower of London.

Table 1. *The Early Plantagenets*

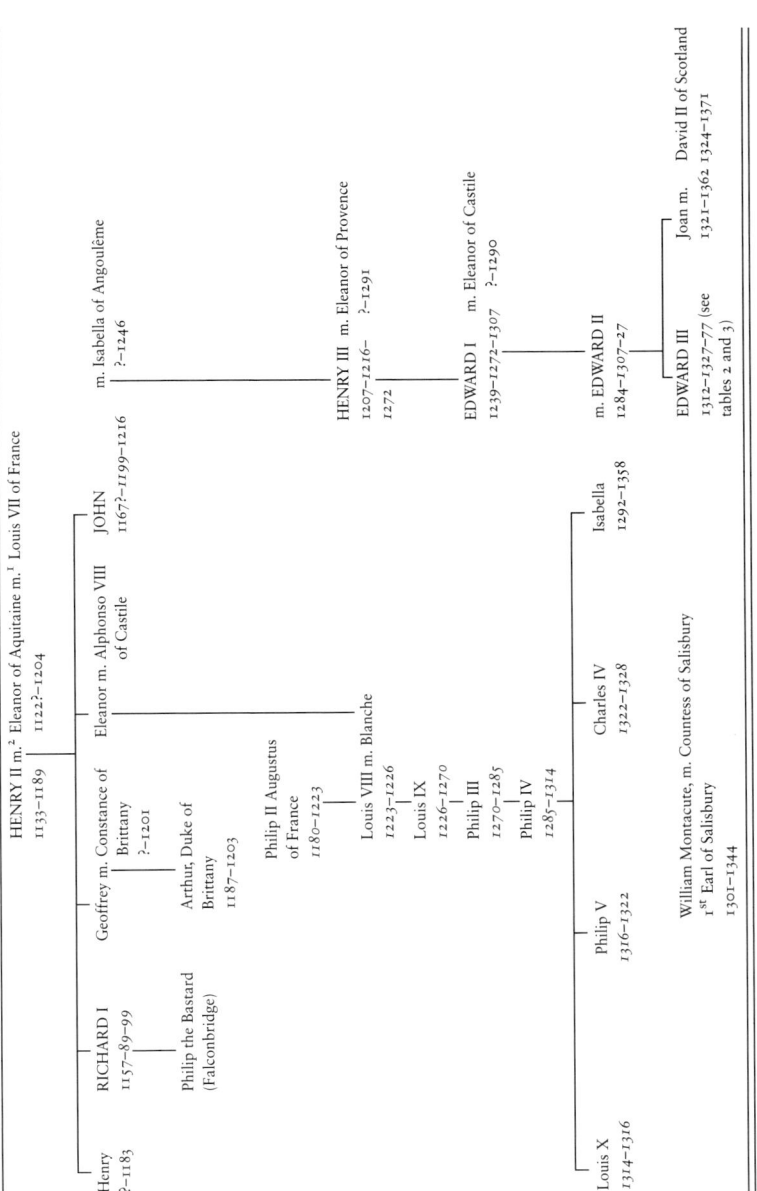

Italicised dates are those of reigns.

Table 2. *The House of Lancaster*

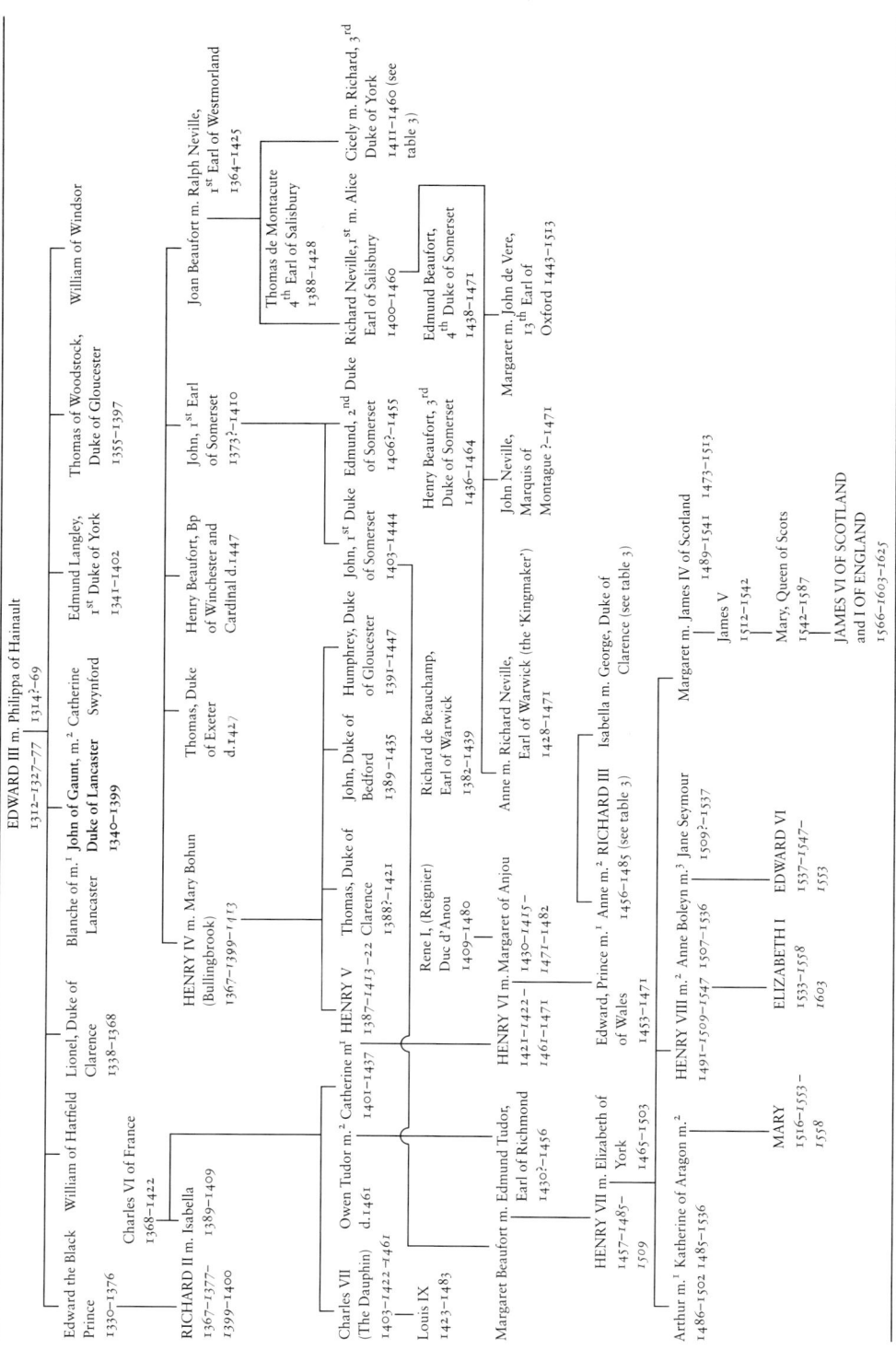

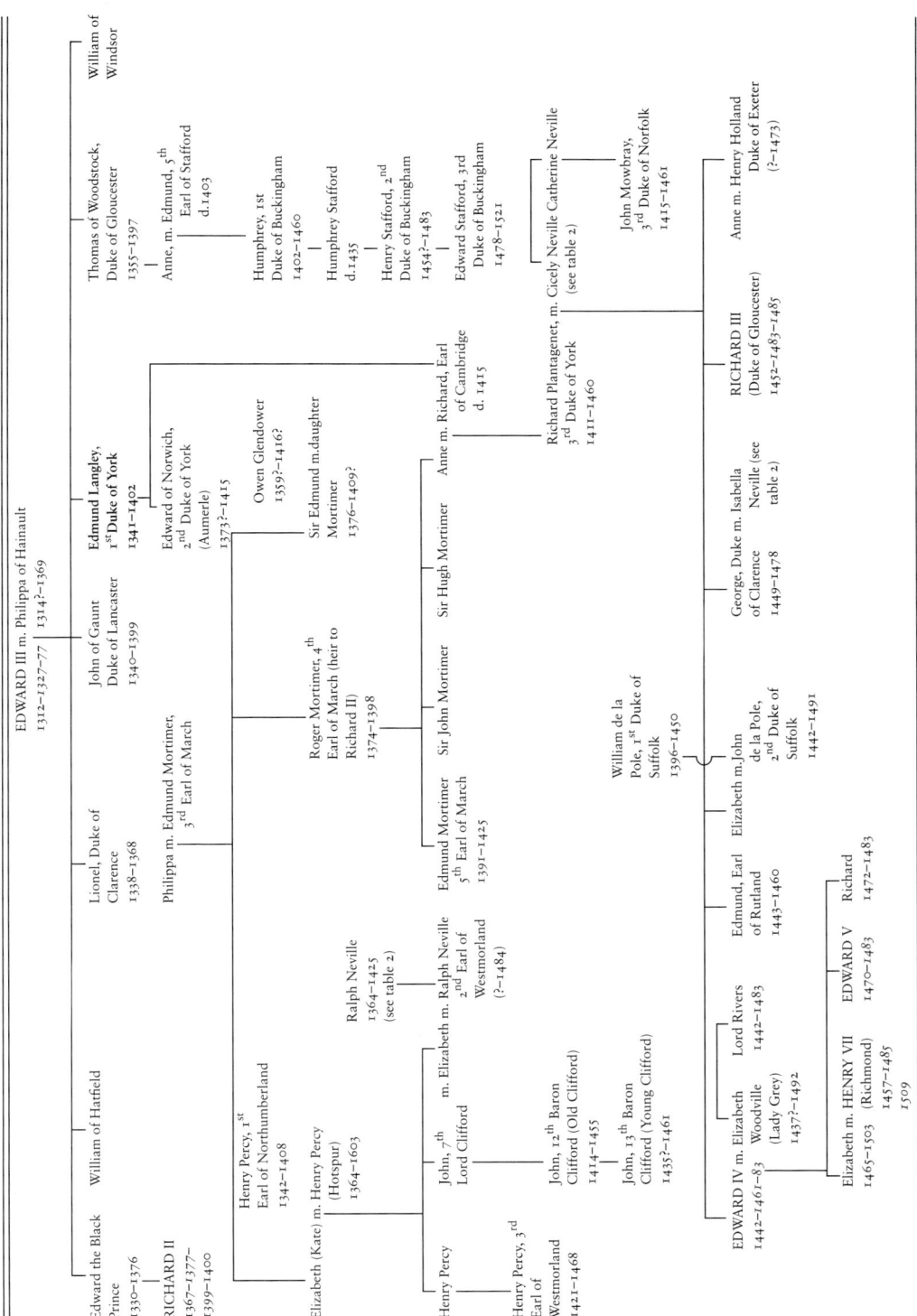

Italicised dates are those of reigns.

All books and articles cited in abbreviated form in the notes to the essays in this volume are listed here in full. The list also includes useful compilations of essays, reference works, and a selection of readings which may be found useful for further study of the plays.

Albright, E. M. 1927, 'Shakespeare's *Richard II* and the Essex Conspiracy', *Publications of the Modern Language Association* 42: 686–720.

Allen, J. W. 1928, *A History of Political Thought in the Sixteenth Century*. London.

Anderson, J. 1983, *Biographical Truth: The Representation of Historical Persons in Tudor/Stuart Writing*. New Haven.

Archer, Ian W. 1999, 'Shakespeare's London', *A Companion to Shakespeare*, ed. David Scott Kastan. Oxford, pp. 43–56.

Aristotle 1920, *On the Art of Poetry*, trans. Ingram Bywater. Oxford.

    1955, *The Ethics of Aristotle*, trans. J. A. K. Thomson. Harmondsworth.

Armstrong, W. A. (ed.) 1972, *Shakespeare's Histories: An Anthology of Modern Criticism*. Harmondsworth.

Ashton, R. (ed.) 1969, *James I by his Contemporaries*. London.

Augustine, Saint 1967, *The City of God: John Healey's Translation of 1610*. London.

Axton, Marie 1977, *The Queen's Two Bodies: Drama and the Elizabethan Succession*. London.

Bacon, Francis 1865, *Essays*, ed. W. Aldis Wright. London.

    1900, *The Advancement of Learning*, ed. W. Aldis Wright. Oxford.

Baker, Herschel 1967, *The Race of Time: Three Lectures on Renaissance Historiography*. Toronto.

Bakhtin, M. M. 1981, *The Dialogic Imagination*, ed. Michael Holquist, trans. Caryl Emerson and Michael Holquist. Austin, TX.

    1984, *Rabelais and his World*, trans. Hélène Iswolsky. Bloomington, IN.

Baldwin, T. W. 1944, *William Shakspere's 'Small Latine & Lesse Greeke'*, 2 vols. Urbana, IL.

Barber, C. L. 1959, *Shakespeare's Festive Comedy*. Princeton.

Barroll, J. Leeds 1958, 'Shakespeare and Roman History', *Modern Language Review* 53: 327–43.

Barton, Anne 1977, 'He that Plays the King: Ford's *Perkin Warbeck* and the Stuart History Play', *English Drama: Forms and Development. Essays in Honour of Muriel Clara Bradbrook*, ed. M. Axton and R. Williams. Cambridge, pp. 69–93.

1981, 'Harking Back to Elizabeth: Ben Jonson and Caroline Nostalgia', *English Literary History* 48: 706–31.

1990, *The Names of Comedy*. Toronto.

Barton, Anne Righter, Richard Pasco, *et al.* 1990, 'The Royal Shakespeare *Richard II*', *Staging Shakespeare: Seminars on Production Problems*, ed. G. Loney. New York, pp. 19–56.

Barton, John and Peter Hall 1970, *The Wars of the Roses: Adapted for the Royal Shakespeare Company from William Shakespeare's 'Henry VI Parts I, II, III' and 'Richard III'*. London.

Bate, Jonathan 1993, *Shakespeare and Ovid*. Oxford.

1997, *The Genius of Shakespeare*. London.

Beauman, Sally 1982, *The Royal Shakespeare Company: A History of Ten Decades*. Oxford.

Becon, Thomas 1844, *Prayers and Other Pieces of Thomas Becon STP*, ed. John Ayre. Cambridge.

Belsey, Catherine 1991, 'Making Histories Then and Now: Shakespeare from *Richard II* to *Henry V*', *Uses of History: Marxism, Postmodernism and the Renaissance*, ed. Francis Barker, Peter Hulme and Margaret Iversen. Manchester, pp. 24–46.

Bergeron, David M. 1971, *English Civic Pageantry 1558–1642*. London.

(ed.) 1985a, *Pageantry in the Shakespearean Theater*. Athens, GA.

(ed.) 1985b, *Pageants and Entertainments of Anthony Munday: A Critical Edition*. New York.

1985c, *Shakespeare's Romances and the Royal Family*. Lawrence, KS.

1991, '*Richard II* and Carnival Politics', *Shakespeare Quarterly* 42: 33–43.

Berry, Edward I. 1975, *Patterns of Decay: Shakespeare's Early Histories*. Charlottesville, VA.

1986, 'Twentieth-century Shakespeare criticism: The histories', *The Cambridge Companion to Shakespeare Studies*, ed. Stanley Wells. Cambridge, pp. 249–56.

Bevington, David 1966, 'The Domineering Female in *1 Henry VI*', *Shakespeare Studies* 2: 51–8.

1968, *Tudor Drama and Politics*. Cambridge, MA.

Bevington, David and Peter Holbrook (eds.) 1998, *The Politics of the Stuart Court Masque*. Cambridge.

Bliss, Lee 1975, 'The Wheel of Fortune and the Maiden Phoenix of Shakespeare's *King Henry the Eighth*', *ELH* 42: 1–25.

Bloch, Marc 1973, *The Royal Touch. Sacred Monarchy and Scrofula in England and France*. London.

Bogdanov, Michael and Michael Pennington 1990, *The English Shakespeare Company*. London.

Bolton, W. F. 1992, *Shakespeare's English: Language in The History Plays*. Cambridge, MA.

Bonjour, Adrien 1951, 'The Road to Swinstead Abbey: A Study of the Sense and Structure of *King John*', *Journal of English Literary History* 18: 253–74.

Boswell-Stone, W. G. (ed.) 1896, *Shakespeare's Holinshed, the Chronicle and the Historical Plays Compared*. London.

Bradley, A. C. 1909, *Oxford Lectures on Poetry*. London.

1957 edn, *Shakespearean Tragedy*. London.

Branagh, Kenneth 1989, *'Henry V' by William Shakespeare: A Screen Adaptation by Kenneth Branagh*. London.

Braunmuller, A. R. and Michael Hattaway (eds.) 1990, *The Cambridge Companion to English Renaissance Drama*. Cambridge.

Bristol, Michael D. 1985, *Carnival and Theatre: Plebeian Culture and the Structure of Authority in Renaissance England*. London.

Brown, John Russell 1973, 'Narrative and Focus: *Richard II*', *Richard II: A Casebook*, ed. Nicholas Brooke. London, pp. 82–98.

Brownlow, E. W 1977, *Two Shakespearean Sequences*. London.

Bullough, Geoffrey (ed.) 1957–73, *Narrative and Dramatic Sources of Shakespeare*, 7 vols. London.

Burden, Dennis 1985, 'Shakespeare's History Plays: 1952–1983', *Shakespeare Survey* 38: 1–18.

Bury, John B. 1920, *The Idea of Progress: An Inquiry into Its Origin and Growth*. London.

Calderón de la Barca, Pedro 1990, *The Schism in England* (*La cisma da Inglaterra*), trans. Kenneth Muir and Ann L. Mackenzie, ed. Ann Mackenzie. Warminster.

Campbell, Lily B. (ed.) 1938, *The Mirror for Magistrates*. Cambridge.

  1947, *Shakespeare's 'Histories': Mirrors of Elizabethan Policy*. San Marino.

Campbell, Oscar James 1971, *The Position of the 'Roode en Witte Roos' in the Saga of King Richard III*. New York.

Candido, Joseph (ed.) 1996, *Shakespeare: The Critical Tradition King John*. London.

  (ed.) 1998, *'Richard II', 'Henry IV, Parts I and II', and 'Henry V': An Annotated Bibliography of Shakespeare Studies 1777–1997*. Asheville, NC.

Cantor, Paul A. 1976, *Shakespeare's Rome: Republic and Empire*. Ithaca, NY.

Carlyle, Thomas 1973, 'The Hero as Poet', *Shakespeare Criticism: A Selection, 1623–1840*, ed. D. Nichol Smith. London.

Cespedes, Frank V. 1980, ' "We are one in fortunes": The Sense of History in *Henry VIII*', *ELR* 10: 413–48.

Chambers, E. K. 1923, *The Elizabethan Stage*. 4 vols. Oxford.

Champion, Larry S. 1980, *Perspective in Shakespeare's English Histories*. Athens, GA.

  1990, *The Noise of Threatening Drum: Dramatic Strategy and Political Ideology in Shakespeare and the English Chronicle Plays*. Newark, DE.

Charney, Maurice 1961, *Shakespeare's Roman Plays: The Function of Imagery in the Drama*. Cambridge, MA.

Cicero, Marcus Tullius 1558, *Marcus Tullius Ciceroes thre bookes of duties, to Marcus his sonne, turned out of latine into english*, trans. Nicholas Grimald. London.

Clare, Janet 1990, *'Art Made Tongue-tied by Authority': Elizabethan and Jacobean Dramatic Censorship*. Manchester.

Clark, Peter 1983, *The English Alehouse: A Social History 1200–1830*. London.

Clegg, Cyndia Susan 1997, ' "By the choise and inuitation of al the realme": *Richard II* and Elizabethan Press Censorship', *Shakespeare Quarterly* 48: 432–48.

Cohen, Derek 1993, *Shakespeare's Culture of Violence*. New York.

Cohen, Walter 1985, *Drama of a Nation: Public Theater in Renaissance England and Spain*. Ithaca, NY.

Coignet, Matthieu 1586, *Politic Discourses upon Truth and Lying*, trans. Sir Edward Hoby. London.

Coleridge, Samuel Taylor 1836, *Literary Remains*, ed. H. N. Coleridge, 4 vols. London.

1930, *Shakespearean Criticism*, ed. Thomas Middleton Raysor, 2 vols. London.

Colley, Scott 1992, *Richard's Himself Again: A Stage History of 'Richard III'*. New York.

Collinson, Patrick 1986, *From Iconoclasm to Iconophobia: The Cultural Impact of the Second English Reformation*. Reading.

2000a, 'History', *A Companion to English Renaissance Literature and Culture*, ed. Michael Hattaway. Oxford, pp. 58–70.

2000b, 'English Reformations', *A Companion to English Renaissance Literature and Culture*, ed. Michael Hattaway. Oxford, pp. 27–44.

Contamine, P. 1984, *War in the Middle Ages*, trans. Michael Jones. Cambridge, MA.

Corbin, Peter and Douglas Sedge (eds.) 1991, *The Oldcastle Controversy: 'Sir John Oldcastle, Part 1' and 'The Famous Victories of Henry V'*. Manchester.

Cousin, Geraldine 1994, *King John. Shakespeare in Performance*. Manchester.

Cox, John D. 1989, *Shakespeare and the Dramaturgy of Power*. Princeton.

Coyle, Martin (ed.) 1998, *William Shakespeare: 'Richard II'*. Duxford, Cambs.

Crowl, Samuel 1992, *Shakespeare Observed: Studies in Performance on Stage and Screen*. Athens, OH.

Cunliffe, John W. 1893, *The Influence of Seneca on Elizabethan Tragedy*. London.

Curran, John E., Jr 1997, 'Royalty Unlearned, Honor Untaught: British Savages and Historiographical Change in *Cymbeline*', *Comparative Drama* 31: 278–303.

Daniel, Samuel 1958, *The Civil Wars [1595]*, ed. Laurence Michel. Newhaven.

David, Richard 1953, 'Shakespeare's History Plays – Epic or Drama?', *Shakespeare Survey* 6: 129–39.

Davies, Anthony and Stanley Wells (eds.) 1994, *Shakespeare and the Moving Image*. Cambridge.

Davies, H. Neville 1985, 'Jacobean *Antony and Cleopatra*', *Shakespeare Studies* 17: 123–58.

Debax, Jean-Paul 1987, *Le théâtre du vice*. Paris.

1999, '"The Formal Vice Iniquity" – Traditions dramatiques dans *Richard III*', *William Shakespeare, Ellipses*, ed. H. Suhamy. Paris.

Dekker, Thomas 1953–70, *The Dramatic Works*, ed. Fredson Bowers, 4 vols. Cambridge.

Dollimore, J. and A. Sinfield (eds.) 1994, *Political Shakespeare: Essays in Cultural Materialism*. Manchester.

Donawerth, Jane 1984, *Shakespeare and the Sixteenth-Century Study of Language*. Urbana IL.

Downie, Penny 1993, 'Queen Margaret in *Henry VI* and *Richard III*', *Players of Shakespeare 3*, ed. Russell Jackson and Robert Smallwood. Cambridge, pp. 114–39.

Driver, Tom F. 1960, *The Sense of History in Greek and Shakespearean Drama*. New York.

Dryden, John 1912, 'The Grounds of Criticism in Tragedy', *Essays*, ed. W. H. Hudson. London.

Duits, H. 1990, *Van Bartholomeusnacht tot Bataafse opstand: Studies over de relatie tussen politiek en toneel in het midden van de zeventiende eeuw*. Hilversum.

Edwards, Philip 1979, *Threshold of a Nation*. Cambridge.

Ellis-Fermor, Una 1964, 'Shakespeare's Political Plays', *The Frontiers of Drama*. London, pp. 34–55.

Felperin, Howard 1966, 'Shakespeare's *Henry VIII*: History as Myth', *Studies in English Literature 1500–1900* 6: 224–46.

Ferguson, Arthur B. 1979, *Clio Unbound: Perception of the Social and Cultural Past in Renaissance England*. Durham, NC.

Figgis, John Neville 1896, *The Theory of the Divine Right of Kings*. Cambridge.

Forker, Charles R. (ed.) 1994, Christopher Marlowe, *Edward the Second*. Manchester.

   1996, 'Marlowe's *Edward II* and its Shakespearean Relatives: The Emergence of a Genre', *Shakespeare's English Histories: A Quest for Form and Genre*, ed. John W. Velz. Binghamton, NY, pp. 55–90.

Forse, J. 1993, *Art Imitates Business: Commercial and Political Influences in Elizabethan Theatre*. Bowling Green, OH.

Fortescue, J. W. 1916, 'The Army: Military Service and Equipment', *Shakespeare's England: An Account of the Life and Manners of his Age*, ed. Sidney Lee and C. T. Onions. 2 vols. Oxford, I, 112–26.

Fox, Adam 1999, 'Remembering the Past in Early Modern England', *Transactions of the Royal Historical Society* 6th Series, 9: 233–56.

Freytag, Gustav 1896, *Technique of the Drama* [1863], trans. Elias J. MacEwan. Chicago.

Froissart, Sir John 1884, *Chronicles of England, France, Spain, and the Adjoining Countries from the Latter Part of the Reign of Edward II, to the Coronation of Henry IV*, ed. T. Johnes, 2 vols. London.

   1901, *Chronicle [1523–1525]*, trans. Sir John Bourchier Lord Berners, ed. William Paton Ker. London, reprinted in Metz 1989.

Fussner, Frank S. 1970, *Tudor History and the Historians*. New York.

Gasper, Julia 1993, 'The Reformation Plays on the Public Stage', *Theatre and Government under the Early Stuarts*, ed. J. R. Mulryne and Margaret Shewring. Cambridge, pp. 190–216.

Geoffrey of Monmouth, 1958, *The History of the Kings of Britain*, trans. Lewis Thorpe. Harmondsworth.

Gibbons, Brian 1993, 'Fabled *Cymbeline*'. *Shakespeare and Multiplicity*, Cambridge, pp. 18–47.

Gilbert Allan H. 1962, *Literary Criticism: Plato to Dryden*. Detroit.

Gowing, Laura 1996, *Domestic Dangers: Women, Words, and Sex in Early Modern London*. Oxford.

Goy-Blanquet, Dominique 1992, '"Two Kingdoms for Half a Crown", Shakespeare and Politics', *Shakespeare Survey* 44: 53–63.

   1995, 'Sad Stories', *French Essays on Shakespeare and his Contemporaries*, ed. J-M. Maguin and Michèle Willems. Newark, DE, pp. 139–52.

   1997, *Shakespeare et l'invention de l'histoire*. Bruxelles.

Greenblatt, Stephen 1980, *Renaissance Self-Fashioning from More to Shakespeare*. Chicago.

1985, 'Invisible Bullets: Renaissance Authority and its Subversion, *Henry IV* and *Henry V*', *Political Shakespeare: New Essays in Cultural Materialism*, ed. Jonathan Dollimore and Alan Sinfield. Manchester, pp. 18–47.

Greene, Robert 1592, *Greene's Groat's Worth of Wit*. London.

Groenveld, Simon 1984, *Verlopend getij: De Nederlandse Republiek en de Engelse burgeroorlog, 1640–1646*. Dieren.

Gurr, Andrew 1992, *The Shakespearean Stage 1547–1642*, 3rd edn. Cambridge.

  1996a, *Playgoing in Shakespeare's London*, 2nd edn. Cambridge.

  1996b, *The Shakespearian Playing Companies*. Oxford.

Gurr, Andrew and Mariko Ichikawa 2000, *Staging in Shakespeare's Theatres*. Oxford.

Gutierrez, Nancy A. 1990, 'Gender and Value in *1 Henry VI*: The Role of Joan de Pucelle', *Theatre Journal* 42: 183–93.

Hall, Edward 1809, *The Union of the Two Noble and Illustre Families of Lancaster and York* [1548]. London.

Halverson, John 1994, 'The Lamentable Comedy of *Richard II*', *English Literary Renaissance* 24: 343–69.

Hamilton, Donna B. 1983, 'The State of Law in *Richard II*', *Shakespeare Quarterly* 34: 5–17.

Happé, Peter 1966, 'The Vice 1350–1605', unpublished Ph.D. thesis. University of London.

  (ed.) 1979, *Four Morality Plays*. Harmondsworth.

  1989, *English Drama Before Shakespeare*. London.

Harbage, Alfred 1941, *Shakespeare's Audience*. New York.

  (ed.) 1989, *Annals of English Drama 975–1700*. London.

Harding, D.W. 1969, 'Woman's Fantasy of Manhood', *SQ* 20: 245–54.

Hart, Jonathan 1992, *Theater and World: The Problematics of Shakespeare's History*. Boston.

Hattaway, Michael 1982, *Elizabethan Popular Theatre*. London.

  2000, 'Allegorising in Drama and the Visual Arts', *Allegory in the Theatre*, ed. Peter Happé. Berne, pp. 187–205.

Hattaway, Michael, Boika Sokolova, and Derek Roper 1994, *Shakespeare in the New Europe*. Sheffield.

Hawkes, Terence (ed.) 1969, *Coleridge on Shakespeare*. Harmondsworth.

Hay, Denys 1977, *Annalists and Historians: Western Historiography from the Eighth to the Eighteenth Centuries*. London.

Healy, Margaret 1998, *William Shakespeare: Richard II*. Plymouth.

Heinemann, Margot 1990, 'Political Drama'. *The Cambridge Companion to English Renaissance Drama*, ed. A. R. Braunmuller and Michael Hattaway. Cambridge, pp. 161–205.

Helgerson, Richard 1992, *Forms of Nationhood: The Elizabethan Writing of England*. Chicago.

  2000, 'Writing Empire and Nation'. *The Cambridge Companion to English Literature, 1500–1600*, ed. Arthur F. Kinney. Cambridge, pp. 310–29.

Helms, Lorraine 1992, 'The High Roman Fashion': Sacrifice, Suicide, and the Shakespearean Stage, *Publications of the Modern Language Association* 107: 554–65.

Henderson, Diana E. 1997, 'The Theater and Domestic Culture'. *A New History of Early English Drama*, ed. John D. Cox and David Scott Kastan. New York.

Hodgdon, Barbara 1972, '*The Wars of the Roses*: Scholarship Speaks on the Stage', *Deutsche Shakespeare-Gesellschaft West Jahrbuch*, 172: 170–84.

1983, 'Two *King Lears*: Uncovering the Filmtext', *Literature and Film Quarterly* 11: 143–51.

1991, *The End Crowns All: Closure and Contradiction in Shakespeare's History*. Princeton.

1993, *Henry IV, Part Two. Shakespeare in Performance*. Manchester.

1997, *The First Part of King Henry the Fourth. Texts and Contexts*. Boston.

Hoenselaars, A. J. 1992, *Images of Englishmen and Foreigners in the Drama of Shakespeare and His Contemporaries: A Study of Stage Characters and National Character in English Renaissance Drama, 1558–1642*. Rutherford, NJ.

Holderness, Graham 1981, 'Shakespeare's History: *Richard II*', *Literature and History* 7: 2–24.

1985, *Shakespeare's History*. New York.

(ed.) 1988, *The Shakespeare Myth*. London.

1992, *Shakespeare Recycled: The Making of Historical Drama*. London.

2000, *Shakespeare: The Histories*. London.

Holinshed, Raphael 1808, *Chronicles of England Scotland, and Ireland* (Reprinted from the second edition of 1587). 6 vols. London.

Holland, Peter 1994, 'Shakespeare Performances in England, 1993', *Shakespeare Survey* 47: 181–208.

1997, *English Shakespeares: Shakespeare on the English Stage in the 1990s*. Cambridge.

Honigmann, E. A. J. 1987, '*King John, The Troublesome Raigne* and "documentary links": A Rejoinder', *Shakespeare Quarterly* 38: 124–30.

Hooker, Richard 1907, *Of the Laws of Ecclesiastical Polity*, 2 vols. London.

1989, *Of the Laws of Ecclesiastical Polity*, ed. Arthur Stephen McGrade. Cambridge.

Hortmann, Wilhelm 1998, *Shakespeare on the German Stage: The Twentieth Century*. Cambridge.

Howard, Jean E. 1994, *The Stage and Social Struggle in Early Modern England*. London.

Howard, Jean E. and Phyllis Rackin 1997, *Engendering a Nation: A Feminist Account of Shakespeare's English Histories*. London.

Hunter, G. K. 1997, *English Drama 1586–1642: The Age of Shakespeare*. Oxford.

Hunter, Robert G. 1976, *Shakespeare and the Mystery of God's Judgments*. Athens, GA.

Huston, Nancy 1986, 'The Matrix of War: Mothers and Heroes', *The Female Body in Western Culture: Contemporary Perspectives*, ed. Susan Rubin Suleiman. Cambridge, MA, pp. 119–36.

Hutcheon, Linda 1988, *A Poetics of Postmodernism*. London.

Innes, Christopher 1979, *Modern German Drama: A Study in Form*. Cambridge.

Iser, Wolfgang 1993, *Staging Politics: The Lasting Impact of Shakespeare's Histories*, trans. David Henry Wilson. New York.

Jacks, Philip J. 1993, *The Antiquarian and the Myth of Antiquity: The Origins of Rome in Renaissance Thought.* Cambridge.

Jackson, Gabriele Bernhard 1988, 'Topical Ideology: Witches, Amazons, and Shakespeare's Joan of Arc', *English Literary Renaissance* 18: 40–65.

Jackson, Macd. P. 2001. 'Shakespeare's *Richard III* and the Anonymous *Thomas of Woodstock*', *Medieval and Renaissance Drama in England* 14: 17–65.

James, King 1994, *Political Writings*, ed. Johann P. Sommerville. Cambridge.

James, Heather 1997, *Shakespeare's Troy: Drama, Politics, and the Translation of Empire.* Cambridge.

James, Mervyn 1986, *Society, Politics, and Culture: Studies in Early Modern England.* Cambridge.

Jenkins, Harold 1953, 'Shakespeare's History Plays: 1900–1951', *Shakespeare Survey* 6: 1–15.

1956, *The Structural Problem in Shakespeare's Henry IV.* London.

Jones, Emrys 1961, 'Stuart *Cymbeline*', *Essays in Criticism* 11: 84–99.

1977, *The Origins of Shakespeare.* Oxford.

Jones, Robert C. 1991, *These Valiant Dead: Renewing the Past in Shakespeare's Histories.* Iowa City.

Jonson, Ben 1925–52, *Works*, ed. C. H. Herford and P. and E. M. Simpson. 11 vols. Oxford.

1969, *The Complete Masques*, ed. Stephen Orgel. New Haven.

Jorgenson, Paul A. 1947, 'Accidental Judgments, Casual Slaughters, and Purposes Mistook: Critical Reactions to Shakspere's [sic] *Henry the Fifth*', *Shakespeare Association Bulletin* 22: 51–61.

Kahn, Coppélia 1997, *Roman Shakespeare: Warriors, Wounds, and Women.* London.

Kamps, Ivo 1996, *Historiography and Ideology in Stuart Drama.* Cambridge.

Kantorowicz, Ernst H. 1957, *The King's Two Bodies: A Study in Mediaeval Political Theology.* Princeton.

Kastan, David Scott 1986, '"Proud Majesty made a Subject": Shakespeare and the Spectacle of Rule', *Shakespeare Quarterly* 37: 459–75.

1999, '"Killed with Hard Opinions": Oldcastle and Falstaff and the Reformed Text of *1 Henry IV*', *Shakespeare after Theory.* London, pp. 93–106.

Kaula, David 1982, '"Let Us Be Sacrificers": Religious Motifs in *Julius Caesar*', *Shakespeare Studies* 14: 197–214.

Kelly, H. A. 1970, *Divine Providence in the England of Shakespeare's Histories.* Cambridge, MA.

Kennedy, Dennis 1993a, *Looking at Shakespeare: A Visual History of Twentieth-Century Performance.* Cambridge.

1993b, *Foreign Shakespeare: Contemporary Performance.* Cambridge.

Kernan, Alvin 1995, *Shakespeare, the King's Playwright: Theater in the Stuart Court, 1603–1613.* New Haven.

Kiernan, Pauline 1999, *Staging Shakespeare at the New Globe.* London.

Kirk, Andrew M. 1996, *The Mirror of Confusion: The Representation of French History in English Renaissance Drama.* New York.

Knight, G. Wilson 1948, '*Cymbeline*', *The Crown of Life.* London, pp. 129–202.

Knights, L. C. 1959, *Some Shakespearean Themes.* London.

Kolin, Philip C. (ed.) 1995, *Titus Andronicus: Critical Essays*. New York.

Kott, Jan 1964, *Shakespeare our Contemporary*, trans. Boleslaw Taborski. London.

Kreps, Barbara 1999, 'When all is True: Law, History and Problems of Knowledge in *Henry VIII*', *Shakespeare Survey* 52: 166–82.

Latimer, Hugh 1968, *Selected Sermons*, ed. Allan G. Chester, Charlottesville, VA.

Le Goff, Jacques 1980, *Time, Work and Culture in the Middle Ages*, trans. Arthur Goldhammer. Chicago.

Lee, Sidney 1900, *Shakespeare's 'Henry V': An Account and an Estimate*. London.

Leggatt, Alexander 1977. 'Dramatic Perspective in *King John*', *English Studies in Canada* 3: 1–17.

  1988, *Shakespeare's Political Drama: The History Plays and the Roman Plays*. London.

Levin, Harry 1954, *Christopher Marlowe: The Overreacher*. London.

  1970, *The Myth of the Golden Age in the Renaissance*. London.

Levine, Nina S. 1998, *Women's Matters: Politics, Gender, and Nation in Shakespeare's Early History Plays*. Newark, DE.

Levy, F. J. 1967, *Tudor Historical Thought*. San Marino, CA.

Liebler, Naomi Conn 1992, 'The Mockery King of Snow: Richard II and the Sacrifice of Ritual', *True Rites and Maimed Rites: Ritual and Anti-Ritual in Shakespeare and His Age*, ed. Linda Woodbridge and Edward Berry. Chicago, pp. 220–39.

Limon, Jerzy 1985, *Gentlemen of a Company: English Players in Central and Eastern Europe, 1590–1660*. Cambridge.

  1986, *Dangerous Matter: English Drama and Politics 1623/4*. Cambridge.

Lindenberger, Herbert 1975, *Historical Drama: The Relation of Literature and Reality*. Chicago.

Loehlin, James N. 1996, *Henry V. Shakespeare in Performance*. Manchester.

  1997, '"Top of the World, Ma": *Richard III* and Cinematic Convention', *Shakespeare the Movie*, ed. Lynda E. Boose and Richard Burt. London, pp. 67–79.

Loftis, John 1987. *Renaissance Drama in England and Spain: Topical Allusion and History Plays*. Princeton.

Loomba, Ania 1989, *Gender, Race, Renaissance Drama*. New York.

MacCallum, M. W. 1910, *Shakespeare's Roman Plays and Their Background*. London.

Machiavelli, Niccolò 1950, *The Prince and the Discourses*, ed. Max Lerner. New York.

Manheim, M. 1973, *The Weak King Dilemma in the Shakespearean History Play*. Syracuse, NY.

Marcus, Leah S. 1988, 'Elizabeth', *Puzzling Shakespeare: Local Reading and its Discontents*, Berkeley, pp. 51–105.

Marienstras, Richard 1985, *New Perspectives on the Shakespearean World*, trans. Janet Lloyd. Cambridge.

  1995, 'Of a Monstrous Body', *French Essays on Shakespeare and His Contemporaries*, ed. J. M. Maguin and M. Willems. Newark, DE, pp. 153–74.

Martindale, Charles and Michelle 1990, *Shakespeare and the Uses of Antiquity*. London.

McCabe, Richard A. 1981, 'Elizabethan Satire and the Bishops' Ban of 1599', *Yearbook of English Studies* 11: 188–94.

McCoy, Richard C. 1989, *The Rites of Knighthood: The Literature and Politics of Elizabethan Chivalry*. Berkeley.

McEachern, Claire 1996, *The Poetics of English Nationhood 1590–1612*. Cambridge.

McFarlane, K. B. 1972, *Lancastrian Kings and Lollard Knights*. Oxford.

McMillin, Scott 1991, *Henry IV, Part One. Shakespeare in Performance*. Manchester.

McMullan, Gordon 1995, 'Shakespeare and the End of History [*Henry VIII*]', *Essays and Studies* 48: 16–37.

Meagher, John C. 1966, 'Hackwriting and the Huntingdon Plays', *Elizabethan Theatre*, ed. John Russell Brown and Bernard Harris. London, pp. 197–219.

Mehus, Donald V. 1975, *Shakespeare's English History Plays: Genealogical Table*. Charlottesville, VA.

Melchiori, Giorgio 1994, *Shakespeare's Garter Plays: 'Edward III' to 'Merry Wives of Windsor'*. Newark, DE.

Metz, G. H. (ed.) 1989, *Sources of Four Plays Ascribed to Shakespeare: 'The Reign of King Edward III', 'Sir Thomas More', 'The History of Cardenio', 'The Two Noble Kinsmen'*. Columbia, MS.

Mikalachki, Jodi 1995, 'The Masculine Romance of Roman Britain: *Cymbeline* and Early Modern Nationalism', *Shakespeare Quarterly* 46: 301–22.

Miles, Geoffrey 1996, *Shakespeare and the Constant Romans*. Oxford.

Miller, Shannon 1992, 'Topicality and Subversion in William Shakespeare's *Coriolanus*', *Studies in English Literature 1500–1900* 32: 287–310.

Miola, Robert S. 1983, *Shakespeare's Rome*. Cambridge.

1985, '*Julius Caesar* and the Tyrannicide Debate', *Renaissance Quarterly* 38: 271–89.

2000, *Shakespeare's Reading*. Oxford.

Montrose, Louis 1996, *The Purpose of Playing: Shakespeare and the Cultural Politics of the Elizabethan Theatre*. Chicago.

Moore, Jeanie Grant 1991, 'Queen of Sorrow, King of Grief: Reflections and Perspectives in *Richard II*', *In Another Country: Feminist Perspectives on Renaissance Drama*, ed. Dorothea Kehler and Susan Baker. Metuchen, NJ, pp. 19–35.

More, Thomas 1963, *The History of King Richard the Third*, vol. II of *The Complete Works of St. Thomas More*, ed. Richard S. Sylvester. New Haven.

Morey, James H. 1994, 'The Death of King John in Shakespeare and Bale', *Shakespeare Quarterly* 45: 329–31.

Mullaney, Steven 1988, *The Place of the Stage: License, Play and Power in Renaissance England*. Ann Arbor.

Mulryne, J. R. 1995, 'Transformations: European History in the Plays of Shakespeare's Contemporaries', *L'Histoire au temps de la Renaissance*, ed. M. T. Jones-Davies. Paris, pp. 59–70.

Myers, Norman J. 1996, 'Finding "a Heap of Jewels" in "Lesser" Shakespeare: *The Wars of the Roses* and *Richard Duke of York*', *New England Theatre Journal* 7: 95–107.

Nashe, Thomas 1904–10, 1958, *Works*, ed. R. B. McKerrow, rev. F. P. Wilson, 5 vols. Oxford.

Nelson, Thomas 1590, *The Device of the Pageant*. London.

Nichols, John 1783, 1823, *The Progresses and Public Processions of Queen Elizabeth*, 3 vols. London.

Nichols, Nina da Vinci 1997, '*Henry VI*', *Shakespeare Bulletin* 15: 10–12.

Noble Adrian (intro.) 1989, 'The Plantagenets' adapted by the Royal Shakespeare Company from [. . .] *Henry VI parts I, II, III and Richard III.* London.

Norbrook, David 1996, '"A Liberal Tongue": Language and Rebellion in *Richard II*', *Shakespeare's Universe: Renaissance Ideas and Conventions*, ed. John M. Mucciolo, with Steven J. Doloff and Edward A. Rauchut. Aldershot, pp. 37–51.

Norwich, John Julius 1999, *Shakespeare's Kings: The Great Plays and the History of England in the Middle Ages, 1337–1485.* New York.

Olivier, Laurence 1984, *Henry V.* London.

Orgel, Stephen 1965, *The Jonsonian Masque.* Cambridge, MA.

Orgel, Stephen and Sean Keilen (eds.) 1999, *Shakespeare and History.* New York.

Ornstein, Robert 1972, *A Kingdom for a Stage: The Achievement of Shakespeare's History Plays.* Cambridge, MA.

Osborn, James M. (ed.) 1960, *The Quenes Majesties Passage.* New Haven.

Painter, William 1575, *The Palace of Pleasure*, reprinted in Metz 1989.

Paris, Bernard J. 1991, *Character as a Subversive Force in Shakespeare: The History and Roman Plays.* Rutherford, NJ.

Parker, Patricia 1996, *Shakespeare from the Margins.* Chicago.

Parry, Graham 1981, *The Golden Age Restor'd: The Culture of the Stuart Court 1603–1642.* Manchester.

Patterson, Annabel 1989, *Shakespeare and the Popular Voice.* Oxford.

1996, '"All is True": Negotiating the Past in *Henry VIII*', *Elizabethan Essays in Honor of S. Schoenbaum*, ed. R. B. Parker and S. P. Zitner. Newark, DE, pp. 147–66.

Peacock, John 1995, *The Stage Designs of Inigo Jones: The European Context.* Cambridge.

Pearlman, E. 1992, *William Shakespeare: The History Plays.* New York.

Pearson, Jacqueline 1982, 'The Influence of *King Leir* on Shakespeare's *Richard II*', *Notes and Queries* 29: 113–15.

Pettet, E. C. 1950, '*Coriolanus* and the Midlands Insurrection of 1607', *Shakespeare Survey* 3: 34–42.

Plutarch 1895–6, *Plutarch's Lives of the Noble Grecians and Romans* (1579), ed. George Wyndham, *Tudor Translations*, trans. Thomas North, 6 vols. London.

Poole, Kristen 1995, 'Saints Alive! Falstaff, Martin Marprelate, and the Staging of Puritanism', *Shakespeare Quarterly* 41: 47–75.

Prior, Moody Erasmus 1973, *The Drama of Power: Studies in Shakespeare's History Plays.* Evanston, IL.

Pugliatti, Paola 1996, *Shakespeare the Historian.* New York.

Puttenham, George 1589, *The Arte of English Poesie.* London.

Pye, Christopher 1990, *The Regal Phantasm.* London.

Rabkin, Norman 1967, *Shakespeare and the Common Understanding.* New York.

Rackin, Phyllis 1990, *Stages of History: Shakespeare's English Chronicles.* London.

Raleigh, Walter 1829, *The Works of Sir Walter Raleigh*, ed. William Oldys and Thomas Birch, 8 vols. Oxford.

Richmond, Hugh M. 1989, *King Richard III. Shakespeare in Performance.* Manchester.

1994, *King Henry VIII. Shakespeare in Performance.* Manchester.

Rickey, Mary E. and Thomas B. Stroup (eds.) 1968, *Certaine Sermons or Homilies Appointed to be Read in Churches in the Time of Queen Elizabeth I [1547–1571], A Facsimile Reproduction of the Edition of 1623*. Gainesville, FL.

Riggs, David 1971, *Shakespeare's Heroical Histories: 'Henry VI' and its Literary Tradition*. Cambridge, MA.

Roberts, Josephine A. (ed.) 1988, *'Richard II': An Annotated Bibliography*. New York.

Robinson, Marsha 1989. 'The Historiographic Methodology of *King John*', *'King John': New Perspectives*, ed. Deborah T. Curren-Aquino. Newark, DE, pp. 29–39.

Rogers, Thomas 1854, *The Catholic Doctrine of the Church of England: An Exposition of the Thirty-Nine Articles*, ed. J. J. S. Perowne. Cambridge.

Ronan, Clifford J. 1995, *'Antike Roman': Power Symbology and the Roman Play in Early Modern England, 1585–1635*. Athens, GA.

Rous, John, John Leland and Thomas Hearne 1716, *Joannis Rossi antiquarii warrvicensis Historia regum Angliæ* (1483). Oxford.

Rutter, Carol Chillington 1997, 'Fiona Shaw's *Richard II*: The Girl as Player–King as Comic', *Shakespeare Quarterly* 48: 314–24.

Saccio, Peter 1998, *Shakespeare's English Kings: History, Chronicle, and Drama*, 2nd edn. New York.

Sanders, Wilbur 1968, *The Dramatist and the Received Idea: Studies in the Drama of Marlowe and Shakespeare*. Cambridge.

Sarlos, Robert K. 1964, 'Dingelstedt's Celebration of the Tercentenary: Shakespeare's Histories as a Cycle', *Theatre Survey* 2: 117–41.

Saul, Nigel 1999, *'Richard II' and Chivalric Kingship*. London.

Schama, Simon 1987, *The Embarrassment of Riches: An Interpretation of Dutch Culture in the Golden Age*. London.

Schenkeveld, Maria A. 1991, *Dutch Literature in the Age of Rembrandt: Themes and Ideas*. Amsterdam.

Seneca 1927, *His ten tragedies translated into English, edited by Thomas Newton, anno 1581*, trans. Jasper Heywood et al, ed. C. Whibley, 2 vols. London.

Shakespeare, William and Royal Shakespeare Company 1989, *The Plantagenets*. London.

Shapiro, S. C. 1987, 'Amazons, Hermaphrodites, and Plain Monsters: The "Masculine" Woman in English Satire and Social Criticism from 1580–1640', *Atlantis* 13: 65–76.

Shaughnessy, Robert 1994, *Representing Shakespeare: England, History And The RSC*. New York.

Shepherd, S. 1981, *Amazons and Warrior Women: Varieties of Feminism in Seventeenth-Century Drama*. Brighton.

Shewring, Margaret 1996, *King Richard II. Shakespeare in Performance*. Manchester.

Sidney, Philip 1965, *An Apology for Poetry*, ed. G. Shepherd. Manchester.

Siegel, Paul N. 1986, *Shakespeare's English and Roman History Plays: A Marxist Approach*. Rutherford, NJ.

Simmons, J. L. 1973, *Shakespeare's Pagan World: The Roman Tragedies*. Charlottesville, VA.

Skinner, Q. 1978, 'Calvinism and the Theory of Revolution', *The Foundations of Modern Political Thought: The Age of Reformation*. Cambridge, pp. 187–358.

Skura, Meredith 1997, 'Marlowe's *Edward II*: Penetrating Language in Shakespeare's *Richard II*', *Shakespeare Survey* 50: 41–55.

Smallwood, Robert 1986, 'Shakespeare's Use of History', *The Cambridge Companion to Shakespeare Studies*, ed. S. Wells. Cambridge, pp. 143–62.

Smits-Veldt, Mieke B. 1991, *Het Nederlandse Renaissancetoneel*. Utrecht.

Spencer, T. J. B. 1957, 'Shakespeare and the Elizabethan Romans', *Shakespeare Survey* 10: 27–38.

Spencer, T. J. B. and Stanley Wells (eds.) 1967, *A Book of Masques. In Honour of Allardyce Nicoll*. Cambridge.

Spikes, Judith Doolin 1977, 'The Jacobean History Play and the Myth of the Elect Nation', *Renaissance Drama* n.s. 8: 117–50.

Spivack, Bernard 1958, *Shakespeare and the Allegory of Evil: The History of a Metaphor in Relation to his Major Villains*. New York.

Sprague, A. C. 1964, *Shakespeare's Histories: Plays for the Stage*. London.

Stirling, Brents 1951, 'Or else this were a Savage Spectacle', *Publications of the Modern Language Association* 66: 765–74.

Stríbrný, Zdenek 1964, '*Henry V* and History', *Shakespeare in a Changing World*, ed. Arnold Kettle. London, pp. 84–101.

2000, *Shakespeare and Eastern Europe*. Oxford.

Strong, Roy 1977, *The Cult of Elizabeth: Elizabethan Portraiture and Pageantry*. Berkeley.

Sullivan, Garrett A. 1998, *The Drama of Landscape: Land, Property, and Social Relations on the Early Modern Stage*. Stanford, CA.

Tacitus 1591, *The End of Nero and Beginning of Galba. Four Books of the Histories of Cornelius Tacitus*, trans. Sir Henry Savile. London.

1598, *The Annales of Cornelius Tacitus*, trans. R. Greneway. [London].

Taylor, Gary 1985, 'The Fortunes of Oldcastle', *Shakespeare Survey* 38: 85–100.

Tennenhouse, Leonard 1986, *Power on Display: The Politics of Shakespeare's Genres*. London.

Thomas, Vivian 1989, *Shakespeare's Roman Worlds*. London.

Thomson, W. H. 1951. *Shakespeare's Characters: A Historical Dictionary*. Altrincham.

Thucydides 1550, *The Hystory*, adapted from the French translation of Claude de Seyssel. London.

Tillyard, E. M. W. 1943, *The Elizabethan World Picture*. London.

1944, *Shakespeare's History Plays*. London.

Traversi, Derek 1958, *Shakespeare from 'Richard II' to 'Henry V'*. London.

1963, *Shakespeare: The Roman Plays*. Stanford.

Tuck, Richard 1993, *Philosophy and Government 1572–1651*. Cambridge.

Vaughan, Virginia Mason 1984, 'Between Tetralogies: *King John* as Transition', *Shakespeare Quarterly* 35: 407–20.

van de Water, Julia C. 1960, 'The Bastard in *King John*', *Shakespeare Quarterly* 11: 137–46.

Velz, John W. 1978, 'The Ancient World in Shakespeare: Authenticity or Anachronism? A Retrospect', *Shakespeare Survey* 31: 1–12.

(ed.) 1996, *Shakespeare's English Histories: A Quest for Form and Genre*. Binghamton, NY.

Venezky, Alice S. 1951, *Pageantry on the Shakespearean Stage*. New York.

Vergil, Polydore. 1844, *Three Bookes of Polydore Vergil's English History, Comprising the Reign of Henry VI, Edward IV, and Richard III*, ed. Henry Ellis, Camden Society. London.

Vergil, Polydor 1950. *The Anglica Historia of Polydor Vergil, A.D. 1485–1537*, ed. Denys Hay, Camden Series, 74. London.

Waage, Frederick O. Jr 1976, 'Henry VIII and the Crisis of the English History Play', *Shakespeare Studies* 8: 297–309.

Waith, Eugene 1978, 'King John and the Drama of History', *Shakespeare Quarterly* 29: 192–211.

Walker, Greg 2000, 'Richard III: The Shape of History', *William Shakespeare, 'Richard III': Nouvelles Perspectives Critiques*, ed. Francis Guinle and Jacques Ramel, *Astrea*, 10: 31–48. Montpellier.

Warner, William 1586, *Albion's England*. London.

Watson, Donald G. 1990, *Shakespeare's Early History Plays: Politics at Play on the Elizabethan Stage*. Athens, GA.

Webster, John 1927, *The Complete Works*, ed. F. L. Lucas. 4 vols. London.

Weimann, Robert 1978, *Shakespeare and the Popular Dramatic Tradition in the Theater*, trans. Robert Schwartz. Baltimore.

Wells, Charles 1993, *The Wide Arch: Roman Values in Shakespeare*. New York.

Wells, Stanley (ed.) 1997, *Shakespeare in the Theatre: An Anthology of Criticism*. Oxford.

Wells, Stanley and T. J. B. Spencer (eds.) 1967, *A Book of Masques*. Cambridge.

Wells, Stanley and Gary Taylor 1987, *William Shakespeare: A Textual Companion*. Oxford.

Welsford, Enid 1927, *The Court Masque: A Study in the Relationship between Poetry and the Revels*. Cambridge.

White, Paul Whitfield 1993, *Theatre and Reformation: Protestantism, Patronage, and Playgoing in Tudor England*. Cambridge.

Wickham, Glynne, Herbert Berry and William Ingram (eds.) 2000, *English Professional Theatre, 1530–1660*. Cambridge.

Wiener, Philip P. 1973, *Dictionary of the History of Ideas: Studies of Selected Pivotal Ideas*, 4 vols. New York.

Wilders, John 1978, *The Lost Garden: A View of Shakespeare's English and Roman History Plays*. London.

Wiles, David 1981, *The Early Plays of Robin Hood*. Cambridge.

   1987, *Shakespeare's Clown: Actor and Text in the Elizabethan Playhouse*. Cambridge.

Williams, Simon 1990, *Shakespeare on the German Stage. Volume 1: 1586–1914*. Cambridge.

Wilson, John Dover 1945, 'The Origins and Development of Shakespeare's *Henry IV*', *The Library* 4th Series, 24: 2–16.

Winny, J. 1968, *The Player King: A Theme of Shakespeare's Histories*. London.

Womersley, David 1991, 'Sir Henry Savile's Translation of Tacitus and the Political Interpretation of Elizabethan Texts', *RES* 42: 313–42.

Woodbridge, Linda 1991, 'Palisading the Elizabethan Body Politic [*Cymbeline*]', *Texas Studies in Literature and Language* 33: 327–54.

Woolf, D. R. 1999, 'The Shapes of History', *A Companion to Shakespeare*, ed. David Scott Kastan. Oxford, pp. 186–205.

Wymer, Rowland 1999, '*The Tempest* and the Origins of Britain', *Critical Survey* 11: 3–14.

Yates, Frances A. 1975, *Astraea: The Imperial Theme in the Sixteenth Century*. London.

Zeeveld, Gordon W. 1940, 'Richard Morison, Official Apologist of Henry VIII', *P.M.L.A.* 406–25.

   1948, *Foundations of Tudor Policy*. Cambridge, MA.

   1962, '*Coriolanus* and Jacobean Politics', *Modern Language Review* 57: 321–34.

INDEX